The Politics of Social Risk

The book provides a systematic evaluation of the role played by business in the development of the modern welfare state. When and why have employers supported the development of institutions of social insurance that provide benefits to workers for various employment-related risks? What factors explain the variation in the social policy preferences of employers? What is the relative importance of business and labor-based organizations in the negotiation of a new social policy? This book studies these questions by examining the role played by German and French producers in eight social policy reforms spanning a century of social policy development. The analysis demonstrates that major social policies were supported by cross-class alliances comprising labor-based organizations and key sectors of the business community.

Isabela Mares is assistant professor of political science at Stanford University. She is the author of articles on social policy and political economy that have appeared in *World Politics, Politics and Society, Governance, Journal of Public Policy*, and edited volumes. She has been awarded the Sage Prize by the Comparative Politics section of the American Political Science Association for her research on the role of business in the development of the modern welfare state.

D1158650

Cambridge Studies in Comparative Politics

General Editor

Margaret Levi *University of Washington, Seattle*

Assistant General Editor

Stephen Hanson *University of Washington, Seattle*

Associate Editors

Robert H. Bates *Harvard University*
Peter Hall *Harvard University*
Peter Lange *Duke University*
Helen Milner *Columbia University*
Frances Rosenbluth *Yale University*
Susan Stokes *University of Chicago*
Sidney Tarrow *Cornell University*

Other Books in the Series

Stefano Bartolini, *The Political Mobilization of the European Left,
    1860–1980: The Class Cleavage*
Mark Beissinger, *Nationalist Mobilization and the Collapse of the Soviet State*
Carles Boix, *Political Parties, Growth, and Equality: Conservative and Social
    Democratic Economic Strategies in the World Economy*
Catherine Boone, *Merchant Capital and the Roots of State Power in Senegal,
    1930–1985*
Michael Bratton and Nicolas van de Walle, *Democratic Experiments in
    Africa: Regime Transitions in Comparative Perspective*
Valerie Bunce, *Leaving Socialism and Leaving the State: The End of
    Yugoslavia, the Soviet Union, and Czechoslovakia*
Ruth Berins Collier, *Paths toward Democracy: The Working Class and Elites
    in Western Europe and South America*
Donatella della Porta, *Social Movements, Political Violence, and the State*
Gerald Easter, *Reconstructing the State: Personal Networks and Elite Identity*
Robert F. Franzese, *Macroeconomic Policies of Developed Democracies*
Roberto Franzosi, *The Puzzle of Strikes: Class and State Strategies in
    Postwar Italy*

Continues after the Index

The Politics of Social Risk

BUSINESS AND WELFARE STATE DEVELOPMENT

ISABELA MARES

Stanford University

CAMBRIDGE
UNIVERSITY PRESS

PUBLISHED BY THE PRESS SYNDICATE OF THE UNIVERSITY OF CAMBRIDGE
The Pitt Building, Trumpington Street, Cambridge, United Kingdom

CAMBRIDGE UNIVERSITY PRESS *Cau*
The Edinburgh Building, Cambridge CB2 2RU, UK
40 West 20th Street, New York, NY 10011-4211, USA
477 Williamstown Road, Port Melbourne, VIC 3207, Australia
Ruiz de Alarcón 13, 28014 Madrid, Spain
Dock House, The Waterfront, Cape Town 8001, South Africa

http://www.cambridge.org

First published 2003

Printed in the United States of America

Typeface Janson Text Roman 10/13 pt.   *System* LaTeX 2$_\varepsilon$ [TB]

A catalog record for this book is available from the British Library.

Library of Congress Cataloging in Publication data

Mares, Isabela.
        The politics of social risk: business and welfare state development / Isabela Mares.
              p.   cm. – (Cambridge studies in comparative politics)
        Includes bibliographical references and index.
        ISBN 0-521-82741-8 – ISBN 0-521-53477-1 (pb.)
        1. Employee fringe benefits – France – History.   2. Employee fringe
benefits – Germany – History.   3. Social security – France – History.   4. Social
security – Germany – History.   5. Welfare state – France – History.   6. Welfare
state – Germany – History.   I. Title.   II. Series.
        HD4928.N62M37   2003
        330.12′6–dc21   2002041557

ISBN 0 521 82741 8 hardback
ISBN 0 521 53477 1 paperback

For my parents

Contents

Contents

Figures and Tables

Figures

Figures and Tables

Tables

Acknowledgments

It is my great pleasure to be able to thank the persons who have provided in-tellectual support and friendship during the period of research and writing. My greatest intellectual debt goes to Peter Hall, the chair of my dissertation committee. Peter has encouraged me to pursue this project and has offered advice and guidance at every critical juncture in its development. Peter's thoughtful, extensive comments on several versions of the manuscript (that are now buried on my hard drive) could easily constitute a book on their own, undoubtedly a better book than the present one. I am extremely grate-ful to David Soskice – whose research has reoriented comparative political economy research during the past decade – for sparking my interest in the study of business and for many, many long hours of conversation. The other members of my dissertation committee, Suzanne Berger, Torben Iversen, and Paul Pierson, generously shared their time with me and helped me avoid many wrong turns along the way. Their work continues to be a source of inspiration for me.

The core research material for this book comprises archival data on business preferences. I have collected these data during an extensive period of travel and have incurred numerous debts at the research stage. In France, my thanks go to Robert Salais, for having hosted me at IRESCO, and to many librarians and archivists at the Archives Nationales, Archive de la Chambre de Commerce de Paris, the Bibliothèque Nationale, and the Centre des Archives Contemporaines for their help in identifying pre-viously unexplored sources. I also want to thank Marcel and Tamara Bene and Alexandra and Olivier Contemine for hosting me during the period of my research in France. In Germany, I would like to thank archivists at the Zentrales Staatsarchiv in Potsdam and Koblenz, the Archive of the Friedrich Ebert Foundation in Bonn, the Rheinisch-Westfälisches

Wirtschaftsarchiv, and the archive of the Bundesvereinigung der Deutschen Arbeitgeberverbände in Cologne. During the period of fieldwork, I had the extraordinary opportunity to be a guest researcher in the stimulating research environment of the labor market unit of the Wissenschaftszentrum Berlin. I want to thank Robert Hancké, Steven Casper, Karl-Orfeo Fioretos, and Stewart Wood for patiently listening to my preliminary ideas and for their research suggestions and leads. At the Max-Planck Institute in Cologne, I am grateful to Philip Manow, Anke Hassel, Philip Genschel, Steffen Ganghoff, Jim Mosher, and Bernhard Ebbinghaus for extremely insightful comments.

The first version of the manuscript was completed at the Center for European Studies at Harvard. At this stage, I benefited from advice from many friends, who were pursuing similar intellectual projects. Many thanks to Carles Boix, Pepper and Mary-Louise Culpepper, Keith Darden, Robert Franzese, Margarita Estevez-Abe, and Gunnar Trumbull. I am also indebted to a large number of colleagues who have commented on the manuscript at various seminars, workshops, and conferences. I am grateful to Richard Deeg, Marie Gottschalk, Peter Gourevitch, Peter Katzenstein, Peter Lange, Jonah Levy, Herbert Kitschelt, Cathie Jo Martin, Jonas Pontusson, Kathleen Thelen, John Stephens, Peter Swenson, Wolfgang Streeck, Margaret Weir, and Nicholas Ziegler for comments. The department of political science at Stanford University provided a highly stimulating environment for the final completion of the manuscript. I am especially grateful to David Abernethy, David Laitin, and Jim Fearon for reading several versions of the manuscript and to Alberto Diaz-Cayeros, Claudine Gay, Steven Haber, Beatriz Magaloni, Jean Oi, Mike Tomz, and Anne Wren for many helpful comments. I would like to thank Paul Sniderman for his advice and for helping me overcome many unexpected adversities in the final preparation of the manuscript.

Several institutions have provided financial assistance during the period of research and writing: the Mellon Foundation, the Krupp Foundation, the Center for European Studies at Harvard University, the American Institute for Contemporary German Studies, the Center for European Studies at Georgetown University, and the Department of Political Science at Stanford University. Parts of this book have been published as articles or book chapters, and I gratefully acknowledge the willingness of their publishers to allow the publication of revised versions. At Cambridge University Press, I am grateful to Margaret Levi and Lewis Bateman for their help in clarifying some ideas and for improving the book manuscript.

Acknowledgments

I have continuously derived strength and inspiration from my family. My husband, Radu, has accompanied me during this long intellectual journey and has participated in all the stages of the project. My brother, Vlad, has always offered the right mix of support and criticism. Finally, my parents have always encouraged me to let my intuition guide me in the choice among competing intellectual projects. This book, which follows this simple advice, is dedicated to my parents.

The Politics of Social Risk

1

The Welfare State

A WORLD AGAINST EMPLOYERS?

During recent decades, welfare states in advanced industrialized societies have experienced a bifurcated trajectory of reform (Kitschelt et al. 1999, Huber and Stephens 2001, Pierson 2000b). A number of countries have enacted radical measures of social policy retrenchment that have restricted the generosity and tightened the eligibility criteria for social policy benefits. In other countries, welfare state and labor market reforms have been more limited in scope. Social policy reforms have only attempted to strengthen the actuarial soundness of social insurance and to put existing social insurance programs on a firmer financial basis.

The bifurcation of these reforms is intriguing for a number of reasons. The first is that the magnitude of social policy retrenchment was much larger in the less generous and more market-conforming welfare states, such as the United Kingdom or New Zealand (Huber and Stephens 2001: 6). In contrast, the depth of retrenchment experienced by the generous welfare states of continental Europe has been more modest. The evolution of wage-bargaining arrangements and other institutions protecting labor, such as employment security regulations, reveals a similar pattern. Liberal market economies – such as the United Kingdom or the United States – have introduced the most dramatic measures deregulating labor markets and weakening the rights of organized labor (King and Wood 1999: 371). In contrast, reforms have been more modest in continental welfare states and a number of countries (such as Norway or Italy) have experienced a recentralization of the institutions of wage bargaining. The trajectory of these reforms has strengthened rather than undermined existing cross-national variation among welfare states.

A second surprising finding of these recent political developments is the broad cross-national variation in the political coalitions forged in support

1

of or opposition to these reforms. The response of employers to these reforms has varied widely across countries. In the United Kingdom, for example, employers have strongly embraced proposals for labor market deregulation and social policy retrenchment (King and Wood 1999, Thelen 2001: 72). In contrast, employers in continental or Northern European economies have "shown only lukewarm support for attempts at profound social insurance reform" (Manow 2000b: 161) and have often defended the core institutional features of their welfare states (Giaimo and Manow 1999). Thus, many scholars have attributed the relatively stronger resilience of welfare states in continental European economies to the presence of cross-class alliances among trade unions and important sectors of the business community strongly supporting the policy status quo (Kitschelt et al. 1999, Manow 2000b: 146–164, Rhodes 2000: 165–196).

The finding that business associations supported existing institutions of social insurance poses, however, a challenge to welfare state scholars. Existing research on the development of the welfare state had been premised on the assumption of business opposition to social insurance. A class-based perspective that has dominated social policy studies for several decades posited that employers have played a reactive role in the political history of the welfare state, by opposing the demands of labor associations for the expansion of social programs and by counteracting the administrative largesse of bureaucratic officials. This research perspective has characterized the expansion of the welfare state as "politics *against* markets," the political triumph of labor-based organizations on a business community forced into retreat (Esping-Andersen 1985). Given this assumption, most scholars of the welfare state lack the analytical tools allowing them to explain the conditions under which employers support the development of social policies. Without a theory specifying the social policy preferences of employers – and the conditions under which the benefits of social insurance outweigh the costs of social policy for firms – the notion of cross-class alliances, which is often invoked in current research on the welfare state, lacks analytical precision.

In an effort to fill the existing gap in our understanding of the political role played by employers in the development of the welfare state, this book has two broad analytical objectives. First, I develop a theoretical model specifying the sources of business preferences toward different institutions of social insurance and the conditions under which profit-maximizing firms – facing competition in domestic or international markets – nevertheless support social policies. Under what conditions can policies designed to compensate employees for the risks encountered during the employment relationship generate positive externalities and tangible benefits for employers? What precisely are the institutional advantages provided by social policy to firms? When do these benefits outweigh the costs of social insurance to firms? What set of factors explains the conflict and disagreement among employers during social insurance reforms?

This model generates the necessary microfoundations allowing us to introduce employers into political analyses of the bargaining over the design of institutions of social insurance. Rather than regarding capital and labor as unified actors involved in a zero-sum conflict over the design of a new social policy, the analysis specifies more rigorously the conditions under which cross-class alliances among sectors of capital and labor form. I distinguish among *prestrategic* and *strategic* alliances. The former are formed if unions and employers support their preferred outcome, the latter if either unions or employers support a social policy that is their second-best choice. I specify the broader political and institutional conditions that contribute to the formation of these alliances and the range of social policy outcomes supported by various cross-class alliances.

In exploring these questions empirically, I examine the role played by employers during the development of the major institutions of social insurance in France and Germany during various episodes spanning more than a century of policy development. I investigate the development of accident, unemployment, and old-age insurance and the development of early retirement policies in recent years. The findings disprove the proposition that business has opposed the development of social insurance, a view that (until recent years) has been widely shared by welfare state scholars. Instead of a monolithic business community uncompromisingly opposing social policies, I find a widespread but clearly predictable divergence among employers when faced with the introduction of a new social policy. Instead of irreconcilable class-conflict, I find that cross-class alliances among parts of the labor movement and some sectors of the business community have played a critical role in the development of policies of social protection.

This chapter situates the analysis of this book within existing research on the welfare state. I begin by discussing the causes accounting for the misunderstanding of the political role of employers in the development of modern institutions of social insurance. Next, I review the most significant recent challenges to the class-based perspective on the development of the welfare state. The chapter concludes by previewing the argument developed in this book.

Class Conflict and the Development of the Modern Welfare State

The literature examining the causes of welfare state development is one of the most developed subfields in comparative politics, a genuine laboratory of research for some of the most influential theories of the determinants of public policy (Köhler 1979, Shalev 1983, Uusitallo 1984, Skocpol and Amenta 1986, Skocpol 1992: 1–66). During the past four decades, an overwhelming number of explanations have been formulated to account for broad aggregate patterns and minute characteristics in the institutional design of many existing social programs. Yet despite the significant achievements of this research, we still lack a systematic account of the role played by employers in the development of the modern welfare state. We lack a broad comparative theory that identifies the variation in the social policy preferences of firms and the mixture of support and opposition in the social policy demands of employers. What explains this paradoxical situation? Why have welfare state scholars ignored or mischaracterized the role played by employers during the process of social policy development? What are the consequences of this analytical omission?

Beginning in the 1970s, the power resource perspective was the dominant analytical perspective informing comparative research on the welfare state (Korpi 1978, 1983, Stephens 1979, Esping-Andersen and Korpi 1984, 1985, Esping-Andersen 1985). The crucial theoretical proposition advanced by this approach was that cross-national differences in social policies resulted from differences in the political "balance of power" between working-class parties and bourgeois or conservative political forces. Power resource scholars have attributed changes over time in the generosity of social insurance programs to factors that contributed to sudden increases in the organizational resources of labor or to exogenous political shocks – such as wars or depressions – that reduced the capacity of employers to oppose reforms (Swenson 2002: 12, Block 1977). Quantitative applications of this theory have been used to explain cross-national variation in the design of social policy programs using various measures of labor strength – such as union density, centralization of wage bargaining, or participation of social democratic parties in the governments (Stephens 1979, Castles 1982, Huber and Stephens 2001, Hicks 1999).

An important limitation of the power resource scholarship is the strong disjunction between the *theoretical* claim that class conflict is crucial for the understanding of social policy development and the *empirical* analysis of this conflict. In fact, power resource scholars provide empirical evidence documenting only one aspect of their theoretical claim, namely that labor-based parties have actively supported the expansion of the welfare state. Most studies devote only a very limited attention to the role played by employers in the deliberations preceding the introduction of a new social policy (Esping-Andersen and Korpi 1985). Employers' opposition to a new social policy is often *assumed*, rather than documented. These analyses fail to examine the causes of intersectoral disagreements among employers when faced with the introduction of a new social policy. In short, the empirical analysis of the social policy preferences and political strategies of employers developed by power resource scholars is often superficial, ad hoc, and unsystematic. Thus, the question about the importance of class-based conflict in the development of modern institutions of social insurance remains an empirically open question.

Often, the specification of the functions of social policy proposed by power resource scholars is premised on the assumption that employers are opposed to the introduction of a new social policy. According to Walter Korpi, the aim of social policy is to "compensate labor for its disadvantaged position in the labor market ..., by redistributing income between different groups or citizens and between different periods of an individual's life" (Korpi 1983: 83). As Michael Shalev remarks, this restrictive conception of the welfare state that "places much emphasis on the modification of distributional inequalities ... invites a class-based analysis" – in other words, an analysis premised on the assumption that labor has a strong interest in the expansion of social insurance, whereas capital opposes social policy (Shalev 1983: 320). The most ambitious theoretical conceptualization of the functions of social policies proposed by power resource scholars is Gøsta Esping-Andersen's notion of "decommodification." According to Esping-Andersen, the aim of social policy is to "emancipate workers from market-dependence" and to "minimize the importance of market-generated income" (Esping-Andersen 1990: 26). As this definition implies, "decommodification strengthens the worker and weakens the absolute authority of the employer. It is exactly for this reason that employers have always opposed decommodification" (Esping-Andersen, 1990: 22). Thus, the very definition of social insurance proposed by power resource scholars precludes an empirical examination of the policy preferences of employers. By narrowly focusing only on those aspects of social insurance premised on a zero-sum conflict between capital and labor, power resource scholars fail to identify aspects of social policy design around which cross-class alliances among unions and employers can form.

Recent Challenges to the Power Resource Perspective

In *The Politics of Social Solidarity*, Peter Baldwin has formulated an important empirical and theoretical challenge to the power resource perspective (Baldwin 1990). By examining the historical experience of five European nations for nearly a century, Baldwin demonstrates that parties and other political organizations representing middle classes – and not labor-based parties alone – have, on numerous occasions, pushed for the expansion of social insurance. Although Baldwin's effort to describe the interests of middle classes in social insurance and to expand our "understanding of the 'social bases' of the welfare state" is extremely persuasive, Baldwin is less successful in identifying the interests of employers in the development of institutions of social insurance.

Baldwin challenges both the empirical and the theoretical propositions of the power resource perspective. First, he shows that the key institutional features of the Scandinavian welfare states were not established during the 1930s or 1940s, thus, during a period of Social Democratic governments. Tax-financed, universalistic pensions were introduced at the turn of the century by parties representing the rural countryside, "in an effort to reduce expenses of poor relief and the pressure it put on local land taxes.... Tax financing spoke to agrarian interests, by shifting burdens from local land taxes to the central authority's indirect consumption levies. A universalistic approach was necessary to ensure that social policy benefitted the farmers' heterogenous labor force" (Baldwin 1990: 74–75). Second, Baldwin argues that even during the postwar years, Social Democratic parties were highly ambivalent about the proposals to remove means testing (due to the concerns about the financial implications of this measure) and only "grudgingly" accepted the proposals to introduce universalistic reforms (Baldwin 1990: 137). Thus, as Baldwin argues, "the view of an essential link between Social Democratic power and the apparent solidarity of early Scandinavian welfare policy is misleading.... It anachronistically reads back a misunderstanding of postwar reforms to an earlier period when other factors were at work" (Baldwin 1990: 62).

On theoretical grounds, Baldwin challenges the assumption of power resource scholars that labor is the only political agent having an interest in the expansion of social insurance. In his elegant formulation, the "proletariat has had no monopoly on uncertainty" nor "has the industrial working class been the risk-prone group in every country at the time social insurance was first developed" (Baldwin 1990: 12). According to Baldwin,

6

in specific historical circumstances, various segments of the middle classes – such as farmers, artisans, liberal professionals, shopkeepers – also had pressing needs for social insurance programs, "not as Bonapartist manipulators but as creatures subject to misfortune surpassing their capacity for self-reliance" (Baldwin 1990: 9). Thus, power resource scholars mischaracterize the major dimensions of political conflict formed during the introduction of a social policy. According to Baldwin, political conflict along class lines is only one line of conflict formed during the extension of policies of social insurance. The social policy preferences of various groups emerge as a result of the interaction among class and a range of additional variables, such as the "capacity of a group for self-reliance," the "demographic outlook," "risk incidence," and "economic prospects" of a group (Baldwin 1990: 12).[1] Baldwin suggests that the structure of existing policies also influences the policy demands of various groups and the political coalitions that can form during the introduction of social insurance.

Baldwin's analysis is successful in specifying the concern of middle classes in the provision of social insurance and in demonstrating that parties representing middle classes have played a critical role in the expansion of the welfare state. However, he remains largely uninterested in exploring the social policy preferences of employers. Important questions concerning firms' preferences in the development of institutions of social insurance remain unexplored. What are the specific policy considerations of firms during the process of social policy reform? Do we encounter variation in the policy preferences of employers, and, if so, what variables explain this variation? One important cause of this omission is the selection of cases. Baldwin's analysis focuses primarily on the development of public pensions and leaves out other important policies, such as unemployment or sickness insurance, policies with significant labor market implications for firms. The justification for this selection of cases presented by Baldwin is rather problematic. "Many aspects of the welfare state are clientelistic, in the sense that their constituencies have largely been set by definition. The issues they raise have therefore rarely passed beyond the calculations of how generous a treatment a particular group can wrest from society as a whole. That unemployment insurance has, until recently, been the concern mainly of wage earners or that measures against work accidents are a matter of most pressing concern

---

[1] As Baldwin points out both the "capacity for self-reliance" and the "incidence of a risk" of a particular group can evolve over time. These variables also vary between nations (Baldwin 1990: 16–18).

to the industrial proletariat will come as no surprise. There has been little to distinguish the politics of implementing or resisting these initiatives from the battles surrounding other, equally clientelistic measures aimed at different social groups: tariffs, for example, or the subsidies, price supports, protection against foreclosure and other generous measures responsible for channeling substantial public resources in the direction of agrarian classes. Disputes of this sort ... were in *no sense specific to social policy*" (Baldwin 1990: 50). Dismissing the politics surrounding the development of crucial institutions of the welfare state – such as disability or unemployment insurance – as "uncharacteristic for social policy" is an unnecessary self-limitation of Baldwin's approach.

During recent years, the study of employers has moved to the forefront of research in comparative political economy (Hall and Soskice 2001a, Hollingsworth and Boyer 1997, Crouch and Streeck 1997, Kitschelt et al. 1999). In part, this revival of interest in the political role of business is a consequence of the inability of labor-centered explanations to account for recent patterns of change in the institutions of wage bargaining (Thelen 1994: 107). Differences in the organizational resources of labor movements or in the political strategies pursued by trade union organizations remained insufficient in explaining the resilience or transformation of corporatist institutions during the recent two decades. The greatest shifts in the level of centralization of the institutions of wage bargaining involving either a decentralization from national-level to industry-level bargaining (experienced by some Northern European economies) or a recentralization of wage bargaining (experienced, for example, by Italy), were the result of the political moves of employers' associations (Thelen 2001). Similarly, as Kathleen Thelen argues, despite the current strains, the resilience of the German institutions of wage bargaining is the consequence of the "unwillingness of German employers to abandon the German model" due to the high vulnerability of German firms to overt labor conflict (Thelen 2000: 167, Thelen and van Vijnbergen 2000). As Thelen remarked, "a fact that became painfully clear in the dynamics of corporatism's breakdown" was that "scholars had misunderstood the genesis of corporatism" (Thelen 1994: 107). Peter Swenson's pioneering research has corrected this misunderstanding. Swenson's analysis shed important light on the role played by large export-dependent firms in bringing about the centralization of wage-bargaining systems in Sweden and Denmark as a means to contain the wage militancy of unions in the sheltered sectors (Swenson 1991: 513, 544).

This new, business-centered literature has made important contributions to the analysis of labor-based institutions in advanced industrialized societies. First, these studies have shown that centralized institutions of wage bargaining provide important policy benefits to firms (as well as labor-based organizations). Among these benefits are wage restraint and labor peace. Second, these studies have described a range of policy trade-offs faced by employers during the process of design of these institutions and have developed specific hypotheses about the policy preferences of different sectors when choosing between firm-level and national-level wage bargaining institutions. Finally, this literature has contributed to our understanding of the conditions facilitating the formation of cross-class alliances in support of or opposition against centralized institutions of wage bargaining.

Given the pivotal role played by employers in the centralization of wage bargaining, what is the importance of business in the development of policies of social insurance? For power resource scholars, the answer to this question seemed unproblematic. A new wave of empirical research has begun to challenge this proposition, suggesting that the answer is far from self-evident. A number of studies have pointed to the beneficial economic consequences of social insurance for firms. Scholars of Japan have suggested that the extensive provision of social policy benefits at the firm level was an important factor accounting for the unique combination of high levels of employment and high levels of provision of firm-specific skills (Estevez-Abe 1999). Recent historical research has documented the support shown by employers of key policies of the Swedish and American welfare states, challenging the assumption of monolithic business opposition to social insurance proposed by power resource scholars (Swenson 1997, 2002, Gordon 1994, Jacoby 1997, Martin 2000). The goal of this book is to contribute to this new direction of research and to develop a systematic account of the role of employers in the development of modern institutions of social insurance.

A Preview of the Book

When and why do employers develop an interest in social insurance? I argue that social policies play an important economic role for the labor market strategies of firms: they reduce the reluctance of workers to invest in skills. To illustrate this statement, consider the following example. Both a worker and a firm face an initial choice whether to invest in some skills, but they both face a high level of uncertainty about the expected return on these skills over various employment states. Investment in skills may bring higher returns to the worker and the employer in the form of higher productivity and higher wages. To make these investments, the worker needs some guarantees that during periods of nonemployment – such as sickness, disability, and unemployment – she will be able to retain a relatively higher wage than low-skill workers. I suggest that the presence of public and private social policies helps workers and employers solve this problem and make these investments in skills. Private social policies lower the mobility of workers across firms and increase the incentives of workers to invest in firm-specific skills. Contributory insurance, policies with earnings-related benefits, that replace a significant part of the income lost by the workers also increase some of the incentives of workers to invest in skills. These policies, which are often administered, in a corporatist fashion, by associations of capital and labor, also allow employers to influence the operation of labor markets and reduce the pressure on high-skill workers to accept jobs that are in conflict with the preexisting skill qualifications of workers (Mares 1997). As existing scholarship has pointed out, policies of social insurance protect workers for the loss of income experienced during employment-related risks. However, they also protect the investment in skills made by *employers*.

These observations are the starting point of the model of business preferences toward different social insurance policies developed in Chapter 2. This model studies two questions. First, what are the social policy outcomes preferred by different firms? What are the most significant variables that affect the social policy preferences of firms and that predict the cleavages in the business community during the introduction of various social policies? The preceding discussion has suggested that in the presence of skilled workers, the benefits of social policies for various firms can outweigh the costs of social insurance of employers. The model suggests that additional variables that affect the social policy of employers are firm size and the relative incidence of risk facing a firm. (The latter variable is defined as the difference in the incidence of risks of workers facing a firm and the economy-wide incidence of risk.)

What is the relative role of unions and employers during the process of bargaining over a new social policy? Incorporating the predictions about the social policy preferences of employers, I characterize the conditions under which cross-class alliances among trade unions and employers will form. I distinguish among prestrategic alliances, in which unions and employers support their preferred outcome, and strategic alliances, in which unions and employers support a social policy that is not necessarily their preferred outcome. I develop a number of propositions about the material and informational consequences of existing private and public policies and their impact on the formation of these strategic alliances. The analysis also points to the critical importance of policy entrepreneurs who can rely on a variety of policy resources to facilitate the formation of these strategic alliances.

Chapters 3 through 6 explore the empirical implications of the model. I test the hypotheses developed in the first part of the book in a large number of cases, spanning nearly a century of social policy development. Germany and France have been selected as country cases in an effort to maximize the variation along crucial independent variables – in this particular case, the relative balance of power of large and small firms (King, Keohane, and Verba 1994). As the empirical chapters illustrate, beginning with the second half of the nineteenth century, France and Germany have differed strongly along several variables of interest – such as the distribution of skills in the economy, the strength and organizational centralization of the labor movement, and the fiscal and bureaucratic capabilities of the state. This variation has played a critical role in shaping the strategic alliances among capital and labor and the resulting social policy outcomes.

Chapter 3 analyzes the introduction of social insurance compensating victims of workplace accidents during the last two decades of the nineteenth century. Whereas Germany introduced compulsory social insurance providing benefits to industrial workers, French policy makers settled for a more modest reform of existing liability laws. Chapter 4 analyzes the role played by German and French employers in the development of policies of unemployment compensation. In Chapter 5 I examine the defeat of proposals to develop universalistic insurance during the first years of the postwar period. Chapter 6 studies the evolution of early retirement policies during recent decades and the systematic failure of German and French policy makers to stop the process of early exit from the labor market. The final chapter summarizes the implications of the analysis.

2

Interests and Coalitions in the Development of the Modern Welfare State

> Joseph Schumpeter once claimed to be able to detect the thunder of world history in accounts of public finance. Fiscal topics – issues of the budget, taxation, the growth of state spending – best revealed the spirit of a people, its cultural level, its social structure. The development of the welfare state is a topic which similarly conceals questions of utmost importance under matters that may at first seem merely technical and abstruse. Social insurance, old-age pensions, workers' compensation, actuarial risk, waiting time, point indexation and cost-of-living differentials rarely seem the stuff of dramatic narrative. In fact, approached from the right angle, the nuts and bolts of social policy testify to the heated struggles of classes and interests. The battles behind the welfare state lay bare the structure and conflict of modern society.
>
> Peter Baldwin, *The Politics of Social Solidarity*

Chapter 1 has analyzed the main reasons for the recent resurgence of interest in the study of employers by comparative political economists (Hall and Soskice 2001a, Hollingsworth and Boyer 1997, Crouch and Streeck 1997, Kitschelt et al. 1999). Employers occupy again a central stage in most comparative studies of public policy after a long period of time in which debates about the role of business in modern capitalist societies "had reached an intellectual *cul-de-sac*" and in which labor-centered or state-centered analyses occupied a prominent place (Pierson and Hacker 2000: 1). The new business-centered literature resolves many of the intractable analytical questions that were the subject of heated debates among pluralists and neo-Marxists during the 1960s and 1970s. It has made significant progress in identifying the sources of cross-national differences in the preferences and organizational capabilities of employers and the role of business in the development of wage-bargaining institutions, institutions of corporate governance, policies of training and skill formation, and industrial policies (Culpepper 1998, Gordon 1994, Jacoby 1997, Martin 1995a, 2000, Pontusson and Swenson 1996, Swenson 1991, 2002, Soskice 1994, 1997, Thelen 2000, Thelen and Kume 1999, Ziegler 2000). The goal of this chapter is to develop a framework that allows us to specify the role played by employers in the development of policies of social insurance.

This broad theme can be, in turn, disaggregated into several narrower questions. The first objective of the chapter is to identify the determinants of business preferences toward different social policy arrangements. Can policies that compensate employees for the loss of income during periods in which the employment relationship is temporarily interrupted – due to sickness, disability, or unemployment – also provide direct and tangible *benefits* to employers? What precisely are the "institutional advantages" social policies can offer to firms? Under what conditions do these benefits exceed the costs of social policies that, for employers, come in the form of social insurance contributions or as constraints on firms' discretionary ability to "rely on the labor input during the production process," to use the impersonal language of economists? In short, the analysis of business preferences toward different institutions of social insurance seeks to uncover the factors affecting the cost-benefit calculations made by different firms when faced with the introduction of a new social policy.

In examining the policy preferences of employers, I develop specific propositions about the precise details of policy design favored by different firms. Thus, the goal is not only to explore why, under particular circumstances, employers have an interest in the provision of social insurance but also to develop an analysis of the *institutional* preferences of firms. Under what conditions do employers favor private, firm-level programs of social insurance? How do employers regard proposals that attempt to socialize risks? Under what conditions do employers oppose the enactment of social policy programs? In specifying the social policy preferences of firms, I will also examine the factors accounting for the cleavages within the business community during different episodes of social policy reform. What explains the policy disagreement among employers during the introduction of a new social policy? Can certain structural characteristics of a firm such as its size or the skill level of the work force predict the policy preference of the firm? Do firm preferences vary across different subsystems of the welfare state, for example, old-age and unemployment insurance? If so, what factors explain these differences?

In the first part of the chapter, I characterize the most significant factors shaping the social policy preferences of firms and specify the conditions under which self-interested, profit-maximizing firms – facing competition in domestic or international markets – nevertheless support social policies. Relying on these insights, the second part of the chapter reexamines the political cleavages and coalitions that emerge during the introduction of a new social policy. If employers are not *a priori* opposed to the introduction of social policies, as previous scholarship assumed, what is the role of class conflict in the historical evolution of the welfare state? Even if employers support some social policies, what questions of policy design continue to be the object of distributional conflict among capital and labor? When should we expect the formation of political coalitions among capital and labor, and what are the broader political and institutional factors facilitating the formation of these cross-class coalitions?

The chapter begins by identifying the broad range of social policies that are historically possible. The following section identifies the most salient issues of policy design confronted by employers and unions during the development of a new social policy and the variety of trade-offs faced by these actors.

The Universe of Social Policies

Social insurance policies come in a variety of institutional forms. Some policies are organized by private actors, such as trade unions, mutual aid societies, firms, or associations of producers. Other policies are exclusively administered by the state. Some policies have narrow pools of beneficiaries, "a small circle, sometimes self-selected to its advantage, sometimes isolated to its own peril" (Baldwin 1990: 2). In some cases, different occupational groups – peasants, miners, doctors – have their own institutions of social insurance. In other cases, the entire population is eligible for benefits. Some policies provide meager benefits and are characterized by stringent eligibility conditions. Other social policies attempt to replace most, if not all of the income lost by workers due to sickness, disability, or other factors that temporarily diminish their opportunities for employment.

A set of simplifications is necessary to guide us through this thick institutional terrain. In an effort to compress this empirical diversity, I begin by assuming that social policies can be mapped in a two-dimensional social policy space (see Figure 2.1). I define social policy broadly, to include both private and publicly financed social insurance. The two axes of

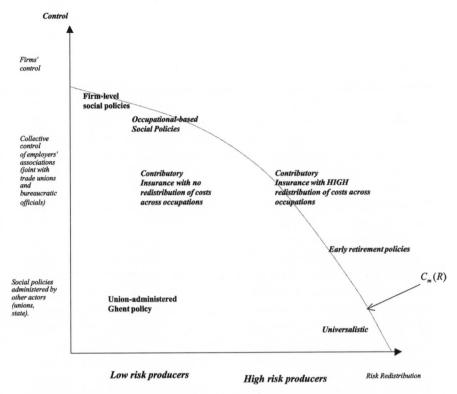

Figure 2.1 The social policy space

the social policy space represent the two issues of policy design that were politically most contested in the history of the welfare state.

The first of these issues concerns the scope of social policy coverage. The percentage of the population that has access to social benefits varies considerably over time, across countries, and, within the same country, across different labor market risks. As Peter Baldwin reminds us, only some welfare states "went from Bismarck to Beveridge. . . . Insurance has existed for millennia; social insurance developed in response to the widespread and multiple uncertainties attendant on modern economies, while the solidaristic welfare state of a Marshallian kind has been the exclusive preserve of only a few nations at certain times in the twentieth century" (Baldwin 1990: 5). A few examples can illustrate this remark. At the turn of the century, after a first wave of social policy reforms pioneered by the Bismarckian legislation, the percentage of the labor force entitled to policy benefits in case of occupational injuries was as high as 71 percent in Germany, 39 percent in Britain, and around 15 percent in Austria, Denmark, Norway, and Switzerland. At the onset of the Great Depression, the percentage of the work force eligible for unemployment benefits was 58 percent in the United Kingdom, 44 percent in Germany, 34 percent in Austria, and around 20 percent in Belgium, Denmark, Italy, and Switzerland. Following World War II, a number of countries such as Denmark, Finland, Sweden, Norway, Switzerland, and the United Kingdom extended sickness and old-age benefits to the entire population. Similar efforts to expand insurance failed in France, Germany, or Austria, countries in which, for the first decades of the postwar period, the percentage of the work force eligible for social insurance benefits was as high as 70 percent (cf. Flora and Alber 1983: 460–461).

The horizontal axis of the social policy space represented in Figure 2.1 is labeled "risk redistribution." This dimension of the social policy space captures both the variation in the scope of insurance and the diversity in the mode in which social policies reapportion the incidence and costs of various risks among labor market participants. The positioning of various social policies along this horizontal axis of the social policy space is affected by a combination of decisions on two interrelated questions of policy design. The first concerns the "boundary" of the risk pool. How broad is the risk pool of social insurance and who is eligible for policy benefits? Is social policy restricted to the participants of a single firm? Is it restricted to workers in one industry, as is the case with many occupational social policies or policies established by individual trade unions or employers' associations? Is the insurance mandatory for the entire population of a country – or are certain groups or occupations excluded from social insurance coverage? Second, additional policy decisions that determine the relationship between the incidence of a risk and the level of social insurance contributions affect the degree of risk redistribution of a social policy. Does the calculation of insurance contributions respect actuarial principles? Does the state subsidize the policy of social insurance (using additional sources of revenues) or are these policies "self-financing," relying exclusively on the contributions of labor market participants? The degree of risk redistribution of a social policy is lower if social insurance contributions are tightly coupled to the incidence of a risk; it is higher for those social policies that loosen this relationship.

The second politically divisive question in the history of the welfare state concerns the distribution of policy responsibilities in the administration of social insurance among unions, employers, and state bureaucrats. The sheer amount of financial resources collected in the form of social insurance contributions and the numerous labor market implications of social policies increased the political significance of these questions for all participants in social insurance reform. Beginning with the earliest social policy reforms, conflict over these questions has been a central component of the politics of social policy reform. In 1902 the main publication of the Federation of German Trade Unions referred to these "administrative questions" (*Verwaltungsfragen*) as the "key element of the entire social insurance" (Allgemeiner Deutscher Gewerkschaftsbund 1902a: 308). French trade unions also regarded questions of control over the allocation of social insurance benefits as policy issues that were on "a par with questions of wages" (Hatzfeld 1971: 220). A key motivation accounting for the participation of employers in the deliberations over a new social policy was the desire to preempt the "meddlesome interference" of trade unions or bureaucrats in the determination of social insurance contributions and allocation of social policy benefits (*Deutsche Arbeitgeberzeitung* 6 December 1925).[1]

I label the vertical axis of the social policy space in Figure 2.1 "control." We can think of "control" as authority over policy decisions concerning the determination of the level of insurance contributions and benefits, adjustments in the financing of the social policy in response to the expansion or contraction of the contributory base of social insurance, the modification of administrative criteria defining the entitlements for social policy benefits, and so on. The axis captures the distribution of responsibilities in the administration of different social policies among unions, employers, and representatives of the state. Without any loss of generality, we can recode this axis as measuring responsibilities in the administration of social insurance retained by one of these three actors. To simplify the presentation, I recode this axis to denote the relative share of the policy responsibilities of firms. Thus, for policies taking high values along this axis, individual firms retain a high level of discretion over all important social policy decisions.

---

[1] See, for example, the statement of the main publication of the Federation of German Employers' Associations regarding the design of unemployment insurance. "Unemployment insurance cannot remain in the same hands as communal social assistance.... A sharp and clear separation must take place. Insurance has to be conducted based on the policy needs of the economy [*Bedürfnisse der Wirtschaft*] and based on the needs of insurance. All other interests that are in conflict with this goal have to be excluded." *Deutsche Arbeitgeberzeitung* 6 December 1925.

Policies taking intermediate values along this dimension of the social policy space are administered by associations of employers and trade unions. This principle of the "corporatist" organization of social insurance was pioneered during the early social policy reforms in Germany during the 1880s and adopted by a large number of countries in the design of their social insurance systems. Finally, in social policies that take extremely low values along this dimension of the social policy space, employers are entirely absent from the administration of social insurance. The most significant policy decisions remain in the hands of either trade unions or government officials.

In Figure 2.1 I position a variety of social policies within the policy space bounded by the two axes "risk redistribution" and "control." At one extreme of the social policy space, we find universalistic social policies that take high values on the risk redistribution axis and low values on the control dimension. The entire population is entitled to social insurance benefits, guaranteeing de facto that the "community of risks coincides with the entire human community" (Baldwin 1990: 2). Business plays no role in the administration of universalistic social policies. Consequently, these policies take zero values along the control axis of the social policy space. At the other extreme, we find firm-level social policies. In those policies that take the lowest value along the risk redistribution axis, the risk pool is restricted to the members of a single firm. Because these policies are administered exclusively by employers, who retain a high level of discretion in initiating and withholding social insurance benefits and in targeting these benefits to a particular subset of their employees – the highly skilled or the highly productive workers – these policies take high values along the control dimension of the social policy space.

Various forms of contributory social insurance can be situated along an imaginary line linking private-type social policies to universalistic social policies. Some of these policies are, de facto, closer to the universalistic pole of the social policy space. In this case, employers retain only a very limited (and sometimes only "ceremonial") role in the institutions administering social insurance. But the level of risk redistribution of these policies can be very high, if, for example, social insurance contributions are uniform across occupations and not tied to the level of risk affecting the particular occupation. Conversely, we find different types of contributory insurance that, from the point of view of policy design, are closer to private-type social policies. These include institutions in which, although social insurance is mandatory, there is no interoccupational redistribution of risks and there are no subsidies directed at high-risk occupations that attempt to compensate for the higher costs associated with the provision of social benefits. There are several ways in which the responsibilities in the administration of these policies can be divided among unions, employers, and the state. In some cases, these actors share policy responsibilities; in other cases, either unions or employers retain an exclusive monopoly over the administration of social insurance. A policy administered by an industry association of employers but whose benefits go to all (or nearly all) workers of an industry takes high values along the control dimension of the social policy space. Examples of these social policies are the *Knappschaften*, social insurance funds established by German employers in the mining industry beginning in the second half of the nineteenth century or the Caisse des Forges, an institution established by French employers in the mining and metalworking industry (Geyer 1987, Hatzfeld 1971, Pinot 1924).

In addition to these three major types of social insurance – private-type social policies, contributory insurance, and universalistic social policies – Figure 2.1 situates a number of other policies within the social policy space bounded by the two axes, risk redistribution and control. Let me discuss the positioning of two additional policies within this social policy space. Ghent policies of unemployment insurance are situated in the lower left-hand quadrant of the social policy space. As Chapter 4 shows, these policies resulted from political decisions of governments to subsidize pre-existing institutions of unemployment support organized primarily by trade unions. An important feature of policy design that explains the positioning of these policies in the lower left-hand corner of the social policy space is the monopoly held by trade unions in the administration of unemployment benefits. A number of variables affecting the strength of the labor movement (such as the degree of centralization of the labor movement and trade union density) influence the location of these policies along the horizontal axis of the social policy space. If a more centralized labor movement administers these policies, the degree of risk redistribution of a Ghent policy of unemployment insurance is higher.

Early retirement policies also occupy a special position within the social policy space. In the case of these policies, individual firms initiate the early retirement case and play a very significant role determining the level of social policy benefits, which often consist of a combination of unemployment and disability benefits and a lump-sum payment made by the firm. Thus, along the control axis of the social policy space, these policies can be situated in the immediate vicinity of private social policies. As is

argued in Chapter 6, what is unique to early retirement policies is a "diffu-
sion" of the costs across a large number of subsystems of the welfare state –
most often unemployment, old-age, and disability insurance (Gaullier 1992,
Guillemard 1997). It follows that early retirement policies take higher values along the horizontal axis of the social policy space than the values taken
by a contributory insurance policy. Early retirement policies are, in fact,
characterized by a unique combination of risk redistribution and control
that positions them in the upper right-hand corner of the social policy
space.

An additional consideration about Figure 2.1 is necessary at this point.
It is important to point out that there are no social policies taking simultaneously high values along both axes, risk redistribution and control. A
hypothetical example of a policy situated in the upper right-hand corner
of the policy space would be a social policy entirely administered by a firm
with no participation of labor representatives or the state, but which remains
universalistic in character. In other words, the risk pool of social insurance
would include the entire population, the policy would be tax-financed, the
level of insurance contributions would not be differentiated across occupations, yet, at the same time, all administrative decisions would remain in the
hands of one single firm! Such policies are historically unknown. I model
the nonexistence of these policies as a constraint on the set of possible social policies. The upper boundary of the social policy space in Figure 2.1
represents this policy constraint graphically.[2]

---

[2] We can provide a more formal characterization of this constraint on the social policy space
(which will be important in the derivation of the maximum of the utility of employers).
More formally, we can regard the upper boundary of the social policy space as the graph
of a function $C_m = C_m(R)$, which models the maximum level of control (C) available to
employers for social policies with a given level of risk redistribution (R). To characterize the
behavior of this function $C_m(R)$, three additional assumptions are necessary at this stage.
First, at the origin of the social policy space, the function $C_m(R)$ takes the value 0. This
policy outcome – in which control and risk redistribution take the value 0 – will be also
labeled as *None*. Second, I assume that in the case of universalistic social policies (at the
point $R_{UNIVERSALISTIC}$), the function $C_m(R)$ takes again the value of 0. This assumption,
again, is a very natural one. In universalistic social policies, employers play no role in the
administration of social insurance. Third, I assume that $C_m(R)$ is concave as a function of R.
This is equivalent to asking that the social policy space be convex. The underlying justification for this assumption is that the social policy space can be thought of as a continuum and
not as a discrete collection of social policies. By definition, the assumption of convexity of
the social policy space requires that if two social policies SP_1 and SP_2 exist, then all policies
situated on the line segment linking SP_1 and SP_2 are also situated in the social policy space.
This requirement is satisfied, because all social policies on the line segment between SP_1
and SP_2 can be thought of as weighted combinations of SP_1 and SP_2.

A final observation about the structure of the social policy space is important at this point. The diagonal axis in Figure 2.1 – linking private social policies to contributory insurance and universalistic programs – points to the existence of a policy trade-off between risk redistribution and control. When confronted with the introduction of a new social policy, employers are never able to achieve a maximal level of risk redistribution and control at the same time. Policies in which employers' control is maximal (private social policies) remain ultimately incompatible with a very high degree of risk redistribution. Conversely, in policies characterized by a high degree of risk redistribution (universalistic social policies), control remains very low.[3] The existence of this policy trade-off raises, however, the interesting question, What actors are more interested in the advantages of risk redistribution and what actors are more interested in the advantages of control? In examining the policy preferences of unions and employers, I seek to formulate a number of hypotheses about the conditions under which different actors prefer different policy combinations of risk redistribution and control.

The Social Policy Preferences of Employers

The proposition that the welfare state impacts in numerous ways the activities of firms is relatively uncontroversial (Pierson 2000a, Manow 2000a, 2000b). Depending on the method of financing social policy commitments in advanced industrialized countries, employers' contributions to social insurance constitute somewhere between 28 (France) and 7 (United States) percent of the nonwage labor costs of firms (OECD 1999: 15).[4] Social policies impact the ability of firms to hire or dismiss workers. The structure and design of social policies have important effects on the ability of firms to train new apprentices or retrain existing workers. The relative generosity of disability, unemployment, or pension benefits affects the "labor market exit strategies" of elderly workers and, thus, indirectly the employment strategies of firms. As Peter Swenson's research has pointed out, the design of social policies affects not only the labor market strategies pursued by firms, but also the nature of competition in product markets. As Swenson suggests,

---

[3] Note that trade unions are confronted with a similar policy constraint. To visualize the constraint, one needs to relabel the control axis as measuring the maximum control retained by trade unions.

[4] Data are for 1998 and represent the social security contributions of employers as a percentage of labor costs. See OECD 1999: table 1.3 (p. 15).

minimum wage standards and social policies "are a regulatory instrument in ruinous product market competition" and "prevent the kind of product market competition enabled by downward wage flexibility" (Swenson 1997: 74, Swenson 2002: chap. 2).[5] Swenson's argument implies that in economies in which cartel-type agreements restricting the level of product-market competition are illegal (such as the United States), the welfare state provides institutional benefits to employers that are otherwise provided by protective product market regulations. Finally, the welfare state can affect the costs and availability of capital to firms and, thus, the broader investment strategies pursued by different sectors. A number of scholars have pointed to the importance of funds of the second-tier pension system as an important source of "patient capital," stimulating the development of particular sectors of the Swedish economy (Pontusson 1992). Similarly, students of the Japanese political economy have highlighted the pervasive regulation of private pension funds by the Japanese government in an effort to channel cheap capital to targeted industrial sectors (Estevez-Abe 1999, 2001).

What *is* controversial is the question of the magnitude of the benefits and costs of social policies for different firms. In most economic analyses, social policies enter the utility of employers with a negative sign.[6] In simpler terms, social policies raise the labor costs of firms, decreasing overall profitability. Other economic analyses regard labor market and other provisions of social insurance as an impediment on the ability of firms to deploy their labor market resources flexibly and, thus, as a source of "welfare losses" for the firms. In short, the presumption of most economic analyses is that the costs of social policies always outweigh the benefits of social policies to employers. The predictions developed by these economic models can be regarded as the null hypothesis of the analysis developed in this section.

Numerous empirical studies, however, provide strong systematic evidence disconfirming this proposition. The first empirical anomaly is the voluntary introduction of private policies by employers in most industrializing societies *prior* to the adoption of compulsory social policies. According to a survey of private institutions of social insurance carried out by the Prussian Ministry of Trade in 1876, 4,850 enterprises (employing

---

[5] As Swenson argues, the role of the welfare state in regulating product market competition is particularly important for American employers, given that cartelist agreements are illegal in the United States. Swenson 1997.

[6] When writing of the utility of employers, economists generally assume that firms maximize total revenues (price times output) minus total labor costs (wages and social security contributions).

over 620,000 workers) had established 11,771 private institutions of social insurance (Fischer 1978: 41). In addition to these firm-level social policies, German employers participated in the financing and administration of "societal insurance funds" (*Unterstützungsvereine*). These institutions experienced a rapid growth in the period prior to the first wave of social policy reforms. In 1860 Germany had 776 insurance funds (with over 170,000 members). The number increases to 1,654 funds (and 420,000 members) in 1874 (Fischer 1978: 41). In France, the mining, railway, and metalworking industries were a laboratory for experimentation with private social policy arrangements during the early period of industrialization. According to a survey commissioned by the Labor Office of the Ministry of Commerce in 1898, 72 percent of the workers (around 184,789 workers) in mining were eligible for private pension policies (Office du Travail 1898, Gibon 1895). Other historical lines of analyses have argued that, on numerous occasions, employers have actively supported various forms of social insurance and rejected private policies. Peter Swenson's pioneering research has identified the strong support of Swedish employers for the centralization of the wage bargaining system and for key policies of the Swedish welfare state (Swenson 2002). Historians of the German welfare state have argued that, on numerous occasions, important segments of the business community have supported institutions of the German system of social protection (Ullmann 1979b, 1981, Breger 1982, 1994). Other studies of the development of social policies in interwar France have attached significance to the role played by employers, most notably in the development of natalist policies (in an effort of firms to retain women workers) (Pedersen 1993). Although the subject of the role played by American employers in the introduction of the Social Security Act is still the object of considerable academic controversy, most studies agree that *some* segments of the American business community supported elements of the New Deal (Skocpol and Ikenberry 1983, Skocpol 1992, Swenson 1997).

These significant examples illustrate that, under some conditions, social policies provide distinct institutional advantages to firms. To put it more simply, the costs of social policy for employers do not always outweigh the benefits provided by social policy to firms. It appears, thus, that the assumption of business opposition to social insurance is too strong to capture the broad empirical variety in the social policy preferences of employers.

What is the underlying motivation for business interest in social insurance? What are the institutional benefits provided by social policies to firms? The starting point of my analysis is the observation that social policies help address market failures in skill formation (Mares 1999, Estevez-Abe et al. 2001). To illustrate this problem, consider the following situation. Let us assume that a worker maximizes an expected utility over various employment states that includes, in addition to the wage, income received during periods of nonemployment, such as sickness, disability, and unemployment. Assuming similar probabilities of "nonemployment," a high-skill worker faces a higher loss in income than a low-skill worker during periods in which the employment relationship is interrupted. Thus, before investing in skills, a worker will demand a guarantee that her income during periods of employment losses will be higher than the income received by a low-wage worker. More specifically, a worker will make investment in skills only in the presence of a social policy with earnings-related benefits that guarantees a higher reservation wage than for low-skill workers. It follows that it is rational for a firm to commit resources to these policies to induce workers to overcome their reluctance to invest in skills.

This example has a number of important implications. First, it suggests that social policies can be regarded as institutional solutions to a "prior game" between firms and employees over investment in skills. From the perspective of the firm, the primary function of social policy is to make workers overcome their initial reluctance to invest in skills. Social policies have fulfilled their key economic function if investment in skills takes place. Whether the worker returns to the firm after a period of long-term unemployment or disability is only a secondary concern to firms. Second, this example suggests that the most significant policy instrument that mitigates the reluctance of workers to invest in skills is the indexation of the social policy benefits to wages, thus, the *gradation of the reservation wage*. Other policy instruments – such as restrictions on the type of jobs that nonemployed workers can accept – further raise the reservation wage of high-skill workers, lowering the incentives of these workers to accept jobs that do not correspond to their skill qualifications. The more general implication is that social policies with earnings-related benefits provide the institutional foundation for investment in skills. This reconceptualization of the function of social insurance suggests that social policies that protect the relative income losses of high-skill workers provide, in fact, important economic advantages to firms as well.

These general hypotheses suggest that under some conditions, such as skill shortages in the economy, the benefits provided by social policies to employers *can* outweigh the costs imposed by social policies on firms.[7] This section develops a model of the social policy preferences of employers that builds on this insight and specifies more rigorously the benefits and costs of different social policies to firms. Should firms provide social policy benefits privately, or should they support the development of "socialized" insurance? To examine these questions, I return to the social policy space outlined in the previous section. The analysis proceeds in two steps. First I examine the cost-benefit calculations made by firms toward policies characterized by different combinations of risk redistribution and control. Next I seek to identify the most significant firm-level characteristics that affect the variation in the utility of firms along the social policy space.

As discussed earlier, the vertical axis of the social policy space measures the residual responsibilities in the administration of social insurance retained by employers. We can think of control as a bundle of institutional features that captures the authority retained by employers over policy decisions involving the determination of the level of social insurance contributions and benefits, incremental adjustments in the financing of social policy in response to the expansion or contraction of the contributory basis of social insurance, the modification of administrative criteria defining the entitlement for social policy benefits, and so on. To analyze the variation in the utility of a firm along the control axis of the social policy space, it is important to compare the relative magnitude of the benefits and costs of an increase in control.

What are the costs for an individual firm associated with an upward movement along the vertical axis of the social policy space? The most direct implication of this increase in the level of 'control' retained by employers in the administration of social insurance is an increase in firms' share in the financing of the respective social policy. The contributions of employers to the financing of the social policy increase proportionally with an increase in employers' control in the administration of social insurance. Universalistic social policies are generally financed by income taxes and thus affect

---

[7] Several economic historians have explained the origin of private, firm-level policies in Germany as a response of employers to the disruptive turnover rates. According to Mary Nolan, "between 1870 and 1890, fluctuation rates for the unskilled were between 70 and 80 percent and for the industrial labor force as a whole between 40 and 50 percent. Although mines and factories made little effort to retain the unskilled, who often left within a few months, they did build a small stable core of skilled workers, who were tied to the firm by high wages, company housing and welfare programs." Nolan 1986: 369.

employers only indirectly, via their impact on the general price level of the economy. In contrast, contributory insurance policies are financed by payroll taxes. Generally, the distribution of the tax burden among employers and employees is proportional to the responsibilities of these actors in the administration of the particular branch of social insurance.[8] Finally, private social policies can be financed through a combination of contributions of employers and employees or, in some particular circumstances, by employers' contributions alone.

What benefits do employers derive from an increased involvement in the administration of social insurance? The most obvious advantage is an increase in their *discretion* over the determination of the social policy benefits. Social policies can become an important instrument complementing the employment practices of firms. Firms gain additional flexibility to rely on social policies during periods of both labor market shortages and unemployment. Employers' own deliberations contain numerous references to the importance of high levels of discretion over the level, duration, and structure of social policy benefits. During the deliberations preceding the introduction of old-age insurance in France, the peak association representing French employers – the Union of Metallurgical and Mining Industries (Union des Industries Métallurgiques et Minières, or UIMM) – worried that a mandatory policy might displace existing private institutions of social insurance established by employers (Dumons and Pollet 1993, 1994: 82, UIMM n.d., Villey 1923a). Opposing the solutions considered by French lawmakers, these employers considered that firm-level social policies alone could guarantee to employers the necessary "flexibility [*souplesse*] and autonomy" (UIMM n.d.).[9] Discussing the relative merits and disadvantages

---

[8] To illustrate this statement, let us compare the distribution of financial responsibilities and control in two subsystems of the German welfare state, sickness and accident insurance, which were established in 1883 and 1884, respectively. In the case of compulsory health insurance, workers' contributions financed two-thirds of the costs of the policy, while contributions from employers covered the remaining one-third of the costs. The administrative setup of this subsystem of the German welfare state reflected the distribution of these financial responsibilities among unions and employers. In this case, trade unions and other labor associations elected two-thirds of the number of representatives to the sickness insurance funds, while employers elected the remaining one-third. In the case of accident insurance, employers financed two-thirds of the costs of the policy, while the state financed the remaining part. The administration of this subsystem of the German welfare state was delegated to liability associations (*Berufsgenossenschaften*), institutions that were staffed exclusively by employers.

[9] At this point, the UIMM claimed to represent "1,200 associations of employers grouping over 380,000 firms" (UIMM n.d.).

of compulsory old-age insurance, the Central Federation of German Industrialists (Centralverband Deutscher Industrieller) expressed concerns about the potential loss of employers' control over the distribution of social policy benefits. As these employers argued, "it might not be desirable in the interest of the stability of our relationship to the work force to have in the future the law alone stand between employers and employees. It is undesirable that the law alone should determine everything that workers should receive during sickness, old-age, and need" (Breger 1982: 136–137).

During the first years following World War II, German and French employers strongly opposed policies that proposed to give labor representatives a two-thirds majority in all institutions administering social insurance and that threatened to undermine a large number of private, firm-level institutions of social insurance. The Federation of German Employers' Associations (Vereinigung der Deutschen Arbeitgeberverbände) defended a social policy based on "parity representation of capital and labor in the administration of social insurance" as the only solution that could "avoid the concentration of economic power of one group over another" and invoked the important economic benefits of social policies "situated in close proximity to the firm" (*betriebsnahe Sozialversicherung*) (Vereinigung der Arbeitgeberverbände 1949d, Landesverband Südwestdeutschland der gewerblichen Berufsgenossenschaften 1946, Arbeitsgemeinschaft der bayerischen Industrie- und Handelskammern, 1947).

Policies taking high values along the control dimension of the social policy space – private-type social policies or contributory social insurance – provide a second distinct advantage to employers. This derives from the tight coupling between the social insurance benefits and the wage hierarchy established within the firm. Earnings-related social policy benefits raise the relative reservation wage of high-skill workers (relative to low-skill workers), lowering the incentives of these workers to take up jobs that do not correspond to their level of skill qualifications. Thus, earnings-related social policy benefits provide indirect institutional guarantees to *employers* that their investment in skills will not be undermined during periods in which their workers are temporarily out of work – such as moments of sickness, unemployment, or disability. Earnings-related benefits act, de facto, as a mechanism of skill retention.

The policy recommendations formulated by associations representing producers during numerous episodes of social policy reform stress the impact of the design of social policies on the decisions of workers to invest in skills and, thus, on the broader skill composition of the work force.

For example, in 1925 the Federation of German Employers' Associations expressed the following considerations about the consequences of rising unemployment: "The condition of unemployment leads to a change in the profession of the unemployed, which is an extremely unfavorable situation for the training of workers and for employers who can hold on to their skilled workers only with great difficulty" (Vereinigung der Deutschen Arbeitgeberverbände 1927: 136). To counteract these labor market developments, German employers recommended a dual change in the institutions administering unemployment insurance. First, they proposed an increase in the role of employers' representatives in the administration and distribution of unemployment benefits. Employers regarded this change in "control" as a guarantee that decisions over the structure and generosity of unemployment benefits "would be in agreement with the labor market conditions of the firm" (Vereinigung der Deutschen Arbeitgeberverbände 1920). Second, to increase the potential of the policy of unemployment insurance to protect the investment in skills of their employees, employers demanded to link the unemployment benefits to the wages of the unemployed (Vereinigung der Deutschen Arbeitgeberverbände 1920). The combination of these policy changes implied a transformation of the existing policy of unemployment assistance into a policy of unemployment insurance. Large German manufacturing employers endorsed this policy change, despite the increase in the payroll taxes of firms associated with the policy of unemployment insurance.

The implication of the preceding discussion is that the utility of a firm along the horizontal dimension of the social policy space can have both a positive and a negative sign, depending of the relative magnitude of the benefits and costs of control to a firm. If the benefits exceed the costs, the utility of firms will be increasing along the vertical axis of the social policy space. If the costs exceed the benefits, the utility of firms will decrease along this dimension. We can define the sensitivity to control of a firm (λ_C) as the partial derivative of the utility of the firm along the control dimension of the social policy space – in other words, $\lambda_C = \frac{\partial U}{\partial C}$.

What factors affect the sensitivity to control of a firm? A first variable that is very likely to influence the sign of the utility along the control dimension of the social policy space is the skill profile of a firm. The percentage of skilled workers in the total work force or the strength and the development of internal labor markets are empirical measures of the skill profile of a firm. A natural hypothesis is that the presence of skilled workers within the firm increases the importance of those features of policy design that "protect" the investment in skills. These features of policy design, in turn, increase the incentives of workers to invest in these skills. Discretion over the determination of social policy benefits also becomes important for firms that have invested significant resources in the skills of their workers. It is likely that these employers will favor social policies that will allow them to *target* benefits to a selective group of their workers and reward their job performance. These considerations allow us to hypothesize that for firms that have invested resources in the skills of their employees, the benefits of social policies characterized by high levels of control often outweigh the costs of these policies. In other words, I hypothesize that the sensitivity to control of these firms is positive.

A second hypothesis of this study is that firm *size* is a factor affecting a firm's sensitivity to control. This hypothesis is based on underlying considerations about differences in the relative market power of large and small firms. A number of empirical studies have demonstrated that firm size is a strong predictor of the degree of market power (Carlton and Perloff 1992: 187–188). Thus, assuming a higher market power of large firms, we can hypothesize that these firms will have a greater capacity than small producers to shift an increase in the nonwage labor costs onto consumers, in the form of higher prices.[10] This severely constrains the ability of many small producers to invest resources in the creation of social policy programs. Due to these financial constraints, small firms are more likely to discount the potential advantages of many social policies and focus primarily on the "unbearable burden" of social policies. In contrast, we expect large firms to discount more readily the effects of an increase in the level of payroll taxes. We can thus hypothesize that the sensitivity to control (λ_C) is positive for large firms and negative for small firms.

The empirical prediction following from the preceding discussion is that large firms employing skilled workers will favor social policies characterized by higher levels of control, whereas small firms employing low-skill workers will discount the potential institutional advantages of control. The analysis does not generate unambiguous predictions for small firms employing skilled workers and large firms whose work force consists, preponderantly, of low-skill workers. We can predict, however, that small firms employing high-skill workers will experience very strong policy dilemmas and a strong tension between the potential institutional advantages of social policies and

[10] This is a standard comparative statics result in a Cournot model of competition. See Carlton and Perloff 1992: 233–234.

the costs of social insurance. Hence, we can predict a stronger variability in the social policy preferences of these firms.

How does the utility of different firms vary along the risk redistribution dimension of the social policy space? How do employers choose among different social policies characterized by similar levels of control but different levels of risk redistribution? What variables affect firms' preferences along this dimension of the social policy space? As discussed earlier, a movement along the horizontal dimension of the social policy space from private to universalistic social policies involves an expansion of the level of coverage – and the inclusion of additional occupations as part of social insurance – and a weakening of the insurance principle in the determination of the level of contributions of the employer and employee. In policies that take high values along this axis, the level of insurance contributions and benefits is not based on actuarial criteria alone. To characterize the preferences of employers along this policy dimension, we need to specify the relative magnitude of two separate effects: the setup costs of a social policy versus the benefits associated with the participation in a broader pool of risks. Let λ_R denote the sensitivity to risk redistribution of a firm (defined as $\lambda_R = \frac{\partial U}{\partial R}$). We are interested in examining the firm-level characteristics that affect the magnitude and sign of λ_R.

The main hypothesis is that firms' preferences on issues of risk redistribution are affected by the *relative* incidence of the labor market risks affecting their work force. A measure of the relative incidence of a risk that will be used in the empirical tests of this proposition is the deviation of the risk facing the firm's work force from the average risk profile of the economy. A central hypothesis of the model is that an increase in the relative incidence of a risk may increase the benefits of risk redistribution for the individual firm. For these firms, private forms of insurance are often costly and extremely ineffective because sharing "good" and "bad" risks is rarely possible in these narrow risk pools. As the size of the risk pool increases, however, the advantages of interoccupational risk redistribution gradually begin to outweigh the initial setup costs of a social policy. It follows that firms facing a high incidence of a risk will support social policies taking high values along the risk redistribution axis. The related hypothesis implies that a decrease in the relative incidence of a risk will lower the benefits of risk redistribution for the firm. For employers in low-risk industries, social policies characterized by high levels of risk redistribution will be unattractive, since these policies turn these firms into subsidizers of high-risk industries.

It follows that the utility of a firm's facing a relatively lower incidence of risk will decrease along the risk redistribution dimension of the social policy space.

The factors affecting incidence of a labor market risk vary across the different risks that are covered by different social policies. For example, the level of mechanization and other variables characterizing the level of technological development of a particular industry affect the incidence of a risk of workplace accidents. Iron and steel producers or producers employing mechanical equipment or complex technologies are high-risk producers; artisans or producers in industries characterized by a lower level of mechanization are low-risk industries. The incidence of the risk of old age is affected by the demographic composition of the workers in a firm. In this case, high-risk producers are those firms employing a higher percentage of elderly workers, whereas low-risk producers rely on a younger work force. The most salient factor affecting the variation in the incidence of the risk of unemployment is the volatility in the demand for a firm's product, which, in turn, can be affected by the volatility in the terms of trade. In the case of the risk of unemployment, employers in seasonal occupations (such as construction) or employers facing wide swings in the prices of their products are high-risk producers. In contrast, employers facing stable and predictable product markets are low-risk producers.

These distinctions have specific implications for the details of policy design favored by different producers. We expect low-risk producers to favor occupational social policies, or contributory policies in which the social insurance contributions of employers is based on strict actuarial considerations – thus policies that involve no attempts to "redistribute" risks among occupations. In contrast, the model predicts that high-risk producers will favor social policies characterized by a high "redistribution of risks" in which the level of insurance contributions is not linked to the incidence of a risk. Given the significant consequences of these choices of policy design for the future social insurance contributions of employers, one expects to encounter a strong conflict and disagreement among producers over these details of the social insurance legislation.

To recapitulate, the analysis has hypothesized that the relative incidence of a risk affects the sensitivity to risk redistribution of a firm ($\lambda_R = \frac{\partial U}{\partial R}$). The sensitivity to risk redistribution is expected to be positive for firms in industries characterized by a high incidence of a labor market risk and negative for firms in industries facing a low incidence of a risk. High-risk

Table 2.1. *Predicted Effect of Incidence of Risk, Size, and Skill Intensity on Firms' Sensitivities for Risk Redistribution and Control*

	Size and Skill Intensity	
	Low	High
Incidence of Risk		
High	$\lambda_R > 0, \lambda_C < 0$	$\lambda_R > 0, \lambda_C > 0$
Low	$\lambda_R < 0, \lambda_C < 0$	$\lambda_R < 0, \lambda_C > 0$

industries are expected to favor highly redistributive social policies, such as universalistic social policies or contributory insurance solutions characterized by high interoccupational risk redistribution, whereas low-risk industries are expected to favor occupational social policies and oppose policy instruments that increase the degree of risk redistribution of a social policy.

The preceding two sections have identified a number of independent variables influencing the utility of firms toward the two dimensions of the social policy space. An increase in the incidence of a risk is expected to increase the benefits of risk redistribution for the firm. This implies that the sensitivity to risk redistribution (λ_R) of a firm in a high-risk industry will be positive, but that the sign of this sensitivity will be negative for employers in low-risk industries. The model has also hypothesized that both the size and skill intensity of a firm will increase the benefits derived by the firm from control, implying that the sensitivity to control (λ_C) of large firms and of firms employing high-skill workers will be positive. Table 2.1 summarizes these hypotheses about the impact of size, skill intensity, and incidence of a risk on the sensitivities for control and risk redistribution of different firms.

Relying on these hypotheses, we are now ready to analyze the preferences of firms in the entire social policy space. Due to the existence of a policy trade-off between risk redistribution and control, we can explore the conditions under which firms will prefer more "private-type" social policies (characterized by high levels of control and low levels of risk redistribution) and contrast them to cases in which firms will favor more redistributive social policies. Summarizing the analysis of the previous two sections, we can write the objective function modeling the utility of a firm over the entire social policy space as

$$U(R, C) = \lambda_R R + \lambda_C C,$$

in other words as a linear combination of R and C.[11] This specification of the utility function makes the important assumption that the sensitivity to risk redistribution (λ_R) and the sensitivity to control (λ_C) have constant sign throughout the social policy space. As discussed, firm-level characteristics, such as size, skill level, and incidence of risk, are expected to influence the magnitude and sign of both λ_R and λ_C. In other words,

$$U(R, C) = \lambda_C(\textit{size of firm, skill level}) \, C + \lambda_R(\textit{relative incidence of risk})R.$$

An analysis of the indifference curves of different firms allows us to locate the maximum of the utility function of firms in the social policy space. Let $C = C(R)$ be an indifference curve, such that $U[R, C(R)] = \textit{constant}$.[12] By implicit differentiation, we obtain

$$\frac{\partial C}{\partial R} = -\frac{\frac{\partial U}{\partial R}}{\frac{\partial U}{\partial C}} = -\frac{\lambda_R}{\lambda_C}.$$

This implies that the slopes of the indifference curves ($\frac{\partial C}{\partial R}$) have constant sign throughout the social policy space. If both the sensitivity to risk redistribution (λ_R) and the sensitivity to control (λ_C) have the same sign, the indifference curves of firms will be upward sloping throughout the social policy space. If the sensitivity to risk redistribution (λ_R) and the sensitivity to control (λ_C) have opposite signs, the indifference curves of firms will be downward sloping throughout the social policy space. Figure 2.2 represents these two separate cases.

The signs of the sensitivities toward risk redistribution (λ_R) and control (λ_C) predict both the slopes of the indifference curves of firms but also the *direction* along which the utility of firms increases throughout the social policy space. Consider first the case in which both the sensitivity to risk redistribution (λ_R) and the sensitivity to control (λ_C) have the same sign. As represented in Figure 2.3, if both λ_R and λ_C are positive, the utility of firms increases upward toward social policies characterized by high levels of control. If both the sensitivity to risk redistribution (λ_R) and the sensitivity to control (λ_C) have a negative sign, the utility of firms decreases, as control increases. The analysis is analogous for the case in which firms' sensitivities

---

[11] A more elaborate analysis of the utility of firms that involves a more complicated functional form of the sensitivity to risk redistribution (λ_R) can be found in Chapter 2 of my dissertation (Mares 1999). I am extremely grateful to David Soskice for suggesting a simplification of the functional form of λ_R.

[12] This analysis of the shape of the indifference curves of firms follows from the assumption of constant sign of $\frac{\partial U}{\partial C}$ and $\frac{\partial U}{\partial R}$.

34

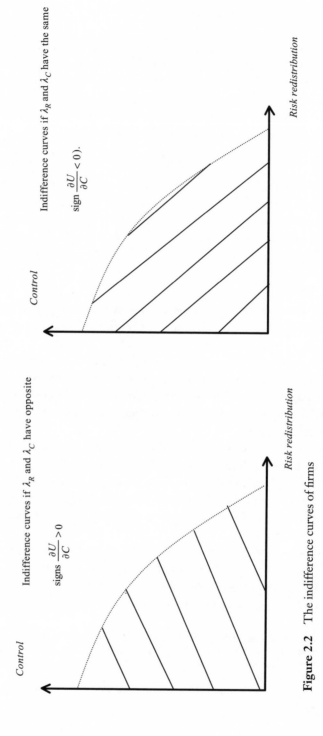

Figure 2.2 The indifference curves of firms

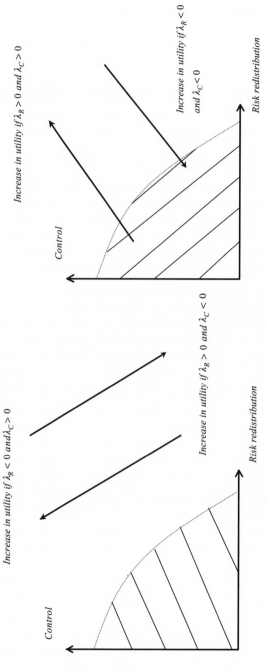

Figure 2.3 The location of the maximum of the utility of firms

to risk redistribution and control have opposite signs. We can distinguish two additional cases. If the sensitivity to risk redistribution (λ_R) is negative, but the sensitivity to control (λ_C) is positive, the utility of firms will increase in the direction of the upper boundary of the social policy space. If the sensitivity to risk redistribution (λ_R) is positive, but the sensitivity to control (λ_C) is negative, the utility of firms will increase in the direction of the horizontal axis of the social policy space. Figure 2.3 represents these predictions about the direction of increase in the utility of firms in the social policy space.

This analysis allows us to determine the location of the maximum of the utilities of firms throughout the social policy space. The pairwise combination of sensitivities to risk redistribution (λ_R) and control (λ_C) with different signs allows us to situate the maximum of the utility of firms at four different points in the policy space: two points on the upper boundary of the social policy space (corresponding to private-type social policies and contributory social insurance) and two points located at the two extremes of the horizontal dimension of the social policy space. Let me discuss the conditions characterizing these four different maxima.

Firms will prefer a private-type social policy if the sensitivity to control (λ_C) takes positive values and the sensitivity to risk redistribution (λ_R) takes negative values. The model predicts that large firms or firms relying on skilled workers will more likely discount the costs associated with the provision of social insurance and will favor a high amount of discretion in the determination of the conditions of eligibility for social policy benefits. However, firms will prefer private-type social policy arrangements *if and only if* the sensitivity to risk redistribution is negative. In other words, "high-risk producers" will find private-type social policies unattractive and will demand the expansion of the level of social insurance coverage.

Second, the model derives the conditions under which contributory insurance is the preferred social policy outcome. Firms will favor these policies if both the sensitivity to risk redistribution (λ_R) and the sensitivity to control (λ_C) are positive. The positive sign of the sensitivity to control indicates that these firms derive significant institutional advantages from policy instruments shared by private policies and contributory insurance, such as earnings-related insurance contributions that reproduce existing wage and skill differences or a relatively high discretion retained by firms in the administration of social insurance. The risk profile of a firm is the significant variable accounting for the divergence in preferences among employers who favor private-type social policies and those producers who prefer contributory insurance. The model predicts the emergence of an important cleavage among high- and low-risk producers. I predict that high-risk industries will favor policies that socialize risks, while low-risk producers will oppose any redistribution of risks, fearing to become subsidizers of high-risk industries.

A third possible outcome is the case in which the sensitivity to risk redistribution (λ_R) takes positive values, while the sensitivity to control (λ_C) is negative. An implication of the analysis is that these firms will favor the introduction of a universalistic social policy. These employers are generally small firms, who prefer tax-financing to contribution-based financing. The positive sign of the sensitivity to risk redistribution implies that these producers find occupationally based social policies characterized by narrow levels of coverage as too costly and unattractive and favor highly redistributive social policies.

Finally, the model implies that firms will reject all social policies if both the sensitivity to risk redistribution (λ_R) and the sensitivity to control (λ_C) take negative values. This analysis predicts this outcome if (a) the firm is small or does not employ skilled workers *and* (b) if the incidence of the labor market risk facing it is small. If both conditions hold, it is likely that the costs of social policies will outweigh their potential advantages for this employer. Table 2.2 and Figure 2.4 summarize the major conclusions of the analysis.

The model generates simultaneously a number of comparative statics results specifying the changes in the location of the ideal policy preferred by a firm as a result of changes in the relative magnitude of the sensitivity to risk redistribution (λ_R) and the sensitivity to control (λ_C). To illustrate these results, let us start from a situation in which both sensitivities are positive. As argued earlier, in this case the firm will prefer contributory social insurance. Assume now that the sensitivity to risk redistribution (λ_R) increases, while

Table 2.2. *Predictions about Social Policy Outcomes Preferred by Different Firms*

	Size and Skill Intensity	
	Low $\lambda_C < 0$	High $\lambda_C > 0$
Incidence of Risk		
High $\lambda_R > 0$	Universalistic	Contributory
Low $\lambda_R < 0$	"None"	Private

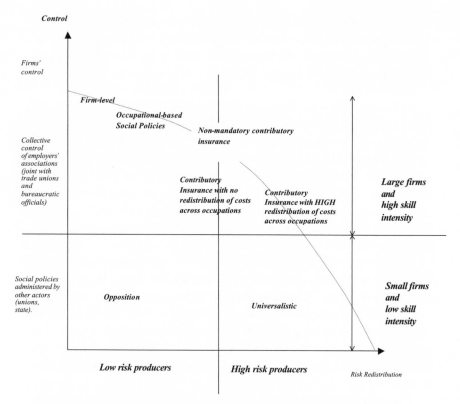

Figure 2.4 Predictions about the policy preferences of firms

the sensitivity to control (λ_C) remains unchanged. A number of factors can increase the benefits of risk redistribution for the firm and thus increase the parameter λ_R. For example, the demographic profile of the workers of the firm might worsen over time or the relative incidence of the risk of unemployment can increase, as a result of a sudden drop in the demand for the products of a firm. Conversely, the costs of highly redistributive social policies can decrease, as a result of a decrease in the incidence of a risk faced by other high-risk industries. The consequence of the increase in the sensitivity to risk redistribution is a change in the slope of the indifference curves of the firm ($\frac{\partial C}{\partial R}$). The slope becomes more negative. Figure 2.4 illustrates this change graphically. The consequence of an increase in the parameter λ_R is a shift in the maximum of the utility of the firm toward universalistic social policies.

Conversely, we can analyze a second case in which the sensitivity to control (λ_C) increases, while the sensitivity to risk redistribution (λ_R) remains unchanged. This change in the parameter λ_C might be the result of an increase in the skill intensity of a firm or of an increase in its profitability, which, in turn, affects the ability of the firm to discount the costs of various programs provided to its workers. As in the previous example, let us take as the starting point the case in which both sensitivities are positive. An increase in the parameter λ_C shifts the maximum toward private social policies. Occupationally based forms of social insurance or private policies become more attractive to the firm than policies more redistributive social policies. Figure 2.5 summarizes these comparative statics results.

The model implies that we should encounter a significant division, disunity, and disagreement among producers during the negotiation of a new social policy. Social policies confront employers with a set of questions that are distributionally divisive. An important reason accounting for this heterogeneity among the preferences of employers is the emergence of two overlapping cleavages among producers: a cleavage among large and small firms (over the policy advantages of control) and a cleavage among high-risk and low-risk producers (over the policy advantages of risk redistribution). One single variable – such as the size of the firm, its skill intensity, or the relative riskiness of the occupation – is insufficient to predict the social policy preference of a firm.[13] Firm size, the skill profile of a firm, and the incidence of a risk *interact* in determining the policy preferences of firms and in predicting the variation in the policy preferences of employers.

What are the consequences of these findings for predictions about the broader political coalitions that can form during the process of social policy reform? I turn to these questions next.

---

[13] On this point, the predictions of the model are in disagreement with the predictions of Estevez-Abe, Iversen, and Soskice 2001. Estevez-Abe et al. argue that the mix between firm-specific and general skills is sufficient in predicting the policy preferences of a firm: employers with high percentages of workers that have made investments in firm-specific skills will prefer more "private-type" social policies, whereas firms employing workers with general skills will favor more redistributive social policies. In contrast, the foregoing analysis suggests that the skill profile of a firm alone is insufficient to predict the social policy preferences of a firm. In contrast to Estevez-Abe et al., this model predicts that firms employing a high percentage of workers with firm-specific skills but which have a high incidence of risk will favor a contributory insurance and *not* a private-type social policy. Firms with general skills but with a low incidence of risks are predicted to oppose the introduction of a social policy.

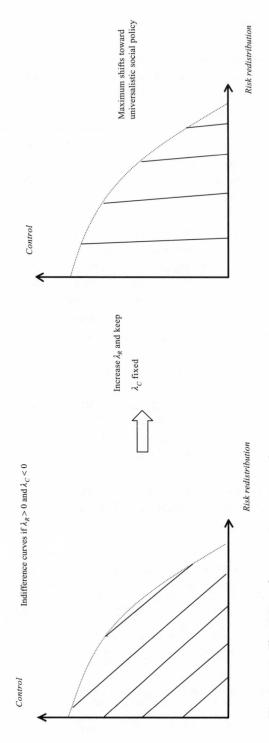

Figure 2.5 Illustration of comparative statics results

Political Coalitions and Social Policy Reform

The preceding analysis provides microfoundations for understanding the policy considerations motivating the involvement of employers in the process of social policy development. But what is the importance of various associations representing employers in the political processes leading to the formulation of a new social policy? What political factors shape the variation in the political influence of employers? What are the implications of this emphasis on employers for our understanding of the relative role played by business and labor associations in the development of the modern welfare state?

Bringing employers back into our analysis of the development of the modern welfare state does not imply that labor associations or political parties representing labor-based constituencies were inconsequential or epiphenomenal for the enactment of policies of social protection. It implies, however, that those approaches premised on a *zero-sum conflict* between capital and labor over the introduction of a new social policy mischaracterize the political process leading to the enactment of institutions of social insurance. Studies premised on the assumption of business opposition to social insurance fail to identify both the range of political cleavages and also the room for potential cross-class alliances emerging during the introduction of a new social policy.

A few additional theoretical observations are necessary to characterize the political influence of employers during the process of social policy development – and to move from an analysis of policy preferences to predictions about the resulting social policy outcomes. First, we need to specify the policy preferences of political associations representing labor. What are ideal social policy choices favored by various trade union associations? How do trade unions choose among various social policies characterized by different combinations of risk redistribution and control? Do we encounter significant disagreement among trade unions over the introduction of a new social policy – and, if so, what variables can explain this disagreement? By locating the policy preferences of trade unions in the social policy space and by specifying the variables predicting cleavages among labor associations, we can identify the conditions under which pre-strategic alliances among unions and employers can form. Second, we need to specify the policy preferences of elected politicians or bureaucratic policy makers. Finally, to characterize the policy process leading to the introduction of a new social policy, we need to analyze the implications of preexisting public and private

41

social policies and the feedback effects of these policies on the organizational and informational resources available to various actors during the process of social policy reform.

The remaining part of this chapter discusses the broad political and institutional factors that facilitate the formation of political coalitions among various sectors of employers and labor associations. I develop a set of hypotheses about the different cross-class alliances that are historically possible and analyze the social policies supported by these coalitions.[14]

The Social Policy Preferences of Labor Associations

In exploring the factors affecting the policy preferences of trade union associations, we can rely on a large and extensive literature developed by social policy scholars. An important finding of this literature is the existence of a strong variation in the social policy demands of the labor movement. Issues such as the mix between private and public institutions of social insurance, the structure of social policy benefits, and the reallocation of the costs of social insurance across different occupations were highly contested among trade unions. The analysis here attempts to position the policy preferences of trade unions in the two-dimensional policy space.

---

[14] The starting point of the analysis is the observation that these political coalitions are vital for the long-term sustainability of a social policy. The preceding discussion of the policy constraints characteristic of social policies has identified two reasons justifying the political importance of these coalitions. First, both trade unions and employers have the policy capability to develop private-type institutions of social insurance. These private-type policies can at times undermine the effectiveness of a statutory social policy, if this policy was enacted without the prior support of unions or employers. Thus, to minimize this "policy slippage" during the implementation of a social policy, a high degree of coordination among policy makers and representatives of unions and employers is important. Second, a large number of social policies are administered in a corporatist fashion by business and labor representatives. Thus policy reformers must ex ante secure the *extraparliamentary* political support of leading associations of unions and employers to guarantee the ex post support of these actors in the implementation of a social policy. As Peter Swenson expresses the political constraint faced by reformist policy makers: "Though politicians may see in electoral and parliamentary majorities a chance to impose reform, they know they cannot necessarily count on sustaining these majorities against a business community crouched and waiting to strike back at the propitious moment. . . . Politicians' desire for robust policy – legislation secure from future attack from businessmen once the social emergency and electoral mobilization of supportive populist pressures inevitably passes – motivated their design of legislation that would engender post facto cross-class alliances reaching into the business community" (Swenson 1997). The definition of strategic coalitions is in agreement with the definition proposed by Swenson.

Trade unions are confronted with several questions of policy design that affect the distribution of control in the administration of social insurance. What should be the importance of preexisting institutions of support administered exclusively by trade unions? How should unions allocate their resources among various risks, such as sickness, disability, or unemployment? Should unions continue to develop voluntary union-based institutions of social support even after a statutory social policy is in place, or should they devote these resources to other purposes, such as support for strikes? Should unions accept employers' control over some social policies, or should these instances of paternalism be rejected? Finally, what should be the role and responsibilities of labor representatives in the administration of the major subsystems of the welfare state? As one of the most prominent scholars of the German labor movement noted:

No other theme was discussed as heatedly in the associational publications and in the trade union meetings as the question about the place of union-based institutions of support in the emancipatory struggle of the labor movement. No other internal associational questions elicited such passionate interventions of trade union members as the debates about the expansion of trade union institutions of support. After all, these were problems with an immediate impact on the everyday life of union members.... In no other sphere of union activity can we observe the practical development of the solidaristic ideals of the union movement more intensely than in the provision of collective benefits by trade unions, since social expenditures constituted the largest part of trade union expenditures. (Schönhoven 1980: 147)

Union-based institutions of social support providing social policy benefits for various employment-related risks go back to the second half of the nineteenth century. A survey conducted in 1877 among thirty German trade unions found that nine trade unions offered sickness benefits to their members, five unions provided disability benefits, and only three unions provided benefits in case of unemployment (Müller 1878: 468).[15] These numbers experienced a dramatic increase during the decades preceding World War I. In 1891, ten trade union associations (with a total membership of 35,792 members) provided unemployment benefits to their members and in 1913 the number increased to forty unions (with a total membership of 2,071,657 members) (Schönhoven 1980). On the eve of World War I, 81.3 percent of members of the German socialist trade union movement

---

[15] Müller's study is based on a survey by August Geib conducted among twenty-five union federations with members in more than one city and five local associations of trade unions (in Hamburg and Munich) (H. Müller 1878: 468).

were eligible for unemployment benefits that were financed exclusively by trade unions, while 97.5 percent of union members were eligible for union-financed sickness benefits (Schönhoven 1980: 174, 180). In France, we find a large number of trade unions offering unemployment benefits to their members. In 1862, 200 unions provided unemployment benefits to their members. The number increased to 334 in 1872, and 627 in 1881 (Ministère du Commerce 1903). The majority of these associations were local unions, with very small membership. Consequently, the percentage of French workers receiving union-based social support remained relatively low (Topalov 1985). In Belgium around the turn of the century, 107 out of 200 socialist trade unions operated an unemployment insurance fund (Vanthemsche 1990: 356).

As several historians of these institutions noted, the *skill intensity* of the occupation remained the strongest predictor of the timing of the introduction of these institutions and of the generosity of the policy benefits offered by unions. Prior to World War I, only unions "which organized highly qualified workers in skilled professions" such as "printers, glove makers, coppersmiths, glaziers, and porcelain workers" provided social policy benefits to their members (Schönhoven 1980: 168). In contrast, during the same period, unions representing workers in low-skill occupations – such as textile or transportation workers – offered no unemployment benefits. In Britain union-based institutions of social support "insured primarily a privileged elite, mainly composed of skilled and highly paid workmen" (Harris 1972: 298, Topalov 1985). In contrast, unions in "industries where the work force was weakly qualified" offered no benefits in case of unemployment (Topalov 1985, Krieger 1980:146). Social policy developments in France reveal a similar pattern. The voluntary institutions of social support were developed by highly skilled unions, such as "Paris workers of precision instruments, ceramic makers of Limoges, hat makers, bookbinders and jewelers" (Fédération du Livre 1895, Rougé 1912: 73). Union-based social support is absent among unions in low-skill occupations or "in a very dispersed industry, such as the clothing industry" (Topalov 1985).

What are the preferences of trade unions along the control dimension of the social policy space? A clear hypothesis is that trade unions will support an increase in their policy responsibilities in the administration of social insurance and distribution of social policy benefits. Cross-national studies of the social policy preferences of labor organizations provide preliminary support for this hypothesis (Topalov 1985, Vanthemsche 1990). Hatzfeld's study of the political development of the French welfare state suggests that "the participation of workers in the administration of institutions of social insurance" was an important demand of the labor movement going back in time to the strikes of the 1870s (Hatzfeld 1971: 67). According to Hatzfeld, a conflict with employers emerged over issues concerning the "orientation, financing of social insurance funds, and the level of social policy benefits" (Hatzfeld 1971: 67). Control over the administration of social insurance was also an important policy issue for the German labor movement. Bismarckian reforms had given labor representatives a two-thirds majority in the administration of the institutions of sickness insurance. As pointed out by several scholars of the German welfare state, this "offered unprecedented opportunities for patronage to the unions. . . . The elections for the social insurance administration offered a first opportunity to practice democratic influence in an area of immediate interest. It was an instance of basic democratic self-determination in a nation where democratic rights were far from being universally granted" (Manow 2000: 24, Tennstedt 1977, Steinmetz 1991: 38, 1993: 43). According to calculations of these scholars, unions delegated between 100,000 and 120,000 representatives to the assemblies of social insurance. Given that the total trade union membership of free trade unions at the beginning of the century was about 480,000, it follows that every fourth union member participated on the executive board of a sickness fund (Manow 2000a: 25). The Belgian Christian Democratic union federation, the General Christian Trade Union (ACV), also sought a prominent role for the labor movement in the administration of compulsory institutions of social insurance, beginning in 1944 (Vanthemsche 1990: 370). Current social policy reforms testify to the importance of "control" for trade union organizations in many European countries. Unions in countries as diverse as Italy, Sweden, or France were more willing to accept changes in the mode of financing of eligibility criteria for many social policies if governments were willing to guarantee their continuing involvement in the administration of social insurance institutions (Anderson 2001, Bonoli 2000, Baccaro 1999).

What factors influence unions' preferences for different institutions of risk redistribution? The historical literature on the development of union-based institutions of social support suggested that the incidence of a labor market risk is a critical factor affecting the ability of unions to provide social policy benefits to their members (Faust 1981, 1986). "Unions in industries with low but predictable risk of unemployment" were more likely to develop union-based institutions of social support. In contrast, union-based unemployment policies "were less frequent among union federations with regularly constant high levels of unemployment, such as construction ... or among organizations with a heterogenous membership structure that was difficult to control, such as sailors" (Faust 1986: 135). A study of the distribution of union-based institutions of social support among British trade unions found very little provision of unemployment benefits among unions in textiles or construction (Robinson 1913: 290).

The transition from craft-based unions to larger, more encompassing trade unions had important consequences for the social policy demands of the labor movement. Historically, the process of centralization of the labor movement coincides with the articulation of political demands for comprehensive institutions of social insurance. In part, this change in the policy preferences of labor associations is caused by the worsening of the risk profile of these trade unions. The growing inroads of trade unions among low-skill workers that accompanied the transition from craft to industrial unions lowered the ability of these labor federations to offer union-based social policy benefits to their members (Topalov 1985, Allgemeiner Deutscher Gewerkschaftsbund 1902b: 278). Sudden exogenous employment shocks, such as World War I, crystallized unions' beliefs that union-based social policies were too fragile to cope with the massive increase in risks. Following "the most acute commercial depression since 1879," the British Trade Union Congress voted by an overwhelming majority in 1908 to demand goverment "grants-in-aid" to trade unions that paid out-of-work benefits (Harris 1972: 273). Following World War I, the main publication of German trade unions expressed worry that union-administered institutions of social support were unable to cope with the massive disturbances of World War I. Abandoning the earlier demands for a Ghent policy of unemployment assistance, the Federation of German Trade Unions (ADGB) began to militate for the introduction of compulsory unemployment insurance (Allgemeiner Deutscher Gewerkschaftsbund 1920a: 159–161, Potthoff 1979, Bieber 1981: 360–415). A recent study of the social policy preferences of American trade unions argued that the U.S. labor movement faced similar considerations.

In the early part of this century, the American Federation of Labor (AFL) held fast to the belief that workers' organizations could better meet the social policy needs of union members than government or employer-sponsored programs. It viewed union-run plans as an important selling point to recruit new members and a way to tie the rank and file more closely to the union. In the 1930's organized labor threw its support solidly behind government programs like Social Security and National Health Insurance only after union-run social welfare plans, ethnic mutual benefit associations, and employers' social welfare schemes proved wholly inadequate in the face of the economic devastation wrought by the Depression. (Gottschalk 2000: 42)

Contributory insurance or universalistic social policy? This question – affecting key dimensions of policy design of the welfare state – posed distributionally divisive issues for the labor movement. In most societies, we observe the emergence of a political conflict over the relative advantages of these policy solutions among trade unions representing higher-skill, higher-earning employees and the broader confederation of the labor movement. The skill profile of the union is a key predictor of the preferences of unions along this policy dimension. As compared with the "median member" of a union representing higher-earning workers (or high-skill workers), the median representative of a larger trade union federation is a lower-skill worker. Reflecting these divergent profiles, unions representing higher-earning employees defended a contributory insurance solution characterized by earnings-related social policy benefits and the differentiation of insurance benefits across occupational groups.

In many European countries, unions representing white-collar employees opposed plans calling for the introduction of flat-rate social policy benefits and jealously defended the occupational autonomy of their own sickness and old-age insurance institutions (Ritter 1933: 51, Hockerts 1980: 97, Kocka and Prinz 1983). In contrast, trade union federations pushed for social policies that equalized benefits across all union members.[16] Several examples provide preliminary support for these hypotheses. Beginning with the first years of the Weimar period, an important policy goal of the ADGB was the demand to end the institutional and organizational decentralization of the German welfare state. These proposals of reform had two different policy components. On the one hand, the ADGB demanded the equalization of the level of insurance contributions across industries characterized by different occupational risks (Allgemeiner Deutscher Gewerkschaftsbund 1903: 177–180). The second goal was the effort to unify all institutions of social insurance. German trade unions pursued these goals calling for the creation of an *Einheitsversicherung*, beginning with the first years of

---

[16] This partially confirms the claim of power resource scholars that trade union federations demand "institutional structures which unify as large sectors of the population as possible into the same institutional contexts" (Esping-Andersen and Korpi 1984: 181). As the foregoing discussion has pointed out, these demands are historically more contingent (emerging as a result of the transition from craft unions to industrial unions) and are generally characteristic of a trade union association that has a more heterogenous risk profile.

Table 2.3. *Predictions about Preferred Social Policy of Trade Unions*

	Skill Intensity	
	High	Low
Incidence of Risk		
High (industrial unions)	Contributory	Universalistic
Low (craft unions)	Union-Administered Social Policies	

the Weimar period. During the first years following World War II, both German and French union federations succeeded in placing these policy proposals on the agenda of reform.

Table 2.3 summarizes the discussion of the factors affecting the policy preferences of trade unions. Note the interesting parallelism between the set of variables predicting the variation in the social policy demands of trade unions and the factors affecting the policy preferences of employers. The incidence of a risk predicts the ability of both firms and trade unions to establish private-type institutions of social insurance, or to demand social policies characterized by broad levels of coverage and pooling of risks. Similarly, the skill intensity of firms or trade unions explains the preferences for social policies with earnings-related or flat-rate benefits. Thus, skill incidence and risk level are factors that explain cleavages among both unions and employers.

Summarizing the preceding analysis, Figure 2.6 situates the policy preferences of various trade unions and associations representing employers in the social policy space. A few observations about Figure 2.6 are important at this point. First, as the discussion has pointed out, the possibility for pre-strategic agreement among employers and unions is higher along the risk redistribution dimension of the social policy space. In contrast, the control issue of the social policy space remains always distributionally divisive among unions and employers. Unions and employers will seek to maximize their role in the adiministration of social insurance even if they agree on the level of social insurance coverage and the degree of redistribution of a social policy. One exception to this statement is the case of a universalistic social policy. In the case of a universalistic social policy, the administration of social insurance is in the hands of state bureaucrats. A universalistic social policy offers other policy advantages to unions and employers, such as tax financing and a broad redistribution of costs. Some sectors of unions

Political Coalitions and Social Policy Reform

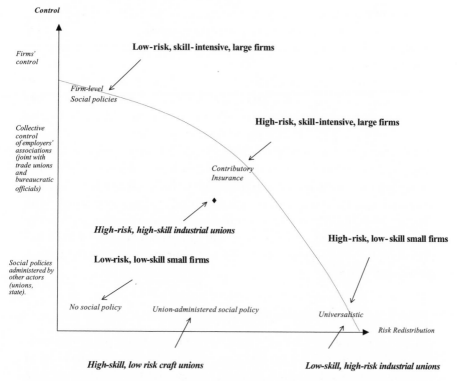

Figure 2.6 The policy preferences of employers and trade unions

and employers will favor a universalistic social policy if their sensitivity to risk redistribution is very high. It follows that a prestrategic alliance among unions and employers in support of a universalistic social policy remains theoretically possible.

Peter Baldwin's study on social policy developments in Denmark at the turn of the twentieth century provides an example supporting this hypothesis about the importance of cross-class alliances in the formation of universalistic social policies. In Baldwin's account, the political coalition supporting an all-inclusive, noncontributory, tax-financed pension consisted of workers and small agrarian producers. The latter hoped "to improve labor market conditions and attract workers to the country-side during the agricultural crisis of the nineteenth century.... Because farmers sought to please a labor force that included both wage earners and smallholders, limiting welfare to the dependently employed, not to mention the urban working class, was out of the question" (Baldwin 1990: 75). Tax financing, another important feature of policy design of the universalistic social policy, was also particularly attractive to Danish farmers who were dependent on world markets, because it avoided an increase in their nonwage labor costs (Baldwin 1990: 66).

The foregoing analysis implies that prestrategic alliances among trade unions and employers' associations are historically relatively rare. It follows that the majority of cross-class alliances that we encounter during the process of social policy development are *strategic* alliances. These alliances form when either unions or employers support a social policy that is not necessarily their preferred outcome. What factors facilitate the formation of strategic alliances among capital and labor during the introduction of a new social policy? Are some alliances more likely to form than others? The remainder of this chapter will identify the set of factors contributing to the formation of strategic alliances and will formulate a number of hypotheses about the types of institutions of social insurance supported by various cross-class alliances.

Policy Legacies and Strategic Alliances

Incorporating insights from the existing literature on comparative systems of social protection, I suggest that two additional factors affect the political bargaining during the introduction of a new social policy and the formation of strategic alliances. The first variable is the credibility with which social policy entrepreneurs, who can be either elected or bureaucratic officials, can commit to a change in the policy status quo. Business and labor representatives are more likely to compromise on their preferred social policy outcome and accept a social policy that is not their preferred outcome when faced with a credible policy change. The second important factor affecting the formation of cross-class alliances concerns preexisting social policies, which shape the political context for strategic interaction. This section discusses the importance of these factors in the formation of strategic alliances and will formulate a number of predictions about the policy outcomes that will be supported by different strategic alliances among various trade unions and sectors of the business community.

Who are policy entrepreneurs? The term has been used rather loosely by social policy scholars to denote "a network of policy reformers inside and outside government ... relatively free from interest-group instrumentalism" (Barenberg 1993: 1403). This definitional laxity tries to accommodate the strong cross-national variation as well as variation across policy areas (within the same country) in the position of policy entrepreneurs in the policy-making process. On some occasions, bureaucrats play a key role in the agenda-setting process and in developing alternative social policy proposals (Heclo 1974, Weir, Orloff, and Skocpol 1988). On other occasions, *elected* politicians use their agenda-setting power to advance a particular direction of reform (Huber and Stephens 2001). We can encounter situations in which reformist policy entrepreneurs move across the bureaucratic and parliamentary arena. Such was the case, for example, during the Third Republic in France, when Alexandre Millerand – an important Radical politician and a key architect of the French policy of unemployment insurance – moved frequently between the Commission of Social Insurance of the Chamber and the Permanent Commission of the Labor Office. Finally, as a large literature on policy networks and "social knowledge" has pointed out, associations of policy experts (such as the English Fabian Society and the German Verein für Sozialpolitik) can play a critical role in placing particular social policy alternatives on the agenda of reform and in initiating a process of policy change (Rueschemeyer and Skocpol 1996, Hall 1989). No general theoretical model exists that predicts the set of conditions under which bureaucrats or legislators or these more diffuse groups of policy experts act as agenda setters in the process of social policy reform. The nitty-gritty details of social policy making are often too messy to allow for these tidy generalizations.

Even if elected policy makers are often not responsible for placing an issue on the agenda of reform, parliamentary majorities are the determining factor in enacting new social insurance legislation. A vast literature has generated predictions about the location of the preferences of political parties in the social policy space and the type of social policies favored by those political parties. Historically, the three broad "families of political parties" – Social Democratic, Christian Democratic, and Liberal – have pursued social policy alternatives differing systematically in their policy design (Huber and Stephens 2001). The political preferences of Social Democratic parties have been directed toward social policies that embrace egalitarian ideals and extend social policy benefits to the entire population (Esping-Andersen 1985, Esping-Andersen and Korpi 1985). Inspired by the principle of subsidiarity – that is, the principle that policy responsibilities should be delegated to the smallest social units capable of carrying out these tasks (family, church, local communities) – Christian Democratic parties have historically favored a high decentralization and fragmentation of institutions of social insurance (Van Kersbergen 1995: 28, Hanley 1994,

Esping-Andersen 1990: 40). In contrast, liberal parties have preferred to enact social policies strengthening the incentives for individual self-reliance.

Yet parties are constrained in their ability to pursue their "ideal" social policy outcome by a range of additional factors, such as the administrative capabilities of the states, fiscal considerations, degree of party competition, and so forth. This suggests that we cannot impute ideal positions to policy entrepreneurs based simply on their partisan affiliation. As Peter Baldwin's research on the origin of universalistic policies in Sweden during the post-war period has illustrated, considerations about the financial implications of these policies contributed to the *initial* decision of Social Democratic policy makers – who controlled the Ministry of Finance – to reject these policy proposals calling for the abolition of means testing (Baldwin 1990: 141).[17] Swedish Social Democratic governments endorsed the universalistic policies *only after pressure* from Swedish conservatives. The weak administrative capabilities of the French state during the Third Republic – and the difficulties encountered in the process of tax collection – severely constrained the range of policy alternatives policy makers could put on the agenda of reform (*Journal Officiel* 1922). The implications of these examples are that fiscal considerations and administrative capabilities can bring about a deviation of policies proposed by various parties from their ideal policy preference.

In attempting to forge a strategic alliance among unions and employers, policy entrepreneurs make strategic use of the policy resources resulting from existing social policies. The observation that preexisting policy structures affect the emerging coalitions around particular social policy outcomes is not new for social policy scholars. During recent years, a large number of studies have begun to explore more systematically the pathways by which preexisting policies influence future political action and have specified a variety of mechanisms by which "policies produce politics" (Lowi 1964, Weir and Skocpol 1985, Skocpol 1992, Pierson 1993, 1994). As Pierson argues, policies have both material and informational consequences (Pierson 1993). Policies affect the material resources of social policy beneficiaries, their organizational capabilities, and the political attachments and the policy preferences of various groups. Social policies have also important informational consequences. By affecting the beliefs of actors about the sustainability of

---

[17] As Baldwin argues, Social Democratic spokesmen such as Per Albin Hansson, Wigforss, and Erlander argued that the means-tested alternative "promised to save the government money. . . . The main effect, the Finance Minister warned, of eliminating need as a condition of entitlement would be to give civil servants and others who were already well-provisioned an additional thousand crowns" (Baldwin 1990: 141).

certain reforms, they facilitate policy coordination around certain policy alternatives, precluding other outcomes. A very influential study linking the *structure* of existing policies to existing coalitions is the analysis of the political responses to the Great Depression developed by Margaret Weir and Theda Skocpol. As Weir and Skocpol argue, the Swedish Social Democrats created a system of price supports without production controls that was attractive to small farmers, contributing, thus, to the formation of the famous "red-green" alliance between workers and peasants. In contrast, the structure of agricultural policies enacted in the United States, characterized by price controls, "ended up joining together larger, commercially well-established, export-oriented southern cotton producers with better-off Midwestern corn and wheat farmers oriented to domestic as well as international markets. This cross-regional alliance, which took shape from the mid 1930's ... frequently cooperated with the conservative alliance of southern Democrats and Republicans in Congress to oppose many urban liberal Democratic initiatives" (Weir and Skocpol 1985: 143–144).

In examining the political consequences of existing social policies, my analysis proposes a twofold extension of the findings of the literature stressing policy feedbacks. First, I intend to explore more systematically the implications of preexisting *private* policies on the political coalitions formed during the process of social policy reform. So far, existing studies of policy feedbacks have exclusively focused on the impact of *public* policies on the future direction of social policy reforms. Such an emphasis is understandable, given the larger scale and visibility of most public social insurance programs. It is important, however, to extend the insights of these analyses and focus on the political consequences and policy feedbacks exercised by private social policies. As I argue, the lower visibility of private policies often increases the resiliency of these programs, hampering the ability of policy makers to dislodge political equilibria based on private policies. Second, my analysis attempts to examine more systematically the mechanisms by which preexisting social policies facilitate unions' and employers' support for a policy that is not necessarily their preferred outcome. I argue that policy feedbacks play an important role in facilitating the formation of *strategic* cross-class alliances. After examining the material and informational consequences of private policies, I turn to an examination of policy feedbacks of public policies.

The design of private policies has a strong impact on the policy preferences and political strategies of the beneficiaries of these policies. If benefits are meager, employees will very likely reject the private policy option, demanding its substitution by a public policy alternative. A similar backlash against the private policies can occur if employees resent the paternalism resulting from the large discretion retained by employers in the provision of private-level social policies. For example, French trade unions in the mining and railway industries rejected the arbitrariness exercised by employers over the allocation of social policy benefits (Hatzfeld 1971: 214–228). Private policies can have the opposite effect on the policy preferences of beneficiaries. If these policies provide generous benefits, beneficiaries might be indifferent to the public provision of insurance or, in some instances, oppose the socialization of risk. Thus, in some cases, employers can be successful in cementing a stable attachment of their employees to private policies that can undercut the support for redistributive social policies. German employers in mining and railways remained extremely successful in creating a long-term attachment of the workers of these industries to existing occupational-based institutions of social insurance. During the immediate years of the postwar period, German trade unions in the mining and railway industries strongly defended the institutional autonomy of the industry-level social policy arrangements (Zentralamt für Arbeit in der britischen Zone 1947). The preferences of these unions diverged from the policy advocated by the main association of the German labor movement, which demanded the administrative unification of all institutions of social insurance and the creation of universalistic social policies.

Several scholars of the American welfare state have noted the attachment of significant segments of the labor movement to private social policies. According to Marie Gottschalk, policies such as the Taft Hartley funds "solidified the commitment of organized labor to the private welfare state.... This alliance persists to this day and is a major obstacle to establishing either national health insurance or single-payer medical systems at the state level" (Gottschalk 2000: 37, 44). As scholars of the Japanese welfare state have pointed out, private social policies have cemented the attachment of Japanese trade unions to firms and preempted policy demands for redistributive social policies even during periods of strong mobilization of unions (such as the first years following World War II) (Dore 1973, Estevez-Abe 1999).

The institutional design of union-based institutions of social support can also affect the policy preferences of the participants in the process of social policy reform. Beginning with the last decades of the nineteenth century, French trade unions had established union-based institutions of social assistance to provide benefits for various employment-based risks to their members. Due to the organizational decentralization of the French labor movement, these institutions were dominant among small, local unions (Rougé 1912, Mossé 1929: 107). According to a survey conducted by French labor market authorities, 49.5 percent of the recipients of union-based unemployment assistance belonged to a union with fewer than one hundred members (Topalov 1985). Because of their extreme decentralization and fragmentation, these "private" union-based institutions of social support posed a lower political threat to French employers. French producers (correctly) estimated that the probability of one peak federation of labor to co-opt these decentralized local unions and turn them into a powerful weapon of class struggle against employers was very low. These policy considerations explain the strategic move of French employers and their acceptance of the Ghent outcome, a policy that institutionalized state subsidies of union-based unemployment funds (Fagnot 1905: 123).[18] During the critical policy deliberations that preceded the introduction of a Ghent policy in 1905, employers attempted to limit the support of the state to those associations that "trouble the relationship between employers and workers" and to larger union federations and to recommend the extension of public subsidies to associations of support "established by chambers of commerce or other associations of employers [*syndicats patronaux*]" (Fagnot 1905). However, French employers tacitly accepted the principle of state subsidy to union-administered unemployment funds (i.e., the Ghent system). This strategic move of employers was the critical factor that facilitated the introduction of this policy in France.

The contrast in the political strategies of French and German employers is remarkable. Given the strength and organizational centralization of the German labor movement, German employers faced a very different strategic choice. They militantly rejected all political demands calling for the subsidization of union-based unemployment funds, denouncing these policies as "subsidization of union strike funds" (*Der Arbeitgeber* 1 October 1911, 1 December 1913). According to the Federation of German Employers' Associations, public support of union-based institutions of unemployment compensation "would sharpen the knife that could be used against employers" (Führer 1990: 89). Similar to German employers, Swedish employers

---

[18] Employers' own statements during the policy deliberations indicate that their acceptance of a Ghent system was a strategic compromise around a policy that was the second-best outcome. A representative of employers during the deliberations of the Conseil du Travail argued that the employers' vote was not "a vote on first principles" (Fagnot 1905: 123).

were also initially opposed to the introduction of a Ghent system, fearing that the subsidization of trade union funds "would bolster union militancy and therefore prop up wages at levels that would harm Swedish industry's competitiveness in international markets" (Swenson 2002).[19] Thus, unions' organizational success in the development of union-based unemployment policies created a policy legacy that precluded the formation of a strategic cross-class alliance around a Ghent system.

Private social policies also have important informational consequences. The lower "visibility" and "traceability"[20] of many private policies can often frustrate the attempts of policy makers to change the policy status quo or undermine their efforts to forge broader political coalitions in opposition to these policies (Arnold 1990). Early retirement policies present the clearest example of private social policies that are extremely sticky. During the past two decades, policy makers in a majority of advanced industrialized countries have been engaged in an effort to undo the process of early exit of elderly workers from the labor market. These efforts have remained largely unsuccessful. The inscrutable density and technical complexity of many early retirement programs have been critical factors accounting for the inability of policy makers to reverse the process of early exit from the labor market. In developing early retirement policies, firms rely on a combination of resources from several subsystems of the welfare state – such as disability, unemployment, and old-age insurance – and put together complex benefit packages that induce elderly employees to retire prior to the official retirement age. The specific financial details of early retirement are not broadly publicized and may even be unknown to trade unions and employers associations. Moreover, the causal chain between firm-level practices and the financial outlook of the old-age insurance system is long, involving complex causal links. Thus, the potential of policy reformers to mobilize public opposition to these policies is severely constrained by the low visibility and traceability of these programs.

In other cases, policy makers can rely on private policies established either by unions or employers and use these as blueprints for the

---

[19] As Swenson points out, the fears of Swedish employers turned out to be unjustified, as the Ghent system did not have its predicted effect on union militancy. Thus, over time, Swedish employers ended up accepting the Ghent system (Swenson 2002). Swedish employers were, however, not part of the initial cross-class alliance that pushed for the introduction of this policy.

[20] Following Arnold, traceability is understood as the link between an identifiable governmental action and a perceptible policy effect (Arnold 1990: 47).

development of national-level social policies. These informational consequences of private policies were particularly important during early
episodes of social policy developments. Private, union-based institutions
of social support served as blueprints to policy makers in countries such as
Belgium, the United Kingdom, France, Sweden, and Switzerland (Varlez
1903, Topalov 1985). As Gustav Schmoller, a prominent German political economist of the nineteenth century, remarked, policies of social insurance established in the mining industry "remained in the eyes of the
German government an ideal model for workers' insurance" (Schmoller
1904: 361, Geyer 1987: 23). Faced with the opposition of the German
parliament to policy proposals that attempted to establish a centralized
system of social insurance, administered entirely by the state, German
Chancellor Bismarck turned to existing institutions of social insurance established by employers and regarded these as an alternative institutional
model. As early as 1880, Bismarck wrote to Louis Baare, a leading representative of the German business community, that he was "willing to
rely on smaller associations to administer accident insurance" (Tennstedt
and Winter 1993: 27). Bismarck also suggested that "there is no doubt
that the accident insurance can be carried out in the most efficient way
by associations that involve representatives of individual sectors or several sectors characterized by similar firm-level conditions" (Tennstedt and
Winter 1993: 81).[21] In many European economies, the institutional origin of corporatist policies of social insurance – that is, those social policies
administered jointly by unions and employers – are occupationally based
institutions of social protection established by these associations. Scholars
of the American welfare state have also pointed out that "existing social
welfare practices of employers and commercial insurance" influenced key
initial institutional features of the Social Security Act, such as "the reliance
on regressive payroll taxes and the initial commitment (reversed in 1939)
to full-reserve financing and strict actuarial criteria" (Hacker and Pierson
2000: 28).

Public social policies – means-tested social assistance, contributory insurance, or universalistic social policies – exercise important feedback effects,
affecting the strategic bargaining during social policy reform and the resulting political coalitions. We can suggest that preexisting public policies can
have ambiguous consequences for the formation of cross-class alliances. If

---

[21] Entwurf für ein Schreiben des Reichskanzlers Otto Fürst von Bismarck an den Staatsminister Albert Schäffle, 19 November 1881, in Tennstedt and Winter 1993: 81.

policy entrepreneurs are skillful in using the material and informational resources of existing policies, they can forge a strategic alliance among unions and employers around a policy that is the second-best choice of these actors. However, these efforts of policy makers aimed at the creation of cross-class alliances can fail. The latter outcome is more likely to occur if policy makers are unable to foreclose the attractiveness of "private policy" alternatives.

The development of German compulsory old-age insurance is an example in which policy makers were successful in bringing about a strategic realignment of the policy preferences of large manufacturing producers, by relying on selective fiscal resources. After the introduction of compulsory sickness and accident insurance in 1883 and 1884, respectively, the interest of German producers in the introduction of compulsory old-age insurance waned (Breger 1982: 133–156, 1994: 38). A number of associations representing key sectors of the German business community expressed worries about the financial implications of this policy and the broader implications of these policies on the competitiveness of the German economy (Breger 1982: 134). The Central Federation of German Industrialists (Centralverband Deutscher Industrieller) protested that employers could not finance this policy unaided by the state (cf. Breger 1982: 146). Other producers – most notably employers in the chemical industry – preferred the provision of old-age benefits at the firm level to a publicly organized public insurance (Kalle et al. 1874: 1–22). To allay the worries of the business community and to induce employers to accept the compulsory old-age insurance project, German Chancellor Bismarck committed the Reich to a sizable subsidy of the costs of this policy (Neuloh 1957: 130). Subsidies from the Reich have covered nearly one-third of the expenditures of Germany's old-age insurance.

On other occasions, the poor design of a public policy, egregious failures of the state in the implementation of a policy, or misallocation of resources by public bureaucrats can contribute to the formation of a strategic alliance in opposition to the particular policy. Thus, actors that initially supported the policy will either push for a reversal in policy or oppose efforts to develop this policy further. As Estevez-Abe argues, during the first years of the postwar period Japanese manufacturing employers were uninterested in the development of corporate-based housing policies for their employees. This outcome was only their second-best choice. They supported it because of the deficiency of the public provision of housing (Estevez-Abe 1999). As Vanthemsche's study of the evolution of a Ghent system in Belgium points out, "the particular organization of unemployment insurance, leading to administrative confusion, concentration of activity on tiresome management tasks, and financial exhaustion, precipitated a real crisis that made many union members reconsider the aims and methods of their organization and the future of unemployment insurance" (Vanthemsche 1990: 363). Consequently, the socialist trade unions shifted their support away from the Ghent system and argued for compulsory unemployment insurance during the postwar years (Vanthemsche 1990: 370). Social policy developments of the French Third Republic provide an additional illustration of this outcome. Throughout this period, the French state suffered from a chronic inability to collect social insurance contributions. Because it was easier to enlist large firms in the financing of existing policies, the financial burden fell disproportionately on large firms as compared with small producers. This contributed to the crystallization of a political coalition among *all* French employers in opposition to the further extension of social insurance. Even high-risk producers that initially supported some contributory disability insurance joined this political coalition in support of purely private social policy alternatives.

One of the implications of the analysis of the previous section has been that a prestrategic alliance among unions and small producers in support of a universalistic social policy is historically possible. If alternative public or private policies contain exceptional provisions for either unions or small firms, however, the interest of these actors in the introduction of a universalistic social policy will decline. Policy developments in postwar Germany show how, under some conditions, "policy feedbacks" undermined the possibility of a cross-class alliance in support of a universalistic social policy. The German National Socialist government introduced for the first time an old-age insurance policy for small producers (*Handwerk*) in 1938 (*Reichsgestzblatt* 1938: 1900, Recker 1985). While the law made old-age insurance mandatory for small firms, it gave employees of the *Handwerk* the choice of contracting private old-age insurance or enrolling in the public insurance of white-collar employees (*Angestelltenversicherung*). This legal provision turned out to be extremely advantageous to small producers, leading to a "self-selection" of the good and bad risks. Young and highly paid small producers ("the good risks") chose private insurance, whereas elderly *Handwerker* (the "bad risks") chose to enroll as part of the white-collar insurance (Zentralamt für Arbeit Lemgo 1948, Post 1956: 7). As a result of the policy advantages of this legal provision, *Handwerk* firms rejected the proposals for a universalistic social policy and argued for the continuation of the status quo.

Both unions and employers form their beliefs about the probability that policy makers will pursue certain avenues of reform from various "cues," such as the length of time policy makers devote to particular reforms, the broad satisfaction of policy makers with the policy status quo, and the results of various surveys carried out by bureaucratic or parliamentary commissions. Thus, policy makers can rely on these signals in their effort to forge an alliance among unions and employers around a public policy that is not the preferred social policy outcome. The introduction of a Ghent policy of unemployment insurance in France in 1905 can illustrate the selective manipulation of information by policy makers about the availability of certain policy options, in an effort to engineer broader alliances in support of this policy. French employers and French trade unions opposed government subsidies to preexisting union-based institutions of social support. Fearing excessive state control over unions' activities, French unions rejected the subsidization of existing unemployment insurance funds by the state and supported instead a contributory unemployment insurance (Varlez 1903, Rougé 1912, Topalov 1985). Yet French labor market authorities were unwilling to place this policy solution on the agenda of reform. Their justification of this policy decision referred to failed attempts of isolated localities (such as the Swiss city St. Gall) to introduce a system of unemployment insurance and to the poor understanding of the causes of unemployment. In several policy statements, French lawmakers signaled to unions and employers their profound hesitation to consider a policy of unemployment insurance (cf. Ministère du Commerce 1903). In response to these signals – and to avoid the breakdown of policy negotiations altogether – French trade unions accepted the Ghent outcome as the second-best choice.

The analysis has developed a number of propositions about the impact of preexisting social policies on the process of bargaining and the formation of *strategic cross-class alliances*. I have analyzed both the material and informational consequences of both private and public social policies. The implication of the analysis is that the structure and design of alternative social policies can alter the strategic calculations of either unions or employers, leading to their support of a policy that is their second-best choice and not their preferred outcome. Figure 2.7 summarizes the analysis of the role of policy feedbacks in facilitating the formation of strategic alliances. The foregoing analysis has established that the range of policies around which strategic alliances can form is potentially very large. Selective incentives provided by employers to unions can undercut labor's support for redistributive social policies and contribute to a strategic alliance around

Political Coalitions and Social Policy Reform

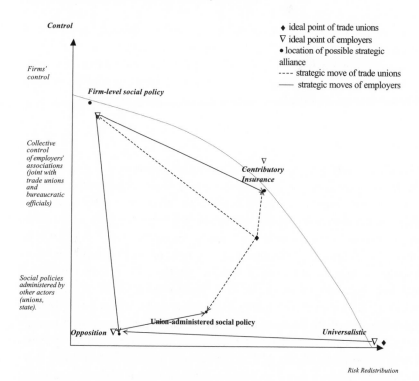

Figure 2.7 Possible strategic alliances

firm-level social policies. Governments can compensate employers for the loss of control over firm-level social policies and induce producers to accept compulsory contributory insurance, despite the initial opposition of firms to these policies. Both the number of strategic alliances and the type of social policies that can be supported by these alliances is very large.

We have established two broad hypotheses about the nature of political coalitions that will form during the introduction of a new social policy. First, prestrategic coalitions – that is, those coalitions in which unions and employers support their preferred social policy outcome – will be relatively infrequent. I have hypothesized that the only theoretical possibility for a prestrategic coalition is a coalition among small, high-risk firms and trade unions in support of a universalistic social policy. In contrast, I hypothesize that strategic coalitions – those coalitions in which unions and employers shift strategically in support of a social policy that is their second-best choice – will be more frequent. Second, I have hypothesized that the structure and design of preexisting private and public social policies will influence the strategic bargaining among employers and unions during the introduction of a new social policy. I have developed a number of propositions about the material and informational consequences of preexisting policies and their political consequences during the process of bargaining.

Looking Ahead

This chapter has developed a set of propositions that allow us to reevaluate the role played by employers in the development of the modern welfare state. The first objective of the analysis has to been to specify the conditions under which employers favor the introduction of particular social policies and to spell out the details of social policy design that have a high salience for producers. Social policies provide a variety of institutional benefits to employers: they protect firms' investments in the skills of their employees and they respond to a variety of other labor market needs of firms. The model developed in this chapter predicts that size, incidence of risks, and skill intensity remain the most important variables predicting the disagreement among firms formed during the process of social policy development. These propositions, showing that even profit-maximizing firms have (under specific circumstances) an interest in the provision of social insurance, allow us to reject a class-based perspective on the development of the modern welfare state, according to which labor favors and employers oppose the introduction of social insurance.

The second objective of this chapter has been to formulate a set of propositions about the political coalitions that will form during the process of social policy development. By bridging approaches interested primarily in specifying the preferences of actors and institutional approaches that focus on the material and informational consequences of existing public and private policies, this chapter has formulated a number of hypotheses about the prestrategic and strategic alliances that will form during the process of social policy development. These propositions point simultaneously to the critical importance of policy entrepreneurs who can rely on a variety of policy resources to deepen initially fragile alliances among trade union associations and key sectors of the business community.

Chapters 3 through 6 test the propositions developed in this chapter in a variety of policy contexts, spanning more than a century in the political history of the French and German welfare states. These cases investigate social policies covering the most significant social risks – old-age, disability, and unemployment – together with an analysis of the development of early retirement policies during recent years. In analyzing each episode of social policy reform, I first test the propositions about the determinants of business preferences toward different social policies. I rely on a newly assembled data set based on archival sources and contemporary publications of producers. Next, I test the propositions about the most significant factors accounting for the formation of various political alliances. Chapter 7 summarizes the findings and their implications for the relative role of class conflict and cross-class alliances in the formation of the modern welfare state.

3

Workplace Accidents as Social Risk

EMPLOYERS AND THE DEVELOPMENT OF ACCIDENT INSURANCE

Workmen's compensation laws mark the political origin of institutions socializing risks. In a majority of countries, accident insurance policies were enacted prior to the introduction of social policies compensating against other risks, such as old-age, sickness, or unemployment (Alber 1982: 49).[1] Institutional solutions that were invented during the policy deliberations surrounding the introduction of this policy – such as the concession of a monopoly over the organization of insurance to the state – served as a blueprint to politicians and lawmakers during subsequent episodes of social policy reform (Ewald 1986).

The political process that led to the introduction of accident insurance differs from the institutionalization of other social risks within the welfare state in one important respect. A crisis of private law served as the catalyst of the process of social policy reform. In the case of the other major social risks – old age, sickness, or unemployment – social insurance was established to complement or replace preexisting institutions and practices of social assistance. In the case of workmen's compensation laws, social insurance emerged as a political solution to the legal crisis of the civil code. At first, political reformers attempted to change the judicial process through which victims of workplace accidents could seek compensation from their

---

[1] In eight out of fifteen countries, accident insurance was the first social insurance, while it was the second branch of social insurance in four other countries (Alber 1982: 49). Alber argues that the sequence accident insurance, sickness insurance, old-age insurance, and unemployment insurance is the normal sequence for West European countries. In Germany, compulsory accident insurance was the second major piece of social legislation, introduced one year after sickness insurance, which was legislated in 1883. Deliberations in the Reichstag about compulsory accident insurance began, however, in 1881, before deliberations about sickness insurance.

64

employers. These piecemeal attempts at reform exposed the important political limitations of all legal solutions that relied on the principle of individual responsibility as the basis of compensation of the victim of workplace accidents. What began as an attempt to find a new legal justification under private law culminated with the introduction of social insurance.

What was the role played by employers during this episode in the political history of the welfare state? What were the policy demands articulated by different firms? What were the most important issues of policy design that were salient for employers? Can the model developed in Chapter 2 explain the variation in the policy preferences of firms? How influential were employers during these political reforms? What policy and institutional factors enhanced the influence of employers during these deliberations? This chapter examines these questions, by analyzing the role played by French and German employers in the negotiation of accident insurance legislation during the last decades of the nineteenth century. In the first section, I analyze the factors that contributed to the politicization of the issue of workplace accidents during the last decades of the nineteenth century and discuss the policy alternatives that were on the agenda of reform of policy makers. I turn next to an analysis of the policy preferences articulated by German and French firms. By relying on a collection of archival sources and publications of employers, I test the main predictions of the model developed in Chapter 2. Next, I examine the role played by employers during the broader political negotiations leading to the introduction of accident insurance legislation. A final section summarizes the main findings of this chapter.

Setting the Stage for Reform: German Private Law and Its Contradictions

Throughout the nineteenth century, the German legal system confined the risk of workplace accidents to the domain of private law. More specifically, workplace accidents were understood as being no different than any other liability issue. This implied that victims of workplace accidents could only be compensated after proving either the "intentionality" or "negligence" of the employer (Piloty 1890). This assimilation of the problem of workplace accidents within preexisting categories of private law was, in many ways, an understandable response of the courts and of lawmakers in a period in which liberal beliefs in individual responsibility, self-help, and self-determination were dominant (Gitter 1969: 6). It remained, however, a highly reductionistic solution. German private law was unable to distinguish among accidents resulting from the intentionality or negligence of an injurer and involuntary or unforeseeable events. As pointed out by numerous legal experts of the period, the civil code lacked a crucial distinction between accidental damages (*Unglücksschaden*) and unjust damages (*Unrechtsschaden*) (Esser 1941: 2, 51). As a result, the preexisting category of "unjust damages" was, artificially, extended to all workplace accidents, even to accidents whose causes remained unknown (Esser 1941: 51). The possibility of liability with no fault was a priori excluded.

This legal presumption that all workplace accidents were "unjust damages" carried, however, tremendous implications for victims of accidents. The legal burden of proof was shifted entirely to workers. The proof of the liability of employers was the precondition of workers' compensation. Thus, courts imposed on workers a nearly impossible task. According to a much quoted official statistic of the period over 60 percent of all workplace accidents were the result of "unknown causes" (*Journal Officiel* 1888a: 1434). The complexity of the causal structure of a workplace accident added to the legal difficulties encountered by victims of workplace accidents. Thus, given the legal hurdles raised by private law, it was almost impossible for victims of workplace accidents to receive compensation (Heinz 1973).

Prior to the emergence of radical proposals to solve this legal conundrum, which culminated with the introduction of compulsory accident insurance, policy makers attempted, at first, to reform the legal process by which victims of workplace accidents could seek compensation. In contrast to the social policy solution, which *eliminated* the question of liability altogether, these proposals for reform remained confined to the framework of the Civil Code. These political initiatives attempted to develop new legal justifications on the basis of which an accident victim could seek compensation, expand the liability of employers, or shift the legal burden of proof from the employee to the employer.

The first avenue of reform pursued by nineteenth-century legal experts was the extension of the liability of employers to a notion that included liability for the accidents resulting from the errors of the supervising personnel. Although this solution was stretching the liability principle quite a bit, this interpretation could find some legal justification in very paternalistic theories that considered employers responsible for work safety and for the protection of workers. Initially, German courts ruled very conservatively and excluded the possibility of liability of employers for third persons, limiting the liability principle only to persons who committed the injury

(Gitter 1969: 15). The principle of employers' liability for the action of third persons was introduced by the Employers' Liability Act (Reichshafts-pflichtgesetz) of 1871 (*Reichsgesetzblatt* 1871: 207).

A second direction of reform attempted to reinterpret the contractual obligations of the employer toward his employees. Based on this enlarged notion of employers' responsibilities, workplace accidents were regarded as a breach of the contractual obligations of the head of the enterprise. This solution was advocated by *Kathedersocialists*, such as Gustav Schmoller, Lujo Brentano, or Victor Mataja. One influential line of argument formulated by these scholars suggested that labor market contracts implied a long-term responsibility of employers for the damages that occur at the workplace (Mataja 1888: 103). Other *Kathedersocialists* based their proposals for reform on a critique of the assumption that labor was a commodity like any other commodity (Brentano 1877a, 1877b: 305). The reforms proposed by these scholars aimed at the creation of incentives for employers to assume long-term responsibilities toward their employees and their incorporation as part of labor market contracts. Higher wages could insure workers during periods in which workers were unable to work. Higher wages could act as a "risk premium."

The third avenue of political reform attempted to reverse the burden of proof from the employee to the employer. In Germany, this avenue of reform was undertaken in the Employers' Liability Act (Reichshaftpflicht-gesetz) of 1871. This piece of legislation remained, in many ways, a legal experiment – innovative, but incomplete, and full of inner contradictions. In attempting to remedy the shortcomings of the private law solution to the issue of workplace accidents, German lawmakers decided to experiment with a legal idea that had been pioneered in the Swiss legislation of the period: the "reversal of the burden of proof." The law introduced the presumption of employer liability for only a limited number of industries. In the case of a workplace accident, employers carried the legal obligation to prove their innocence. Employers were liable until they could prove that the accident resulted from the error of negligence of the employee or from "higher forces." In addition, the law also expanded the liability of employers to the action of third persons. Employers were liable for the accidents that were caused by the errors of the supervising personnel during the execution of their duties (*Reichsgesetzblatt* 1871: 207, Heinz 1973: 27).

An examination of the industries for which the legal burden of proof was shifted toward employers reveals, however, some of the contradictions of this solution. Lawmakers singled out railways as an industry prone to very high risks of workplace accidents and as an occupation in which employers could potentially control those "exterior forces" that had caused the accident (Gitter 1969: 17). Consequently, lawmakers decided to reverse the burden of proof in the case of railways. In the case of mining, another industry characterized by a high incidence of the risk of workplace accidents, workers remained responsible for proving the fault of employers. Lawmakers considered that, in the case of mining, workers "enter the job with full knowledge of the danger that can result from the cooperation with other employees" and that shifting the risk toward employers would impose an unnecessary burden on producers.

As this example indicates, the entire approach was not premised on compelling theoretical criteria that could unambiguously distinguish among industries in which this expanded liability of employers applied and those industries in which the civil code should be still in force. Even proponents of an immediate reform of the private law had to admit the inconsistency of the solution introduced in the Employers' Liability Act. According to Julius Baron, a *Kathedersocialist*, there was no compelling theoretic reason that could justify the separate legal situation of an industry such as railways. Consequently, the Employers' Liability Act had either to be eliminated or extended to all industries (Heinz 1973).

The process of policy experimentation that characterized legal and political developments during the last decades of the nineteenth century incrementally shifted the policy status quo toward an outcome that was highly unfavorable to employers. Suddenly, both courts and policy makers were improvising and defining new legal arguments and justifications that departed from a strict implementation of the liability principle. All proposals for reform – either the expansion of employers' liability for the action of their immediate subordinates or the reversal of the burden of proof – undermined the advantageous situation hitherto enjoyed by employers. These difficult and seemingly unsolvable questions suddenly "opened up" the factory to broader public scrutiny, an intrusion that was unwelcome, for most nineteenth-century employers. As Anson Rabinbach summarized this state of affairs, "these conflicts ... brought the expertise of insurance companies (public and private), legal theorists, legislators, doctors, and scientists to a sphere previously regarded as the private terrain of conflict between employer and employee. By opening the factory to the scrutiny of these competing discourses, the workplace became the scene of empirical investigation, legal theorizing, statistical review, juridical decision and medical supervision" (Rabinbach 1996: 53).

German employers regarded the situation resulting from the introduction of the Employers' Liability Act as extremely disadvantageous. A German industrialist from Cologne characterized the act as "a poisonous plant" (Heinz 1973: 89). The lowering of the legal barriers faced by the employees increased the number of cases taken to a court (Vogel 1951: 25, Breger 1982: 80). Other employers considered that this law contributed to an increase of conflict within the firm (Breger 1982: 83). This, in turn, fueled workers' militancy and contributed to an increase in membership of the working class parties (Breger 1982: 83).[2] As a result of the introduction of the Employers' Liability Law, the insurance premiums demanded by private insurance companies also increased, which contributed to an increase in the labor costs of firms (Breger 1982: 83).

The starting point of the policy proposals developed by German employers during this period was the observation that all legal attempts to address the issue of workplace accidents presupposed a relationship between proof of individual fault or negligence (of either employer or of employee). This link between fault and compensation transformed the relationship between employers and workers into a zero-sum situation. To avoid this zero-sum outcome, employers proposed to sever the relationship between fault and compensation, by compensating victims of workplace accidents *without* requiring any proof of the individual fault of employers. The legal implications of this apparently simple solution were radical. The liability principle was a key organizing principle of private law and could not simply be "abolished" by a political decree. But, as proposed by employers (and only later by other German lawmakers), the liability principle could be circumvented, if the institution granting benefits to victims of workplace accidents was functioning under *public law*.

This idea became the key organizing framework of a policy proposal formulated by Louis Baare, the president of the Chamber of Commerce of Bochum (Industrie und Handelskammer Bochum 1881: 15–22). The origin of these ideas among Bochum employers is not accidental. This Chamber of Commerce was located in the heartland of the Ruhr region, the motor of Germany's industrialization. The most representative firms belonging to this chamber were mining and steel producers, representing industries characterized by a high incidence of workplace accidents that experienced most strongly the disadvantages of the Employers' Liability

---

[2] Breger's analysis is based on the petition submitted by the Chamber of Commerce Essen to the Reichstag on 19 April 1881 (Breger 1982: 83).

Law (Mariaux 1956: 537, 544). The Baare proposal recommended the creation of an insurance fund (*Arbeitsunfallversicherungskasse*) compensating victims of workplace accidents (or members of their families) (Industrie und Handelskammer Bochum 1881: 15, para. 1). Bochum employers proposed to extend the scope of social insurance to workers in the entire Reich employed in "construction, agricultural occupations (which do not rely exclusively on human effort), mines and quarries" (Industrie und Handelskammer Bochum 1881: 15, para. 1). Baare recommended financing this accident insurance fund by relying on contributions of employers (covering half of the costs of this policy), on contributions from workers (covering one-quarter of the costs), with communes financing the remaining share of the costs (Industrie und Handelskammer Bochum 1881: 19, para. 10). The key departure from the policy status quo was the removal of the obligation on the part of victims of workplace accidents to prove the fault of employers as a precondition for their compensation.[3]

Baare's proposal for the development of compulsory accident insurance had a dual impact during the policy deliberations of the period. First, it served as the basis of the social policy demands formulated by the Central Federation of German Industrialists (Centralverband Deutscher Industrieller). The organization had been founded in 1876 as a result of the unification of several sectoral associations of producers, such as the Association of German Iron and Steel Industrialists (Verein Deutscher Eisen- und Stahlindustrieller) and the Langnamverein (the Association for the Preservation of Common Economic Interests in Rheinland Westfalen) (Ullmann 1983: 77: 85, Kaelble 1967, Hentschel 1978: 99–103). The Baare bill was widely circulated among the members of this association and served as the blueprint for the version of accident insurance legislation endorsed by the Federation of German Industrialists during its meeting on 30 January 1881 (Centralverband Deutscher Industrieller 1881).

The Baare bill had also an impact during the process of policy formulation of the first accident insurance draft bill, prior to the deliberations in the Reichstag. During no other episode in the political history of the German welfare state did employers play such a strong role in the initial "agenda-setting" stage of policy formation. During a meeting on 18 September 1880, Bismarck asked Baare to recommend possible alternatives to the revision of existing legislation on liability in the case of workplace accidents (Tennstedt

---

[3] The only exception was if the accident was a major fault of the victim; in this case, no benefits were paid (Industrie und Handelskammer Bochum 1881: 343, paras. 5 and 6).

and Winter 1993: 242, 277, 320).[4] In response to this request, German employers formed a policy committee – which included Baare; Beutner, the president of the Central Federation of German Industrialists; August Servaes, the president of the Langnamverein; and other employers representing the interests of the iron and steel, mining, and textiles (Tennstedt and Winter 1993: 242). The committee endorsed the Baare proposal and submitted the results of its policy deliberations to Bismarck on 6 November 1880 (Tennstedt and Winter 1993: 349).[5]

The Baare bill reflected the interests of iron and steel producers and other industries facing a high incidence of the risk of workplace accidents. However, not all German producers were ready to endorse this bold policy move. In contrast to large firms, many small producers did not see the immediate advantages provided by a contributory accident insurance. For many of these producers, public insurance organized by the state implied "police-like supervision and administrative interference of the state" (Breger 1982: 81). The following section examines the most significant factors explaining the policy disagreement among German employers.

The Social Policy Preferences of German Firms

How can we explain the disagreement among German producers during the process of reform of the liability law? To test the main propositions of the model developed in Chapter 2, I have relied on a combination of archival collections and other publications of employers of the period. The first source is a survey among German chambers of trade and commerce, commissioned by the Prussian Statistical Bureau in 1881 (Francke 1881). This survey documents and analyzes the statements of sixty-one chambers of commerce toward the social policy alternatives that were under consideration during the period. This survey provides invaluable insights into the process of preference articulation of employers and of the details of policy and institutional design considered significant by these producers. In addition to these data collected by the Prussian Statistical Office, I have

---

[4] See the follwing documents in Tennstedt and Winter 1993: (a) Sitzungsprotokoll einer Bochumer Industriellenversammlung, 22 September 1880; (b) Brief des Kommerzienrats Louis Baare an den Reichskanzler Fürst Otto von Bismarck, 30 September 1880; (c) Brief des Kommerzienrats Louis Baare an den Reichskanzler Fürst Otto von Bismarck, 20 October 1880 (Tennstedt and Winter 1993: 242, 277, 320).

[5] See Baare's letter to Bismarck, Brief des Komerzienrats Louis Bare an den Reichskanzler Fürst Otto von Bismarck, 6 November 1880 (Tennstedt and Winter 1993: 349).

examined the records of the policy deliberations of several associations of employers representing large, manufacturing firms, such as the Central Federation of German Industrialists (Centralverband Deutscher Industrieller), periodicals published by different sectoral associations of German employers (iron and steel producers and the federation of employers in the chemical industry), and the collection of documents published by the historical commission of the German Academy in recent years (Verhandlungen, Mitteilungen und Berichte des Centralverbandes Deutscher Industrieller 1881–1887, Tennstedt and Winter 1993, 1995).[6]

A first implication of the model developed in Chapter 2 suggests that we should encounter disagreement among employers over the degree of risk redistribution of different social policies. The model predicts that industries facing a low incidence of the risk of workplace accidents will oppose the socialization of risks and any measures uniformizing social insurance contributions across industries. In contrast, occupations characterized by a high incidence of workplace accidents are expected to favor social policies pooling the risk across a very large number of occupations as well as a number of measures that sever the link between the contribution of employers to social insurance and the incidence of a risk. These firms are expected to support compulsory social insurance and even more radical proposals calling for the universalization of social policy. The crucial implication of the model is that the incidence of a risk of an industry remains the key predictor of the sensitivity toward risk redistribution (λ_R) of a firm: λ_R is expected to be positive for high-risk industries and negative for low-risk industries.

Statistical data on the number of workplace accidents collected by private insurance companies during the period provide a measure of the distribution of this risk across different industries (Tennstedt and Winter, 1993: 537). An average for the period between 1876 and 1878 – two years before the formulation of the first draft of accident insurance legislation – reveals the uneven distribution of the risk of workplace accidents across occupations. At one extreme of the spectrum, we find high-risk industries – such as railways, mining, the metallurgical industry, and construction. The number of deadly accidents per 100,000 workers in these industries was 597 in railways, 261 in mining, 160 in steel production, and 125 in construction. In contrast, for low-risk industries the number was 18 in textiles, the paper industry, and leather industry and 17 in agriculture (Tennstedt and Winter

---

[6] Among the publications of employers I have consulted are *Stahl und Eisen, Zeitschrift des Vereins Deutscher Eisenhüttenleute*, and *Die Chemische Industrie*.

1993: 537). We expect a stronger dissatisfaction with the policy status quo (the Employers' Liability Act of 1871) among high-risk producers. Employers in industries strongly affected by the risk of workplace accidents are expected to favor policies socializing insurance that allow them to shift some of the costs to low-risk producers. In contrast, we expect low-risk producers to oppose policy decisions by which they become subsidizers of high-risk industries.

The data reveal a significant disagreement among employers over the relative advantages of compulsory social insurance as compared with the existing policy status quo. Iron and steel producers were the strongest supporters of a *compulsory* accident insurance (Verein Deutscher Eisen- und Stahlindustrieller 1884a, 1884b). These employers supported a policy solution in which all industries paid similar insurance contributions, irrespective of the incidence of risk of workplace accidents (Verein Deutscher Eisen- und Stahlindustrieller 1884a). Associations of employers representing the mechanized industries of the Ruhr region, such as the association of German employers of Bochum, also supported the creation of compulsory accident insurance (Industrie und Handelskammer Bochum 1881).

Employers in high-risk industries also called for a broad and expansive definition of the risk pool of social insurance – a measure that had the obvious advantage of lowering their social insurance contributions (Breger 1982: 90, Tennstedt and Winter 1993: 338–342).[7] A letter of Josef Massenez, a director of a steel plant, to Louis Baare expressed the worry that the definition of the risk pool of social insurance that was proposed in the original Bismarckian proposal was too narrow. "I see no reason," Massenez added, "why agricultural workers should not enjoy the benefits of the law" (Tennstedt and Winter 1993: 338–342). The original draft bill formulated by Baare recommended the inclusion as part of the compulsory accident insurance of "all workers employed in factories, construction sites and in all agricultural occupations which do not rely entirely on human effort" (Industrie und Handelskammer Bochum 1881: 16). During their encounters with Bismarck, these producers pressed arguments stressing the need to extend social insurance to agriculture, but their recommendations remained unsuccessful. In October 1880, Baare resignedly observed that "Bismarck does not want to hear anything about the insurance of agricultural workers" (Brief des Komerzienrates Louis Baare and

---

[7] Breger's analysis is based on a publication of the association representing iron and steel producers, the Verein Deutscher Eisen- und Stahlindustrieller (Breger 1982: 90).

den Rittergutsbesitzer Ferdinand Knaur, 1 October 1880, in Tennstedt and Winter 1993: 279, Breger 1994: 32).

In contrast to these producers in high-risk industries, employers in industries facing a lower incidence of risks viewed the proposals to socialize insurance with considerable worry and distrust, denouncing the Baare draft bill as a plot of iron and steel producers or as a "conspiracy of large firms" (Ullmann 1979b: 588). In a petition to the Bundesrat, the Federation of Cotton Employers of Southern Germany (Verein Süddeutscher Baumwollindustrieller) expressed the concern that the first version of accident insurance legislation that was under discussion in the Reichstag placed a disproportionately higher burden on employers in textiles as opposed to iron and steel producers (Tennstedt and Winter 1993: 554–556). The main association representing agricultural employers, the German Agricultural Council (Deutscher Landwirtschaftsrat), worried about the costs resulting from the extension of social insurance to agriculture (Tennstedt and Winter 1993: 531–538). In a writing addressed to the Reich Ministry of Interior Affairs (Reichsamt des Innern), these employers emphasized the existence of strong differences among industry and agriculture with respect to the incidence of workplace accidents. "In industry, workers are always employed in the same location and are, thus, incessantly exposed to the risk of workplace accidents. In agriculture, workers exchange their jobs. For several months during the year, they do not come into contact with motors, machines, or traction forces. This circumstance has to be taken particularly into account in determining the level of risk of the agricultural enterprise and in the calculation of the insurance contributions" (Tennstedt and Winter 1993: 533). Agricultural employers hoped that lawmakers would consider "the peculiarities of the various occupations as well as their differences."

But while these producers protested against a perceived absence of fairness in the allocation of the costs of social insurance among occupations, they insisted that it was important to extend some of the advantages of social insurance to agriculture. To avoid the migration of workers to more attractive industrial occupations, it was important that agriculture shared the benefits of the new institutions of social insurance. "The introduction of compulsory accident insurance creates a better situation for the industrial worker. There is no doubt that agricultural employees will try to find a job in these professions as soon as the opportunity will present itself, even if this change will not bring about an increase in their wages. A similar example is the migration of workers to mining, namely to the old mines with well-endowed miners' insurance funds [*Knappschaftskassen*]. The prospect of sufficient and secure support in case of accidents, sickness, and disability exerts a strong attraction on the workers, leading easily to labor shortages. If agricultural employers remain outside the contemplated accident insurance, then we have to worry that agricultural employers will lose a fraction of their employees, if they do not offer to workers a remuneration that is higher than the wages paid by other occupations" (Tennstedt and Winter 1993: 533).

During this early episode in the political history of the German welfare state we found a disagreement among German employers over the distribution of responsibilities in the administration of social insurance among the state and private actors. Chapter 2 has suggested that firm size should be a strong predictor of the *intensity* in the policy preferences of firms toward these questions of policy design (λ_C). All things equal, the model has hypothesized that large firms will more likely discount the costs imposed by social policies characterized by higher levels of control and support either private type social policies or a corporatist organization of social insurance. In contrast, Chapter 2 has suggested that "control" is relatively unimportant for small firms ($\lambda_C < 0$). The records of the policy deliberations of German employers largely confirm this theoretical prediction.

Associations of producers representing large manufacturing producers argued for the introduction of an insurance policy administered by employers. A meeting of the Central Federation of German Industrialists devoted to the study of alternative proposals of institutional design of the new policy concluded that a "corporatist" organization of social insurance that entrusted significant administrative responsibilities to employers remained the preferable form of institutional design (Centralverband Deutscher Industrieller 1883: 149). These producers strongly opposed the monopolization of social insurance by the state. This solution was regarded as an "unnecessary form of state socialism, given the dense network of preexisting institutions of social insurance existing in German society." One of the strongest worries of employers about the monopoly of the state over the administration of insurance was that bureaucratic officials could gain access to sensitive information of individual firms, "which were in strong competition for their existence" (Centralverband Deutscher Industrieller 1884: 34).

Thus, for large firms, employers' participation in the administration of social insurance was a critical issue of policy design. These employers were ready to accept higher insurance contributions in exchange for higher "control." Small producers had the opposite policy priority. For these firms, the dominant policy consideration was the minimization of their social insurance contributions (Handel und Gewerbe 1888: 373–374). These firms were ready to support any social policy that guaranteed a containment of their costs. Among the sixty-one chambers of commerce surveyed by the Prussian Statistical Office, only five (8 percent of the sample) voiced concerns about the absence of representation of employers in the new institutions of social insurance; more than half of these producers continued to express concerns about the costs of the new social policy (Francke 1881). According to the Chamber of Commerce of Braunsberg, "the consequences of the new social insurance legislation were incalculable and highly dangerous" (Francke 1881: 399). Similarly, the chambers of commerce of Breslau and Stralsund worried that "unlike private insurance companies," the state "would not be able to keep social insurance contributions low." The Chamber of Commerce of Stettin regarded the introduction of this legislation as "an economic event of incalculable consequences" and deplored the elimination of competition in the provision of insurance (Francke 1881: 405). The Chamber of Commerce Osnabrück argued that the law weakened German industry vis-à-vis its foreign competitors (Francke 1881: 401). Of the chambers of commerce surveyed in the sample, 39 percent did not regard compulsory accident insurance as preferable to the existing legislation, whereas 26 percent regarded a reform of the employers' liability law as preferable to the introduction of a new accident insurance.

Figure 3.1 summarizes the findings on business preferences. The preceding analysis points to the existence of a profound disagreement among German producers over the reform of existing liability laws. The introduction of a compulsory accident insurance was the desirable policy outcome for large, manufacturing employers and primarily for producers in industries characterized by a high incidence of workplace accidents. Not all employers, however, supported these radical reforms. But what was the importance of the different sectors in the German business community during the policy-making process that culminated with the introduction of compulsory accident insurance? The following section analyzes this question.

The Negotiation of Accident Insurance

In October 1880 Georg Ferdinand Beutner, the president of the Central Federation of German Industrialists (Centralverband Deutscher Industrieller) wrote to Louis Baare: "Within the time-frame that I have allotted myself, I have completed the project for the worker insurance legislation. Admittedly, I did not approach this job with particularly strong enthusiasm

Negotiation of Accident Insurance

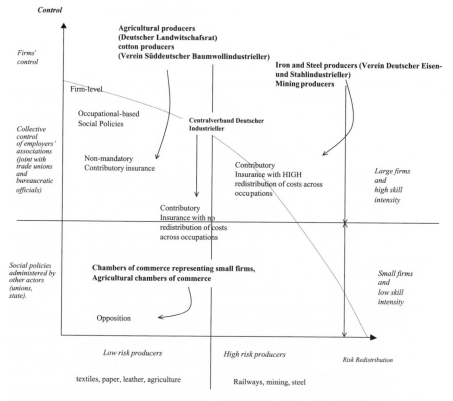

Figure 3.1 German employers and the introduction of accident insurance

because the government has already completed its draft bill and thus we arrive too late" (Tennstedt and Winter 1993: 294). Beutner's worries were not entirely justified. Based on the archival evidence available to us, it is quite certain that employers did not "arrive too late." As many participants in the policy-making process remarked and as Bismarck himself admitted, the Baare draft bill had a tremendous policy impact on the initial proposal of reform, which formulated a clear legal and political alternative to the re- form of the liability laws. Beutner's note expresses a more pervasive worry of German employers about the long-term sustainability of their political alliance with Bismarck around common policy principles.

The Central Federation of German Industrialists, the main association representing large manufacturing producers, supported the introduction of a contributory accident insurance. A policy committee representing employers played a consultative role in the initial process of agenda-setting and formulation of the social policy alternative to private law solutions. But how significant was the influence of German employers, once policy making moved from a narrow and restricted circle surrounding Bismarck to the broader arena of the Reichstag?

To answer these questions and to determine the role played by German employers during the broader long process of reform leading to the final acceptance of compulsory accident insurance by the Reichstag in June 1884, this section reconstructs the process of policy deliberation between 1881 and 1884. The analysis points out that employers' political influence decreased throughout the period. A number of factors characterizing the initial political context – most significantly the policy disagreement among the Liberals, Conservatives, and the Catholic Zentrum, the three largest political "blocs" represented in the Reichstag – increased employers' influence during the early stages of the policy-making process. Relying on business opposition to a reform of private law, Bismarck remained successful in forging a political alliance in the Reichstag that blocked reforms recommending an expansion of the Liability Act of 1871 initiated by the liberal parties. This "defensive" alliance that brought together the conservative parties and the Zentrum succeeded in blocking a further expansion of the Employers' Liability Law. During these early stages of reform Bismarck remained, however, less successful in crafting a majority *supporting* the introduction of a compulsory accident insurance. As a result, he was compelled to accept policy changes that modified his initial policy proposal in important ways. These policy changes responded to demands of elected politicians but also to policy recommendations formulated by the Central Federation of German Industrialists. Once a winning political coalition among the conservatives and the Zentrum (the so-called clerical-conservative compromise) in support of social insurance was formed, the political support of employers was no longer important to Bismarck. A statement of Bismarck points to this diminished political influence of employers during the final stages of reform. In response to the recommendations of the Central Federation of German Industrialists calling for additional policy changes that went beyond the policy agreement reached in the Reichstag, Bismarck remarked that "the objections of employers are no longer to be considered" (Tennstedt and Winter 1995: XXXIII). Broad political support among the leading political parties made nonparliamentary reliance on the support of German employers, which had characterized the early stages of policy development, less essential.

The first accident insurance draft bill was submitted to the Reichstag in March 1881 (Deutscher Reichstag 1881b: 1–66). Building on the crucial legal innovation of the Baare proposal, Bismarck seized the immense political opportunities that resulted from employers' attempts to depart from the preexisting legal tradition that linked compensation of the victims of workplace accidents with the proof of absence of individual fault. A large number of legal obstacles to the compensation of the victim of workplace accidents – which under private law could result in a denial of accident benefits – were simply eliminated, *aufgehoben* in the public law solution. Compulsory insurance under public law replaced the liability principle (Heinz 1973: 108).[8] It was Bismarck's hope that the "paternal care of the state for its citizens [*Fürsorgepflicht*] would replace the bitterness of the conflicts between employers and employees that were a by-product of the private law regime" (Quandt 1938: 18).

Despite the fundamental agreement on the need to replace the liability principle, which was at the basis of the original informal alliance among Bismarck and large manufacturing producers, the bill departed, in significant ways, from the ideal policy preferences of employers. Bismarck and the Central Federation of German Industrialists disagreed on three critical issues of policy design: the administration of accident insurance, the possible extension of insurance to agricultural occupations, and the financing of the new policy. The bill submitted by Bismarck to the Reichstag proposed the creation of an Imperial Insurance Board (Reichsversicherungsanstalt) responsible for the administration of accident insurance (Industrie und Handelskammer Bochum 1881: para. 2). The justification for this strong administrative centralization was Bismarck's consideration that this institution would have greater administrative capabilities to monitor the cases of accidents. This proposal departed in significant ways from the initial Baare bill. The latter had recommended the creation of "administrative subdivisions [*Unterabteilungen*] situated in close proximity to existing administrative districts" (Industrie und Handelskammer Bochum 1881: 16, para. 2). On the policy question concerning the scope of social insurance, the draft bill submitted to the Reichstag recommended the extension of the risk pool of social insurance to all employees (whose yearly income

---

[8] Heinz refers to this policy change as the "replacement of the liability principle through guarantee of insurance" (*Haftungsersetzungsprinzip durch Versicherungsschutz*) (Heinz 1973: 38).

did not exceed two thousand Reichsmark) working in "mines, saltworks, purification works, marshes, mines, shipyards, construction sites, factories, and iron- and steelworks" (Deutscher Reichstag 1881a). This definition of the risk pool of social insurance was narrower than the proposal envisaged by large manufacturing employers. The Central Federation of German Industrialists had recommended the extension of social insurance to agricultural occupations that were dependent on machines in their production process (Industrie und Handelskammer Bochum 1881: para. 1). Finally, the *Bismarckian* bill proposed that employers' contributions financed two-thirds of the costs of accident insurance, with a subsidy of the central government covering the remaining one-third of the costs. In an effort to increase the feeling of dependency on the generosity of the state among German workers, Bismarck explicitly rejected the participation of employees in the financing of social insurance (Quandt 1938: 25).[9] In contrast, the Baare bill favored a mode of financing in which one half of the costs were divided among workers and communes, with employers financing the remaining half of the costs (Industrie und Handelskammer Bochum 1881: 16).

A large majority of the members of the Reichstag opposed the first accident insurance bill. Representatives of left-liberal political parties – such as the German Progressive Party (Deutsche Fortschrittspartei) and the Liberal Union (Liberale Vereinigung) – expressed the strongest hostility toward the accident insurance legislation, denouncing it as "the last clash among the absolutist state and the state of free development" (Quandt 1938: 33). Deputies representing the more centrist National Liberal Party (Nationalliberale Partei) remained, in principle, more open to the introduction of compulsory insurance but rejected the monopolization of insurance by the state and regarded the creation of the *Reichsanstalt* as an "illegitimate form of state socialism" (Deutscher Reichstag 1881c: 673). The draft bill found the strongest potential support among the conservative parties, the Conservatives (Konservativen) and the German Reichparty (Reichspartei). Although these parties were ready to endorse the introduction of a legislation that went beyond the extension of the liability law, they rejected the state contribution to social insurance (Quandt 1938: 42–53).

---

[9] See, for example, a note of Bismarck rejecting the contributions of workers to accident insurance. Randbemerkung zu einem Bericht des preussichen Gesandten in Stuttgart, 8 December 1880 in Reichsarchiv des Deutschen Ministeriums 129 (quoted in Quandt 1938: 25).

The "pivotal" legislators in both chambers of the German Reichstag were deputies representing the Catholic Zentrum. Beginning with the elections of 1881, the Zentrum had become the largest party in the Chamber of Deputies, occupying 100 out of the 397 seats (Ritter 1980: 39). (A similar electoral result was achieved in the 1884 election, when the Zentrum won 24.9 percent of the popular vote, which was translated into 99 seats.) The Zentrum supported a "positive policy imbued by Christian principles" that extended social policy benefits to the workers. Thus, representatives of this party remained, in principle, ready to cooperate with Bismarck in the development of the legislation of accident insurance. But they expressed a profound uneasiness toward the proposal of the bill that aimed at the administrative centralization of social insurance. Zentrum deputies characterized the *Reichsanstalt* as a "concentration of power suffocating all forces" that created "an alien and mechanical relationship between workers and employees" (Deutscher Reichstag 1881c: 689–690). A second, related motivation for their rejection of administrative centralization concerned the regional distribution of power among the federal government and the *Länder*. Due to its strong regional presence in Bavaria and other southern German states, Zentrum politicians opposed the creation of institutions strengthening the role of the Reich, depicting the Bismarckian proposal as a project "that creates nightmares for every Bavarian patriot" (Quandt 1938: 36). In the Bavarian parliament, the Zentrum party warned against the rapid "consolidation of the Reich into a unitary state" and pledged to veto any proposals encroaching on the ability of the *Länder* to maintain independent institutions of social insurance" (Quandt 1938: 36).

Representatives of the Zentrum developed an alternative project for the institutional design of social insurance that departed significantly from the reforms envisaged by Bismarck. In sharp contrast to the draft bill that was under discussion in the Reichstag, the Zentrum recommended the delegation of the administration of social insurance to associations representing employers and employees. These suggestions calling for the introduction of a "corporatist" system of social insurance were inspired by policy ideas that were widely influential in Catholic milieus (cf. Hitze 1880). According to deputies of the Zentrum, the preconditions of these institutions existed already in German society. Preexisting associations covering against the risk of accident insurance (*Unfallgenossenschaften*) "created a common link [*gemeinsames Band*] among employers and employees." The role of the new policy of accident insurance was to create a framework that "strengthened, supported, and extended these corporatist associations that had arisen naturally" (Deutscher Reichstag 1881c).

During the deliberations of the social policy committee of the Chamber, members of the Conservative Party attempted to forge a coalition with representatives of the Zentrum in support of a modified version of the bill submitted by Bismarck. The political composition of this commission reflected the distribution of power in the Reichstag, with policy members of the Zentrum occupying a pivotal role between conservative parties who supported compulsory accident insurance and the liberals who were in favor of an expansion of the liability law.[10] The result of the deliberations of the commission was a solution recommending the regional decentralization of accident insurance and the elimination of the subsidy of the state (Deutscher Reichstag 1881a: 846, 1881b).[11] However, this clerical-conservative compromise forged in the commission of the chamber was ephemeral. Skepticism about the de facto decentralization of the new social policy continued to be pervasive. Reflecting these worries, the Bavarian representative in Berlin wrote to Munich that "Bismarck had fooled the *Zentrum* and that the latter had not obtained from Bismarck the corresponding reward" (Tennstedt and Winter 1993: 613).[12] This led to a reversal in their position of *Zentrum* politicians. Once the bill moved to the floor of the *Bundesrat*, the *Zentrum* joined again the opposition to the bill and helped defeat the first version of the accident insurance legislation.[13]

Bismarck's frustration with the defeat of the bill in the "parliamentary sand"[14] – as he disparagingly referred to the Reichstag – enhanced the

---

[10] The social policy commission of the Reichstag that convened on 6 April 1881 had twenty-eight members. Its composition was as follows: ten representatives of liberal parties (Progressive Party and the Nationalliberals), eight representatives of the conservative parties, eight politicians of the Zentrum, and two representatives of regional parties from Alsace (Quandt 1938). This implies that the pivotal legislator of the commission was a Zentrum politician, the same as in the Reichstag.

[11] Seventeen members of the commission, representing the Conservatives and the Zentrum, voted in support of this proposal (see Deutscher Reichstag 1881b).

[12] Reference is to the correspondence between the Bavarian representative in Berlin. See Bericht des Bayerischen Gesandten in Berlin Graf Hugo von und zu Lerchenfeld-Koefering an den Bayerischen Staatsminister des königlichen Hauses und Aussenminister Freiherr Krafft von Crailsheim, 16 June 1881 (Tennstedt and Winter 1993: 619–621).

[13] On this rejection, see the following sources in Tennstedt and Winter: Bericht des Bayerischen Gesandten in Berlin, 25 June 1881, and Brief des Geheimen Oberregierungsrats Theodor Lohmann an den Schuldirektor Dr. Erst Wyneken (Tennstedt and Winter 1993: 618).

[14] Reference to a speech to the representatives of Innungen (Vertreter Deutscher Innungen) on 17 April 1895 (Tennstedt and Winter 1995: XXIX).

importance of extraparliamentary support of this policy (Tennstedt and Winter 1995: XXIX). During this period, the consultation among Bismarck and leading associations of employers remained intense. As early as September 1880 Bismarck signaled to Baare that he was willing to consider a policy alternative that "relied on smaller associations to administer accident insurance" (Tennstedt and Winter 1995: 27). After the defeat of the first version of accident insurance in the Reichstag, the idea of a *corporatist* organization of social insurance moved to the foreground and became the "focal solution" that was acceptable to *both* large producers and the Catholic Zentrum. The core of this policy idea was to delegate the administration of social insurance to employers. As Bismarck argued, "there is no doubt that the accident insurance can be carried out in the most efficient way by associations that involve representatives of individual industrial sectors or of several sectors characterized by similar firm-level conditions" (Tennstedt and Winter 1995: 81).[15]

In May 1882 the government submitted to the Reichstag a second draft bill of accident insurance (Deutscher Reichstag 1882). In this draft bill, Bismarck abandoned his plan to centralize the administration of social insurance at the level of the Reich. Instead, the bill proposed a very cumbersome system encompassing multiple organizations characterized by overlapping jurisdictions and unclear prerogatives. Based on their risk profile, firms were, at first, divided into different "classes of danger" (*Gefahrenklassen*) (Deutscher Reichstag 1882). These administrative units were responsible for financing nearly two-thirds of the benefits of a victim of workplace accidents (Deutscher Reichstag 1882). But in *addition* to these classes of danger, the draft bill proposed the creation of liability associations (*Berufsgenossenschaften*), encompassing firms of the *same* industry (Deutscher Reichstag 1882). These "corporatist" occupational funds took over organizational responsibilities that had been assigned to the Imperial Insurance Board in the first draft bill (such as the collection of accident insurance contributions) (Deutscher Reichstag 1882).

The peak association representing large manufacturing employers welcomed the "corporatist" administration of accident insurance as organizationally superior to the administrative centralization by the state (Centralverband Deutscher Industrieller 1883, Tennstedt and Winter

---

[15] Entwurf für ein Schreiben des Reichskanzlers Otto Fürst von Bismarck an den Staatsminister Dr. Albert Schäffle, 19 November 1881 (Tennstedt and Winter 1995: 81).

1995: 253–261).[16] According to these employers, liability associations (*Berufsgenossenschaften*) allowed both the necessary decentralization and self-administration. They were regarded as important institutions that could counterbalance the increase in power of the German state. Nevertheless, employers expressed profound worries about potential problems in the implementation of this new insurance law. For employers, the division of industries into different "classes of danger" appeared as a capricious and arbitrary exercise of lawmakers. "What do these firms have in common? What are the similarities between shipbuilding and the fabrication of noodles, between the chocolate industry and blast furnaces, which belong to the same class of danger?" (Centralverband Deutscher Industrieller 1883: 153). To economize on administrative costs, employers recommended the elimination of the two-tiered system that administered the new social insurance. As employers concluded, "the implementation of a corporatist administration of social insurance does not appear possible in the complicated way in which the administration has envisaged this goal" (Centralverband Deutscher Industrieller 1883: 150).

Employers were not the only actor that regarded the proposal of the second draft bill as unnecessarily cumbersome. Policy makers in the Reichstag raised similar objections. A number of politicians worried that the blurring of responsibilities among the liability associations and the classes of dangers would diminish the capacity of these institutions to collect insurance contributions (Quandt 1938: 90). In response to these objections, the government submitted yet another draft bill that eliminated the chaotic system in the administration of social insurance (Deutscher Reichstag 1884b). This third draft bill retained only the liability associations (*Berufsgenossenschaften*) as the institutions administering accident insurance (Deutscher Reichstag 1884b: para. 11–33).[17] The preface to this draft bill acknowledged that the broad delegation of power to "corporative associations was in general harmony with the development of public life" and that it corresponded to the "practical needs" as well as to the "desires of the industrial circles" (Deutscher Reichstag 1884b: 38). Employers were given broad prerogatives in the administration of these occupational risk pools – among others, the freedom to determine the regional scope of a risk pool (Syrup and Neuloh 1957: 122).

---

[16] See Entwurf einer Stellungnahme des Zentralverbandes Deutscher Industrieller zur zweiten Unfallversicherungsvorlage (Tennstedt and Winter 1995: 253–261).

[17] In contrast to the occupational associations of the second draft bill, these liability associations (*Berufsgenossenschaften*) included only firms belonging to the *same* industry.

84

The role of the state in the administration of social insurance was severely curtailed. The only remaining administrative responsibility of the Imperial Insurance Office was to supervise the adequacy of the safety measures introduced by individual firms (Deutscher Reichstag 1884b: paras. 87–91).

This third draft bill found a stronger support in the Reichstag. Pivotal legislators representing the Zentrum welcomed the solution that blended the principle of compulsory insurance – supported by Catholic policy makers – and the coveted administrative decentralization (Deutscher Reichstag 1884b: 62). In the Reichstag, the final objections of politicians centered around the proposed subsidy on the part of the state to the new social insurance. In defense of this subsidy, Bismarck argued that he attempted to prevent the "burdening of the industry with the full costs of social insurance" (Gitter 1969: 28).[18] The Centralverband Deutscher Industrieller supported the state subsidy and voiced strong concerns about the ability of industry to carry the entire costs of a contributory insurance unaided (Centralverband Deutscher Industrieller 1882: 25). However, all political parties with the exception of the Conservatives opposed the participation of the state in the financing of social insurance (Quandt 1938: 115). This political opposition led to the final elimination of the state subsidy from the final version of the accident insurance draft bill. Compulsory accident insurance became a policy financed entirely by employers.

The final choice of policy design reflected thus a strategic compromise among Bismarck, large manufacturing producers, and the pivotal politicians of the Zentrum. Due to the opposition of employers and the Zentrum, Bismarck was unable to achieve his preferred social policy outcome, characterized by the administrative centralization of social insurance in the hands of the state. The final policy outcome delegated all administrative responsibilities for the new insurance to liability associations (*Berufsgenossenschaften*), consisting entirely of business representatives. Thus, along the "control" dimension of the social policy space, the final policy outcome came closest to the ideal policy point of producers. Large manufacturing producers were unable to achieve similar success along the second dimension of the social policy space. The risk pool of social insurance excluded agricultural employers. The proposals of large manufacturing employers to "extend the advantages of social insurance to all occupations" remained unsuccessful.

---

[18] This is a reference to Bismarck's speech in the Reichstag on 9 January 1882, mentioning that he lacked the courage to burden the industry with the full costs of this policy.

Legal and Political Developments in France

French political efforts to find a solution to the problem of workplace accidents paralleled developments in Germany. For most of the nineteenth century, the Napoleonic Civil Code of 1804 provided the legal basis for the resolution of questions of workplace accidents (Dupeyroux 1995, Namgalies 1981). Article 1382 of the Civil Code stated an unequivocal relationship between individual liability and compensation. "Any action that causes a damage to somebody else demands reparation" (Jaillet 1980: 17–19). In the case of workplace accidents, French law applied similar legal requirements regarding the burden of proof as for any other liability issue. This implied that victims of "accidental accidents" (*accidents accidentels*) – those accidents for which the exact responsibility could not be determined with precision – remained uncompensated (Hesse and Le Gall 1999: 181).

The second half of the nineteenth century ushered in an intense search for legal and political reforms. The first avenue of reform pursued by legal experts of the period remained an expansion of the liability of employers. In their rulings on cases of workplace accidents, French courts began to rely increasingly on another article of the Civil Code, article 1384 (Jaillet 1980: 25–29). Based on this article, the responsibility of employers extended to objects and persons situated under the authority of the head of the enterprise.[19] A number of important court decisions of the period ruled also that employers were liable for accidents resulting from "external circumstances," such as breakdowns in machines (Arrêt du Conseil dÉtat, 21 June 1895, in Jaillet 1980: 28).

A second avenue of reform attempted to redefine the basis of legal responsibility of employers toward their workers. Proponents of the legal theory of contractual responsibility (*responsabilité contractuelle*) argued that employers had the obligation to "take all necessary measures to safeguard the life and health of their employees" (Sauzet 1883: 621, Pic 1895: 502–517, Pascaud 1885: 365–371). Thus, workplace accidents reflected a breakdown of the contractual obligations of employers. Article 1382 of the Civil Code was inapplicable because it was premised on the criminal responsibility (*responsabilité délictuelle*) of employers. Another implication of this legal theory of contractual responsibility was that victims of workplace accidents

---

[19] Article 1384, paragraph 1, of the French Civil Code was formulated as follows. "On est responsable non seulement du dommage que l'on cause part son propre fait, mais encore de celui qui est causé par le fait des personnes dont on doit répondre ou des choses que l'on a sous sa garde."

were no longer required to prove employers' fault as a precondition of their compensation. In contrast, the legal burden of proof was reversed and employers were now required to prove their innocence. During the second half of the nineteenth century, a number of French courts began to apply the legal doctrine of contractual responsibility of employers in their decisions. Two higher courts (Dijon and Beçanson) ruled that employers are "obliged to protect the workers against dangers that may result from workplace accidents" and that "this obligation entails the necessity to foresee all possible causes of workplace accidents" (Sauzet 1883: 621).[20]

Policy makers and politicians in the French Chamber of Deputies also attempted to explore the possibility of a reversal of the burden of proof in case of workplace accidents. The earliest draft bills of accident insurance legislation discussed in the French parliament proposed a reversal of the burden of proof (*renversement de la preuve*) similar to the German Employers' Liability Act of 1871. The first draft bill of the law of workplace accidents, submitted by deputy Nadaud to the Chamber of Deputies in May 1880, consisted of a single article: "If a person, lending his work to another person is injured or killed, the employer will be fully responsible, unless he proves that the accident has resulted from an error caused by the victim" (*Journal Officiel* 1880). A number of other draft bills introduced variations on this common legal theme. One draft bill suggested shifting liability to employers for all accidents whose causes remained unknown (*Journal Officiel* 1882a). This proposal was far more radical than the solution introduced in Germany. It recommended to shift the liability for workplace accidents to *all* employers and not only to a limited number of industries that were more prone to workplace accidents.

In 1882 the Chamber of Deputies appointed a parliamentary commission to examine the different proposals recommending the reversal of the burden of proof (*Journal Officiel* 1882b). The commission proposed to amend article 1384 of the civil code, by specifying those industries for which the reversal of burden of proof applied, but also to define the circumstances when this presumption of employers' fault did not apply. The latter were accidents "caused by 'external forces' [*force majeure* or *cas fortuit*]" (*Journal Officiel* 1882c: 1882).

Beginning with the mid 1880s, a new set of policy ideas began to gain increasing ground among policy makers of the Chamber of Deputies. This legal doctrine was known as the *théorie du risque professionnel* (Eycken 1900,

---

[20] Refers to the decision of the Dijon court of 27 April 1877 (Sauzet 1883: 616).

Dejace 1889, Bellom 1899, Hubert-Valleroux 1896). As a result of the acceptance of this new legal theory by an increasing number of policy makers, efforts to design legislation similar to the German Employers' Liability Act were gradually abandoned. Proponents of the *théorie du risque professionnel* argued that workplace accidents were a "new risk," specific to modern industry. Accidents were "the sad, but inevitable tribute in human blood paid in exchange for the wonders of industry" (Dejace 1889: 12). Searching for individual fault or responsibility in the case of workplace accidents was simply beside the point. "The risk specific to each profession is *independent of the fault* of workers and employers" (Cheysson 1895: 416, Ewald 1996: 250). This implied that the legal requirement – of either employer or worker – to prove responsibility in causing workplace accidents had to be abandoned. Both critics and proponents of the theory admitted that by severing the relationship between personal responsibility and compensation, the *théorie du risque professionnel* stood in sharp discontinuity to the entire legislation (*Journal Officiel* 1882b).[21] As Léon Say eloquently formulated this issue on the floor of the Senate, "there is no point of contact between the civil law and the *théorie du risque professionnel*: one is founded on the principle of responsibility, the other on the principle of solidarity" (Ewald 1996: 249).

The first reform bill that incorporated new legal theory was submitted to the Chamber of Deputies in 1882 (*Journal Officiel* 1882c).[22] The author was Félix Faure, an important radical politician of the period. Faure's bill differed from existing proposals to solve the problem of workplace accidents in several important respects. First, it proposed to eliminate trials as the basis of compensation of the victims of workplace accidents. As the justification prefacing the draft bill stated, "because workplace accidents are the inevitable consequence of work, work itself is responsible for workplace accidents" (*Journal Officiel* 1882c: 357). According to Faure, this justified shifting to employers the costs of compensating victims of workplace accidents. Faure's bill proposed to grant compensation to all victims of accidents, without requiring any proof of liability. The costs had to be financed entirely by employers. This idea had been widely endorsed by other proponents of the *théorie du risque professionnel*. As one legal expert of the period argued, "the worker bears a part of the *risque professionnel*

---

[21] The parliamentary commission appointed to examine the first projects of law based on the *théorie du risque professionnel* observed that "this legislation situates itself beyond the existing legislation, leaving it intact …, but establishing for other cases of accidents a parallel legislation" (*Journal Officiel* 1882b: 1008).

[22] *Journal Officiel* 1882a, 1882c.

through his physical and moral suffering; employers also have to sacrifice a part of their advantages by compensating the victims" (Eycken 1900: 72). The draft bill proposed the creation of private institutions of insurance, which could aid employers in coping with "the risk generated by their own enterprise" (*Journal Officiel* 1882c: 359). It also recommended classifying industries into "categories of danger," based on their risk profile and specified the maximal amount of compensation that could be received by the victims of accidents.

These efforts to find a new legal and political solution to the problem of workplace accidents that attempted to redefine the legal responsibility of employers toward workers or to spell out possible exemptions to the civil code reveal the profound legal and political crisis of French private law, when confronted with the question of workplace accidents. The rulings of the courts and the incipient process of political reform shifted the policy outcome away from the nineteenth-century status quo. The political uncertainty resulting from the process of policy experimentation had profound implications for French employers.

The Preferences of French Employers

French employers were strongly involved in the political and legal debates surrounding the reform of liability laws. Numerous producers regarded the aggravation of their liability that was the cumulative effect of court decisions with understandable worry and nervousness. As a member of the steering commission of the Association of French Industry (Association de l'Industrie Française) characterized the policy environment faced by employers: "This set of circumstances constitutes the most absolute arbitrariness. All the associations representing employers and workers alike are unanimous in their belief that any regulation is preferable to this uncertain situation, which gives rise to the most contradictory decisions" (Jourdain 1899: 35).[23] Although a majority of French employers agreed that the legal responsibilities of producers in the case of workplace accidents had to be clarified, profound disagreement persisted over the desirable direction of reform. Three policy questions were the object of disagreement among employers. Was a reform that embraced the new *théorie du risque profession-nel* preferable to a legal reform that remained entirely consistent with the

---

[23] Jourdain was a member of the steering commission of the Association of French Industry.

Civil Code? Should the obligation to insure against the risk of workplace accidents be mandatory for all employers? What should be the mix between institutions of social insurance administered and supervised by the state and "private-type" social insurance institutions organized by individual firms or associations of employers?

The goal of this section is to test the main propositions specifying the sources of intersectoral disagreement among producers developed in Chapter 2. My analysis of the policy preferences of French employers is based on two primary sources. I rely on archival records of the internal deliberations of various employers' associations on the question of social insurance reform.[24] An additional invaluable source is a collection of contemporary publications of employers analyzing various aspects of these political reforms, found at the French National Library (Dada and Proutière 1980).

The sample – consisting of thirty-seven observations – is a representative cross-section of the French business community during the last two decades of the nineteenth century. The defining characteristic of the French economy of the period was the predominance of small producers (Fridenson and Straus 1987, Dansette 2000). According to the social census of 1851, around 4.7 million employees in France were employed in small enterprises, with only 1,330,000 workers employed in large manufacturing firms (Woronoff 1998: 221). Similarly, a survey conducted in 1860 among Parisian employers found only 7,500 firms that had a work force larger than 10 workers; 31,000 firms that employed between 2 and 10 workers; and 62,000 firms that employed 1 worker (Woronoff 1998: 221). Finally, the labor market data quoted during the parliamentary deliberations of the period suggested that more than 60 percent of the French labor force was employed in small enterprises (with less than 10 employees) (*Journal Officiel* 1889: 200).[25] To reflect this economic structure of the French economy, most observations in my sample reflect the policy preferences of small firms. In addition, the sample includes the most representative associations grouping large manufacturing producers. This includes the Iron Works Committee (Comité des Forges) and the Committee of Producers in Coal Mining (Comité de

---

[24] A collection of these records can be found in the archive of the Paris Chamber of Commerce. See Chambre de Commerce de Paris 1880–1890.

[25] The official statistical sources of the period define large enterprises as enterprises with more than ten employees, thus I infer that the same criterion was used by policy makers during the parliamentary debates (see Woronoff 1998: 221).

Houillières (cf. Villey 1923b, International Labor Organization 1927: 50–77, Priouret 1963, Lefranc 1976).[26]

These records of employers' deliberations reveal a profound disagreement among French producers on the question of the reform of the liability law. The large majority of small producers opposed a reform that was based on the *théorie du risque professionnel*. Many individual chambers of commerce regarded the *risque professionnel* as an incomprehensible legal fiction. "What is this new legal entity situated between employers and employees?" asked the Chamber of Commerce of Beauvais and Oise (Chambre de Commerce de Beauvais et de l'Oise 1895). Other employers regarded the new justification for the compensation of the victims of workplace accidents as ill-defined. As employers of the Chamber of Commerce of Nevers argued: "If the *risque professionnel* is a risk that is inherent to a profession, independent of the fault of both employers and employees, why are employers held liable for this risk?" (Chambre de Commerce de Nevers 1895). According to employers of Chalon-sur-Saone, Autun, and Louhan, Félix Faure's draft bill created a "shocking and revolting inequality" by introducing the "a priori guilt of employers" (Chambre de Commerce de Chalon-sur-Saone, Autun et Louhan 1884).

In March 1893, during a meeting with Félix Faure, employers from the Paris region expressed their support of the "principle to provide compensation to the victims of workplace accidents" but disagreed with the method proposed by the law, which "imposed an absolute responsibility on employers" (Chambre de Commerce de Paris 1883a). Employers recommended that the solution to the problem had to be searched "within the laws that govern us" (Chambre de Commerce de Paris 1883a). In a later meeting of 1883, the Commission of Social Affairs of the Paris Chamber of Commerce rejected a solution based on the *théorie du risque professionnel* (Chambre de Commerce de Paris 1883b). Employers argued that this theory contradicted the principle of equality before the law of employer and employee, because it made employers liable for "an accident that is independent of any fault or negligence on their part" (Chambre de Commerce de Paris 1883b). These objections were simply missing the point of the new legal solution. Based on the *théorie du risque professionnel*, employers were *stricto sensu* not liable for workplace accidents, but they remained responsible for the compensation of victims.

---

[26] The Comité des Forges and the Comité des Houillierès are among the founding federations of the Union des Industries Métallurgiques et Minières in 1901 (Lefranc 1976: 39).

In contrast to associations representing small producers, large manu-facturing employers supported proposals of reform put forward by the Chamber of Deputies as early as 1888. Representatives of the Iron Works Committee (Comité des Forges), the peak federation representing iron and steel producers, expressed their "unhesitant support" for the principle of the *risque professionnel,* "a principle that calls necessarily for the insurance of employers" (Comité des Forges 1891). Similarly, the Comité Central des Houillières de France, an association representing employers in min-ing, supported the "the principle of the project submitted for deliberation to the parliament" (Darcy 1898: 3). Finally, the Association of French Industry (Association de l'Industrie Française) supported "the *théorie du risque pro-fessionnel,* namely the fact that the head of the enterprise [*chef d'industrie*] should pay for the benefits of victims of workplace accidents" and demanded that "the amount of benefits should be determined by lawmakers to avoid future legal controversies" (*Journal Officiel* 1893: 1592). This association signaled to French lawmakers that it preferred a reform based on the *théorie du risque professionnel* to the policy status quo characterized by a "profound legal uncertainty" (*Journal Officiel* 1889: 240).

Large firms, however, did not support the proposals of French lawmakers without qualifications. For these producers, the ideal social policy outcome was one that guaranteed the autonomy of preexisting *private* institutions of social insurance. Beginning with the second half of the previous century, large firms and sectoral or regional associations of producers had estab-lished private-type institutions of social insurance providing social policy benefits to the victims of workplace accidents or their families. For exam-ple, as early as 1859, large manufacturing firms in Paris had established a private insurance fund (Caisse d'assurance mutuelle) for the victims of workplace accidents (Comité des Forges 1891: 220). Employers in the con-struction industry had established a similar institution in 1869. The largest private institution of social insurance compensating victims of workplace accidents – the Caisse d'assurance mutuelle des Forges de France – had been established by the Iron Works Committee in 1891 (Réforme Sociale 1894: 344). In 1892 thirty-one firms participated in the financing of this insurance solution (Réforme Sociale 1893: 961). As Henri Hatzfeld, a historian of the French welfare state commented on these institutions, "they satisfied labor market imperatives of large firms and their needs for recruitment, stabil-ity, and discipline" (Hatzfeld 1971: 123). Faced with proposals to socialize insurance, large employers strongly defended the autonomy of these pre-existing institutions and argued in favor of granting exceptional status to these institutions as part of social insurance (Réforme Sociale 1894: 345). These findings confirm one of the hypotheses of Chapter 2, suggesting the importance of control for large firms.

While large firms took an active role in defending the autonomy of these private institutions of social insurance, small producers militated for the freedom to opt out of social insurance. The dominant theme expressed by the deliberations of various chambers of commerce was concern about the "prohibitive costs" of the new insurance law. As an association of employers formulated these worries, "by preoccupying itself exclusively with the situation of workers, the draft bill neglects the numerous and interesting class of employers who will not be able to afford these costs and will succumb as victims of the new incurred responsibility" (Chambre de Commerce de Paris 1883b). Another association of producers stated that it was "inequitable and impracticable" to ask small producers to finance social insurance (Darcy 1896). Small producers who "hire a journeyman for a more or less transitory job do not have more resources than the latter. In fact, they are not different from a simple worker" (Darcy 1896). Other associations also voiced concerns about the potential increase in their non-wage labor costs. "The law will provoke a state of chronic misery in rural industry," wrote one chamber of commerce (Chambre de Commerce de Nevers 1895). Other producers wrote, "We beseech the lawmakers not to inflict a new charge on French industry, on our large and small enterprises, so courageous in their fight against foreign competition, in general so benevolent toward the workers. Under the impact of this new charge a large number of these will inevitably succumb" (Chambre de Commerce d'Abbeville 1898a).

The model developed in Chapter 2 has hypothesized that questions about the scope of social insurance and the interoccupational redistribution of risks are also distributionally divisive for employers. An implication of the model has been that employers in industries facing a high incidence of risks will favor highly redistributive social policies and will favor the expansion of social insurance to include large segments of the population, whereas low-risk producers will oppose a high redistribution of risks. The records of the policy deliberations of French producers support this hypothesis. Iron and steel producers and employers in mining and other industries facing a high incidence of the risk of workplace accidents supported a wide scope for the new insurance legislation. In a policy statement submitted to the Chamber of Deputies, the Central Committee of Coal-Mining Producers (Comité Central des Houillières de France) opposed the intention of French lawmakers to apply the *risque professionnel* only to industries relying on mechanical tools. As these employers argued, the arbitrary distinction between "mechanized and nonmechanized industries was based on the erroneous assumption of the harmlessness [*innocuité*] of nonmechanical professions" (Darcy 1896: 6). In contrast to the policy proposal formulated in the Chamber of Deputies, these employers demanded the "the extension of the law to all occupations" (Darcy 1896: 6, *Journal Officiel* 1888a). Employers brought their demands to the floor of the French parliament. During the deliberations in the Chamber of Deputies, representatives of employers (de Clerq) opposed the intention of lawmakers to restrict the accident insurance legislation to a limited number of industries. "We want to pay our part," argued employers. "This will be done through insurance societies organized at the regional level, through private insurance through other solutions. But I think that you are wrong to enumerate the industries [referring here to the first draft bill of accident insurance, which enumerated the industries for which the *théorie du risque professionnel* applied]. It is much better to apply the principle indicated by us, namely to apply the law to all workers" (*Journal Officiel* 1888b: 1467).

In contrast to high-risk producers, employers in industries facing a lower incidence of risk protested against the expansive definition of the risk pool of social insurance. "What will happen to the small industrialists included in this dangerous association?" asked the Chamber of Commerce of Marseille (Chambre Syndicale de Marseille 1897). The most vocal opponents of the introduction of compulsory accident insurance were agricultural producers (Augé-Laribé 1950: 109–117). The Society of French Agricultural Employers (Société des Agriculteurs de France) opposed the intention of lawmakers to enlist agricultural producers as part of social insurance, denouncing these plans as a measure that protected manufacturing producers but disfavored agriculture (Augé-Laribé 1950: 112). Due to their lower incidence of risk for workplace accidents, these producers regarded the introduction of compulsory insurance as a policy that brought no immediate advantages but created only unbearable financial burdens. "The agricultural employers will be unable to finance social charges that are this heavy. There is no agricultural employer who can provide the necessary capital" (Augé-Laribé 1950: 113).

These surveys of the voices of French producers support the main hypotheses developed in Chapter 2. Figure 3.2 summarizes the findings. We find a strong disagreement among French firms over the ideal design of the institutions of social insurance. Risk incidence and firm size remain the two

Preferences of French Employers

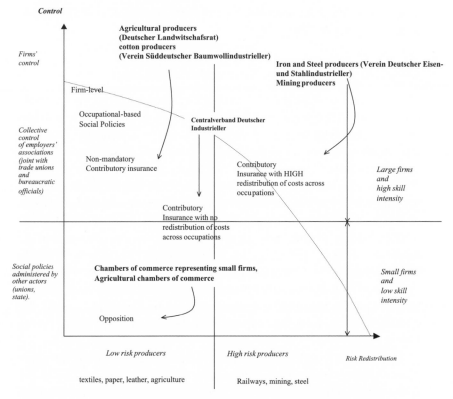

Figure 3.2   French employers and the introduction of accident insurance

variables that have the strongest effect in explaining the social policy preferences of French employers. Existing sources do not allow us to test the impact of the skill composition of the work force on the social policy preferences of employers. While supportive of the *théorie du risque professionnel* and of compulsory accident insurance, large firms called for the introduction of a social policy that encouraged and relied on preexisting private institutions of social insurance. To minimize the costs of social insurance, small firms demanded purely voluntary private institutions of social insurance. High-risk producers (such as employers in mining and steel) favored an extensive application of the new social insurance law, whereas low-risk producers (such as those in agriculture) preferred to remain outside of the scope of social insurance.

How did French policy makers respond to the demands of French employers? I turn to this question next. The following section reconstructs the process of political deliberations leading to the introduction of an accident insurance policy in 1898.

Compulsory Insurance or a Reform of Liability Law?

The *théorie du risque professionnel* that was formulated by French policy makers as early as 1880 was a bold attempt to solve the intractable legal issues posed by the compensation of victims of workplace accidents. However, a political consensus about the design of the institutions of social insurance that reflected or implemented this theory was reached only with great difficulty. The parliamentary deliberations about the accident insurance legislation lasted eighteen years. During this period, countless proposals, draft bills, and parliamentary reports were exchanged between the Chamber of Deputies, the Senate, and various political associations interested in the outcomes of these reforms (Bellom 1894, Eycken 1900, Ewald 1996). As one member of the Chamber noted with irony in 1888, ten years *before* the introduction of the accident insurance legislation: "If we have been the first to consider the need to reform the problem of workplace accidents, we have been almost the last to solve the problem" (*Journal Officiel* 1888b: 1434).

This long and protracted political process that preceded the introduction of accident insurance in 1898 was the consequence of a strong policy disagreement among the two chambers of parliament over the design of the institutions of social insurance. French policy makers struggled with the same issues of policy design as French employers. How broad should be risk pool of social insurance? What should be the contribution of each occupation in the financing of the new policy? What should be the role of the state in the administration of the new insurance? What responsibilities should be delegated to preexisting, private institutions of support and those institutions of social insurance that had been already established by employers? Throughout these policy deliberations, policy makers in the Chamber of Deputies pursued an agenda of reform that favored a stronger role of the state as guarantor of the new insurance solution. In contrast, the Senate opposed far-reaching social insurance reforms and proposed only modest, incremental reforms of existing liability laws.

The divergence in the policy outcomes espoused by "median representatives" in the two chambers of the French parliament was the consequence of different electoral rules for the two chambers (Goguel 1946, 1952). Representatives in the Chamber of Deputies were elected through universal suffrage. Despite the fragmentation of the political landscape during the Third Republic, the elections between 1880 and 1898 yielded significant majorities for the political forces that were supportive of social insurance reform – the Moderate Republicans, Radicals, and Radical Socialists.[27] In stark contrast to the Chamber, the Senate remained the bastion of conservative opposition to far-reaching social reforms (Hutton 1986, Pactet 1995).[28] While 75 out of the 300 senators (the so-called *sénateurs inamovibles*) were elected for life by representatives of the National Assembly, the remaining 225 senators were selected by an electoral college that disproportionately favored representatives of communes. This election mechanism to the upper chamber introduced a strong bias favoring small rural communities and a broader constellation of interests opposed to a compulsory social insurance: agricultural producers, small landowners, the provincial bourgeoisie (Chevalier 1998: 47, Marichy 1969: 206).[29] Léon Gambetta's famous characterization of the Senate of the Third Republic as the "the grand council of the communes" aptly and concisely summarized this state of affairs.

In the Chamber of Deputies, the first debate of the accident insurance legislation took place between May and July 1888 (*Journal Officiel* 1888a, 1888b). The first difficult issue that confronted policy makers was whether the *théorie du risque professionnel* should be at the basis of the new insurance legislation. The *risque professionnel* was defined as "a risk inherent to a determined profession" that was independent of the fault of employers or workers (*Journal Officiel* 1893: 1583).[30] Proponents of this theory argued that this risk was "real, precise," and pervasive (*Journal Officiel* 1893: 1583). Because statistical data on the most important causes of workplace accidents

---

[27] On the existence of these majorities in support of reform, see Goguel 1952, Mackie and Rose 1974: 119–121. Between 1881 (the year in which the first draft bill that recommended a reform based on the *théorie du risque professionnel*) and 1898 (the year in which the accident insurance legislation was adopted), the combined number of deputies occupied by Republicans, Radicals, Radical Socialists, and Socialists was as follows: 455 (out of 541) between 1881 and 1885, 367 (out of 569) between 1885 and 1889, 463 (out of 566) between 1893 and 1898, and 472 (out of 572) between 1898 and 1902.

[28] In the words of Pierre Pactet, a French expert on constitutional government, the Senate was "politically republican and socially conservative" (Pactet 1995: 288).

[29] An expert on the French Senate discussed this bias in favor of small localities: "A city with a population of 100,000 has the same number of delegates [to the senatorial college] as two cities of 10,000 inhabitants, four small towns of 2501 inhabitants, and 24 villages of 200 inhabitants, despite the fact that its population is 5, 10, or 25 times higher" (Marichy 1969: 206).

[30] This was the definition provided by a renowned legal expert of the period, Emil Cheysson (Cheysson 1895a, 1895b).

were unavailable in France, French policy makers relied on data collected by the German social insurance administration. According to these data, 12 percent of workplace accidents resulted from the negligence of employers, whereas around 20 percent of accidents could be attributed to the fault of workers. However, in 68 percent of the cases, the responsibilities could not be imputed to workers or to employers. In the legal jargon of the period, these were referred to as the "accidental accidents." They marked the limitations of a private law solution.

Proponents of the *théorie du risque professionnel* recommended to shift to employers the responsibility to compensate the victims of workplace accidents. In contrast to alternative policy solutions, this shift in the costs of social insurance to employers was not based on the presumption of the liability of producers. As Félix Faure, a member of the social policy commission of the Chamber argued, "we act in this way, because we estimate that the head of the enterprise is the natural distributor of costs. More than anyone else, he has the ability to shift a fraction of this new charge either to the work force, to the profit of the enterprise, or even to consumers" (*Journal Officiel* 1893: 1583).

A second difficult question faced by French lawmakers was to determine the scope of application of the new law. The argument invoked on the floor of the Chamber was that the *risque professionnel* was a consequence of mechanization. "The *risque professionnel* exists today, but did not exist in 1804, the moment when the Civil Code was written. In 1804 we did not have what we have now: the large murderous machines used by industry. The accidents were less numerous and one could rely on the rigor of the principles inscribed in the Civil Code" (*Journal Officiel* 1888a: 1434). Consequently, the first draft bill of the law recommended to restrict the scope of the law to industries "in which mechanical forces are used, such as quarries, mines, and transportation."

In numerous writings addressed to lawmakers and during encounters with members of the Social Policy Commission of the Chamber, associations representing large manufacturing producers supported the *théorie du risque professionnel*. As large firms argued, the policy was preferable to the policy status quo characterized by absolute arbitrariness. "The Association of French Industry accepts the principle that implies that worker victims of workplace accidents should be compensated by the head of the enterprise. This association demands that the amount of benefit for each type of workplace accident is established to prevent, as much as possible, further legal wrangles" (*Journal Officiel* 1893: 1582). According to this association, one of the advantages of the law was its potential to bring about labor peace between capital and labor. What is remarkable about the early debates in the Chamber is that a representative of employers (and not a reformist policy maker) submitted the proposal calling for "an extension of the advantages of the law to *all* workers" (*Journal Officiel* 1888a: 1467). "Why limit the law?" asked employers (*Journal Officiel* 1888a: 1467). "Why introduce arbitrary distinctions and limitations?" As discussed, this policy preference of manufacturing industries for the extension of the scope of social insurance was motivated by the understanding that socialized forms of insurance implied lower costs than purely private social policies.

The third important policy question faced by policy makers in the Chamber concerned the role of the state in the organization of social insurance. Recognizing that a dense network of private institutions of social insurance established primarily by large manufacturing producers was already in place, lawmakers attempted to encourage the proliferation of these institutions under the auspices of the new law. The draft bill gave employers the freedom to "form among themselves mutual institutions of insurance [*caisses d'assurance mutuelle*]" (article 28) (*Journal Officiel* 1888a). However, firms were allowed to join these private institutions of insurance only if they could demonstrate the availability of sufficient resources to compensate victims of workplace accidents. Lawmakers imposed similar conditions on firms that wanted to remain their own insurers. If employers lacked these financial resources, they were required to join a public institution of social insurance, the Caisse d'assurance contre les accidents (*Journal Officiel* 1888a). In contrast to the design of the institutions of social insurance favored by German lawmakers, where the state held the de facto monopoly over the administration of social insurance, policy makers of the Chamber of Deputies were ready to accommodate a greater role for private institutions of social insurance.

The draft bill of the Chamber encountered profound opposition on the floor of the Senate (*Journal Officiel* 1889).[31] Senators attempted to conserve the "just and beneficial aspects" of this legislative project, but also remove its "dangerous and excessive elements" (*Journal Officiel* 1889: 251). The main objection to the policy solution of the Chamber raised by members of the Senate was the insufficient attention to the distinct policy needs of small producers. As senators argued, small producers operated

---

[31] In the words of an opponent of the law, the proposal of the Chamber of Deputies was "ridiculous, impracticable, and impossible" (*Journal Officiel* 1889: 202).

under fundamentally different constraints than did large firms. Many large manufacturing employers had already voluntarily established private-type institutions of social insurance which provided benefits to the victims of workplace accidents (*Journal Officiel* 1889: 200). Thus, the draft bill of the Chamber did not affect in significant ways the social insurance charges faced by these large firms. In contrast, an increase in the level of social insurance charges could "bring about immediate financial ruin" for many small producers. "In a majority of small workshops, employers are only a more intelligent worker, who succeeded in establishing a modest capital as a result of their savings. Thus they were able to enlist the help of two or three workers. According to this legal project, an employer becomes liable for all accidents that can occur in his workshop, even for those accidents caused by the errors of his aides. For small producers, the law inevitably entails financial ruin" (*Journal Officiel* 1889: 200).

To protect small producers against an increase in their social charges, the Senate endorsed only the creation of voluntary private insurance. This policy solution accommodated the differential social policy needs of large and small firms. Thus, senators recommended eliminating the requirement for producers to obtain insurance through the Accident Insurance Fund (Caisse d'assurance d'Accidents), if no private insurance was available. The accident insurance fund administered by the state was depicted as a source of "abuses and a danger for the public finances" and an illegitimate form of state socialism imported from 'authoritarian Germany' (*Journal Officiel* 1890a: 120–121). The "state will take everything and pay everything. This institution will destroy the existing private insurance industry and will inevitably lead to the introduction of compulsory social insurance" (*Journal Officiel* 1890a: 120). These considerations led to the rejection of the proposal of the Chamber to assign a partial (albeit limited) responsibility of the state in administering social insurance.

Finally, the Senate took explicit steps to protect *agricultural* producers against the potential aggravation of their legal responsibility toward their employees and against a potential increase in their nonwage labor costs. While endorsing the *théorie du risque professionnel* – understood as the general obligation of the head of the enterprise to compensate victims of those accidents for which responsibility could be imputed to neither employers nor employees – senators made a concerted effort to limit the application of this theory to *manufacturing* employers alone. Policy makers in the Chamber had proposed to apply the law to industries in which "mechanical tools were used" (article 1, Project of the Chamber). This implied that the

100

théorie du risque professionnel affected those agricultural employers who relied on machines in their production process, but not employers "relying on
nonmechanical, animal forces." Senators raised two objections to the classification of producers proposed by the Chamber. First, no evidence existed
to demonstrate that the number of workplace accidents in "mechanized"
agricultural enterprises was higher than in enterprises that did not use
these machines extensively. Thus, the law introduced an arbitrary distinction between "enterprises belonging to the same industry" (*Journal Officiel*
1889: 220). Second, numerous policy makers of the upper chamber argued
that agricultural employers "used mechanical forces only intermittently"
(*Journal Officiel* 1889: 301). "Should an agricultural producer that had made
use of machines only for one week during the harvest period be responsible
for compensating victims for workplace accidents?" asked a member of the
Senate (*Journal Officiel* 1889: 301). The implication of this line of reasoning
was that the distinction among "mechanized and nonmechanized producers" that had been established by the Chamber was spurious. In lieu of the
proposal of the Chamber, the Senate recommended the explicit exclusion
of agriculture from the scope of the new law.

The project voted by the Senate endorsed only a very limited reform of
the status quo (*Journal Officiel* 1890a). The Senate rejected all proposals
to impose on employers the obligation to insure against the risk of workplace accidents. With respect to the future organization of social insurance,
the Senate recommended the elimination of all forms of state supervision
of the voluntary institutions of social insurance established by employers.
With respect to the scope of the new law, the Senate explicitly rejected the
application of *théorie du risque professionnel* to agricultural producers. Thus,
on all major questions of policy design, the final proposal of the Senate
was much closer to the policy demands that had been formulated by French
small producers.

But policy makers in the Chamber of Deputies were not ready to endorse this minimalist view about the scope of accident insurance proposed
by the Senate. The major objection raised by deputies of the French lower
house was that private voluntary insurance did not provide sufficient guarantees to workers that they will be compensated after a workplace accident.
The first endemic problem of voluntary private insurance was a problem
of self-selection of employers: only "good risks" had an incentive to join an
insurance company. As a French policy maker formulated this issue: "There
are both careful and careless employers, or what in insurance terms could
be called the good and the bad risks. On the one hand, one finds those

important industrialists who can apply with relative ease all methods of prevention against workplace accidents. These employers will join a private insurance [*mutualité*] to avoid the annoying formality of compulsory insurance. On the other hand, we find the bad risks, the small and medium enterprises" (*Journal Officiel* 1893: 1581). The latter were unlikely to join social insurance voluntarily.

According to the policy makers of the Chamber, the idea of voluntary insurance that was supported by the Senate conflicted with and undermined the commitment of the state to guarantee benefits to the victims of social policy. "Leaving employers the freedom not to insure would distort the principle of responsibility established in the law. After having recognized the right of an allowance for workers who are victims of workplace accidents, it is not enough to regulate private insurance societies, or to organize a state institution in competition with these societies. It is not enough to design ingenious measures facilitating insurance" (*Journal Officiel* 1890b). Policy makers in the Chamber envisioned only one potential remedy against the endemic limitations of private insurance. This solution was to introduce compulsory social insurance. Jules Roche, the minister of trade and industry, justified his recommendation for this radical policy move by noting that "compulsory insurance is both in the interests of workers and of employers."

A final important question of policy design considered by policy makers in the Chamber of Deputies concerned the relationship between preexisting private institutions of social insurance and insurance administered by the state. A separate draft bill submitted by Jules Roche to the Chamber in 1890 expressed the reluctance of the French bureaucracy to assume greater responsibilities over the administration of insurance. "If the state were to monopolize the provision of insurance, the government would face the difficult task of administering substantial amounts of capital. It might, thus, find itself exposed to considerable losses" (*Journal Officiel* 1890b). To avoid this financial overextension of the state, policy makers in the Chamber recommended the delegatation of greater responsibilities to private institutions of social insurance organized by employers. French policy makers in the Chamber considered the existing private institutions of social insurance as the "only rational solution." "The only rational system is the mutual insurance system organized by employers. This mutual insurance takes as the basis of the contribution of employers not the possibility of an accident, but the accident itself and the obligations incurred as a consequence of this accident. The charges are distributed among all employers of the industry in proportion to the total costs paid by each firm" (*Journal Officiel*

1890b: 1427). This particular institution of insurance thus allowed a very low interoccupational redistribution of the costs of each policy.

The new draft bill of the Chamber of Deputies allowed individual employers to choose among various forms of insurance. Employers were given the freedom to remain their own insurers or to join private-type institutions of social insurance. Alternatively, employers could join one of the risk pools administered by the state. The draft bill recommended the creation of the Conseil Supérieur des Accidents du Travail, established as part of the Ministry of Industry and Commerce. The role of this new institution was "surveillance, guaranty, and control, combined to render the principle of universal compensation more effective" (Cheysson 1895a).

The Senate was unwilling to accept the principle of compulsory insurance. In a second round of policy deliberations, the Senate reiterated its minimalist view of the scope of insurance, arguing that the obligation of insurance "will create excessive charges for employers, becoming the cause of financial ruin of small producers" (*Journal Officiel* 1895: 582). After an intense political struggle (in which the commission that endorsed the proposals of the Chamber was forced to resign), the Senate rejected the proposals for compulsory accident insurance (Pic 1898: 520). The policy solution adopted by the Senate in 1897 had a deep impact on the insurance bill that was finally adopted by the Chamber in May 1898 (Pic 1898).[32] The final legislation accepted the *théorie du risque professionnel* as the legal basis for the compensation of the victims of workplace accidents.[33] The scope of the law was extended to include agricultural employers who relied on mechanized forces, an outcome that had been favored by policy makers in the Chamber.[34] Employers were given significant latitude to choose among the type of institutions of social insurance: they could remain their own insurer or join mutual insurance companies or other sectoral or regional institutions of insurance. As an observer of the law pointed out, it was the belief of French lawmakers that these institutions could flourish "without any guidance" from the state and without "a unique direction" (Pic 1898: 526). Summarizing these policy deliberations, an important participant in

[32] As Pic points out, "On 26 March 1898, the Chamber adopted unanimously (with 520 votes) and without debates the project on accident insurance that emerged, on 19 March, from the deliberations of the Senate" (Pic 1898: 512).
[33] Compulsory accident insurance was introduced by French lawmakers only in 1905 (Join-Lambert 1997: 367, Saint-Jours 1982: 94).
[34] Technically, the law covered these employers only beginning with June 1899 (Hesse and Le Gal 1999: 199).

all stages of reform pointed out that the final policy outcome, which guarantees to employers an unrestricted freedom of choice over the institutions of social insurance, accommodated the policy concerns of "*boutiquiers* and small industrialists." In an effort to accommodate the policy needs of small producers, French lawmakers compromised on the principle of compulsory social insurance.

French political developments thus stand in sharp contrast to the evolution of policies in Germany. In Germany, large manufacturing employers exerted a critical influence in the negotiation of institutions of accident insurance. In contrast, the policy outcome enacted by French lawmakers came much closer to the ideal policy preference of small firms. Several factors account for the greater political influence exerted by small producers in France. As discussed earlier, during the last decades of the nineteenth century, the French economy was an economy dominated by small producers. Most significantly, French political institutions amplified the political influence exerted by small producers. The system of representation to the Senate transformed the French upper chamber into the arena voicing the demands of rural producers and small employers. As this section demonstrated, the Senate repeatedly blocked all policy proposals that called for the introduction of compulsory insurance or of any measure raising the nonwage labor costs of firms. This additional veto position of French small producers prevented the enactment of German-type social policies of social insurance.

Conclusion

In this early episode in the political history of the welfare state, the institutions of social insurance resulted from a political negotiation among employers and reformist elites. In both France and Germany, labor representatives did not participate in the legal struggles that led to the transition from private law to social insurance (Benöhr 1981, Hofmann 1982, Ewald 1996). Most explanations of these reforms (which, in fact, originated with Bismarck's contemporaries) have examined the social policy intentions of reformist elites (Schmoller 1899, Rothfels 1938, Vogel 1951, Born 1957, Ritter 1986). The evidence presented in this chapter suggests that a broader analysis that pays closer attention to the demands articulated by key sectors of the business community is necessary to account for the institutional design of social insurance that was chosen in each country.

The analysis of the policy preferences of German and French employers confirms a number of the propositions formulated in Chapter 2. Confronted with questions about the design of the new institutions of social insurance, employers' concerns centered around the distribution of responsibilities in the administration of social insurance and the "redistribution of risks" across different occupations. The findings confirm two of the hypotheses concerning the impact of firm size and incidence of risks in affecting the policy preferences of firms along these dimensions of the social policy space. In both France and Germany, large manufacturing producers favored a policy outcome giving employers a level of discretion in the administration of social insurance. For small firms, issues of control were relatively unimportant and were outweighed by considerations about the costs of the new social policy. Employers in industries exposed to a high incidence of workplace accidents – such as iron and steel producers and employers in mining – supported a broad and expansive definition of the risk pool of social insurance. In contrast, low-risk producers (such as agricultural employers) opposed these expansive views of the scope of social insurance, preferring social policies characterized by a low redistribution of risks.

Finally, the preceding analysis has suggested that employers have played a critical role during the political negotiation of the institutions of social insurance. The difference between the German and French institutions of social insurance can be attributed to differences in the political strength of different sectors of the business community. In Germany, large manufacturing producers played a decisive role in the initial stages of policy reform and exerted a significant constraint on the policy objectives pursued by Bismarck. The final social policy outcome delegated responsibilities for the administration of social insurance to employers' representatives alone. Thus, this policy outcome was very close to the ideal policy preference of these producers. By contrast, in France small producers exerted a decisive political influence and successfully blocked policy proposals calling for the introduction of compulsory social insurance. In France, the final policy outcome was much closer to the ideal point of small producers.

4

Is Unemployment Insurable?

EMPLOYERS AND THE
DEVELOPMENT OF
UNEMPLOYMENT INSURANCE

Unemployment was, undoubtedly, the most "problematic" social risk. National-level policies compensating against the risk of unemployment were introduced, in a majority of countries, several decades *after* the creation of other branches of social insurance (Alber 1982: 49). This lag in timing was in many cases the consequence of a profound uncertainty about the commensurability between unemployment and other labor market risks and about the possibility of applying traditional insurance techniques to situations of temporary loss of work (Leibfried 1977: 189–201). As pointed out by a recent wave of scholarship, the political struggles surrounding the institutional design of a system of unemployment insurance were embedded in and inextricably linked to a broader set of political deliberations about the *causes* of unemployment, feasible remedies for it, and, more broadly, the place of unemployment in modern industrial society (Salais et al. 1986, Piore 1987, Topalov 1994a, 1994b).

The notion of unemployment underpinning the classificatory and redistributive practices of institutions of social insurance remains a category of relatively recent origin. In contrast to beliefs and practices that viewed unemployment as an individual risk, resulting from the idleness, unwillingness to work, or moral shortcomings of the worker, the "modern" notion of unemployment sees unemployment as a natural and regrettable by-product of a particular organization of work in the modern enterprise (Piore 1987). Thus, broad changes in the organization of work, such as the emergence of the stable employment relationship, as well as other institutional changes, such as modifications in private and public institutions of poor relief and the dissolution of older forms of solidarity, contributed to this change in the societal understanding of the notion of unemployment.

These changes served as preconditions for the policy debates that are the subject of the present chapter.

Policies insuring against the risk of unemployment were the result of a protracted and highly disputed process of political negotiation. The frequent change of system in many countries and the intense experimentation, by most governments, with a variety of different policies reflect these political conflicts. Prior to World War I, only a few German cities had established a Ghent system of unemployment insurance. The onset of World War I brought about the introduction of the first national-level policy of unemployment assistance in 1914. In 1918 the first government of the Weimar period reorganized the policy of unemployment assistance. Finally, German policy makers introduced a contributory unemployment insurance in 1927. In contrast to Germany, France introduced a Ghent system in 1905. Plans to introduce contributory unemployment insurance as part of the general social insurance legislation of 1928 remained unsuccessful. France introduced compulsory unemployment insurance only in 1958.

As the analysis in Chapter 2 has pointed out, the choice of a system of unemployment insurance posed two overarching questions of policy design. The first politically contested issue concerned the political boundary of the risk pool (which occupations should participate in the policy of unemployment insurance?) and the degree of risk redistribution among different occupations that face different incidences of unemployment. The second issue, control, concerned the distribution of administrative responsibilities among unions, employers, and the state. The different systems of unemployment insurance that were introduced during this period institutionalized different political compromises on questions of risk redistribution and control. In a means-tested system of unemployment assistance, stringent eligibility tests restricted the number of beneficiaries of unemployment benefits. In this policy, the majority of administrative decisions over the duration and level of social policy benefits remained in the hands of bureaucrats and local government officials. This solution to the problem of control made the system vulnerable to multiple and contradictory complaints from unions and employers, who resented their absence of involvement in the administration of a policy with far-reaching consequences for the labor market. In a Ghent system of unemployment insurance, all administrative decisions remained in the hands of trade union organizations. This resolution of the problem of control was highly problematic for employers. In a Ghent system, the redistribution of risks among the different occupations remained very low: each individual trade union determined the level of unemployment insurance contributions and benefits for its members who were temporarily out of work and no attempts to achieve a broader pooling of risks were made. In a contributory unemployment insurance, administrative responsibilities were shared among unions and employers.

The case of unemployment insurance provides us an opportunity to test the propositions about the determinants of employers' preferences toward different social policy arrangements developed in Chapter 2 and to explore the different pathways of business influence during deliberations about different systems of unemployment insurance. Did employers reject all policies of unemployment compensation or did they express an interest in the development of these policies? Do we find intersectoral disagreement among employers over the introduction of this policy, and, if so, what factors explain this disagreement? What is the relative role of labor organizations and employers' associations in the development of these policies?

To answer these questions, the chapter is organized as follows. A first section discusses social policy developments in France and analyzes the political factors that have facilitated the introduction of a Ghent system in 1905. In a following section, I turn to the analysis of social policy deliberations surrounding the development of social insurance during the decade following World War I. I test the main propositions concerning the determinants of the social policy preferences of firms when faced with different social insurance projects and analyze the political influence of employers during this episode of social policy development. Next, I turn to the analysis of social policy deliberations in Germany and examine the role played by employers during the protracted policy negotiations that culminated in the introduction of contributory unemployment insurance in 1927.

An Early Success: The Introduction of a Ghent System in France in 1905

France, a country considered by social policy scholars as a welfare state laggard, played in fact a pioneering role in the introduction of social policies compensating for the effects of unemployment (Flora and Alber 1981: 37–80, Jallade 1988). By introducing a Ghent system in 1905, France became the first country to establish a *national*-level policy of unemployment assistance. Reformist policy entrepreneurs of the period brought these policy issues on the broader political agenda, in an effort to consolidate a vast array of preexisting institutions of unemployment assistance and to "regularize the existing forms of societal support." As is shown later in the chapter, the Ghent system was not the preferred social policy alternative of the French labor movement. French trade unions favored a contributory unemployment insurance. Employers also opposed the Ghent outcome and regarded unions' control over the distribution of unemployment benefits with considerable worry and mistrust. The institutionalization of this policy outcome in France can be attributed to the ability of skillful political entrepreneurs to forge a cross-class alliance among representatives of capital and labor around a policy outcome that was the *second-best* choice of both unions and employers.

Although the preoccupation of French policy makers with the question of unemployment goes back to the 1870s,[1] a more sustained political effort that culminated in the introduction of a national-level system of unemployment assistance developed only during the last two decades of the nineteenth century (*Journal Officiel* 1879: 220). In 1895 the French Labor Office (Office du Travail) initiated a number of studies about possible solutions to the problem of unemployment (Office du Travail 1896: 5–10).[2] The question facing the Permanent Commission of the Labor Office concerned the role of the national government in the provision of "insurance against involuntary unemployment" and the relationship between public support and individual insurance. In the words of the commission, the immediate question was whether "a third level of public intervention that regularized and generalized the isolated efforts of the unions and communes remained a necessary and worthy goal of the government" (Office du Travail 1896: 8–9). In an effort to develop policy recommendations on these issues, the Permanent Commission of the Labor Office devoted its attention to two interrelated questions: the understanding of the lessons of foreign policy experiences and the measurement of preexisting societal institutions of support in case of unemployment.

---

[1] See *Journal Officiel* 1879, 1884.

[2] The Office du Travail (which was part of the Ministry of Commerce and Industry) appointed a permanent commission to study policies attenuating the consequences of involuntary unemployment during periods of industrial crises. The results of the activities of this commission can be found in Office du Travail 1896. For an overview of the conclusions of this commission, see Projet des voeux ayant pour but d'attenuer les consequences du chômage involontaire pendant les periodes de crise industrielle présenté à la Commission Permanente par M. Auguste Keufer (Office du Travail 1896: 5–10).

To this end, the commission conducted a first survey among French trade unions. This study attempted to evaluate the nature and level of support offered by workers' associations (Office du Travail 1896: 45–77). In 1852 a ministerial decree placed an interdiction on the attempts of the *mutualités* to offer assistance in case of unemployment (Rougé 1912: 52).[3] Beginning in 1852, union-based policies of unemployment assistance remained the predominant form of societal support (Rougé 1912: 51). The results of this first major survey among trade unions proved, however, inconclusive. The commission examined the statutes of 2,178 unions comprising 408,500 members (Office du Travail 1896: 45–77). Out of these numerous associations (many of which had an ephemeral existence), 487 unions had formulated as one of their goals to offer some support to their members in case of unemployment, while 184 unions had established the level of assistance offered to the unemployed. This remained, however, only a proclamation of first principles which did not necessarily reflect unions' practices. Out of the 246 unions that responded to an additional survey of the Labor Office, 159 unions had abandoned this initial goal, while 87 continued to offer some form of unemployment assistance. There was only one national federation – the Federation of Workers in the Printing Industry (Fédération des Travailleurs du Livre) comprising 147 local unions (and 7,000 members) – that offered financial support to its members in case of unemployment (Fédération du Livre 1895, Varlez 1903, Rougé 1912).[4]

The inconclusiveness of these statistical findings brought these bureaucratic reformist efforts to a temporary stop in 1895 (Conseil Supérieur du Travail 1897: 30). The members of the Permanent Commission of the Labor Office found themselves in a profound dilemma, unable to formulate a clear policy recommendation, and suggested only a "further study and investigation" of the causes of unemployment and the possibilities of insurance against its consequences (Conseil Supérieur du Travail 1897: 31). A few years later, the question of unemployment insurance resurfaced, this time in the parliamentary arena. This initiative can be attributed to the political activism of Alexandre Millerand. Millerand, an important radical politician and a (later) republican socialist, brought high political visibility to the question of unemployment insurance and helped forge a public consensus around the necessity of public intervention (Topalov 1985). As

---

[3] Instruction aux préfets of 29 May 1852 (Rougé 1912: 51).
[4] The unemployment fund of the Fédération du Livre was established in 1892 (Fédération du Livre 1895).

minister of commerce in the cabinet of Waldeck-Rousseau, Millerand introduced a first draft bill of unemployment legislation and brought the issue of the organization of a system of unemployment compensation back on the political agenda of the Labor Office.

This second wave of policy reform began during the summer of 1903. An earlier bill of 1899 had reorganized the Conseil du Travail within the Ministry of Commerce, transforming it into a "genuine economic parliament," a "protocorporatist" institution representing the interests of unions, employers, and chambers of commerce, as well as representatives of political parties and social reformers (Topalov 1985).[5] During a number of deliberations that took place in 1903, the Conseil Supérieur du Travail turned to the question of the organization of unemployment insurance. A policy consensus around a Ghent solution to the problem of unemployment emerged gradually during these meetings (Ministère du Commerce 1903, Fagnot 1905). Paradoxically, the actors favoring most strongly the introduction of a Ghent system of unemployment insurance were reformist political entrepreneurs and not trade unions. As the records of these deliberations indicate, reluctant trade union representatives, prodded by reformist policy makers, accepted a Ghent system of unemployment insurance.

Trade union representatives came to the deliberations of the Conseil du Travail demanding the introduction of a compulsory unemployment insurance. According to one of their spokesmen, Victor Dalle – a member of the National Federation of Employees (Conseil de la Fédération Nationale des Employés) – unemployment insurance had to be extended to "all human beings, with no exception" (Fagnot 1905: 122). The new insurance was to be financed by contributions from employees and employers and through a subsidy from the state (Ministère du Commerce 1903: 22). According to unions' plans, the contributions of employers had to be raised in the form of a tax on patents (Ministère du Commerce 1903: 42). Any intermediary solution that fell short of being a compulsory insurance and that did not require any financial sacrifice from employers was viewed by unions

---

[5] During the meetings of 1903, which endorsed the Ghent solution, the Conseil Supérieur du Travail had the following composition: eight members of parliament, nineteen representatives of the chambers of commerce, nineteen representatives of trade unions, eight representatives of employers, eight representatives of the Conseils des Prudhommes, one representative of the Chamber of Commerce of Paris, one delegate of the associations of production, and two professors of law.

as a "partial and fragmentary remedy," as "a palliative"[6] (Fagnot 1905: 122, 124).

During the early stages of the deliberations, trade union representatives saw no direct advantage in a system that institutionalized public subsidies to preexisting union unemployment funds. Such a solution was viewed by trade unions as a double-edged sword, weakening the control of trade unions in the administration of unemployment insurance and bringing, thus, a severe blow to union autonomy (Ministère du Commerce 1903: 30, Fagnot 1905: 124–126, Confédération Générale du Travail 1904: 235).[7] Unions attempted to minimize the intervention of the state in the administration of unemployment insurance, even if the price for unrestricted union autonomy was the rejection of the financial subsidies (Topalov 1985: chap. 2).[8]

This rejection of the Ghent solution by the trade unions may appear surprising. A strong assumption in existing welfare state scholarship (which appeared to be self-evident and, thus, has not been tested empirically) has been that the Ghent system of unemployment insurance was unambiguously the preferred outcome of unions, due to the organizational and institutional advantages and the "selective incentives" for union membership created by this system (Rothstein 1992). How can we explain this policy preference of French trade unions? The records and publications of the French labor movement of the period contain several indications about the causes of trade unions' rejection of a Ghent system (Archives Nationales F7 13594). First, unions resented the administrative oversight over their practices of assistance. To receive the subsidies from the state, unions were required to

---

[6] Along the same lines, see the position taken in the debate by Guèrard, the secretary of the National Union of Railway Workers (Fagnot 1905: 124).

[7] As the representative of trade unions in these deliberations argued, "a system of state subsidies implies a rigorous control of the state of all the unemployment insurance funds" (Ministère du Commerce 1903: 30). On unions' fear of state supervision, see Fagnot 1905: 124–126. During the Fourteenth National Congress of the Confédération Générale du Travail that took place in September 1904, union leaders (such as Delassale) protested against the subvention by the government of union unemployment insurance funds. See Confédération Générale du Travail 1904: 235.

[8] As Christian Topalov notes, "this demand is very characteristic of the French trade union movement before 1914 and actually very similar to British and American unions. In this field, as in other social policies, unions do not demand from the outset public intervention. If unions see an advantage to gain, they formulate counterproposals based on the principle of administration of the system of unemployment assistance by trade unions and the refusal of any solution that weakens their autonomy. At the center of the unions' project is the creation of a *pansyndicalisme*, against employers, but also against the state" (Topalov 1985: chap. 2).

pay benefits only in cases of involuntary unemployment and to withhold them in the case of sickness, invalidity, strikes, or lockouts (Rougé 1912: chap. 9). In exchange for subsidies, the state required trade unions to maintain a certain "separation" between the different risks, a separation unions were unwilling to make (Varlez 1903: 132, Topalov 1985). Second, a Ghent system put unions in the delicate and often unpopular position of withdrawing unemployment benefits (even from union members) in cases of extended unemployment spells. The third reason for the rejection of a Ghent system by French trade unions is linked to the view of the French labor movement that the fundamental goal of union organization is the preparation for class struggle and that any form of collaboration with state officials should be avoided. According to an early debate within the Twelfth National Congress of the Confédération Générale du Travail held in 1902, any acceptance of subsidies from the state marked a detour from the fundamental goal of the labor movement, which engaged trade unions in a "governmentalism" that had to be avoided (Confédération Générale du Travail 1902: 235–238).

Employers came to the deliberations praising the advantages of a private system of unemployment insurance, free of public intervention. On numerous occasions employers invoked the virtues of the British experience, where support in case of unemployment remained in the hands of voluntary associations. "British unemployment funds, which are extremely successful, receive no subvention from the state. This example has to be followed: similar to our neighbor we should leave the organization of unemployment insurance in the hands of private initiatives" (Ministère du Commerce 1903: 6).[9] According to the president of the Chamber of Commerce of Lyon, "the only remedies against unemployment are individual savings, channeled either into saving funds or special unemployment insurance funds" (Fagnot 1905: 111).

Both these alternatives – unions' proposal for a contributory unemployment insurance and employers' demand for purely private provision in case of unemployment – were rejected early on during the deliberations. As union representatives pointed out, the meager wages in most industries left no room for private savings (Fagnot 1905: 112–113).[10] Both reformist

---

[9] Intervention of industrialist Heurteau during the meeting of 4 May 1903 (Ministère du Commerce 1903: 6).

[10] See statement of Coupat, secretary of the Federation of Mechanical Workers (Fédération des Mécaniciens) (Fagnot 1905: 112–113).

policy entrepreneurs and union leaders demanded a certain level of public intervention *beyond* the purely private level of provision (Ministère du Commerce 1903: 25). The primary justification for public support was the fact that involuntary unemployment resulted often from the introduction of new technologies, developments that "benefited society in its entirety" (Fagnot 1905: 114).[11] Even employer representatives conceded that unemployment had among its causes the fact that industrial production remained badly regulated (Fagnot 1905: 112). Once employers accepted the principle of public intervention, their primary concern became the limitation of the scope of the participation of the state (Fagnot 1905: 110–111).[12]

A contributory unemployment insurance that was advocated by trade union representatives met with the strong opposition of employers. The objections of employers centered on the potential costs of this policy (Ministère du Commerce 1903: 26, Fagnot 1905: 123). The new social charges remained both extremely unpredictable and potentially much higher than the contributions to the accident insurance that had been introduced in 1898 (Fagnot 1905: 123, Ministère du Commerce 1903: 26).[13] For employers, a source of these high costs was the pervasive impossibility of distinguishing between real and simulated unemployment and of establishing "the true degree of unemployment" (!) (Fagnot 1905: 123).[14] Having compromised on the principle of public intervention, employers demanded a compromise of the same magnitude from unions. A representative of the cotton industry expressed this point with great clarity: "If you would like to reach an agreement – and on my part I am ready to make a step in this direction, do not ask from us a vote on first principles. If you demand a manifestation of our principles, we will be intransigent and we will be able to accept neither the obligation of insurance nor the direct participation of the state" (Fagnot 1905: 123–124).

Reformist bureaucrats at the Office du Travail also expressed reservations about a contributory unemployment insurance. Invoking the example

---

[11] Position defended by a director in the Ministry of Labor, Arthur Fontaine (Fagnot 1905: 114–116).

[12] Fagnot, a participant in these deliberations points out that employers accepted the principle of public intervention very early during the deliberations (Fagnot 1905: 110–111).

[13] A reference to the comments made by Darcy, president of the Comité Central des Houilières de France (Fagnot 1905: 123).

[14] As a representative of employers formulated this point during the deliberations, "it is not sufficient to recognize the true unemployed, but also identify the true degree of unemployment" (Fagnot 1905: 123).

of the Swiss city of St. Gall – where efforts to organize a contributory unemployment insurance had failed – they considered that this project posed overwhelming administrative questions (Ministère du Commerce 1903: 26–28). As reformers pointed out, solutions to many important problems were still unknown: the monitoring of the unemployed to limit potential fraud, the determination of insurance contribution for professions affected differently by the risk of unemployment, the distribution of the financial obligation among large industrial centers and communes (Ministère du Commerce 1903: 27).

Faced with the double opposition of employers and of reformist policy entrepreneurs, union representatives abandoned their proposal for a contributory unemployment insurance (Fagnot 1905: 127). This strategic move of unions opened the way for negotiations about an institutional alternative to a compulsory insurance and purely private provision (Fagnot 1905: 127).[15] The third type of solution considered during these deliberations was the "generalization of the system introduced in the Belgian city of Ghent." In the Commission of the Labor Office, the actors championing this policy solution were reformist political entrepreneurs (Ministère du Commerce 1903: 23).[16]

According to social reformers, a Ghent system of unemployment insurance, in which the state subsidized preexisting, "societal" unemployment insurance funds, had a number of institutional advantages. The first was that its immediate introduction became possible: "being based on what already existed," and furthering the development of voluntary institutions of social insurance, no additional large-scale bureaucratic apparatus was necessary (Ministère du Commerce 1903: 29). Another advantage of this policy was the institutional solution for monitoring the willingness to work of the unemployed. Because a Ghent system delegated these functions to unions (or other mutual aid societies), the most difficult problem posed by a system of unemployment assistance could be solved "in the most efficient way" and with minimal administrative involvement of the state (Fagnot 1905: 130).

---

[15] As François Fagnot notes, "Once employers accepted the intervention of public authorities and workers abandoned their demands for a contributory unemployment insurance, the discussion was liberated from the two issues of 'fundamental principle' and the practical questions could be approached with more chances to find a common ground" (Fagnot 1905: 127–128).

[16] During the deliberations, the Ghent solution was proposed for the first time by Dubief, a representative of the Chamber of Deputies within the Council (Ministère du Commerce 1903: 23).

The disadvantage of a Ghent system was that it favored only a minority of workers – providing no compensation to workers in low-skilled[17] or nonunionized professions.[18]

The decision to introduce public subsidies (paid by the municipalities) to local associations to distribute unemployment benefits was reached rapidly. But negotiations stumbled on the question of the *kinds* of associations that were eligible to receive subsidies from the state. To limit the influence of trade unions, employers demanded the subsidization of *all* associations offering some form of unemployment assistance (Fagnot 1905: 131). Employers prevailed on this point. The list of associations eligible for subsidies from the state was extended to include philanthropic organizations, the *mutualités*, and even unemployment funds organized by a local chamber of commerce. The most controversial issue during the deliberations was the question whether associations offering unemployment benefits that were not organized at the local but at the *national* level could also become eligible for public support. After all, this remained the point where France could depart from the Belgian model and redesign the Ghent system, transforming it into a national-level policy.

Employers objected to the extension of these subsidies to federations of trade unions that offered benefits to their members (such as the Fédération des Travailleurs du Livre), fearing the increase in union organization and membership that could result from this measure (Fagnot 1905: 140). Subsidizing national organizations of trade unions, rather than local associations, necessitated also a larger financial involvement of the state. During several rounds of negotiation employers resisted this extension of the responsibility of the state (Ministère du Commerce 1903: 44–45). According to employers, policies compensating against the effects of unemployment had to remain "a communal system applied to local associations" (Fagnot 1905: 140). Unions, on the other hand, shared a different view. Advocates of unemployment subsidies for the union federations (coming primarily from the ranks of unions and from the Bourses du Travail) argued that the goal of any system of unemployment insurance remained the job placement of the unemployed. From this perspective, a federation of trade unions had greater resources to support the movement of workers from

[17] Preexisting unemployment funds were predominant among high-skill professions (Topalov 1985: chap. 2).
[18] A point made by union representatives during the deliberations (Ministère du Commerce 1903: 44).

regions with high to regions with low unemployment and a better understanding of the labor market circumstances (Fagnot 1905: 135–139, Ministère du Commerce 1903). Reformist bureaucrats sided with trade unions, supporting the subsidization of trade union federations as well as local associations. The abstention of employers during the final vote led to a narrow victory of unions and social reformers on this point.

The policy recommendations of the Conseil,[19] favoring the introduction of state subsidies to associations distributing unemployment assistance, moved then with great speed through the parliamentary arena, facilitated, in part, by the fact that Alexandre Millerand, the initiator of the policy effort,[20] was now a president of the Commission of Social Insurance (Commission d'Assurance et de Prévoyance Sociale) of the Chamber of Deputies (Conseil Supérieur du Travail 1897: 985). Millerand himself presented the case for these policies in front of the Chamber (*Journal Officiel* 1904b).[21] Encountering no opposition from the deputies of the right, the law was introduced as a supplementary measure to the budget of 1905 and remained the basic element of the French system of unemployment insurance until the Second World War (*Journal Officiel* 1905a: 5510–5512).

The determination of reformist policy entrepreneurs such as Alexandre Millerand, and their ability to place this issue on the agenda of reform remain crucial factors accounting for the formation of this *strategic* cross-class alliance among unions and employers. A second important factor accounting for this political breakthrough and the early introduction of reform was the broader political ascendancy of left-wing forces, grouped within the Bloc des Gauches. This increase in the political strength of the left raised the probability of parliamentary political action in support of a policy of unemployment compensation, lowering the opposition of employers' representatives within the Conseil Supérieur du Travail to a social policy outcome that was not necessarily their first policy choice. Finally, a more distant background factor that affected the formation of this cross-class alliance was the character of French industrial production, which was dominated by small producers. A Ghent system of unemployment assistance posed a lower political threat to small producers than to large manufacturing firms.

---

[19] See Ministère du Commerce 1903: 985.

[20] During the spring of 1904, after these deliberations in the Conseil Supérieur du Travail, Millerand himself initiated a draft bill in the Chamber. See *Journal Officiel* 1904a: 625.

[21] See the speech of Alexandre Millerand during the parliamentary debates on 30 November 1904. In his speech, Millerand considers these measures only "a necessary preface to the organization of an insurance solution" (*Journal Officiel* 1904b).

A counterfactual implication of this observation is that a strategic cross-class alliance around a Ghent system is less likely in an economy dominated by large manufacturing enterprises.

The French policy of unemployment assistance was centered around two *different* kinds of institutions. At the local level, the system delegated responsibility over distribution of unemployment benefits to a vast variety of associations, such as local unions, philanthropic organizations of poor relief, or *mutualités*,[22] that became eligible for subsidies from the municipalities (*Journal Officiel* 1905b: 5511).[23] At the national level, unemployment funds established and administered by a federation of trade unions were eligible for subsidies from the state, if these associations had more than 100 members.[24] As the Report of the Minister of Commerce that prefaced this law pointed out, French reformers considered that "the latter presented the maximum chances of success and the guaranty of control" because "they were in a better position to control the unemployed and secure their job placement" (*Journal Officiel* 1905b: 5510).[25] Correspondingly, the subsidies of the state to the national-level unions were higher than the subsidies to the local associations (*Journal Officiel* 1905b: 5510).[26] The periodic inquiries and surveys on the development of societal forms of unemployment assistance carried out by the French Ministry of Labor (Ministère du Travail et de la Prévoyance Sociale) reveal, however, that a larger number of local-level union organizations took advantage of the Ghent system as compared with national federations of trade unions. The number of local-level trade unions receiving subsidies increased from 36 in 1908 to 54 in 1910 and 62 in 1913. Following World War I, the number of unemployment insurance funds organized by the municipalities decreased to 50 in 1925, increasing again to 69 in 1930 and reaching the level of 135 in

---

[22] *Journal Officiel* 1905b: 5511. To be eligible for these subsidies, these associations had to total at least fifty members.

[23] There was one exception to this general rule. Local unions with more than one hundred members were eligible for a subsidy from the state, if they received no support from the municipalities.

[24] *Journal Officiel* 1905b: 5510, article 2.1.

[25] French authorities also believed that the success of the national unions was premised on the fact that unions "could establish, in an equitable manner, the level of insurance contributions of each of the members and the level of benefits to which they are entitled" (*Journal Officiel* 1905b: 5510). However, the opposite argument could also be made: local unions had a better chance of survival, precisely because they distributed the risk across *several* occupations.

[26] The additional condition was that the union had a presence in at least three *départements* and that it had more than one thousand members (*Journal Officiel* 1905b: 5510).

1934.[27] In contrast to these local-level associations, the number of national-level trade union associations eligible for unemployment benefits experienced almost no increase until the mid 1930s, a period of intense growth of trade union activism (Noiriel 1990: chaps. 4 and 5). Two of the most significant trade unions that administered a union unemployment fund were both in the printing industry – the Federation of Workers in the Printing Industry (Fédération des Travailleurs du Livre) and the French Federation of Printers (Fédération Litographique Française). Another significant national trade union federation receiving subsidies from the state was the Federation of Mechanical Workers (Fédération des Ouvriers Mecaniciens) (Rougé 1912: 157, Mossé 1929). The number of national trade union organizations administering unemployment benefits was 3 in 1908 and 1910, 5 in 1913, 1 in 1921, 4 in 1925, 8 in 1930, and 17 in 1934 and 1937.[28] Thus, despite stronger financial incentives for centralized unions to offer unemployment benefits to their members, the French law of 1905 did not contribute to the organizational centralization of the French labor movement and the formation of centralized union unemployment funds.

Following World War I, French reformers began to pursue the introduction of compulsory social insurance with great intensity. The reannexation by France of Alsace and Lorraine, two provinces that had experienced German institutions of social insurance, was an important factor motivating French politicians to search for this upward harmonization in social insurance benefits (Hatzfeld 1971: 143–144, Immergut 1992: 90). Another important consideration was the perception of failure of previous policy initiatives, most notably the failure of the legislation providing old-age pensions. Alexandre Millerand, the political architect of the unemployment law of 1905, played again a crucial role in the initiation of social insurance legislation in the period following World War I. As president of the Council of Ministers, Millerand "signaled that social insurance was to be a priority of his administration, by appointing an Alsatian, Jourdain, as minister of labor and authorizing Jourdain to prepare a legislative proposal" (Immergut 1992: 90).

Two issues were at the center of the first reform initiatives: the provision of benefits in case of old-age and sickness and the introduction of family benefits. In 1921 a first draft bill of reform was submitted to the

[27] These data have been compiled from *Journal Officiel* 1907: 26–27, 1913: 7585–7588, 1923: 9675: 9680, and Topalov 1985.
[28] For a source of these data, see note 27.

Chamber of Deputies (*Journal Officiel* 1921). This bill, known also as the Vincent Report, recommended the introduction of old-age and sickness insurance financed by equal contributions from employers and employees. This initial project made, however, no recommendation for the development of a compulsory unemployment insurance.

The Commission of Social Insurance (Commission d'Assurance et de Prévoyance Sociale) of the Chamber of Deputies took up the study of the recommendation of the Vincent Report in the following year (*Journal Officiel* 1923b). The conclusions of the deliberations of the commission were published in January 1923 (in a document known as the the Grinda Report). The commission also recommended to omit the risk of unemployment from the general social insurance legislation. The justification for this decision presented in the Grinda Report stressed the absence of a broader understanding of the causes of unemployment. "There is a branch of social insurance," stressed the report of the Commission of Social Insurance of the Chamber, "which we have deliberately eliminated from the reform: the branch that has as its goal the provision of guarantees against the effects of unemployment. This is a risk whose causes and effects are still poorly understood, which has been the object of numerous investigations that have not yet formulated clear evaluations. No probability table allows us to establish a serious basis for the prediction of the incidence of this risk. . . . It appears very imprudent to legislate on this matter before these studies are completed and before the partial experiences attempted in France and abroad identify a method for the practical organization of this policy. It would have been very difficult to attempt to include a compulsory unemployment insurance full of uncertainties in a reform package, which, more than ever, needs to present the highest possible guarantees of security" (*Journal Officiel* 1923b: 58).

The report of the social policy commission of the Senate – known also as the Chaveau Report was published in 1926; it recommended the introduction of compulsory unemployment insurance (*Journal Officiel* 1926: 33–64). This report strongly argued for the inclusion of compulsory unemployment insurance alongside the legislation covering all other social risks. If the aim of the new legislation was the provision of compensation to the worker during times of loss of work, it was vital to develop a compulsory unemployment insurance, since "together with sickness and disability, unemployment was the most dramatic circumstance in the life of the worker" (*Journal Officiel* 1926: 38). The report of the commission proposed the creation of compulsory unemployment insurance covering all workers of French nationality (*Journal Officiel* 1926: 59, article 21). The insurance was to be financed by contributions from employers and employees, supplemented by subsidies from the local and national government (*Journal Officiel* 1926: 59, articles 24 and 25). The Senate recommended that the administrative responsibilities for the new insurance be placed in the hands of labor exchanges and mutual aid societies (*Journal Officiel* 1926: 50, articles 21(2) and 23).

French Employers and the Assurances Sociales

Before discussing the broader political negotiations surrounding the Social Insurance project, I will analyze the positions of French employers in response to these reform initiatives. What were the policy solutions preferred by French employers? Was there significant policy disagreement among French producers and, if so, what are the causes accounting for the differences in their policy preferences? The analysis of the social policy demands of French firms relies on a collection of reports of different business associations found at the Chamber of Commerce in Paris, the Archive of Assembly of Presidents of French Chambers of Commerce, and the archives of the General Federation of French Production (Confédération Générale de la Production Française).

In the French policy debate, the proposals for contributory unemployment insurance were bundled with proposals for compulsory insurance covering other social risks, such as sickness and old age. As pointed out, specific plans for the provision of unemployment insurance were added to this broader legislative project only very late, as part of the draft bill formulated by the social policy commission of the Senate in 1926. Some of the chambers of commerce in my sample do not explicitly discuss the details of the unemployment insurance legislation when discussing the broader project of the *Assurances Sociales*. In addition, it is very likely this late inclusion of unemployment insurance as part of the policy proposals for social insurance impacted the strategic calculations of French producers. Because the commitment of policy makers to this particular branch of social insurance was very low, it was easier for employers to reject the introduction of compulsory unemployment insurance than to oppose compulsory old-age or sickness insurance.

Both large and small firms expressed a vocal opposition to the various projects aiming at the introduction of social insurance legislation, the Vincent project of 1921, the Grinda project of 1923, or the Chaveau

121

Report of 1926. The majority of French business associations regarded these projects as "hasty," "premature," and "incomplete answers" to questions of insurmountable technical difficulty. As the Union of Metallurgical and Mining Industries (Union des Iudustries Métallurgiques et Minières, or UIMM) described the vast legislative ambitions of the project, "this is an impressive juridical monument, which is based on mandatory contributions from employers and the principle of national solidarity and whose goal is to cover against all existential risks more than 25 million French citizens, two-thirds of the population. It seems that after *Salente* by the Abby of Fénélon and the *Utopia* of Thomas More no other project has attempted such a remarkable endeavor for the welfare of entire mankind" (UIMM 1922: 3).

However, large and small firms opposed the social insurance project for different reasons (cf. Hatzfeld 1971). In the case of large firms, the most significant cause of opposition to the project of the Chamber of Deputies was the worry that the socialization of all risks – and the creation of compulsory old-age, sickness, and unemployment insurance – might displace the preexisting "private" social policies established by employers. Institutions such as private pension, sickness funds, and private family benefits that had been established as a result of the policy initiative of employers played an important role in providing social policy benefits to a narrow segment of the French work force. In opposing compulsory insurance, large producers defended existing institutions of private provision and the autonomy of employers to administer social insurance. The amendments and changes to the law proposed by these employers stressed the importance of the "separation of risks" and the creation of occupational risk pools within social insurance and of the limitation of the administrative involvement of the state. Large firms signaled to policy makers that they remained in principle open to the progressive institutionalization of social insurance, if these policies *complemented* existing private institutions of social provision. In contrast to large producers, small firms expressed a more acute concern and worry about the costs of social insurance, rejecting social insurance legislation.

The association that provided the most articulate expression of the concerns of large manufacturing employers was the Union of Metallurgical and Mining Industries (UIMM 1922). This organization (which had been founded in 1901) grouped over 6,000 firms (employing more than 700,000 workers) in "all industries concerning the production and transformation of metals, such as iron mines, hydraulic presses, metallurgy, mechanical construction, and shipbuilding" (UIMM 1922: 1–2, Lefranc 1976: 39). In 1921 representatives of the UIMM were invited by members of the Social Policy Commission of the Chamber of Deputies to present their social policy concerns (UIMM 1922: 2). The report issued by the Union of Metallurgical and Mining Industries during the following year expressed the dissatisfaction of large producers with the draft bill. As this report pointed out, the "fundamental error of the project consists in neglecting and not relying on the existing institutions of social insurance, which would increase the effectiveness of the law in difficult situations" (UIMM 1922: 4). According to employers, the first obligation of the lawmaker was to "interrogate the experience and to investigate if the risks have not been already covered by existing institutions, then to explore the degree of vitality of preexisting institutions, whether they have exhausted their resources and if they could further develop adequately, faced with new demands" (UIMM 1922: 3).

In their defense of private, firm-centered institutions of social insurance, large firms invoked the "visible advantages" of preexisting institutions providing old-age, sickness, and family benefits. The UIMM argued that private institutions of social insurance provided important benefits not only to workers but to *employers* as well, by "creating the attachment of a more stable and satisfied work force, content with its destiny" (UIMM 1922: 5). The surveys conducted by the UIMM suggest a widespread presence of these institutions among large firms. Out of 36 firms (with a total workforce of 80,000 workers), 29 firms had established insurance funds subsidized by employers providing sickness benefits to their workers (UIMM 1922: 5). With respect to firm-level policies providing old-age insurance benefits, the study found that an old-age insurance fund established by the Iron Works Committee (Comité de Forges) in 1894 covered 282 enterprises with over 235,000 insured workers (UIMM 1922: 6). Finally, in the case of institutions providing family benefits, the survey of the UIMM reported the existence of 74 institutions of social assistance (*caisses de compensation*), serving more than 4,000 firms and providing benefits to over 1 million workers (UIMM 1922: 7, Pedersen 1993: 224–285).

By demanding the creation of institutions of social insurance in which either firms or industry-level associations of employers played a large role in administering social insurance, large firms rejected the two major policy principles of the new legislation: the "principle of national solidarity" and the "principle of generalization of insurance." The report of the UIMM argued that "if administered by the state, social insurance would lose an important part of its own character and would acquire certain features characteristic to social assistance" (UIMM 1922: 11). Large French firms objected to the project of the Chamber, calling it "an attempt to bring under the control of the state [*étatiser*] existing private institutions" and to create a "hotbed of public sector employees" (*pépinière des fonctionnaires*). The alternative policy project formulated by employers recommended placing the firm at the foundation of institutions of social insurance: "The firm shapes the existence of the worker in crucial ways, by determining the level of wages and the kinds of risks to which the worker is exposed, and by establishing the strongest bonds of solidarity among workers. It seems natural that the firm should provide the basis for the organization of social insurance. Better than any other social institution, the enterprise can be reconciled with the institutions of the *mutualité* providing family benefits. Enterprises also facilitate the creation of large autonomous and homogenous insurance funds for the provision of old-age benefits" (UIMM 1922: 13).

In contrast to large firms, small firms showed a lower degree of interest in employers' control in the administration of the institutions of social insurance. Commenting on the Social Insurance project of the Chamber of Deputies, which recommended the division of administrative responsibilities among the state and employers, the Chamber of Commerce of Havre exclaimed that this project transformed "industrialists and shopkeepers into collectors of taxes and contributions" (Chambre de Commerce du Havre 1922). The overwhelming majority of chambers of commerce in my sample rejected the social insurance project, invoking concerns about an increase of the social charges. Commenting on the Chaveau report, published by the Senate in 1926, the Chamber of Commerce of Belfort noted that "the charge on enterprises that will result from the introduction of a contribution totaling 10 percent of the wages will have inevitable repercussion on the price level in the entire economy. It seems certain that given the takeoff in economic activity of foreign industries – whose impact is already visible in the notable slowdown of transactions on our national market – a perturbation of the entire production of such a magnitude will place our industry and trade in a visibly unfavorable and dangerous situation. The immediate introduction of a system of insurance covering all social risks will provoke a profound crisis that will compromise the very interests that the new legislation attempts to protect. The workers will be the first to experience the effects of this crisis" (Chambre de Commerce de Belfort 1925). Chambers of commerce from Rennes, Troyes, Belfort, Marseille, and Lyon also objected to the new charges for employers resulting from this legislation and recommended the withdrawal of the project from legislative deliberations (Chambre de Commerce de Rennes 1922, Chambre de Commerce de Troyes 1921, Chambre de Commerce de Belfort 1925, Chambre Syndicale de Marseille 1921, Union des Chambres Syndicales Lyonnaises 1921).

Large and small producers concurred in recommending the abandonment of plans aiming at the introduction of contributory unemployment insurance. "The uncertainty is formidable," wrote the Chamber of Commerce of Paris. "This addition of the risk of unemployment is extremely dangerous, because it goes against the very technique of insurance. It is impossible to apply the law of big numbers. Neither the frequency of the risk, nor the magnitude of the social charges, nor the number of unemployed can be determined. The involuntary unemployment depends on economic causes that are rapid and impossible to determine with precision" (Chambre de Commerce de Paris 1926). Similar arguments were voiced during the General Assembly of Presidents of Paris, in its meeting of March 1927. This meeting was attended by representatives of 102 Chambers of Commerce. While endorsing a "prudent and gradual introduction of the *Assurances Sociales*, . . . appropriate to the risk that is covered," these chambers of commerce unanimously rejected the introduction of compulsory unemployment insurance (Assemblée des Présidents des Chambres de Commerce en France 1927).

The preceding analysis supports one of the propositions of the model developed in Chapter 2. Firm size remains an important predictor of the sensitivity to control (λ_C) of the social policy preferences of firms. The UIMM, an association representing large manufacturing employers, recommended the creation of private-type institutions of social insurance to supplement firm-level policies established by employers. Employers' *control* over the provision of social policy benefits was a crucial policy concern for large firms. These issues are insignificant for small producers. The only policy considerations expressed by small producers were worries about the potential increases in their nonwage labor costs. Thus, as predicted by the model, the sensitivity to control (λ_C) takes positive values for large firms and negative values for small firms.

What are the policy preferences of French employers along the second dimension of the social policy space, a dimension representing the degree of socialization of risks? Do we find disagreement among employers? If so, what variables predict this disagreement? Chapter 2 has hypothesized that the incidence of a risk is a predictor of the sensitivity to risk redistribution (λ_R) of a firm. This hypothesis thus suggests that employers in industries facing a high incidence of the risk of unemployment will favor highly redistributive social policies, whereas "low-risk industries" will reject the socialization of social insurance, preferring narrow occupational risk pools.

According to the study conducted by Robert Salais and his collaborators, we find a strong divergence in the labor market adjustment of French producers during the interwar period (Salais et al. 1986: chap. 3). The major implication of this study is that unemployment is a phenomenon encountered primarily among large manufacturing producers in mechanical and metallurgical industries in the departments of north (Ardennes, Oise, Euse) and northeastern France (Vosges). As Salais argues, "the fluctuations in the volume of work are more often externalized as unemployment by large enterprises. Here we encounter a strong breaking-off [*rupture*] of the relationship between employer and worker" (Salais, Bavarez, and Reynaud 1986: 97). In contrast, "small independent producers of the countryside or of small provincial towns" have responded to changes in the demand for their products not by laying off workers but by adjusting working time. Unemployment was much lower in rural departments, dominated by small family-owned farms, such as Dordogne, Vendée, Creuse, or Ardèche (Salais et al. 1986). Salais's analysis has two implications for the predictions of the social policy preferences of firms. The first is that the strongest predictors of the sensitivity to risk redistribution (λ_R) of a firm are the sector (industry or agriculture) and firm size. We expect large manufacturing producers to support a compulsory unemployment insurance. In contrast, we expect small agricultural enterprises to oppose the introduction of this policy.

The two main associations grouping agricultural producers, the Society of French Farmers (Société des Agriculteurs de France) and the National Confederation of Agricultural Associations (Confédération Nationale des Associations Agricoles) strongly opposed the plans of French lawmakers to extend social insurance to agricultural producers (Augé-Laribé 1950: 109–117). Invoking the existence of strong differences in the character of the employment relationship among agriculture and industry – such as the higher presence of remuneration in kind in agriculture, the reliance of agricultural employers on members of their extended family, and the "strong individualism [*farouche individualisme*] of the peasant, which is the result of the profound isolation of work on the field" – these associations waged a fierce political campaign against the extension of social insurance to agriculture. They preferred a policy outcome relying on voluntary institutions of private insurance, such as mutual aid societies (*societés de secours mutuels*) and agricultural mutual insurance companies (*mutuelles agricoles*) in providing social policy benefits to both workers and small producers in the countryside.

Contrary to the predictions of our model, associations representing large manufacturing producers also rejected the proposals of French lawmakers to socialize insurance. The Union of Metallurgical and Mining Industries opposed the policy proposals to establish a national-level insurance fund, "the Caisse Nationale de Garantie, an organization redistributing the good and bad risks" (UIMM 1922: 13). Employers also opposed policy efforts to unify contributions to social insurance and recommended regional and occupational differentiation in the insurance contributions. "Finally, we have to recognize that various risks affect different professions, environments, and regions in very different ways, and it would be certainly abusive to want to impose a unitary regulation for all provinces of France. Neither the needs, nor the economic conditions, nor the possibilities of realization are identical or even comparable. It appears that a more certain and promising avenue of reform would give social insurance its corporatist form" (UIMM 1922: 12).

Large manufacturing producers admitted that the level of insurance contributions mandated by the legislator were often smaller than the social charges voluntarily accepted by large firms. Why did they oppose the introduction of a compulsory insurance and legislative efforts to socialize risks? The archival records of the deliberations of these producers suggest that an additional factor affected the cost-benefit calculations of these firms (Ministère du Travail 1922). The main reason accounting for a rejection of compulsory insurance was the worry that the French state had a very low ability to collect insurance contributions. These producers estimated that the likelihood of tax evasion of small firms and agricultural producers was very high. This rendered compulsory social insurance unattractive for large manufacturing employers as well. In the words of these employers:

There are no doubts that we would encounter the most severe difficulties in the application of compulsory insurance in the rural world, where the spirit of individualism is so developed and modes in which labor is remunerated are so diverse. The same person is often owner, employer, or employee, depending on the moment of the year or even on the moment of the day. . . . The same difficulties would occur if the law were applied to small and medium industrial and commercial enterprises, in all seasonal trades and generally to all persons who do not have one single occupation or one that is sufficiently stable. As has been already the case with the application of certain fiscal laws and the application of the pension law of 1910, the resistance in

127

certain regions or in certain media will be very strong. The consequence will be that the law will not be applied everywhere to all those that should be subjected to the law, leading to a great material and moral disorder. (Ministère du Travail 1922: 4)

The worries of large manufacturing employers about the low levels of enforcement of a contributory compulsory social insurance in an economy dominated by small and agricultural producers were not entirely unjustified. In his analysis of the application of the social insurance legislation of 1928 to the agricultural world, François Goguel pointed out that "the number of beneficiaries of the law effectively enrolled in the agricultural social insurance was substantively inferior to what the number should have been if the legal dispositions would have been respected. A large number of presidents of agricultural associations convinced employers that the constant diminution of the rural work force justified the nonapplication of social laws in agriculture, while, in fact the improvement of the living conditions of agricultural employees would have been the only means to retain them in the countryside" (Goguel 1946: 274). Thus, the assessment of large manufacturing employers about the social policies that served their interests best was largely correct. These were private, occupationally based social policies.

Figure 4.1 summarizes the main findings on the policy preferences of employers. The analysis supports one of the propositions of the model developed in Chapter 2. We find a disagreement among large and small firms over the importance of private-type social policies and over the advantages provided by these policies to firms. While large and small firms disagreed over the advantages of private-type policies of social insurance, they were united against the proposals of French legislators to introduce compulsory social insurance.

Negotiation and Defeat

These policy considerations were at the basis of the political strategies of French producers during the decade in which the social insurance project was under consideration by French policy makers. As Edmond Villey, a deputy and an important participant in the parliamentary deliberations of the period, pointed out, "all the partisans of the law recognized that an immense majority among employers have been hostile to the project" (Villey 1924: 558). A number of historians of the Assurances Sociales, such as Henri Hatzfeld, François Goguel, Ellen Immergut, or Dominique Simon,

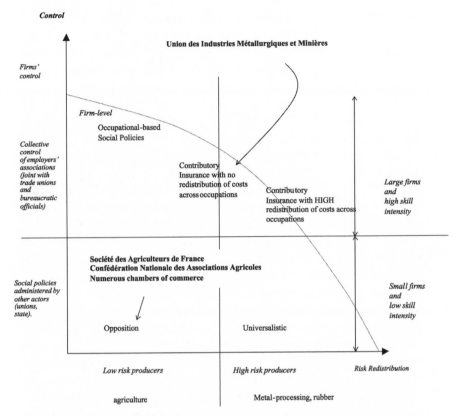

Control

Union des Industries Métallurgiques et Minières

Firms'
control

Firm-level
Occupational-based
Social Policies

Collective
control
of employers'
associations
(joint with
trade unions
and
bureaucratic
officials)

Contributory
Insurance with no
redistribution of costs
across occupations

Contributory
Insurance with HIGH
redistribution of costs across
occupations

Large firms
and
high skill
intensity

Société des Agriculteurs de France
Confédération Nationale des Associations Agricoles
Numerous chambers of commerce

Social policies
administered by
other actors
(unions,
state).

Small firms
and
low skill
intensity

Opposition

Universalistic

Low risk producers

High risk producers

Risk Redistribution

agriculture

Metal-processing, rubber

Figure 4.1   French employers and the introduction of the *Assurances Sociales*

have noted the numerous press campaigns, hostile to the project, that had been financed by some employers (Hatzfeld 1971: 104, Simon 1986: 137, Immergut 1992: 95, Goguel 1958: 267–275). The opposition of a number of associations grouping French producers continued even *after* the approval of the social insurance legislation by both chambers in 1928. The Assembly of Presidents of French Chambers of Commerce continued to express worries about the fragile financial equilibrium of the law, resting only on "conjectures, hypotheses, probabilities, and approximations" (Hatzfeld 1971: 145). Another publication of French employers, *L'animateur des temps nouveaux*, referred to the social insurance legislation as the crazy law, *la loi folle* (*Journal Officiel* 1930: 543, Hatzfeld 1971: 104).

This political episode in the history of the French welfare state allows us to analyze significant questions about the political influence of employers

129

during the institutionalization of social insurance legislation. By what strategies did French producers attempt to influence policy makers? What was the role of French labor organizations during these deliberations? How successful were employers in achieving if not their preferred outcome – the defeat of the law – at least significant concessions regarding the institutional design of the new social policy? Finally, how significant was the retreat of policy makers from their ideal policy outcome, when faced with this formidable opposition of employers?

The most significant arenas where the major decisions regarding the design of the new social insurance legislation have been made were the social policy commissions of the Chamber of Deputies (the Commission d'Assurance and the Prévoyance Sociale) and of the Senate (the Commission de l'hygiène, de l'assistance et de Prévoyance Sociale). As pointed out by Hatzfeld, the "elaboration of the law was the affair of the commissions and of the interest groups involved: agriculture, the *mutualité*, the Confédération Générale du Travail (CGT), the medical profession and employers" (Hatzfeld 1971: 145). The primary cause of this overwhelming political importance of the commissions was the technical complexity of the social insurance law, which necessitated extensive specialization among legislators. The political debates on the floor of the Chamber of Deputies and the Senate were brief and concerned with more abstract philosophical principles – such as the role of individual freedom and responsibility – and made no effective policy changes to the bill. Thus, to understand the political influence of French employers, we need to characterize the magnitude of the policy changes made by these parliamentary commissions in response to the demands raised by business associations. My analysis attempts to reconstruct the response of these policy makers to the considerations expressed by employers, based on the most significant publications of the commissions of social affairs of the French parliament.

The first social insurance draft bill submitted by the government to the commission recommended a radical break with the status quo in the provision of social policy benefits, characterized by incomplete coverage and a profound institutional heterogeneity among providers (*Journal Officiel* 1921). The policy conception underlying this project stressed the importance of the administrative and financial *unification* of institutions of social insurance covering sickness, old-age, and family benefits. It was the belief of policy makers that it would be easier to establish a financial equilibrium of social insurance "if a more general distribution of risks was attempted" and if the resources financing old-age insurance were combined with the resources financing sickness and disability benefits (*Journal Officiel* 1921: 1297, 1302). Reflecting the belief of policy makers that a "flexible, discreet, but firm control of the state" in the administration of social insurance was necessary, the Vincent project recommended the centralization in the collection of insurance revenues at the level of individual regions. In addition, the project recommended the creation of a national guarantee fund (*Caisse Nationale de Garantie*), whose role was to establish a financial balance among the different insurance funds (by subsidizing funds that experienced a temporary deficit) (*Journal Officiel* 1923b: 1305).

The second important policy characteristic of the Vincent project remained the sudden and drastic expansion of the level of insurance coverage. The authors of this bold move regarded the narrow scope of the pension law of 1910 as the primary cause for the failure of this legislation. In a social policy that was not compulsory for the entire population and whose application had been only weakly enforced by the government, the "law of big numbers" could apply only with great difficulty. While it became rational for good risks to opt out of social insurance, only the "bad risks had an interest in joining the risk pool" (*Journal Officiel* 1921: 1301). To avoid the financial problems of a policy prone to endemic problems of self-selection, the draft bill recommended the application of social insurance to all French workers who entered an employment contract and whose yearly income did not exceed 10,000 francs (*Journal Officiel* 1921: 1298). According to the calculations of policy makers, this provision extended the risk pool of social insurance to 8.1 million French employees – covering around 40 percent of the French labor force (and around 22 percent of the entire population) (*Journal Officiel* 1921: 1302).[29] The self-employed and other "small employers of the city and of the countryside, free to choose their occupation and masters of their own work" and who "worked either alone, employing only one single worker or employing the members of their family," were also given the right to join the insurance, if they accepted the full charges (*Journal Officiel* 1921: 1302, 1307). This creation of voluntary insurance added potentially 1.4 million members to the risk pool. Lawmakers were aware that the average age of the participants in this voluntary insurance was higher than the economy-wide average (making it likely that these participants would draw on social policy benefits only after a very brief history of contributions), but they remained relatively confident that a potential

---

[29] Calculations are based on data in Flora and Alber 1983.

deficit of old-age insurance could be compensated from the surplus of the other subsystems of social insurance (*Journal Officiel* 1921: 1304).

The initial Vincent Project was thus highly ambitious. As Ellen Immergut pointed out, this draft bill recommended the creation of a system of social insurance that was "more administratively centralized than comparable legislation in Germany, England, or Scandinavia" (Immergut 1992: 91). As compared to future iterations of this project, the Vincent report was closest to the social policy demands of those segments of the French labor movement that were willing to cooperate in the introduction of social insurance. The Confédération Générale du Travail played a critical role during the policy deliberations and "remained one of the rare and undoubtedly most active groups militating in favor of the Assurances Sociales" (Hatzfeld 1971: 251). Beginning with the Trade Unions Congress of 1921, the CGT demanded the "introduction of a general system of social insurance covering all the risks faced by the employees – accidents, sickness, unemployment, invalidity, and old age" – and a participation of trade unions in the administration of this policy (Confédération Générale du Travail 1921: 19). A 1923 report of the administrative commission of the CGT reiterated the same demands (Confédération Générale du Travail 1923). Noting that the social insurance bill that was under discussion in the Chamber of Deputies left out any compensation during unemployment, the CGT demanded the immediate introduction of unemployment insurance. "We believe that social insurance which does not insure against the risk of unemployment is incomplete. It leaves in suspension, above the head of the worker, a risk that . . . is an evil that hits the worker blindly and sometimes in a rapid and unexpected manner" (Confédération Générale du Travail 1923: 134).

Employers in large firms as well as small producers expressed profound reservations toward this project. A number of the policy recommendations made by business associations during encounters with members of the Commission of Social Insurance of the Chamber had an impact on ulterior projects of institutional design. The most important policy change that was made in response to the worries expressed by large producers was the administrative decentralization of social insurance (*Journal Officiel* 1923b: 41).[30] From the perspective of employers, it was critical to rely on the broad variety of *preexisting* institutions of social insurance and to "realize

[30] The Grinda report itself acknowledged the influence of associations representing employers on these policy decisions (*Journal Officiel* 1923b: 41).

a genuine decentralization of social insurance that is not guaranteed in the existing project" (UIMM 1922: 14–15). In contrast, the UIMM considered that the solution recommended by the Vincent project was "the costliest of all, the system in which the control is the least efficacious and one that leads to the largest number of public employees" (UIMM 1922: 15).

The Grinda report, completed by the Commission of Assistance and Social Insurance of the Chamber during the fall of 1923 formulated the response of policy makers to these demands raised by associations in various economic milieus (*Journal Officiel* 1923b: 37).[31] This report departed from the original Vincent project in two important respects. First, it attempted to reduce the presence of the state in the administration of social insurance and to delegate significantly more responsibilities to the associations representing the employers and employees. Members of the commission seemed to accept the criticism of the Vincent project that had been voiced by employers in its entirety and almost unreflectedly. As the preface to the new bill stated, "This insurance remains impregnated by *étatisme* and by a mechanical automatism. Due to the transformation of institutions of social insurance into organizations of the state, due to the application of administrative and bureaucratic methods and the elimination of emulation among these funds, this policy seems to be permeated by an 'embryo of death' [*germe de mort*]. The new text, which we submit, confides the entire administration of social insurance to the insured, with no intervention from the state" (*Journal Officiel* 1923b: 40). In this new draft bill, the existing private-type institutions of social insurance – the mutual insurance funds and the policies of social insurance established by employers (*caisses professionnelles patronales*) – became the institutional and organizational backbone of social insurance. The state stepped to the background, assuming the more modest role of "coordinator" of these institutions. In response to demands coming from organizations of unions and employers, the draft bill assigned labor representatives one-half of the seats in the administration of social insurance and the remaining half to representatives of employers (*Journal Officiel* 1923b: 40).

The second important issue on which French policy makers retreated from their initial policy aspirations concerned the level of interoccupational redistribution of risks in the new institutions of social insurance. The Grinda report recommended the introduction of a compulsory social

---

[31] As the report pointed out, the commission carried out an investigation (*enquête*) among "all the interested groups" (*Journal Officiel* 1923b: 37).

insurance for all employees (whose income was lower than 10,000 francs), but it proposed the institutional and financial separation of the agricultural insurance (*Journal Officiel* 1923b: 53–54). Lawmakers were ready to admit that this significant policy change was a concession to the "big agricultural associations," such as the Society of French Farmers (Société des Agriculteurs de France) or the National Confederation of Agricultural Associations (Confédération Nationale des Associations Agricoles) (*Journal Officiel* 1923b: 53; cf. Augé Laribé 1950). As noted earlier, agricultural producers strongly opposed the introduction of compulsory insurance. The compromise solution proposed by policy makers was the creation of a *régime special* for agriculture, allowing social insurance contributions to be "in a direct relationship to the risks that are specific to this occupation" (*Journal Officiel* 1923b: 54). The report also recommended a stronger reliance on preexisting institutions of social assistance – such as the mutual aid societies (*societés de secours mutuels*), agricultural mutual insurance companies (*mutuelles agricoles*), the insurance funds of agricultural syndicates, and societies of reinsurance for the provision of social benefits in the countryside. As the authors of the new draft bill argued, "in the countryside, people have a more intimate knowledge of each other than in the city, employers and workers have a much closer access to the institutions of social insurance, and we can anticipate that, given their direct interest in these institutions, they will remain capable to recover the contributions of employers and workers to social insurance without relying on strong formalities and without a very elaborated organizational apparatus" (*Journal Officiel* 1923b: 54). It is important to point out that policy makers severely underestimated the degree of opposition among French farmers to the extension of social insurance. The refusal of many French farmers to enroll in social insurance indicates that even the compromise solution recommending the creation of a special agricultural occupational insurance was ultimately unsatisfactory to agricultural employers.

By acknowledging the importance of private forms of social provision and by delegating stronger responsibilities to these institutions in the administration of social insurance, the Grinda report reflected a significant shift toward the policy outcome preferred by large manufacturing employers, such as the UIMM. Although employers welcomed these policy changes, their opposition to the "introduction of new social charges" surged during this period. This shift in attitude reflects the response of French producers to a new political environment. The elections of May 1924 brought to power a broad coalition of left-wing political forces (grouped within the

Cartel des Gauches) (Goguel 1958: 225–235). The governments of this period – led by Edouard Herriot, Paul Painlevé, or Aristide Briand – remained committed to a policy of fiscal expansion. As pointed out by Henri Hatzfeld, this policy met with a profound opposition of the French business community (Hatzfeld 1971: 144–145). A publication of the Union of Economic Interests (Union des Interêts Economiques) and of the Confederation of Commerical Groups (Confédération des Groupes Commerciaux), two umbrella associations of French producers, expressed this strong hostility of employers toward the policies of fiscal expansion. "The commercialists and industrialists of France are crushed by taxes, exasperated by injustice, and threatened by the introduction of new social charges. They declare that the most certain consequence of the exaggerated fiscal measures is the paralysis of the economic activity of the country and the increase in unemployment and in the general price level of the economy. Employers declare that they will accept new sacrifices only if these sacrifices are indispensable for the financial equilibrium of the budget" (Union des Intérêts Economiques and Confédération des Groupes Commerciaux 1926: 156).

In this political environment characterized by a strong confrontation among the government and employers over the issue of the "appropriate" financial involvement of the state, the Commission of Hygiene of the Senate took up the study of the Social Insurance project. In contrast to policy makers in the Chamber of Deputies, the Commission of the Senate emphasized the importance of fiscal moderation of the state (*Journal Officiel* 1926: 33). Summarizing the conclusions of nearly two years of additional deliberations, the Chaveau Report pointed out that the primary objective of the commission was "to make the system of social insurance more flexible and more practical. To hasten the implementation of the law, one concern has dominated the deliberations, the concern not to appeal to the financial aid of the state" (*Journal Officiel* 1926: 33). To this end, the members of the commission attempted to evaluate the incidence of the risks affecting various groups of the French work force and to develop new forecasts of the magnitude of future financial expenditures of social insurance that were more conservative than the estimates developed by the Chamber of Deputies. The Senate envisaged a policy of social insurance in which the subsystems covering the various risks were in financial equilibrium and which minimized the degree of redistribution among the compulsory and voluntary social insurance. (As discussed earlier, French policy makers expected a high level of "high-risk" workers and independents in the voluntary social insurance and the need for a subsidization of these institutions by the compulsory social insurance.) These financial considerations affected the design of institutions of social insurance. First, the commission attempted to limit the financial transfers of the state to social insurance. Second, this project assigned an even stronger role to the *mutualité* in the administration of the new policy. For the authors of this project, these institutions approximated the policy ideal characterized by a strict actuarial soundness and financial equilibrium that had to be emulated by the new institutions of social insurance on a broader scale.

An important change formulated by the commission of the Senate was the recommendation to add a policy covering the risk of unemployment alongside the insurance subsystems covering the other social risks. The justification for this expansion of the scope of social insurance presented in the Chaveau Report stressed the necessity of an insurance that covered the worker against the risk of unemployment, since, "as in the case of risks such as sickness, maternity, old age, or invalidity, the consequence of unemployment is the interruption of work that is necessary for the existence of the individual and the family" (*Journal Officiel* 1926: 38). Members of the commission believed that it would be rather unproblematic to add the risk of unemployment to the social insurance legislation, given the particularism of labor market developments in France: "An economy with a feeble birthrate, aggravated by the ravages of the war period, France is characterized by an enormous labor shortage. France has become an immigration economy in a truly exceptional manner. It is the only country in Europe that finds itself in this situation" (*Journal Officiel* 1926: 41). Thus, policy makers of the Chamber and the Senate believed that the introduction of compulsory unemployment insurance would not entail an increase in the financial commitment of the state.

This optimism was not shared by broader economic and political circles in France. The proposal for compulsory unemployment insurance met with the strong opposition of the French business community. French employers argued forcefully that the resources needed to finance the other branches of the *Assurances Sociales* – old-age and sickness insurance as well as family benefits – placed "an unbearable burden on French industry" (Union des Corporations Françaises 1926). Significant social policy experts sided with employers, and called for caution before undertaking such a risky enterprise. For example, a report of the Statistical Society of Paris of October 1926 expressed "formal reservations against the extremely dangerous consequences resulting from the introduction of unemployment

insurance" (Bernard 1926). The combination of this profound policy uncertainty about the "insurability" of the risk of unemployment coupled
with the strong opposition of the French business community accounts for
the retreat of French policy makers from this policy goal. In a second draft
bill, the Chaveau commission abandoned the plans to introduce compulsory
unemployment insurance.

The project of the Senate served as the basis for the final version of the
social insurance legislation that was voted into law in March 1928 (*Journal
Officiel* 1928: 4086–4098). Considerations about upcoming elections added
additional urgency to the project and prevented another round of deliberations in the Chamber. The final application of the law was further de-
layed until an additional *réglement d'administration publique* was issued in
April 1930.[32] As several historians of this episode insightfully remarked,
"nearly nine years of parliamentary deliberations converted the initial plan
for simple, rational administration and universal coverage into one of the
most fragmented social insurance schemes in Europe" (Immergut 1992:
97). "French social security is an 'unfinished cathedral' . . . whose edifice itself is of magnificent proportions and provides a wide variety of protection
for nearly the entire population. But within the church there are numerous
altars, each collecting funds for different purposes and dispensing earthly
benefits in different ways. Within the Cathedral grounds, an almost endless
sprawl of cloistered groups obtain special comforts and privileges" (Ashford
1982: 228).

The final insurance bill that was adopted by the French parliament in
1928 reflects an important strategic accommodation to the concerns of
the French business community. We can clearly identify the concessions to
the social policy demands expressed by the business community by comparing the initial Vincent project of 1921 to the final version of this legislation.
First, French policy makers compromised on their goal to centralize the
administration of insurance in the hands of the state. Instead, the French
institutions of social insurance delegated significant policy responsibilities
to preexisting private institutions of social insurance created and administered by employers. Second, French policy makers abandoned their goal
to create a genuine social insurance – that is, a policy in which the level of

---

[32] As pointed out by Hatzfeld, in a highly visible effort to "compensate" employers in large
firms for the increase in social charges resulting from the introduction of the social insurance
legislation, simultaneously with this *réglement d'administration publique*, French lawmakers
introduced another measure reducing the real-estate taxes owed by employers. Hatzfeld
1971: 151–152.

insurance contributions were separated from the incidence of the risk faced by individual occupations. The institutional fragmentation of social insurance into a myriad of "occupational risk pools" represents a clear concession to the social policy demands expressed by the French business community during that period. The convergence of interests among large and small firms around private-type institutions of social insurance decisively influenced the type of institutions of social insurance adopted by French policy makers.

A First Political Experiment: A Means-Tested Unemployment Assistance

Although Bismarckian Germany played a pioneering role in the development of compulsory insurance, covering the risks of sickness, old age, and accidents, it lagged behind most European nations in the development of a national-level policy compensating against the effects of unemployment (Alber 1981, Ritter 1986: 94, Steinmetz 1993: 163). In an effort to cope with the massive labor market disturbances of World War I, German policy makers introduced a means-tested policy of unemployment assistance only in 1914. It took more than ten additional years of policy deliberations until Germany established a policy of compulsory unemployment insurance in 1927.

Due to the absence of significant policy initiatives on the part of the federal government to introduce a policy of unemployment compensation, policy responsibilities were shifted to lower levels of governments, the *Länder* and communes (Faust 1986, Born 1957: 224, Führer 1990: 109–114). As discussed by Georg Steinmetz in his recent research on local-level social policy provision in imperial Germany, cities became genuine laboratories of policy experimentation (Steinmetz 1991: 18–46, 1993, Faust 1986, Henning 1974: 271–287). In 1896 Cologne introduced a voluntary policy of unemployment insurance, subsidized by the municipality, based on a model that had been pioneered in the Swiss city St. Gall (Faust 1986: 139–142, Henning 1974: 280). Sixteen other German localities introduced a Ghent policy of unemployment assistance prior to 1914. Among these, Strassbourg, Stuttgart, Mannheim, Offenbach, and Berlin Schöneberg were the largest cities that subsidized unemployment funds organized by trade unions (Nagel 1921, Henning 1974). The diversity of the economic structure of a city remained the most important economic precondition for the introduction of a local-level policy of unemployment assistance: these policies

138

flourished in localities that were dependent on several different industries allowing for some interoccupational redistribution of this risk (Faust 1986: 146). This explains why no locality in the industrial heartland of Germany, Nordrhein-Westfalen, or in other regions that remained dependent on a single industry (such as the Saar region, Saxony of Silesia) introduced a policy of unemployment assistance prior to 1914. Confirming Gary Herrigel's thesis of the dual character of Germany's industrial structure, we encounter a strong north-south divide in the provision of unemployment policies at the municipal level: fourteen out of the sixteen cities that introduced a Ghent policy of unemployment assistance prior to World War I were south of the river Main (Faust 1986: 146; cf. Herrigel 1995).

The Socialist trade union movement favored the introduction of a Ghent system of unemployment assistance. A policy resolution of the Second Trade Union Congress of 1896 expressed the unions' belief that this "policy would provide an important impulse for trade union organization," disputing the worries of more radical members that a policy of unemployment assistance might "obliterate the militancy and readiness to fight [*Kampfcharacter*] of the labor movement" (Allgemeiner Deutscher Gewerkschaftsbund 1896: 117, 121, Faust 1986: 153–161, Wermel and Urban 1949). During the period prior to World War I, we find a steady increase in the number of trade union associations that offered some form of assistance to their members (IG Metall 1980: 63, Faust 1981, tables 1–4, Schönhoven 1980: 147–193). In 1869 only the union representing workers in the metalworking industry had established an unemployment insurance fund (*Versicherungsgesellschaft gegen Arbeitslosigkeit*). In 1894, 25 percent of trade unions that belonged to the Federation of German Trade Unions (Allgemeiner Deutscher Gewerkschaftsbund) offered unemployment benefits to their members. The number increased to 37 percent in 1899, 65 percent in 1906, and 86 percent in 1912. On the eve of World War I, out of a total of forty-eight unions that were part of the Federation of German Unions, forty-four offered unemployment benefits to their members (Faust 1981).[33]

---

[33] The statistical data reported in Faust show also important differences among trade unions in the magnitude of resources committed to unemployment benefits. Unions' expenditures for unemployment insurance as a percentage of total union expenditures were highest for unions in skilled professions, such as glaziers (54%) and sculptors (50.8%). In the metalworking industry, union expenditures for unemployment insurance constituted 31.8% out of total union expenditures (data are for 1908) (Faust 1981).

While the German trade union movement called for the introduction of a policy of unemployment insurance that built on existing institutions of support, German employers militantly opposed any policy of unemployment compensation. Both representatives of large and small producers denounced any legislative proposals attempting to provide unemployment compensation as the "recognition by the state of a cancer, the sign mark of a crippled condition and of inferiority,"[34] or as "the subsidization of laziness" (*Der Arbeitgeber* 1914; see also *Der Arbeitgeber* 1910b, 1913b, 1913c). The Central Federation of German Industrialists referred to the efforts to establish a policy of unemployment insurance as a "monstrous project" (*ungeheuerliches Projekt*)[35] and argued that the German economy "had reached the utmost limit in affording policies of social insurance" (Faust 1986: 171).[36] From the perspective of employers, the Ghent system of unemployment insurance appeared as especially problematic and was denounced on numerous occasions as "an official reward for entering the social democratic trade unions" (Faust 1986: 174, *Der Arbeitgeber* 1910a, 1913a, 1913b).

The changes introduced by policy makers at the onset of World War I broke this policy stalemate among unions and employers. In response to growth in unemployment that resulted from temporary shortages in raw materials facing Germany's key industries and faced with the threat of the Social Democratic Party to veto additional credits for the war effort, the government introduced a policy of wartime unemployment assistance (*Kriegserwerbslosenfürsorge*) (Lewek 1992: 34). In 1914 the government added a supplement to the budget, totaling 200 million Reichsmark, designed for the provision of benefits in case of unemployment (Wermel and Urban 1949, Lewek 1992). Although a significant part of the costs of the new policy were financed by the Reich, the administration of unemployment assistance was placed in the hands of the communes. To fulfill this role, communes either organized assistance committees (*Fürsorgeausschüsse*) or chose to delegate these administrative responsibilities to local unions, institutions of poor relief, and even to local associations of employers (Wermel and Urban 1949: 13–15, Lewek 1992, Simons 1919). In Saxony and Silesia, for example, employers in the textile industry established a policy of

---

[34] Führer 1990: 212, based on a document of the Chamber of Commerce Hannover.

[35] The formulation belongs to Bueck, the president of the Central Federation of German Industrialists (Faust 1986: 170).

[36] Reference to a publication of German employers, *Industrielle Zeitfragen*.

unemployment assistance (Wermel and Urban 1949: 14). In other regions of Germany, such as Baden, chambers of commerce and trade unions cooperated in the distribution of unemployment benefits (Wermel and Urban 1949: 14). One of the consequences of this heterogeneity among the institutions providing unemployment assistance was the widespread regional disparity in the level and duration of unemployment benefits. The wartime policy of unemployment assistance resembled more a patchwork of isolated and unrelated initiatives than a coherent and unitary policy.

The *Kriegserwerbslosenfürsorge* was intended as a temporary policy solution. Nevertheless, at the end of World War I this policy was not dismantled but reorganized. During the fall of 1918, amid efforts of demobilization, a coalition government that included representatives of the Social Democratic Party and of the Zentrum introduced a policy of unemployment assistance (*Erwerbslosenfürsorge*) (*Reichsgesetzblatt* 1918: 1305–1308). In contrast to the wartime unemployment assistance – in which communes were allowed to decide whether to introduce a policy of unemployment compensation – the provision of unemployment benefits became a compulsory obligation for all communes (*Reichsgesetzblatt* 1918, section 2). To carry out this goal, communes received subsidies from the Reich and from the *Land* totaling five-sixths of the costs of the policy (*Reichsgesetzblatt* 1918, section 4). Unemployment benefits were means-tested but, surprisingly, not temporarily limited. Communes were given wide discretionary authority to determine the level of benefits and to monitor the true "need" of the unemployed and the "willingness" of the unemployed to accept a job (*Reichsgesetzblatt* 1918, sections 8 and 9).

The war brought about a profound change in the preferences of German trade unions. In 1918 unions abandoned demands for a policy of unemployment assistance that placed the entire responsibility for the distribution of unemployment benefits in the hands of labor organizations. Proposals for the introduction of a compulsory unemployment insurance occupied a prominent place in the ten-point Economic and Social Policy Program published by the Federation of German Trade Unions in 1918 (Allgemeiner Deutscher Gewerkschaftsbund 1918: 6, Potthoff 1979: 194, Bieber 1981: 260–415). Unions called for the introduction of a compulsory unemployment insurance, covering all blue- and white-collar employees with a yearly income lower than five thousand Reichsmark. They demanded that the insurance be financed by contributions of workers and employers and supplemented by a strong financial participation of the state.

An additional important policy priority of trade unions was the demand for parity representation among unions and employers in the institutions administering unemployment insurance and of a neutral supervision of the state in these institutions (Allgemeiner Deutscher Gewerkschaftsbund 1920a: 159–161, Lewek 1992: 160). This change in the strategies of German trade unions reflected the realization of the labor movement that the pre-existing union-based networks of support were too fragile to cope with the massive unemployment that accompanied the postwar demobilization. As a publication of the Federation of German Trade Unions (Allgemeiner Deutscher Gewerkschaftsbund) reflected on this change in strategy, "the wartime and transition economy have brought about a far-reaching trans-formation of the economic structure and unemployment of such a mag-nitude, making it impossible for trade unions to take upon themselves the resulting burden" (Allgemeiner Deutscher Gewerkschaftsbund 1920b: 251).

The profound changes in the political context in the period after 1918 – such as the participation of the Social Democratic Party in the postwar governments – brought about a change in the political strategies of the major associations of German producers. Employers' political payoffs as-sociated with the strategy of opposition to all policies of unemployment assistance were lower in the political environment of the Weimar Republic (as opposed to the imperial period). By continuing to oppose all forms of unemployment compensation, employers were running the risk of becom-ing irrelevant bystanders in a political drama whose characters and center of gravity had changed (Vereinigung der Deutschen Arbeitgeberverbände 1919). A publication of German producers suggested that the speed with which policy makers attempted to solve the questions posed by the introduc-tion of a policy of unemployment assistance was "bluffing"(*Der Arbeitgeber* 1920). Expressing a similar disorientation and strategic retreat, the peak federation representing German producers signaled its readiness to par-ticipate, alongside labor organizations, in the deliberations for a policy of unemployment compensation (Feldman and Steinisch 1973: 68).

For German producers, the institutional design of the means-tested policy of unemployment assistance (*Erwerbslosenfürsorge*) was profoundly flawed. Of particular concern for these producers was their lack of in-volvement in the administration of a policy that had significant labor mar-ket consequences, or the absence of employers' "control." Decisions con-cerning the monitoring of the willingness to work of the unemployed or control over need remained in the hands of the communes. A prominent publication of German employers argued that the inability of the communes to test the willingness to work of the unemployed "encourages laziness and leads to the formation of an army of parasites" (*Deutsche Arbeitgeberzeitung* 1920). In addition, employers regarded the widespread disparity in the level of unemployment benefits provided by different communes as the primary cause of the coexistence of high unemployment and labor market short-ages. Numerous publications of large firms decried a situation in which "significant professions of vital significance for the health of the economy, such as mining or agriculture, cry for labor forces, while hundreds of thou-sands are lazy" (*Der Arbeitgeber* 1920). All efforts made by the Imperial Employment Office to curtail the discretionary authority of the communes in the distribution of unemployment benefits and to lower the hetero-geneity in the level of social policy benefits remained insufficient from the perspective of employers (*Der Arbeitgeber* 1927).

These statements allow us to establish a partial preference ordering of German large producers over alternative policies of unemployment com-pensation. Clearly, a Ghent system of unemployment assistance remained the policy outcome ranked lowest by employers. This social policy alter-native was extremely undesirable to employers given the increase in the political strength of the labor movement during the Weimar period. It is very likely that employers ranked a means-tested policy of unemploy-ment assistance higher than a Ghent system. However, as discussed earlier, this policy remained equally undesirable given problems of institutional design of the means-tested solution. A contributory unemployment insur-ance presented the strongest institutional advantages to large producers: as compared with all the other social policy alternatives, employers retained significant control over the distribution of unemployment benefits and the determination of insurance contributions. The strategy of opposition to all policies of unemployment compensation was, in the political environment of the Weimar period, a dominated strategy for German employers. These various considerations explain, why, due to a *combination* of prestrategic and strategic considerations, large German producers began to support a con-tributory unemployment insurance during the first years of the Weimar period.

As early as January 1920, one of the central publications of German employers, the *Deutsche Arbeitgeberzeitung*, voiced the support of large pro-ducers for a contributory solution. "Instead of the policy of unemployment assistance, which is an undifferentiated distribution of money to the de-serving and undeserving, we demand the introduction of unemployment insurance. Such an insurance is possible, and it has been already introduced in several countries" (*Deutsche Arbeitgeberzeitung* 1920). One of the leading associations representing the economic interests of large German firms, the Association of German Industry (Reichsverband der Deutschen Industrie), supported a contributory unemployment insurance beginning with 1920. A statement of the association that dated from this year made the following policy recommendation: "The root of the problems of the means-tested policy of unemployment assistance lies the absence of discrimination in the distribution of unemployment benefits and the inability to distinguish the deserving recipients of benefits. The means-tested unemployment assistance has to be replaced immediately by an unemployment insurance" (Reichsverband der Deutschen Industrie 1920). Did these statements express the views of the entire German business community or was there significant disagreement among employers on questions pertaining to the design of institutions compensating employees in case of unemployment? How does the theoretical framework developed in Chapter 2 explain the policy preferences articulated by different firms?

The Social Policy Preferences of German Employers

To test the theoretical propositions about the determinants of business preferences, I have relied on three distinct types of sources. The most significant records that allow us to explore the considerations about the relative advantages and disadvantages of different policies of unemployment compensation formulated by employers were the internal policy deliberations of the social policy committees of different associations of employers. Fortunately, the records of the most significant associations representing both large firms (Vereinigung der Deutschen Arbeitgeberverbände, or VDA) and small producers (Deutscher Handwerkstag) were available in various business archives in Germany.[37] Second, to examine the policy preferences of individual chambers of commerce, I have examined the collection of yearly reports of German chambers of commerce found at the archives of the German Economic Ministry (Reichswirtschaftsamt) and the German

---

[37] To document the internal social policy deliberations of these organizations, I have used the following sources: *Geschäftsbericht der Vereinigung der Deutschen Arbeitgeberverbände* (Berlin, 1920–1927); *Mitteilungen der Vereinigung der Deutschen Arbeitgeberverbände* (Berlin, 1927–1930); *Mitteilungen des Reichsverbandes des Deutschen Handwerks 1920–1927*; *Verhandlungen des Deutschen Industrie- und Handelstages, Sitzung des Sozialpolitischen Ausschusses* (Berlin: Liebheit und Thiessen, 1922–1927).

Imperial Employment Office (Reichsarbeitsamt).[38] Finally, the analysis relies on the policy recommendations expressed by the main publications of German employers: *Der Arbeitgeber* and *Die Deutsche Arbeitgeberzeitung*, two publications reflecting the views of large producers as well as the publication of employers in the artisanal sector, *Das Deutsche Handwerksblatt*.

Although the large majority of these sources record the internal deliberations of these associations (where, as discussed, the incentives toward a strategic misrepresentation of the interests of firms are lower), it is important to point out that it is extremely difficult to separate the prestrategic and strategic considerations shaping the preferences of these firms. As the foregoing discussion has illustrated, the shift in the position of the Federation of German Employers' Associations from an unconditional opposition to all policies compensating during unemployment to a qualified support of policies of unemployment insurance reflects both prestrategic and strategic considerations of these producers. Would this peak federation of German producers have supported a contributory unemployment insurance without the extremely undesirable *Erwerbslosenfürsorge* and in the absence of a political threat of the Imperial Employment Office and Weimar politicians to introduce a policy of unemployment insurance? Unfortunately, the available data do not allow us to answer these counterfactual questions. It is important to point out that large firms' support of contributory unemployment insurance reflects more than the strategic calculations of producers. As is shown later, these demands reflect considerations of these employers to provide institutional guarantees to their workers that the investments in their skills would not be undermined during periods of unemployment. The available evidence at this point does not allow us to rank unambiguously the first preference of firms; it allows us to establish only that large firms are indifferent between having no policy of unemployment compensation and a contributory insurance *and* that they rank both these alternatives higher than a means-tested policy of unemployment assistance or a Ghent system (cf. Mares 2001: 52–74). In other words, for large firms, (None, Contributory) > Assistance > Ghent.

We do not find a unified response among German producers to the question whether unemployment was an "insurable" labor market risk, necessitating a compulsory unemployment insurance. A large number of associations representing the interests of small firms continued to voice

---

[38] See Zentrales Staatsarchiv Potsdam, Akten betreffend die Berichte der Handwerkskammern, Reichswirtschaftsministerium, 2071–2078, and Reichsarbeitsamt, 4309–4310.

145

opposition against *any* policy of unemployment compensation a long time after the reversal in the position of large firms and even *after* the introduction of compulsory unemployment insurance in 1927. The deliberations of the individual chambers of commerce provide numerous examples of this opposition. The Chamber of Commerce of Altona expressed "fundamental reservations about the introduction of unemployment insurance which creates immense financial burdens for the Reich, *Länder*, and communes" (Handelskammer zu Altona 1922). Similar concerns were voiced by the Chamber of Trade of Hanover. "Germany's economy will be in the near future subjected to strong fluctuations. There is no foundation for a legal regulation of this issue, due to the fact that an accurate estimation of the financial implications of this legislation is not possible. The burdens resulting from this insurance will not be financially viable for employers in periods of economic crises during which the contributions will be extremely high" (Handelskammer zu Hannover 1922). Another association representing producers in Mittelrhein also opposed the "increase of expenditures for unproductive reasons" (Mittelrheinischer Fabrikantenverein 1920).

The two leading associations representing the interests of small firms, the Association of German *Handwerk* (Reichsverband des Deutschen Handwerks) and the Congress of German Industry and Commerce (Deutscher Industrie- und Handelstag, or DIHT), continued to oppose the introduction of compulsory unemployment insurance. In 1920, a resolution of the DIHT expressed the distrust of these employers toward a policy that "weakens the feeling of responsibility and the striving for self-reliance and which fosters the tendency toward idleness" (Deutscher Industrie- und Handelstag 1920a). The Association of German *Handwerk* voted in support of a compulsory unemployment insurance only during its meeting of October 1926, a belated vote that most likely reflects the strategic accommodation of these producers to an imminent political reality, rather than an expression of their underlying preference (Reichsverband des Deutschen Handwerks 1926a).

This division and disunity among large and small firms supports one of the main conjectures concerning the determinants of the utilities of firms toward different social policies. As the analysis developed in Chapter 2 has pointed out, the size and skill requirements of different firms are likely to influence the relative magnitude of the benefits and costs of different policy arrangements. The model has hypothesized that, if large firms are interested in the institutionalization of guarantees for their work force that their investments in skills will not be undermined during periods of unemployment, the *sensitivity to control* (λ_C) of these firms can be positive. Depending on the sign of the *sensitivity to risk redistribution* (λ_R), these firms will prefer either private-type social policy arrangements (if $\lambda_R < 0$) or contributory social insurance (if $\lambda_R > 0$). In Chapter 2 I have argued that small producers have a lower ability to shift an increase in their costs to consumers in the form of higher prices. Thus, small firms are hypothesized to show a higher concern about the consequences of an increase in their social charges associated with new contributions to social insurance. This lowers the likelihood that the "diffuse" benefits provided by social policies to these employers will outweigh the costs of different social policies. It follows that the sign of *sensitivity to control* (λ_C) of these firms will be negative. Depending on the magnitude of the sensitivity to risk redistribution, these firms will either oppose all social policy arrangements (if $\lambda_R < 0$) or will support universalistic social policies (if $\lambda_R > 0$).

Reflecting these different sensitivities to control, large and small firms disagreed over the policy design of the new institutions of unemployment insurance. For large firms, considerations about the need to institutionalize guarantees to their workers that the investment in their skills would not be undermined during periods of unemployment were of paramount importance. A report of the Federation of German Employers' Associations published in 1925 expressed these concerns of large producers about the adverse implications for *employers* of the long-term unemployment of their workers. "The condition of unemployment leads to the change in the profession of the unemployed, which is an extremely unfavorable situation for the training of workers in particular occupations and for employers who can hold on to their skilled workers only with great difficulty. These hardships will become even stronger during the coming years when the problem of skill formation of workers will become extremely severe, due to the decline in birthrates of the wartime period" (Vereinigung der Deutschen Arbeitgeberverbände 1927: 136). These employers considered that a policy of unemployment insurance had to provide stronger institutional guarantees to both employers and employees that the investment in skills would not be undermined during periods of unemployment. The pressure on skilled workers to take up jobs that did not correspond to their skill qualification had to be attenuated.

To increase the potential of the new policy of unemployment insurance to protect the investment in the skills of their employees, large producers stressed the importance of earnings-related unemployment benefits, a system known in the debate of the period as the *Lohnklassensystem.*

147

These employers demanded to link unemployment benefits to the wages of the unemployed and to eliminate the flat-rate benefit structure that had characterized the *Erwerbslosenfürsorge* (Vereinigung der Deutschen Arbeitgeberverbände 1927). The Federation of German Employers' Associations argued that "purely insurance-based considerations call for the importance of the gradation of the insurance benefits based on the level of wages. Our practical experience [with the means-tested policy of unemployment assistance] suggests additional social and economic reasons calling for the elimination of the flat-rate benefit structure" (Vereinigung der Deutschen Arbeitgeberverbände 1927: 164) The important beneficial consequence of the earnings-related benefit structure was that it raised the relative income of high-skill workers during periods of unemployment, lowering the incentives of these workers to accept a wage that did not correspond to their skill qualifications. Earnings-related unemployment benefits *reproduced* the skill and wage qualifications established at the firm level during periods of unemployment.

Large firms' support of a contributory unemployment insurance reflects the concerns of these producers to provide stronger guarantees to their workers that the investment in skills would not be eroded during periods of unemployment. But *political* considerations also played an important role in accounting for the importance attached by these employers to a policy of unemployment insurance administered by representatives of capital and labor, and not by union members alone. Large firms regarded the political access to the administration of social insurance as a *Machtmittel*, an instrument of political power that could alter in fundamental ways the balance between capital and labor (Vereinigung der Deutschen Arbeitgeberverbände 1927: 160). This explains the strong and unequivocal rejection of a Ghent policy of unemployment insurance by all economic associations representing the interests of large firms (*Der Arbeitgeber* 1910a, 1912, Vereinigung der Deutschen Arbeitgeberverbände 1927: 159). A Ghent system of unemployment insurance administered by trade unions was denounced by these employers as a "hidden subsidization of the strike funds of unions" (*verkappte Streikunterstützung*) (*Der Arbeitgeber* 1913c). As the VDA pointed out, the participation of employers in the administration of social insurance was "of vital significance" for two reasons. The first reason was the difficulty to determine the causes of unemployment and the extent to which unemployment was the result of unwillingness to work. Such issues were easier to establish in the case of either sickness or disability, because "the subjective factor was of lesser importance in causing the incidence of these risks" (Vereinigung der Deutschen Arbeitgeberverbände 1927: 159). Thus, employers considered that the monitoring of the "willingness and ability to work of the unemployed" could not be entrusted to trade unions or to bureaucrats. Second, unemployment had a much higher "general political significance during economic clashes as compared with the other labor market risks" (Vereinigung der Deutschen Arbeitgeberverbände 1927: 159). Both these considerations made the question of business involvement in the administration of unemployment insurance a vital policy objective for employers

Small producers expressed different views about the relative advantages and disadvantages of different policies of unemployment compensation. Considerations about the need to reduce the tax burden of social insurance were of paramount importance and outweighed all potential benefits provided by social policy to employers. Almost all policy statements issued by small producers expressed strong worries about the financial implications of the new policy of unemployment insurance. A writing of the Association of German *Handwerk* (dating from 1923) reports on "strong lamentations coming from all circles of the *Handwerk* concerning the burdens resulting from the introduction of the policy of unemployment insurance." As the same memo continues, "countless independent *Mittelstand* firms went under as a result of the immense tax burdens that have been loaded on employers" (Reichsverband des Deutschen Handwerks 1923). A resolution of the DIHT dating from 1920 reflects similar concerns. According to these producers, "the serious economic situation and the expectation of further economic deterioration make these proposals to raise additional financial revenues for social insurance particularly disturbing. The expansion of the existing institutions of social insurance and the introduction of new institutions with a large administrative apparatus and new unproductive expenditures are all incompatible with the precept of prudence and thriftiness" (Deutscher Industrie- und Handelstag 1920a). These worries about the social charges resulting from the introduction of a new social branch of social insurance explain the preference of these employers for a tax-financed policy of unemployment insurance or for a policy characterized by generous financial subsidies of the state (Reichsverband des Deutschen Handwerks 1925: 12–14).

The model developed in Chapter 2 predicts policy disagreement among employers around a second set of questions of policy design. These issues concern the political boundary of the risk pool of social insurance and the redistribution of the costs among different industries. What occupations should become part of the new unemployment insurance? Should industries characterized by a higher incidence of the risk of unemployment pay higher social insurance contributions or should all industries pay equal contributions to unemployment insurance? Chapter 2 has hypothesized that the incidence of the risk of unemployment will predict the cleavage among employers along this dimension of policy design. I hypothesized that industries characterized by lower levels of unemployment will support a lower level of risk redistribution in social insurance and will demand a separation among the social insurance institutions of various occupations. In contrast to these producers, employers in industries facing high and recurrent levels of unemployment will support the introduction of unitary social insurance contributions and favor an expansive definition of the risk pool of social insurance.

Using data collected by German labor market authorities, I have estimated the incidence of the unemployment in various industries.[39] In 1925 occupations experiencing low levels of unemployment were agriculture with an unemployment rate of 0.3 percent, the chemical industry (0.47 percent), the paper industry (1.75 percent), the food-processing industry (1.42 percent) and the textile industry (2.77 percent). In contrast, industries experiencing high levels of unemployment were construction (5.86 percent), mining (8.17 percent), the wood-processing industry (9.08 percent) and the large metalworking sector – with an unemployment rate of 10.7 percent. The available sources do not allow me to estimate the unemployment rate in the German *Handwerk* sector. Qualitative sources indicate a progressive worsening of the economic situation of the *Handwerk* during the period and an increase in the level of unemployment.

As predicted, employers in industries facing a low incidence of unemployment opposed highly redistributive policies of unemployment insurance. The two most important federations representing the interests of agricultural employers – the Reichslandbund and the Association of Employers' Organizations in Agriculture and Forestry (Reichsverband der land- und forstwirtschaftlichen Arbeitgebervereinigungen) – opposed the proposals of lawmakers to include agriculture as part of unemployment insurance. These employers pointed out that agricultural employers paid wages to the workers even during the winter months, despite the high costs associated with these employment practices (Führer 1990: 324). Thus, employers

---

[39] These sectoral unemployment rates have been computed using data from Hoffmann 1965: 198–199 and Deutscher Reichstag 1926: 168–169.

argued "the labor market contract of agricultural employees is the best insurance against the risk of unemployment" (Führer 1990: 323).[40]

Handwerk firms also perceived themselves as losers from the interoccupational redistribution of risks that was contemplated by the policy makers of the Imperial Employment Office. They regarded the measure according to which all employers were required to pay equal contributions to unemployment insurance as a policy decision that favored disproportionately firms characterized by a higher incidence of unemployment (Reichsverband des Deutschen Handwerks 1926b). To avoid this interoccupational redistribution of risks, the major association representing *Handwerk* firms (Reichsverband des Deutschen Handwerks) recommended a policy that was analogous to the solution found in the case of accident insurance. According to these producers, linking employers' social insurance contributions to the incidence of the risk of unemployment affecting different industries guaranteed a "a juster treatment of the *Handwerk*" (Reichsverband des Deutschen Handwerks 1926b). Simultaneously, these employers recommended the inclusion of agriculture in unemployment insurance, as a measure that could "improve considerably the financial aspects of the law" (Reichsverband des Deutschen Handwerks 1926c: 322, 1927: 17–20, Handwerkskammer von Oberbayern 1920). As the main publication of the *Handwerk* pointed out "there is no justification for a special provision (*Sonderfürsorge*) for agriculture, as the labor markets of agriculture and industry are closely integrated" (Reichsverband des Deutschen Handwerks 1926a: 19).

Industries facing a high incidence of a risk of unemployment voiced different preferences with respect to the interoccupational redistribution of risks. The political and economic power of "modern" sectors – such as machine tools, metalworking, and electricals – within the institutions of business representation increased dramatically during the first years of the Weimar Republic. As David Abraham, Gerhard Feldman, and other historians of the period pointed out, the economic and political ascendancy of modern industries during the first decades of the twentieth century culminated with a leadership change within the Federation of German Employers' Association during the mid 1920s (Abraham 1981). The election of Carl Duisburg as president of the leading association of German producers marks "the replacement of authoritarian by the reformed capitalism

---

[40] Statement of president of one of the associations of agricultural employers, Reichsverband der landwirtschaftlichen Arbeitgebervereinigungen.

in Germany" (Führer 1990: 201). Other studies have pointed out that beginning with the mid 1920s, the Federation of German Employers' Associations began to express the policy interests of these dynamic export industries (Führer 1990: 317).

In 1922 the Federation of German Employers' Associations demanded the "expansion of the scope of the unemployment insurance legislation" and "the inclusion of good risks [günstige Risiken] within unemployment insurance, in other words, of occupations in which the danger of future unemployment is lower" (Vereinigung der Deutschen Arbeitgeberverbände 1923: 35). Moreover, these employers opposed the differentiation of unemployment insurance contributions based on the incidence of a risk faced by different industries and rejected "the creation of occupational risk pools [Gefahrenklassen] within unemployment insurance" (Vereinigung der Deutschen Arbeitgeberverbände 1923: 35). In a writing addressed to the Imperial Labor Office in 1920, this association argued that it was impossible for employers in industries characterized by high and recurring levels of unemployment to pay higher unemployment insurance contributions, because "the financial existence of these firms is endangered, both as a result of the uncertainty in their labor relations and as a result of an uncertainty in demand. An additional financial burden that would result from the doubling of the insurance contributions should not be attempted" (Vereinigung der Deutschen Arbeitgeberverbände 1920: 475). During the following year, the Social Policy Committee of the Federation of German Employers' Associations reiterated its demands for a "wide redistribution of risks" (ein möglichst großer Gefahrenausgleich) (Vereinigung der Deutschen Arbeitgeberverbände 1921: 27).

Figure 4.2 summarizes these findings. The analysis of the policy preferences of German employers confirms the central propositions of the theoretical model. We find a profound disagreement among German employers over the optimal design of the future institutions of unemployment insurance. The strongest predictors of the cleavage in the business community are risk incidence and firm size. High-risk industries pushed for a highly redistributive unemployment insurance, whereas low-risk producers opposed their inclusion as part of the common risk pool. Large manufacturing firms demanded special guarantees to their workers that their skills will not be undermined during periods of unemployment and a representation of firms in the institutions administering unemployment insurance. In contrast, the main policy consideration expressed by associations representing small firms remained the minimization of their nonwage labor costs.

Development of Contributory Insurance

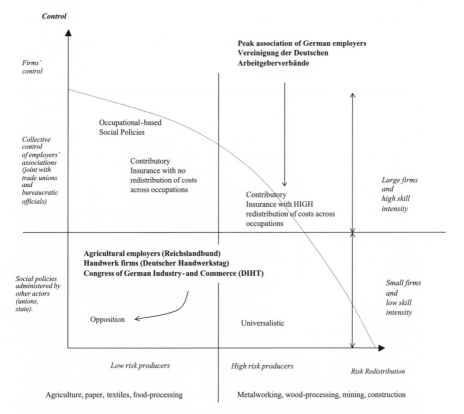

Figure 4.2 German employers and the introduction of unemployment insurance

How influential were employers during the negotiation of the institutions of unemployment insurance? The remaining part of the chapter analyzes these questions.

Cross-Class Alliances and Social Policy Reform: The Development of Contributory Unemployment Insurance

As the preceding sections have established, the main associations representing the interests of large manufacturing producers supported a contributory unemployment insurance beginning in 1920. This stands in sharp contrast to unequivocal rejection of all policies of unemployment compensation by the Central Federation of German Industrialists (Centralverband Deutscher Industrieller) during the imperial period.

Other significant economic associations in Germany voiced a similar dissatisfaction with the means-tested policy of unemployment assistance. The largest trade union federation, the Federation of German Trade Unions (ADGB) called for the introduction of contributory unemployment insurance and abandoned its earlier demands supporting a Ghent system. Trade unions hoped that a policy of unemployment insurance (financed by contributions from employers and employees) would increase the responsibility (*Verantwortlichkeitsgefühl*) of employers toward their employees. As the leading publication of trade unions argued, "due to the fact that employers will be paying contributions to unemployment insurance, they will be interested in lowering the level of unemployment" (Allgemeiner Deutscher Gewerkschaftsbund 1921: 745, 1922: 504). It is significant to point out that the support of a contributory insurance was not a moot point for the entire labor movement but was highly contested politically, at least during the first years of the Weimar period. The Federation of German Trade Unions had to ward off political attacks coming from more radical union associations (such as the Federation of Metalworkers), which regarded the *Erwerbslosenfürsorge* as a stepping-stone toward the introduction of a universalistic social policy and which rejected the insurance solution to the risk of unemployment. The more radical trade union associations regarded any policy of social insurance as an "unjust subsidization of the profit motives of capitalists through contributions of workers" (cf. Führer 1990: 190, Potthoff 1979, Ritter 1933).

The Federation of German Trade Unions recommended the introduction of a policy of unemployment insurance that was jointly administered by representatives of trade unions and employers. These demands were part of broader political demands for "economic democracy" (*Wirtschaftsdemokratie*) and for the institutionalization of a stronger role for the economic associations representing capital and labor in the management of the economy (Potthoff 1979: 177–200). As social policy experts of the Federation of German Trade Unions argued, it was important to clarify the public responsibilities toward the unemployed but also to "guarantee all the *rights* of unions and employers associations" (Führer 1990: 200). The latter part of the statement alluded to the need to clarify the responsibilities of capital and labor in the administration of the new insurance.

German bureaucrats and policy makers showed also a keen interest in the rapid replacement of the policy of unemployment assistance by a policy of unemployment insurance. The most important motivation of this policy preference was the desire to shift the financial burden of this new policy to unions and employers and to relieve the budgets of the Reich, *Länder* and communes from the obligation to finance unemployment relief (Lewek 1990: 161–167, Führer 1990: 171–174). In numerous cabinet meetings of the period, Labor Minister Heinrich Brauns expressed the clear and un-equivocal desire of his ministry to relieve the federal budget of the financial burden of the *Erwerbslosenfürsorge* (Wulf 1972: 165, 205, 436, Erdmann and Vogt 1978: 554). Rudolf Hilferding, a finance minister of the Grand Coalition that took office to overcome the political crisis, called the introduction of the policy of unemployment insurance "an essential political requirement, given the catastrophic financial situation of the Reich" (Erdmann 1978: 274).

In the German bureaucracy, the critical player that remained staunchly dedicated to the development of a policy of unemployment insurance was the Imperial Employment Office (Reichsarbeitsamt, or RAM) (Führer 1990: 174, Manow 2000). In a context characterized by a high political instability and a very short duration of governments, the Imperial Employment Office remained a landmark of stability, pursuing the resolution of the intractable policy questions posed by the development of unemployment insurance.[41] The strong and unwavering policy commitment of the office to the enactment of this policy (which stands in sharp contrast to the indecision of policy makers in France) strengthened an initially fragile cross-class alliance among unions and employers in support of this policy. We can identify two distinct mechanisms by which these reformist policy entrepreneurs cemented this cross-class alliance. The first is informational in nature. The strong commitment to a policy of unemployment insurance by the Reichsarbeitsamt affected beliefs about the likelihood of the implementation of the unemployment insurance law held by both unions and employers and increased the costs incurred by each of these actors if they withdrew their representatives from the common policy deliberations. The archival records of the meeting of the social policy

---

[41] Scholars of this period point out that the strategy pursued by the Imperial Employment Office stands in sharp contrast to the policies desired by the parliamentary majority. Philip Manow correctly points out that strategy of the Imperial Employment Office "of conservative stabilization was not only without the consent of the parliamentary majority, but was pursued against the expressed will of the parliament. The higher civil servants increasingly shared the view of conservative critics and of German employers who blamed an irresponsible and undisciplined parliamentarism (*ungezügelter Parlamentarismus*) and the Weimar party state (*Parteienstaat*) for the grade crisis of the republic and the German economy." Manow 2000a. See also Geyer 1991.

committee of the Federation of German Employers' Associations (VDA) reveal that these considerations played an important role in shaping the political *strategies* of this association during its encounters with bureaucratic officials and elected politicians of the Weimar period. According to the VDA, the strong consensus in support of unemployment insurance of these officials made the opposition to this policy "totally hopeless" (*aussichtslos*). Thus, as the VDA pointed out, it was vital to leave aside any principled objections to the introduction of this legislation and to cooperate in the formulation of the law to guarantee that the organizational and financial concerns of employers were considered (Führer 1990: 218).[42]

The second strategy by which bureaucrats of the Imperial Employment Office strengthened the stakes held by unions and employers in the success of the new policy of unemployment insurance was by increasing the involvement and participation of these actors in the administration of the institutions of the unemployment insurance. The policy principle according to which unemployment insurance had to be administered jointly by associations representing the interests of unions and employers – called during the debates of the period "the principle of self-administration of social insurance" – became a crucial theme in the policy debates of the first years of the Weimar Republic. Numerous pamphlets and publications addressing the question "State administration or self-administration?" published during this period testify to the importance of this policy issue. Successive draft bills of unemployment insurance law strengthened the role and responsibilities of unions and employers in the administration of unemployment insurance. Through these policy choices, the initially fragile cross-class alliance was more firmly anchored in the institutional configuration of the German welfare state.

The policy of unemployment insurance introduced in Germany in 1927 was the political result of a cross-class alliance among unions and employers, an alliance that was forged and strengthened by the skillful political intervention of reformist entrepreneurs (Mares 2000, Faust 1987: 260–279).[43] In the remaining part of this chapter, I attempt to reconstruct the relative influence of unions and employers during the negotiations leading

---

[42] Führer draws here upon a statement of a protocol of the meeting of the Social Policy Committee of the VDA, 27 January 1925, Staatsarchiv Hamburg, Blohm/Voss 1326.

[43] Faust also stresses that the social policy outcome was supported by a "pragmatic coalition among employers and employees" (Faust 1987: 260–279).

to the institutionalization of this policy. It is important to point out that one of the implications of this argument stressing the causal significance of this cross-class alliance among trade unions and employers representing large manufacturing firms is that bureaucratic autonomy alone is insufficient in explaining the emergence of this policy. Despite the strong commitment of the Imperial Employment Office to the introduction of a policy of unemployment insurance, the political and administrative support of unions and employers in the implementation of this policy was essential for the economic viability of this insurance solution. Thus, policy makers of the Imperial Employment Office sought to obtain the political support of unions and employers for the most important details of policy design. As the discussion here points out, at numerous times during these negotiations, both unions and employers had the ability to send a strong "stop signal" to policy makers of the Imperial Employment Office and to block the continuation of the deliberations if a certain policy choice was unacceptable.

The existing archival evidence suggests that the most significant decisions concerning the new unemployment insurance legislation were taken during policy deliberations among representatives of trade unions, employers, and bureaucrats of the Imperial Employment Office. This pattern of policy making, characterized by a stronger relative importance of the bureaucracy as opposed to the parliament during the formulation and clarification of new legislative initiatives, is a defining feature of the policy-making process of the Weimar period. The main cause for this bureaucratic specialization was the parliamentary instability of the period (Witt 1983: 117–149).[44] As a number of studies of the process of policy making in the Weimar Republic have pointed out, most legislative initiatives of the period emerged as a result of a long process of deliberation among the ministries and the relevant interest groups (Stürmer 1967, Witt 1983). The Reichstag took up the discussion of the unemployment insurance legislation during the fall of 1926 and made only few changes to the draft bill that had been submitted by the Imperial Employment Office, before approving the law in January 1927. These policy changes were formulated by the social policy commission of the Reichstag. This commission also involved representatives of unions and employers as part of its policy deliberations (Deutscher Reichstag 1926). Thus, unions and employers were

---

[44] As Witt argues, if we exclude the emergency legislation, "the overwhelming number of all successful legislative initiatives originated in the bureaucracy" (Witt 1983: 139).

involved in both political arenas that designed the policy of unemployment compensation.

During the spring of 1920, the Imperial Employment Office submitted the first draft bill of the unemployment insurance legislation to the cabinet of Gustav Bauer (*Reichsarbeitsblatt* 1920: 391–410). The risk pool of unemployment insurance included both blue- and white-collar workers, but it excluded agricultural employees and employees of the public sector. The defining feature of this draft bill was the proposal to entrust the collection of unemployment contributions and the distribution of unemployment benefits to the local-level sickness insurance funds, the *Ortskrankenkassen* (*Reichsarbeitsblatt* 1920, para. 27/1). The most important reason for this political choice of the Imperial Employment Office was the desire to avoid the creation of another layer of administration in the dense network of institutions of social insurance that made up the German welfare state. Because bureaucratic officials were ready to concede that the institutions of sickness insurance lacked significant policy competency in establishing the eligibility for unemployment benefits of persons temporarily out of work, they recommended that labor exchanges supported the sickness insurance funds in determining the "need and ability to work of the unemployed."

The position taken by the unions and employers in response to this initial draft bill reflects the importance attached by these actors to the principle of self-administration of social insurance. The Federation of German Trade Unions expressed a moderate endorsement of this draft bill, calling it a "useful starting point [*brauchbare Grundlage*] for the future resolution of the problem of unemployment insurance" (Allgemeiner Deutscher Gewerkschaftsbund 1920b: 248–251). Unions advocated the expansion of the risk pool of unemployment insurance to include also agricultural employees (Allgemeiner Deutscher Gewerkschaftsbund 1920b: 251). Initially, unions welcomed the provision of the draft bill that placed the *Ortskrankenkassen* at the center of the new unemployment insurance (due to the strong position held by trade unions in the administration of the institutions of sickness insurance) (Tennstedt 1977: 52–60, 108). A few months after the publication of this original draft bill, unions reconsidered this initial position and called for the organization of unemployment insurance around the labor exchanges (Führer 1990: 256). In contrast to the institutions of sickness insurance, labor exchanges had much more precise information about the organization of the labor market and the ability to "match" the unemployed with available jobs and reduce the level of unemployment in a much shorter period of time.

Employers expressed profound reservations about the resolution of the questions pertaining to the administration of unemployment insurance (Vereinigung der Deutschen Arbeitgeberverbände 1920). From the perspective of firms, the creation of this "dual system" in which both sickness insurance funds and labor exchanges administered unemployment insurance was problematic because of two reasons. First, employers expressed concerns about the reduced political representation of firms in the administration of unemployment insurance. As Rudolf Blohm, an industrialist from Hamburg pointed out, "under the current circumstances, the institutions of sickness insurance are with almost no exception the agents [*die Organe*] of the free trade unions. Thus, in reality, it is not the *Ortskrankenkassen* but trade unions that will be administering unemployment insurance" (Führer 1990: 258).[45] Employers also opposed the introduction of business contributions to unemployment insurance without the delegation of administrative prerogatives and responsibilities to employers. Protesting against this provision of the draft bill, large firms demanded "parity representation in the administration of unemployment insurance" (Nagel 1920).

The second objection of employers toward the first draft bill of unemployment insurance concerned the duplication of administrative duties among labor exchanges and sickness insurance funds. A publication of employers presented a cynical characterization of the future unemployment insurance: "We can imagine how papers will be sent back and forth, how many different times the unemployed will be sent from one institution to another to determine whether they are eligible for unemployment benefits. It is strange that labor exchanges are not the institutions administering the unemployment insurance" (Wagner 1920). In a writing addressed to the Imperial Employment Office, the Federation of German Employers' Associations expressed similar concerns and demanded the centralization of the collection of unemployment insurance contributions and the distribution of benefits in the hands of the same authority (Vereinigung der Deutschen Arbeitgeberverbände 1920).

In response to the concerns expressed by unions and the strong political opposition of employers, Labor Minister Heinrich Brauns withdrew the first draft bill of the unemployment insurance law from public deliberations in 1921 (*Der Arbeitgeber* 1921b). During the following year, the

---

[45] Refers to statement of Rudolf Blohm to the Chamber of Commerce of Hamburg, 6 August 1920, Archive of the Chamber of Commerce Hamburg 66A1.1 (cf. Führer 1990: 258).

Imperial Employment Office submitted a second draft bill tentatively entitled "Provisional Unemployment Insurance" (*Reichsarbeitsblatt* 1921: 839–845, 1922: 329–346, 1923: 187–194). Similar to the provisions of the first project, the risk pool of unemployment insurance included all workers who were covered by sickness insurance, which, in practical terms, implied the exclusion of agriculture from unemployment insurance (*Reichsarbeitsblatt* 1921: 839, para. 2). In contrast to the first draft bill, this second project of the Imperial Employment Office made a more concerted attempt to clarify and distinguish among the responsibilities of the various institutions involved in the administration of unemployment insurance. The responsibility of labor exchanges was to "control the willingness of work and the involuntary unemployment, to end unemployment by directing the unemployed to the suitable job, and finally to limit unemployment through a planned regulation of the labor market." Sickness insurance funds continued to remain responsible for the collection of unemployment insurance contributions. Contributions to unemployment insurance were differentiated across occupations based on the "risk of unemployment in each profession" (*Reichsarbeitsblatt* 1921: 843, para. 65). An important change introduced by this second draft bill concerned the elimination of capital reserves and the transformation of unemployment insurance from a partially funded system to a pay-as-you-go system.

The second draft bill met with stronger enthusiasm from the major associations representing the interests of unions and employers. The leading publication of German employers, *Der Arbeitgeber*, welcomed the efforts of the Imperial Employment Office to clarify future policy responsibilities in the new policy of unemployment insurance and to end the "lamentable *Erwerbslosenfürsorge*" (*Der Arbeitgeber* 1921b). However, employers continued to express dissatisfaction about the institutional design of the new insurance. From the perspective of employers, the most problematic aspect of the new policy was the weak institutionalization of the "disciplining function" of unemployment insurance. According to employers, the legal notions of "willingness to work" (*Arbeitswilligkeit*) and "ability to work" (*Arbeitsfähigkeit*) of the unemployed were improperly defined. This implied that the threat of the termination of unemployment compensation was not credible (*Der Arbeitgeber* 1921a). In addition, the VDA stressed the importance of "widening of the risk pool of unemployment insurance" and opposed the occupational differentiation in the level of unemployment insurance contributions (Vereinigung der Deutschen Arbeitgeberverbände

1923: 35).[46] To succeed, the new unemployment insurance had to include "occupations affected to a lesser extent by the risk of future unemployment" (Vereinigung der Deutschen Arbeitgeberverbände 1923: 35).

On the issue of interoccupational redistribution of the risk of unemployment, the Federation of German Trade Unions and the VDA were in "unanimous agreement" (Spliedt 1924: 257). Trade unions also opposed the creation of occupational risk pools in social insurance. The ADGB considered an unemployment insurance mandating the same contributions from all occupations as the only viable policy alternative. As the ADGB wrote, "We have to reject the creation of different occupational risk pools, especially within the industrial sectors. It is impossible to establish the incidence of the risk of unemployment, especially in the ups and downs of our economy. This division into occupational categories would create many unnecessary differences within occupations and within the same enterprise, raising ultimately the level of contributions and the cost of unemployment insurance. Not only our trade unions but also the large associations of employers have always responded to the variation in the incidence of risk of unemployment in a solidaristic way, through unitary contributions and a unitary level of benefits" (Allgemeiner Deutscher Gewerkschaftsbund 1922b: 521). The joint opposition to the occupational differentiation of unemployment insurance formulated by unions and employers led to the withdrawal of this proposal from future unemployment insurance draft bills.

During the fall of 1925, the Imperial Employment Office published a revised bill of unemployment insurance (*Reichsarbeitsblatt* 1925). This draft bill responded to the calls for simplification of the administrative apparatus and for the parity representation of the interests of capital and labor in the new institutions of unemployment insurance. At the center of the new insurance were unemployment insurance funds organized at the level of individual *Länder (Landesarbeitslosenkassen)*. These most significant responsibility of these institutions was to establish the contributions to unemployment insurance and to monitor the distribution of unemployment benefits by the labor exchanges. The administration of the unemployment insurance funds was placed in the hands of a committee consisting of an equal number of representatives of unions and employers. In contrast, labor exchanges remained responsible for the distribution of unemployment

---

[46] As this report points out, employers expressed these considerations during the encounters with representatives of trade unions and representatives of the Imperial Employment Office (Vereinigung der Deutschen Arbeitgberverbände 1923: 36).

benefits, the monitoring of the willingness to work of the unemployed, the determination of need, and so on.

This third draft bill of the unemployment insurance law thus made a decisive step toward the introduction of the self-administration of unemployment insurance by representatives of capital and labor. Both the Federation of German Trade Unions and the Federation of German Employers' Associations welcomed this change in institutional design. As *Die Arbeit*, the leading theoretical publication of German trade unions, pointed out, "these institutions create neutral zones in which the interests that are being expressed are not the social particularistic interests of employers and employees, but the common interests in production [of these actors]. The participation in these corporations of self-administration have to be understood as a practical education for the democratic understanding of the common goals of capital and labor" (Erdmann 1925: 390–392). As several studies of the social policy position of the German trade union movement during the Weimar period pointed out, "the planned construction of insurance was a practical application of the demands raised at the 1925 trade union congress to 'cooperate with the capitalists as economic agents enjoying equal rights in the codetermination of the German economy'" (Potthoff 1979).[47] The Federation of German Employers' Associations also welcomed the decision of the Imperial Employment Office to accept the policy principle of "self-administration" of social insurance but demanded that these self-governing bodies "be entrusted with special authority and power" (Vereinigung der Deutschen Arbeitgeberverbände 1925).

While supportive of the progress in the institutional design made in this draft bill, unions and employers continued to push for additional policy changes. The proposals submitted by trade unions favored an even stronger centralization of the institutions administering unemployment insurance. According to trade unions, the regional unemployment insurance funds could, potentially, destroy the "unity of unemployment insurance at the level of the Reich, in favor of particularistic efforts of small and large *Länder*" (statement of trade unions quoted in Führer 1990: 276). Rejecting the plans for the creation of unemployment insurance funds organized at the level of each individual *Land*, trade unions favored the creation of a single unemployment insurance fund for the entire German economy. The direct implication of trade unions' plan was the unification of the level

---

[47] A statement made by German Trade Unions during the Twelfth Congress of the Federation of German Trade unions (Führer 1990: 276).

of unemployment insurance contributions across all *Länder* (Allgemeiner Deutscher Gewerkschaftsbund 1924: 342). This proposal for a "total equalization of risks" (*völliger Gefahrenausgleich*) between regions with different levels of unemployment had the advantage of broadening the solidarity of social insurance (Allgemeiner Deutscher Gewerkschaftsbund 1924: 342). These proposals of trade unions that called for a "broad solidarity of risks" were also supported by the Social Democratic Party. As a representative of the Social Democratic Party argued during the deliberations of the Reichstag, "no other branch of social insurance calls for a similar solidarity of risks. Contributions to unemployment insurance have to be equalized across the entire Reich" (Deutscher Reichstag 1926: 173).[48]

The Federation of German Employers' Associations supported the proposals of the Imperial Employment Office to introduce regional differentiation in the administration of unemployment insurance. According to the social policy committee of the VDA, the organization of a "community of risks" (*Gefahrengemeinschaft*) had to be guided by two underlying principles: to counteract administrative largesse (*Wirtschaften aus grossen Fonds heraus*) and to increase the administrative responsibilities of the lowest units that distributed unemployment benefits (Vereinigung der Deutschen Arbeitgeberverbände 1924: 101–102). Assigning the power to determine the level of unemployment insurance contributions to a single organization was, according to employers, "unacceptable." In this case, this institution would have the power "to keep unemployment insurance contributions at high levels *ad infinitum*."

The second policy objection to this draft bill that was formulated by the peak association representing large manufacturing firms concerned the administration of unemployment benefits. The plan of the Imperial Employment Office was to place these responsibilities in the hands of the labor exchanges, institutions that included representatives of unions and employers but also of communes. On repeated occasions employers demanded the reduction of the influence of the communes in the administration of unemployment benefits. According to employers, communes lacked the institutional incentives to be "prudent" and cost-effective when distributing unemployment benefits. This was a consequence of multiple fiscal obligations of the communes. Due to the fact that communes were also responsible for the financing and administration of the means-tested

---

[48] This proposal for the equalization of insurance contributions submitted by the Social Democrats in the Reichstag was, ultimately, rejected (Lewek 1992).

policy of poor relief, they had strong incentives to shift some of the recipients of poor relief onto the rolls of unemployment insurance (which
was financed by contributions from employers and unions). To counteract
this situation, employers demanded the introduction of "a sharp and clear
separation between unemployment insurance and the communal policies of
social assistance. Unemployment insurance has only to be conducted based
on the needs of the economy and based on insurance considerations alone.
All actors who have interests conflicting with this goal have to be eliminated from the administration of unemployment insurance" (Deutscher
Reichstag 1926).

The third draft bill was submitted to the Reichstag in December
1926 (Deutscher Reichstag 1926b). In the social policy committee of the
Reichstag, a "grand coalition consisting of representatives of governmental parties, the Zentrum and the German People's Party (DVP), and of
the two opposition parties, the Social Democratic Party and the German
Democratic Party (DDP), made the final changes to the unemployment
insurance draft bill (Führer 1995: 186).[49] The policy recommendations of
this committee became part of the final unemployment insurance draft bill,
which was approved by the Reichstag in January 1927. Some last-minute
modifications introduced by the committee brought about a further centralization in the administration of unemployment insurance and an increase in
the supervision of the state over the administration of this policy. Based on
the recommendations of this committee, communes were removed from the
administration of unemployment benefits, a policy change that responded
to the preferences expressed by employers.

The long and protracted effort that culminated with the introduction
of a compulsory unemployment insurance in 1927 reflected the effort of
German policy makers to forge and sustain a cross-class alliance among
unions and employers around this policy outcome. At the beginning of the
1920s, we find a strategic realignment in the social policy demands of unions
and large manufacturing producers. While unions abandoned their earlier
demands for the introduction of a Ghent policy of unemployment insurance, large manufacturing producers also abandoned their unconditional
opposition to any policy of unemployment compensation. During the mid

---

[49] As Führer argues, the "Deutschnationale Volkspartei DNVP which joined the coalition
government at the beginning of 1927 tolerated this grand coalition in social and economic
policy through its passivity in the deliberations of the activities of the social policy committee" (Führer 1992: 186).

1920s, Labor Minister Brauns used his agenda-setting power to deepen this political compromise among unions and employers. The state withdrew from the administration of unemployment insurance and delegated a large number of policy responsibilities to trade unions and employers. Furthermore, the Labor Ministry accommodated the policy demands of trade unions and large manufacturing employers, calling for a "wide redistribution of the risk of unemployment." These policy choices used the institutional architecture of the policy of unemployment compensation to deepen and anchor the cross-class alliance among unions and employers.

Conclusion

Prior to World War II, France and Germany developed divergent policy responses to the risk of unemployment. By introducing a Ghent policy in 1905, France remained one of the first countries that established a *national-level* policy of unemployment compensation. Proposals aiming at the introduction of contributory unemployment insurance developed during the 1920s remained, however, unsuccessful. In contrast to France, Germany initiated a means-tested policy of unemployment assistance as an attempt to cope with the labor market disturbances of World War I. In 1927, after nearly a decade of policy experimentation, German policy makers established a contributory unemployment insurance.

This chapter has argued that this divergence in outcomes can be attributed to different political alliances supporting these policies. The coalitions are *strategic alliances* formed during the bargaining process around a policy outcome that is often the *second-best* choice for some of the actors. Reformist policy entrepreneurs (such as Alexandre Millerand or Rudolph Brauns) played a critical role in the formation of these strategic alliances by using the process of social policy design to further the political compromise among unions and employers. French policy makers extended similar subsidies to trade unions and employers' associations that provided benefits in case of involuntary unemployment, in an effort to decrease employers' worries vis-à-vis a Ghent system. In France the Ghent outcome was thus the result of a cross-class alliance among important segments of the business community and trade unions. German policy makers involved representatives of both labor and capital in the administration of the new unemployment insurance, thus furthering the strategic alliance among independent trade unions and large manufacturing producers formed during the first years of the Weimar period.

5

Unified or Occupationally Fragmented Insurance?

POLITICAL REFORMS DURING
THE POSTWAR YEARS

During the first years of the postwar period, the success of the Beveridge reforms in Britain triggered an intense process of policy experimentation in a large number of European countries. In both Germany and France, policy makers and military occupation authorities initiated ambitious reforms that challenged the fundamental policy principles of their respective welfare state. The main objectives of these reform proposals were the extension of the provision of social insurance to the entire population and the administrative centralization of various subsystems of the welfare state.

What was the role played by German and French employers during these political episodes? What were the policy demands of different sectors? Can the model developed in Chapter 2 explain the observed variation in the preferences of firms? What role did employers play during the political negotiations of institutions of social insurance and in the political defeat of these policy proposals? This chapter examines these questions, by relying on two types of archival sources. First, I document the social policy preferences of a representative sample of the business community in both France and Germany by relying on a data set assembled from the most significant business and parliamentary archives of these countries. Second, I explore the political bargaining over the design of the institutions of social insurance, in an effort to identify the most important political coalitions formed in support of and in opposition to these reforms. The sources of my analysis are documents found in the parliamentary archives and archives of the social policy commissions of the period.

166

Military Authorities and Social Insurance Reform

The military authorities that governed a defeated and divided Germany during the immediate postwar years regarded reform of social insurance as an issue that could determine Germany's future trajectory of economic and social development (Hockerts 1980). As they immediately discovered, these reforms confronted them with a number of difficult, nearly unsolvable policy questions. The war had depleted the financial resources of the German welfare state. The situation was extremely troubling for Germany's system of old-age insurance, which had been used by the Nazi regime for the financing of the war effort (Manow 1998: 193–211). War devastation, large population transfers, and the collapse of the German economy were all factors straining the budgets of all subsystems of the welfare state to their utmost. In an effort to solve these acute problems, the military authorities of the different occupation zones began to develop proposals for a comprehensive reform of the German welfare state beginning with the spring of 1946.

In the British occupation zone, the initial position of the military authorities was that the principles of social insurance reform were not open to negotiation and that German input was to be confined to the implementation of the reforms (Hockerts 1980: 34–35). In practice, they compromised on this principle. They delegated significant responsibilities in the development of the legislation reorganizing German institutions of social insurance to the Central Labor Office (Zentralamt für Arbeit) in Lemgo and to former bureaucrats of the Imperial Employment Office, such as Wilhelm Dobbernack (Bundesarchiv Koblenz Z40, Dobbernack 1947: 58–63). We find significant consultation among occupation authorities and the newly organized trade union organizations in this zone, due, in part, to the political affiliation of many staffers of the manpower division with the British Labour Party (Hockerts 1980). The visit of Beveridge to Germany during the summer of 1946 further emboldened the German trade union movement to push for the introduction of far-reaching reforms, similar to those that that had been successfully implemented in Britain (Berichte zur Zonenkonferenz 1946). In the southern part of Germany, American military authorities also maintained an extremely close contact to the German labor movement during the initial deliberation over social insurance reform (Landesrat der amerikanischen Besatzungszone n.d.). Union representatives (such as Willi Richter, who later became president of the German Federation of Trade Unions) participated in the social policy committee that was charged with the exploration of reform alternatives facing the German welfare state (Tennstedt 1977: 234, Hockerts 1980: 53–55). As a result of these factors, the balance of influence during the initial deliberations over social insurance reform was tipped toward the trade union movement.

In the fall of 1946, the Manpower Directorate of the Control Council of the Allied Powers published a draft bill outlining a proposal for social insurance reform for the entire German territory (Landesrat der Amerikanischen Besatzungszone 1946a: 39–67, 1946b: 71–89). This draft bill recommended far-reaching changes in the administration of the German welfare state and in the financing of social policy benefits. In an effort to shore up much-needed resources for the payment of current benefits, the draft bill suggested making social insurance mandatory for a number of other occupations in addition to the working class. Consequently, the level of social insurance coverage was expanded to include "nonindependent workers" (*unselbständig Beschäftigte*) as well as "independents" (*Selbständige*) and their families (Landesrat der Amerikanischen Besatzungszone 1946b, 71–89).[1] Abandoning the earnings-related benefit structure that had characterized the German welfare state since Bismarckian reforms, the bill recommended the introduction of flat-rate old-age and disability benefits that consisted of a basic level and a supplement tied to the average income of the economy. With regard to the administration of social insurance, the draft bill recommended the unification of the various risk pools into a unitary institution. This implied the unification of the two separate institutions of old-age insurance of blue- and white-collar workers and also the elimination of a broad variety of institutions administering sickness benefits, such as firm-level sickness insurance funds (*Betriebskrankenkassen*) and private insurance companies (*Ersatzkrankenkassen*). Finally, the draft bill expressed a strong commitment to the reintroduction of the "democratic administration" of social insurance by representatives of capital and labor. In a joint decision of the Allied Powers of February 1947, unions were given a two-thirds majority in the administration of the new unified insurance and employers were assigned the remaining one-third of the seats (Hockerts 1980: 37).

The beginning of political disagreements among the four superpowers eliminated the possibility of an insurance solution for the entire German

[1] The draft bill excluded from compulsory insurance those persons who were engaged in a short-term, temporary occupation (article 4) as well as independent producers in agriculture and forestry.

168

territory. Representatives of the Russian military authorities retreated from the joint deliberations of the Manpower Directorate of the Control Council of Allied Powers. Unilaterally, Russian occupation forces mandated the introduction of universalistic policy in the eastern part of Germany.[2] The important political consequence of the disagreement among the former allies was the increase in political influence of *domestic* groups during the political process of social insurance reform. For the occupation authorities in the western part of Germany, the political costs of ignoring the demands raised by a variety of societal groups – such as trade unions, employers, doctors, and the representatives of the various institutions of social insurance – became prohibitively high. As a result, the Control Council of the Allied Powers began to institutionalize a closer political consultation with groups that had very strong interest in the outcome of these reforms. The earlier attempts to impose far-reaching reforms of social insurance "from above" on a defeated German population gave way to a process of bargaining among the military authorities and the main political associations of German society. Starting with this second stage of the reform process, employer representatives began to play a more active and prominent role during the policy deliberations surrounding social insurance reform.

Employers and Proposals for Einheitsversicherung

This case provides an opportunity to test the model of business preferences developed in Chapter 2. How did employers respond to these political initiatives aimed at the administrative unification of all branches of social insurance? What was the response of firms, when faced with proposals to broaden the level of social insurance coverage? Do we find significant intersectoral disagreement among employers, and if so, what factors explain this policy disagreement? Can the model of business preferences developed in Chapter 2 explain the variation in the preferences of firms? To test this model, I rely on a collection of archival sources documenting the internal policy deliberations of more than twenty associations of German employers. These associations represent a wide variety of sectors (large firms and *Handwerk*, manufacturing and agricultural employers) as well as

---

[2] The reforms introduced in the eastern part of Germany were developed in analogy and direct continuation to the policies that had been introduced in Berlin in 1945.

a high regional diversity (the associations are found both in the American and British occupation zones).[3]

I will start by summarizing the changes to the policy status quo introduced by the draft bill of the military authorities of 1946. These proposals for reform introduced significant policy changes along both dimensions of the policy space, control and risk redistribution. Along the control dimension of the policy space, the first type of institutional change involved an increase in the administrative centralization of the German welfare state. The aim of these reforms was to merge old-age, sickness, unemployment, and accident insurance into a "unified insurance" (*Einheitsversicherung*). The major motivation behind this policy change was the belief of the Council of Allied Powers that centralization would economize on administrative costs. The second change to the policy status quo involved an increase in the role of trade unions in the administration of social insurance. Prior to 1933, the division of responsibilities in the administration of the welfare state among capital and labor differed across the various subsystems of the German welfare state. Employers occupied one-half of the number of seats in the institutions administering old-age insurance and one-third of the number of seats in the supervisory councils of sickness insurance. Accident insurance was the only subsystem of the German welfare state administered by employers alone, with no participation of trade unions. The policy proposals of the occupation authorities gave labor representatives a two-thirds majority in the administrative councils of all branches of social insurance. Finally, the third change to the policy status quo involved the broadening of the risk pool of social insurance. The occupation authorities regarded this solution as a politically expedient way to generate the revenues that were necessary for the financing of the current benefits.

Chapter 2 has hypothesized that we will encounter a variation in the policy preferences of firms along the control dimension of the social policy space. More specifically, the model has predicted that control should be more significant to large firms as compared with small producers. Large firms are expected to support social policies giving employers high levels of discretion over the administration and distribution of social policy

[3] In collecting these data on the preferences of employers, I have used the following archives. The Economic Archive of Nordrhein-Westfalia (Rheinisch-Westfälisches Wirtschaftsarchiv) of Cologne for its collection of reports of various Chambers of Commerce, the Archive of the Bundesvereinigung der Deutschen Arbeitgeberverbände in Cologne, the Archive of the Friedrich Ebert Foundation in Bonn, and the Federal Archive of Koblenz.

benefits to their work force. In contrast, we expect that for small firms considerations about the costs of different social policies will outweigh the policy benefits derived by higher control. Do the empirical findings support these predictions of the model?

The first policy change recommending the administrative unification of all branches of social insurance was opposed by all associations representing German producers and not by large firms alone (Hilbert 1947, *Der Arbeitgeber* 1949a, 1949b). Employers' representatives in the social policy committee of the American occupation zone depicted the "concentration [*Zusammenballung*] of the entire financial apparatus of social insurance in one hand" as a "development with ominous consequences for the creation of democratic institutions" (Schieckel 1947). Other associations of German producers voiced similar arguments. The Federation of Chambers of Commerce of Bavaria drew parallelisms between the postwar proposals for reform and the policy changes introduced during the period of National Socialism, which had removed employers from the administration of social insurance (by abolishing the legal principle of self-administration of social insurance) and had extended the oversight of the Nazi state over all branches of the German welfare state (Arbeitsgemeinschaft der bayerischen Industrie- und Handelskammern, Bayerischer Handwerkskammertag und Arbeitsgemeinschaft der Arbeitgeberverbände-Bayerns 1947). As employers argued, an important lesson of the National Socialist interlude in the political history of the German welfare state was that bureaucratic "centralization does not lead to a reduction in administrative costs" (Landesverband Südwestdeutschland der gewerblichen Berufsgenossenschaften 1946, Die Wirtschaft und die deutsche Sozialversicherung n.d.).

Opposing the proposals of military authorities, German employers recommended the administrative decentralization of social insurance and the separation of the administration of various subsystems of the German welfare state (Hilbert 1947: 287). An association of employers argued that "the decentralization of social insurance and the wide variety of existing organizations is a sign of strength of existing social policies. Different risks necessitate the construction of different social insurance institutions" (Landesverband Südwestdeutschland der gewerblichen Berufgenossenschaften 1946). Defending the prewar status quo, employers called for the creation of social insurance institutions situated in "close proximity to the firm" (*betriebsnahe Sozialversicherung*) (Arbeitsgemeinschaft der bayerischen Industrie- und Handelskammern 1947, Landesverband Südwestdeutschland der gewerblichen Berufsgenossenschaften 1946). In a report entitled *The Economy and the German Social Insurance*, manufacturing employers argued that institutions of social insurance administered by employers had been historically successful in containing the growth in social insurance contributions (Die Wirtschaft und die Deutsche Sozialversicherung n.d.).

Institutions of sickness insurance organized at the firm level [*Betriebskrankenkassen*] as well as the liability associations [*Berufsgenossenschaften*] ... determine the level of insurance contributions and reserves based on the risk profile of the firm, which is influenced by the accident-proneness [*Unfallgefährlichkeit*] and sickness of the work force. This has a strong effect on the level of social insurance contributions, as both employers and employees have an interest in lowering the potential burden of high insurance contributions. The concentration [*Zusammenlegung*] of these insurance branches in large, centralized institutions ... will necessarily decrease the interest of the firm and of its employees to reduce the risk of sickness and accidents. (Die Wirtschaft und die Deutsche Sozialversicherung n.d.)

The second institutional change introduced in the draft bill of the Control Council of Allied Powers increased the role played by trade unions in the administration of social insurance. These policy changes met with the strong opposition of all associations of German producers and not only with the opposition of large firms alone. Both the Federation of German Employers' Associations (Vereinigung der Arbeitgeberverbände), the major association of large manufacturing employers, but also the association of chambers of commerce of the British occupation zone, an association representing primarily small firms, invoked the importance of social insurance institutions situated in "close proximity to the firm" (Vereinigung der Arbeitgeberverbände 1949a, 1949b, 1949c, Vereinigung der Handwerkskammern in der britischen Zone zu der SPD, n.d.). While employers signaled their policy commitment to the "principle of self-administration of social insurance" (*Selbstverwaltung der Sozialversicherung*), they expressed simultaneously strong objections against the increased role of trade unions in the administration of the German welfare state (*Der Arbeitgeber* 1949c, 1949d, 1949e). During its negotiations with the occupation authorities and with the representatives of the Ministry of Labor, the major association representing the interests of large firms called for the introduction of "parity representation" of capital and labor in the administration of social insurance as the only solution that could "avoid the concentration of economic power of one group over another" (Vereinigung der Arbeigeberverbände 1949d). Representatives of small firms also supported genuine "self-representation in the administration of social insurance (Vereinigung der Industrie- und

Handelskammern in der britischen Besatzungszone 1948). These findings partially confirm the first hypothesis of Chapter 2. Control over the administration of social insurance is important for *all* employers and not large firms alone.

The third major policy change recommended the broadening of the risk pool of social insurance. Chapter 2 has suggested that decisions along the risk redistribution dimension of the social policy space are distributionally divisive for employers. "Low-risk producers" are expected to prefer narrow occupational social policies and oppose efforts of lawmakers to socialize risks. In contrast, "high-risk" producers are expected to benefit from a highly redistributive social policy.

What were the distributional consequences of this proposed expansion of the risk pool of social insurance for various sectors of the German economy? Who were the winners and who were the losers of this policy change? According to employers' representatives on the social policy committee of the American occupation zone, the "risk profile of the newly included industries" was significantly worse than the risk profile of the occupations that were currently part of social insurance (Schieckel 1947). Employers' assessment of the risk profiles of various industries was based on a comparison of the old-age dependency ratio of industries that had participated in the financing of the Bismarckian insurance and those occupations that had been excluded from social insurance. Thus, the expansion of the risk pool implied a redistribution of risks favoring the newly included industries. Employers concluded that the broadening of the risk pool would significantly worsen the average risk profile of social insurance. According to an assessment made by employers, "the future average age of the insured will be significantly higher" (Schieckel 1947)

All major associations representing large manufacturing employers in the British and American occupation zone opposed the policy proposal to broaden the level of social insurance coverage. These employers admitted that the solution contemplated by policy makers could solve current financial problems of old-age insurance but expressed significant worries about the capacity of the pension system to finance the benefits of *future* generations of retirees, if this expansion of the risk pool came about (Schieckel 1947: 122–127).[4] The "worsening of the risk" that was now socialized required either higher future social insurance contributions on the part of

---

[4] This viewpoint is expressed by the employers represented in the social policy committee of the American occupation zone. See Erklärung der Arbeitgebervertreter im Sozialpolitischen

all employers or a future reduction in the level of social policy benefits. Employers worried that the first outcome might hamper the competitiveness of German firms, whereas the second possibility would be hard to implement politically. As a result, these firms concluded that the expansion of the social insurance coverage was a decision with potentially ominous implications.

A second important objection to the expansion of the risk pool of social insurance raised by these employers pointed to the effects of this policy change on existing social private policies. These employers argued the most important danger brought about by the creation of the *Volkspension* was that it absorbed a sizable share of resources from both employers and employees, crowding out the resources for an earnings-related pension system and for private provision in case of old age (Schieckel 1947: 122–127). The main association representing employers in Bavaria (Arbeitsgemeinschaft der Arbeitgebervereine Bayern) pointed out that "the expansion of social insurance to segments of the population ... prevents the possibility of an appropriate, individually designed private insurance" (Arbeitsgemeinschaft der bayerischen Industrie- und Handelskammern 1947).

What were the social policy preferences of "high-risk producers," that is, those employers with a more unfavorable age structure? The actuarial calculations of social policy experts of the period suggest that occupations with the more unfavorable age structure were agriculture, mining and railways, and *Handwerk* firms (Schieckel 1947). These estimations correspond with the assessments of these occupational groups about their own demographic predicament. Thus, for example, a document of agricultural interest groups pointed out that "the number of elderly in agriculture is higher than in other occupations. The load of old age is particularly burdensome in agriculture" (Die zwei Seiten der bäuerlichen Altersversicherung n.d.). Commenting on the nature of employment in their profession, "frought with risks and characterized by rather unattractive working conditions," employers in railways and mining also pointed to the premature aging and early retirement among their employees (Wirtschaftsvereinigung Bergbau 1956, Geyer 1987: 395).

What are the preferences of these firms along the risk redistribution dimension of the social policy space? The first important finding is that all these employers demand one or another form of financial compensation

Ausschuss des Länderrats zum Gutachten der Sachverständigen der amerikanischen Zone über die Neuordnung der Sozialversicherung, in Schieckel 1947: 122–127.

for the higher "riskiness" of their occupation. In other words, these employers push for some form of risk redistribution. In the case of agriculture, these demands for social protection stand in sharp contrast to the opposition to all institutions of social insurance that had been espoused by these producers during earlier episodes of social policy reform (Stellungnahme der Landwirtschaft zur Socialversicherung n.d.). However, these employers opposed the proposals of policy makers of the Central Employment Office to unify all occupational-based institutions of social insurance in a single "risk pool." In contrast to these proposals, these employers favored an outcome in which the German government *subsidized* existing occupationally based institutions of social insurance. This preference of high-risk producers of a policy outcome in which the state *subsidized* occupationally based institutions of social insurance follows from the importance attached by German employers to maintaining "control" over the administration of social insurance.

The social policy demands of employers in mining and railways exemplify the preferences for financial subsidization of high-risk producers. Beginning with the mid-nineteenth century, employers in mining had established extensive firm-level and industry-level institutions of social protection (Kammertöns 1952). During the Weimar period, we find sixteen miners' insurance funds, offering social policy benefits to over 700,000 workers (Geyer 1987: 210). Employers in mining regarded these occupational social policies as a "a compensation for the stronger health risks [and] the difficulty of work" in this profession. They were necessary instruments "facilitating the recruitment of new generations of workers to these professions" (Wirtschaftsvereinigung Bergbau 1956). Employers in railways also considered the private social policy arrangements of their industry as "necessary arrangements, given the special working conditions of the railway industry" and as important institutions that "filled important voids in the German system of social provision" (Deutsche Eisenbahnhauptverwaltung 1947a, 1947b, Sozialaussschuss der Hauptpersonalvertretung bei der Reichsbahngeneraldirektion [britische Zone] 1946).

Two special financial arrangements made these private-type institutions of social protection in these high-risk industries possible. The first was a significant wage restraint of workers in these industries. As employers in railways reflected on the situation, "a close connection exists between wage and social policy in the railway industry. The wages of workers in the railway industry are always lower than the comparable wages of workers in other industries. This is justified because railway workers need special institutions of social insurance" (Deutsche Eisenbahnhauptverwaltung 1947a). The second financial arrangement involved significant contributions of the state in the financing of these institutions. A provision of the Social Insurance Code of the Weimar period (the Reichsversicherungsordnung of 1924) stipulated that "the Reich will make available means that are necessary in addition to contributions to maintain the level of benefits of these institutions" (Zentralanstalt für Arbeit Lemgo 1947a).[5] According to estimates of employers in the railway industry, these financial subsidies from the Reich covered 52 percent of the costs necessary to finance occupational pensions in railways (Zentralanstalt für Arbeit Lemgo 1947a and n.d.). In the case of mining, the subsidies from the state covered around one-third of the social policy expenditures.

These preferences of employers for a continuing financial subsidization of occupational social policy led to a significant policy conflict between these producer groups and policy makers of the Central Employment Office. Invoking strong financial difficulties, policy makers in the postwar period intended to eliminate the subsidies to these occupational social policies (Zentralamt für Arbeit in der britischen Zone 1947, Zentralanstalt für Arbeit Lemgo n.d.). Employers in mining and railways disagreed with policy makers, demanding the continuation of these subsidies. According to the peak association of employers in mining (Wirtschaftsvereinigung Bergbau), the policy of subsidization of occupational institutions of social insurance reflected "the duty of the entire community" to finance the "ups and downs in the life of mining, so that employees are not dependent on charities during periods of economic crises" (Zentralanstalt für Arbeit 1947b).

German *Handwerk* firms also demanded a mix of private-public policies of social insurance that combined a large discretion of the firm in the choice of the institutions of social insurance and a financial subsidy from the broader community of taxpayers to those firms with an unfavorable risk profile. A policy memo drafted by the Central Association of German

[5] Reichsversicherungsordnung (RVO) of 1924, paragraphs 1384 and 1385. Quoted in Zentralanstalt fur Arbeit Lemgo n.d., Finanzielle und organisatorische Schwierigkeiten bei der Sozialversicherung der Reichsbahn, in Archive of the Friedrich Ebert Foundation, Auerbach Papers, 208/1. See also Zentralanstalt für Arbeit Lemgo 1947 and Organisation der knappschaftlichen Versicherung bis 1933, Archive of the Friedrich Ebert Foundation, Auerbach Papers, 215.

Handwerk (Zentralverband des Deutschen Handwerks) in the spring of 1949, entitled *The Demands for Old-Age Insurance of the Handwerk*, voiced the importance of social policies for these firms. "The poverty among *Handwerkers* is so pervasive, that we cannot abandon these social policies, despite some worries" (Zentralverband des Deutschen Handwerks 1949). As this document pointed out, *Handwerk* firms continued to support the principle of compulsory insurance, provided it allowed the freedom of choice in the type of institutions of social insurance. "Each *Handwerker* should choose among various insurance solutions based on its own social policy needs" (Zentralverband des Deutschen Handwerks 1949). The Central Association of German *Handwerk* rejected the proposals for the creation of unitary insurance that was contemplated by lawmakers during the postwar period. The latter was derided as "*Eintopf-Versicherung*," a phrase whose approximate translation is "social insurance drawn from a single cookpot" (Schatz 1947: 81). The strongest disadvantages of the universalistic solution was that it could burden some small firms with "excessive" social insurance contributions (Zentralverband des Deutschen Handwerks 1949, Höffner 1959, Abel 1959).

A law introduced during the period of National Socialism created possibilities for *Handwerk* firms to "externalize" some of the costs to the broader community of taxpayers. The law introducing provisions for old-age insurance for the German *Handwerk* of December 1938 had given small firms the choice between enrolling in the public old-age insurance of white-collar employees (*Angestelltenversicherung*) or taking insurance with private insurance companies (*Reichsgesetzblatt* 1938: 1900). The important consequence of this provision that gave *Handwerk* firms the freedom of choice among private and public forms of old-age insurance was the self-selection among "good" and "bad" risks. Young and highly paid small producers (the "good risks") chose private insurance, whereas elderly *Handwerkers* (the "bad risks") chose to enroll as part of the public social insurance (Post 1956: 24–25, Zentralamt für Arbeit Lemgo 1948).[6] According to a study carried out by the Central Employment Office of the British occupation zone, the effect of this "self-selection" among *Handwerk* firms was the "subsidization of the insurance costs of small producers by the social insurance of white-collar employees" (Zentralamt für Arbeit 1948, Post 1956: 7). Another study commissioned by the trade unions of white-collar

---

[6] For the statistical data demonstrating this "self-selection," see Zentralamt für Arbeit 1948 and Post 1956: 24–25.

employees (*Deutsche Angestelltengewerkschaft*) depicted *Handwerkers* as "an alien body (*Fremdkörper*) for the public old-age insurance" (cf. Höffner 1959: 76).[7]

Thus, for *Handwerk* firms the policy status quo established by the 1938 insurance legislation created a highly favorable financial arrangement, protecting high-risk producers from an increase in their social insurance contributions. In an effort to discredit this legislation and implement a policy change, occupation authorities pointed to the infamous collaboration between the peak association of the *Handwerk* and the Nazi government that had resulted in the 1938 social insurance law (Zentralamt für Arbeit n.d.).[8] Despite the unpopularity of the 1938 law, *Handwerk* firms defended it as a preferable social policy alternative to the unification of social insurance.

A few conclusions follow from this analysis. The proposed reforms involving policy changes along both dimensions of the social policy space – control and risk redistribution – posed important issues of policy design to German producers. Employers opposed all changes to the institutional setup of the German welfare state recommended by military authorities, which involved both an increase in the administrative centralization of social insurance and an increase in the role of trade unions in the administration of the German welfare state. Employers' defense of the "Bismarckian" setup of the of the German welfare state is remarkable. In contrast to episodes of social insurance reform analyzed in the previous two chapters, we do not find differences in the intensity of the policy preferences of employers toward policy questions of "control." The *sensitivity to control* (λ_C) takes positive values for *all* employers and not for large firms alone.

Figure 5.1 summarizes the main findings on business preferences. As predicted by Chapter 2, the preferences of high- and low-risk producers differ along the risk redistribution dimension of the social policy space. Large manufacturing employers opposed the policy proposals to broaden the risk pool of social insurance, arguing that these measures will "worsen the risk that is socialized." In contrast, employers with more unfavorable risk

---

[7] Höffner quotes a study commissioned by the trade unions of white-collar employees, entitled "Handwerkerversorgung, soziale Rentenversicherung und Sozialreform" (Höffner 1959: 76).

[8] As the officials of the Central Employment Office pointed out (in an attempt to discredit the 1938 law), the law introducing old-age provision for the *Handwerk* had been introduced "in agreement with the chief associations of German *Handwerk* of the National-Socialist period" (Zentralamt für Arbeit n.d., memorandum).

Control

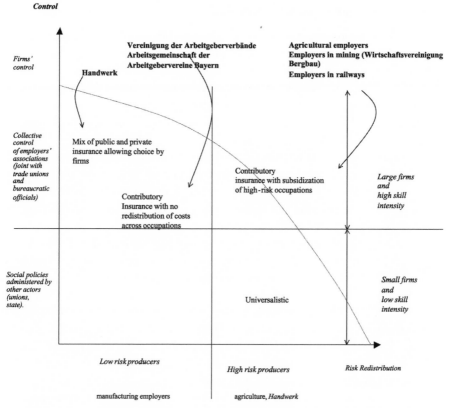

Figure 5.1 German employers and postwar social policy developments

profiles – such as mining, railways, or *Handwerk* firms – preferred a social policy outcome in which the German government compensated them for the higher riskiness of their occupations through financial subsidies to existing occupationally based policies. A significant finding of this analysis is that German high-risk producers preferred this subsidization of existing occupationally based institutions of social insurance to the universalization of social insurance. The important political implication of the analysis is that no single producer association supported a universalistic social policy. This distribution of preferences among German firms had significant implications for the process of negotiation of the institutions of social insurance during the first postwar years. Employers' defense of the Bismarckian status quo remains an important factor contributing to the political defeat of universalistic social policy in postwar Germany.

The Negotiation of Social Insurance

What was the political response of other groups in German society to the social insurance reform bill drafted by military authorities during the first postwar years? As already discussed, beginning in 1947 American and British occupation authorities began to pay closer attention to the preferences for social insurance reform of German economic and political actors. The process of "reform from above" gave way to a process of political consultation with the most significant political forces in German society. The goal of this section is to analyze this political negotiation of social insurance reform during the first years of the postwar period. What were the most important factors that prevented the introduction of a universalistic social policy? Is the opposition of German producers the sole cause accounting for the defeat of universalistic social policy?

Initially, the German trade union movement embraced the efforts of occupation authorities to introduce far-reaching reforms of the German welfare state with great enthusiasm (Industrieverband Bau, Steine und Erde 1947, Württembergischer Gewerkschaftsbund 1947). Trade unions regarded these proposals as a response to a long-standing political desideratum of the labor movement. Historically, both the Social Democratic Party and the Federation of German Trade Unions (Allgemeiner Deutscher Gewerkschaftsbund, or ADGB) had criticized the institutional fragmentation of the German welfare state as the main reason accounting for the disparity in social policy benefits among workers and demanded the centralization of the administration of social insurance (Ritter 1933: 32–43, Kleeis 1911: 5–31). During the first postwar years, the German labor movement took up a similar critique of the "multifaceted and impenetrable" decentralization of the German institutions of social insurance (Vertreter der Gewerkschaften im Länderrat 1947). At the first congress of the Federation of German Trade Unions of the British occupation zone, which was convened in Bielefeld in April 1947, trade unions demanded the unification of the administration of social insurance of each risk at the level of the *Land* in a regional insurance office (*Landesversicherungsanstalt*) to counteract the potential inequalities in the benefits of insurance funds covering "good" and "bad" risks (Deutscher Gewerkschaftsbund der Britischen Besatzungszone 1947: 157). Starting with 1949, successive congresses of the unified trade union movement of West Germany reiterated similar political demands (Deutscher Gewerkschaftsbund der Britischen Besatzungszone 1947: 157).

A second idea that occupied an important place among the demands of the trade union movement was the proposal to restore (and possibly increase) the role of labor representatives in the administration of social insurance. Historically, the administration of local-level sickness insurance funds (*Ortskrankenkassen*) had been the first and most significant avenue of access of the Social Democratic movement to the administrative apparatus of the German state (Tennstedt 1977). As pointed out by Florian Tennstedt, George Steinmetz, and, most recently, Philip Manow, "the principle of self-administration of social insurance which guaranteed the prominent representation of unions in the sickness funds and the new regional insurance offices proved an important organizational stabilizer for union development, giving trade unions unprecedented opportunities for patronage" (Manow 2000; 22; cf. Tennstedt 1977, Steinmetz 1993). By invoking the *Führerprinzip*, the National Socialist regime had ended the self-administration of social insurance by employers and trade unions and had concentrated these responsibilities in the hands of the state.[9] During the first postwar years, trade unions attempted to take advantage of the window of opportunity favorable to far-reaching policy changes and actively pursued a role for labor in the administration of social insurance that went beyond the responsibilities held by trade unions during the Weimar period (Storch 1947: 140, Dobbernack 1947: 61). The Federation of German Trade Unions supported the decision of the Allied powers to recommend a two-thirds majority in the administration of the *Einheitsversicherung* held by labor representatives and opposed employers' demands for "parity representation" of the interests of capital and labor (Gewerkschaftsrat der vereinten Zonen 1948, Gewerkschaftsbewegung der britischen Besatzungszone 1949: 320–321, Deutscher Gewerkschaftsbund n.d., n.d. Tagung). From the perspective of trade unions, the arguments of employers suggesting that responsibilities in the administration of social insurance should be proportional to the share of payroll taxes paid by capital and labor respectively were spurious. As unions argued, "the payroll taxes paid by employers are not personal contributions, diminishing their profits, but parts of the social product that are anticipated by employers as cost factors and which can be shifted upon consumers through the determination of prices" (Killat n.d.).

An additional important demand formulated by the trade union movement during the postwar period called for the universalization of social

---

[9] The law ending the self-administration of social insurance was passed on 5 July 1937. See Dobbernack 1947.

insurance coverage (Deutscher Gewerkschaftsbund der britischen Besatzungszone 1947: 145, Gewerkschaftsbewegung der britischen Besatzungszone 1949: 719). This demand reflected not only the narrow occupational interest of workers to "divide uniformly the *burden of social insurance charges* across the entire population" but also the policy ideal of the Social Democratic movement to provide "existential security" (*Sicherheit der Existenz*) to the entire population (Storch 1947: 139). Anton Storch, who later became first minister of labor in postwar Germany, argued strongly for the inclusion of independents in social insurance: "A part of the independents still believe that they can get along without social insurance benefits. But many of them will realize, once the inevitable monetary reform takes place, how little they are left with and how much they need protection through social insurance" (Storch 1947: 139).

The draft bill of the Control Council introduced a policy mix of "risk redistribution and control" that was close to the political demands of trade unions. It unified all risk pools, gave unions a two-thirds majority in the administration of social insurance, and generalized the provision of social insurance to the entire population. However, other provisions of the bill were highly disappointing for the German labor movement. In an effort to make social insurance self-financing, the occupation authorities recommended significant cutbacks in the level of social policy benefits. The bill reduced the generosity and duration of sickness benefits, eliminated the subsidies of the state to old-age insurance, and increased the stringency of the eligibility conditions for disability insurance (cf. Hockerts 1980). Other cutbacks affected disproportionately particular recipients of social policy benefits. One of the aims of the bill was to unify the old-age insurance of white-collar employees and of workers. In doing so, the occupation authorities did not propose an improvement in the level of old-age benefits of workers (as some trade unions had hoped) but a *reduction* in the benefits of white-collar employees (Hockerts 1980: 33).[10]

The simultaneous pursuit of austerity measures and the universalization of insurance created a strong policy dilemma for the German labor movement. While supportive of the general principles behind the social policy reforms contemplated by the military authorities, a large number of trade union associations were opposed to reductions in the generosity of social policy benefits (Vertreter der Gewerkschaften im Länderrat 1947,

---

[10] The basic pension benefit of white-collar employees was reduced from 37 to 30 Reichsmarks.

Deutscher Gewerkschaftsbund der britischen Besatzungszone 1947: 144). In an effort to avoid these austerity measures, trade unions proposed to increase the financial subsidies of the state to old-age insurance. Trade unions of the British occupation zone were the strongest defenders of these proposals (Baldwin 1990: 193). These unions argued that the German state had a "legal obligation to finance the new old-age insurance out of general tax revenues, contributing an amount that was proportional to the capital reserves that have been destroyed" during the war (Storch 1947: 140). But on this point, the Allies were unwilling to compromise. According to the military authorities, austerity measures were necessary, and financial transfers to cover the deficits of old-age insurance were an unrealistic policy alternative.

The draft bill of the occupation authorities met with the opposition of German employers. An umbrella association for different groupings of employers in the American zone, the Federation of Bavarian Chambers of Commerce and Industry (Arbeitsgemeinschaft der bayerischen Industrie- und Handelskammern), warned against the dangers of political experimentation in questions of social insurance reform in a period of economic and social flux (Arbeitsgemeinschaft der Bayerischen Industrie- und Handelskammern 1947). Other associations representing primarily small producers in southwest Germany also proposed to postpone a reform of social insurance after the monetary reform, in order to "lower the uncertainty about the magnitude of the nonwage labor costs imposed on firms" (Arbeitsgemeinschaft der bayerischen Industrie- und Handelskammern, 1947, Industrie- und Handelskammer München 1947). These associations of employers opposed the centralization of social insurance and demanded the maintenance of existing institutions administering social insurance, such as the liability associations (*Berufsgenossenschaften*) and the firm-level sickness insurance funds (*Betriebskrankenkassen*). Employers in the British occupation zone expressed similar concerns regarding the draft bill. The association of chambers of commerce of the British occupation zone also opposed the extension of social insurance to include the *Handwerk* and invoked the importance of social insurance institutions situated in "close proximity to the firm" (*betriebsnahe Sozialversicherung*) (Vereinigung der Handwerkskammern in der britischen Zone n.d.). An association of producers in Rheinland-Westfalen (Landersverband der gewerblichen Berufsgenossenschaften Rheinland-Westfalen) suggested that a centralized mammoth organization of social insurance that was contemplated by the draft bill "embodied an authoritarian principle of organization, whereas a decentralized system of social insurance divided into different insurance subsystems" was, in essence, more democratic (Schieckel 1947: 100–112).

A commission consisting of independent social policy experts (Sachverständigenkommission) appointed in the summer of 1946 also voiced strong opposition to the proposals aimed at the administrative unification of social insurance (Schieckel 1947: 102). According to the final report of this commission, there were no compelling reasons justifying the unification of all branches of social insurance (Schieckel 1947: 102). The contemplated reforms attempted only to fix the financial problems of one branch of social insurance, by subsidizing it with funds from another system of the welfare state. This cross-subsidization among the different insurance subsystems "had to be rejected." The arguments opposing the centralization of social insurance proposed by the commission were remarkably similar in spirit and formulation to the objections formulated by employers. Unification of social insurance was a problematic exercise, because it "excluded the necessary adaptation to local and occupational needs [*örtliche und berufliche Sonderbedürfnisse*]" (Schieckel 1947: 102).

The widespread opposition to the reform projects "sent a strong stop signal to occupation authorities" (Baldwin 1990). As pointed out by Hockerts and other historians of this political episode, although formal deliberations around the draft bill of the Control Council of Allied Powers continued until the spring of 1948 with the submission of the draft bill to the finance committee and later coordination committee (*Koordinierungsausschuss*) of the bizonal government, "there was no doubt that starting with the fall of 1947 the American and British participated only *pro forma* in the deliberations and that they were determined to prevent the adoption of the law" (Hockerts 1980: 79). General Robertson, the British military governor, expressed this new position of the occupation authorities concerning social insurance reform in the spring of 1948: "There is no justification in the occupying powers concerning themselves with a matter which is the responsibility of the German authorities" (Hockerts 1980: 79).

In the summer of 1947 the British and American military authorities established the economic council (*Wirtschaftsrat*) of the united economic zone, a quasi-parliamentary institution with legislative prerogatives for economic, labor, and social insurance affairs (Hockerts 1980: 85–90). The creation of this institution marks the definite withdrawal of the occupation authorities from decisions regarding the shape of the future institutions of social insurance and the delegation of the responsibilities on these questions to

German politicians and policy experts (Hockerts 1980: 86).[11] Within the economic council, the parties that had supported the draft bill proposing the creation of an *Einheitsversicherung* (Social Democrats and Communists) were outnumbered by a margin of six votes by the "bourgeois" parties, the Christian Democratic (CDU) and Christian Social Union (CSU), the smaller Democratic Party (DP), and the Free Democrats (FDP). These nonsocialist parties were strong defenders of the "Bismarckian" policy status quo. They opposed both the expansion of social insurance and the elimination of distinctions between white- and blue-collar old-age insurance. As an early position paper concerning questions of reform of social insurance, drafted in the fall of 1947 by leading experts of the Christian Democratic Union, argued: "We have to reject the unification of social insurance, due to the concentration of power and the creation of mammoth structures [*Mammutgebilde*]" (CDU 1947).

Until the formation of the Federal Republic in 1949, the economic council remained the main legislative forum of the West German provinces. During this period, lawmakers in the economic council did not formulate further legislative proposals aiming at a fundamental reorganization of the German welfare state. Instead, they confined their activities to social policy reforms that responded to immediate and pressing needs of the German population. Due to the financial collapse of old-age insurance after the introduction of monetary reform, poverty among the elderly reached extremely troubling levels. In December 1948 the Social Democratic faction of the economic council introduced a draft bill whose goal was to bring social insurance benefits in line with the new economic circumstances of the postwar period (Weisz and Woller 1977: Drucksache Nr. 614 and Nr. 796). The law proposed to increase the level of pension, sickness, and old-age benefits; to introduce a minimal pension (*Mindestrente*); to increase the fiscal transfers of the state to old-age insurance; as well as a number of other measures laying the groundwork for the future unification of old-age insurance of blue- and white-collar workers (Dobbernack 1949: 66–68, Hockerts 1980: 91–94). This legislative initiative marks, thus, a significant political retreat of those actors that supported a universalistic social policy. The ambitious plans to unify the administration and to "universalize" the provision of social insurance were temporarily postponed.

---

[11] This delegation of responsibilities was expressed in the monetary reform act: "The reform of social insurance shall be the responsibility of German legislative bodies"; cf. Hockerts 1980: 86.

The law of adaptation of social insurance (*Sozialversicherungsanpassungs-gesetz*) marks the end of Germany's political experiment with universalistic social policies. The law also signals the acceptance of core institutional features of the Bismarckian welfare state by the Social Democratic Party. Among other institutional features of social policy, the Social Democratic Party accepted a high level of heterogeneity in the benefits structure of various occupations and administrative decentralization of social insurance. In exchange for this acceptance of the "Bismarckian" status quo by the Social Democratic Party, the Christian Democratic Party supported an extension in the generosity of social policy benefits as well as an increase in the subsidization of various subsystems of the welfare state through taxes (Baldwin 1990). During the coming decades, the Social Democratic Party attempted to bring these proposals for universalistic social policy back on the policy agenda. During the early 1950s, the SPD initiated legislation recommending a two-thirds majority of labor representatives in the administration of social insurance (Weisz and Woller 1977: Drucksache Nr. 829). During the 1970s, German Social Democrats initiated policy proposals recommending the universalization of social insurance (Bartholomai 1977: 161–172).

Why did Germany fail to adopt a universalistic social policy? As the preceding analysis demonstrates, the most important features of institutional design of the German welfare system were clearly in flux and "up for grabs" during the first years of the postwar period. Thus, an explanation stressing "path dependency" and the stickiness of institutions is clearly insufficient in accounting for the continuity of policy outcomes between prewar and postwar Germany. To account for institutional continuity, we need to examine why an overwhelming political majority in German society found earnings-related, "Bismarckian" social insurance preferable to a universalistic social policy.

The first factor accounting for the failure of policy reform in postwar Germany was the unattractiveness of the policy proposal put on the agenda of reform by military authorities to a broad range of interests in German society. This reform proposal formulated by military authorities combined the universalization of insurance with significant austerity measures, entailing benefit cutbacks and reductions of the financial transfers of the state to institutions of social insurance. As Peter Baldwin summarized these reform ambitions, "the goal was to shift a burden from the state, displacing it directly to the social insurance system" (Baldwin 1990: 191). The unattractiveness of the policy proposal of occupation authorities contributed to the formation of a *strategic* alliance among German trade unions and German employers in defense of the "Bismarckian" status quo. German trade unions and the Social Democratic Party opposed the reduction in the level of social policy benefits of higher-earning employees that was envisaged by military authorities. Abandoning their demands for an administrative centralization of social insurance as a political precondition for the equalization of social policy benefits of all occupational groups, trade unions shifted to a policy position recommending the maintenance of differences in policy benefits among higher-earning and lower-earning employees. Opposing both the institutional centralization of social insurance and an increase in the role of labor representatives in the administration of the German welfare state, the most important economic associations representing German employers supported the Bismarckian status quo and rejected the universalistic social policy.

A second important conclusion of this analysis is that no single group in German society regarded the universalistic social policy proposal as an attractive policy alternative. As Chapter 2 has hypothesized, potential beneficiaries from a universalistic social policy were small firms in high-risk industries. The introduction of uniform insurance contributions allows these employers to shift some of the costs of social insurance to low-risk producers. As the foregoing discussion has illustrated, preexisting social policies enacted during the prewar period and during the period of National Socialism had opened up more favorable policy alternatives for Germany's high-risk producers. In the case of employers in mining and railways, the policy of financial subsidization of preexisting occupational institutions of social insurance was a preferable alternative to the universalization of social policy. In the case of *Handwerk* firms, the optionality of social insurance (guaranteed by the 1938 legislation) was a policy arrangement that protected high-risk producers from an increase in their social insurance contributions. German high-risk producers found these preexisting social policy outcomes preferable to a universalistic social policy. In the end, a large majority of German society comprising both labor and business representatives favored the prewar status quo over a universalistic policy.

An Early Success: The Ordonnance *of 15 October 1945*

During the immediate postwar period, French policy makers attached a decisive priority to the reorganization of the institutions of social insurance

(Join-Lambert 1997, Laroque 1999, Galant 1955, Baldwin 1990, Barjot 1988). The broad ambition of the reforms pursued in France during the first postwar years was to broaden and *universalize* the provision of social insurance benefits to the entire population. It is unquestionable that the ideas of the Beveridge report influenced policy developments in France. Pierre Laroque, the architect of the French postwar reform had spent the wartime period in Britain. French policy makers observed British reforms with strong interest, and the example of the Beveridge plan was often used during the deliberations as a benchmark against which alternative proposals for reform were evaluated (Join-Lambert 1997: 373–378, Baldwin 1990: 164) Nevertheless, one should not overemphasize the importance of this policy model for political developments in postwar France. The most significant commonality between the French and British reforms remained the aspiration to extend social insurance to the entire population. However, the reform objectives of the French policy makers remained more "Bismarckian" in their orientation than the policy goals of the Beveridge plan. French policy makers did not seek to introduce flat-rate social policy benefits but attempted to preserve the linkage between social insurance benefits and the wages of the employees. Pierre Laroque justified the importance of earnings-related social insurance benefits by noting that "there is no true social security for the employees, if the social policy benefits are not, to a certain extent, proportional to the revenues lost" (Laroque 1946: 16). Second, French postwar reformers rejected the method of financing of social insurance through general taxation that was characteristic of the Beveridge plan and of Scandinavian social policy developments. They also opposed an increase of budgetary transfers to the financing of social insurance. Given the lack of financial flexibility resulting from an increase in budgetary subsidies to social insurance, the revenue for potential increases in the generosity of transfers or in the number of social policy beneficiaries had to come from social insurance contributions alone (Archives Nationales C15290, 25 April 1946).

What is remarkable about policy developments in postwar France is the speed with which major decisions were taken during the first few months following the liberation. A first bill of social insurance reform was publicly announced in May 1945 and enacted only four months later. The most important factor accounting for the ability of policy makers to enact this proposal in such a brief time interval was the broad consensus in support of social insurance reform among the three largest political parties – the Socialists, Communists, and Christian-Democratic MRP (Movement

Republican Populaire) – forged during the period of occupation (Michel and Mirkine-Guetzevich 1954, Einaudi and Goguel 1952). Both the charter of the French resistance movement and a number of statements of the Conseil National de la Résistance testify to this political consensus around "a complete social security plan administered by the representatives of interest groups and the state" (Galant 1955: 24, Durand 1953, Barjot 1988: 13).[12] The social insurance draft bill of the first postwar administration attempted to capitalize on this fragile cross-party alliance and translated this general commitment to change into concrete policies and institutions (Barjot 1988: 11–12).[13]

The most important consequence of the strong political consensus among the three major political parties was the weakening of the political groups that either objected to the proposals for reform or that demanded a more careful consideration of other possible policy alternatives. These dissenters from the initial policy consensus included representatives of employers and one trade union confederation, the Confédération Française des Travailleurs Chrétiens (CFTC). Associations representing both employers and trade unions were involved in the policy deliberations, as part of a special extraparliamentary commission – the Comission Délépine – appointed in June 1945 by Labor Minister Alexander Parodi to examine the social insurance plan developed by the administration (Commission Délépine 1945–1946).[14] Their opposition to crucial elements of the proposed social insurance reform was simply ignored by a government that presided over a broad legislative majority. Thus, the political influence of French employers during the early stages of reform remained very low (cf. de Gaulle 1954: 121).[15]

The social insurance draft bill of the administration recommended two broad types of changes to the status quo. First, it proposed to unify the administration of all branches of social insurance – old-age, sickness, accident insurance, and family benefits – into one single insurance fund

---

[12] The detailed social policy program of the Conseil National de la Résistance can be found in Barjot 1988: 13.

[13] Projet d'ordonnance portant l'organisation générale de la Sécurité Sociale. See Barjot 1988: 11–12.

[14] The Commission Délépine included, in addition to representatives of the government and the parliament four representatives of labor organizations, four representatives of employer's organizations, and representatives of the institutions of social insurance.

[15] This is also noted by Charles de Gaulle in his memoirs: "les employeurs ont accuieillit la Sécurité Sociale avec resignation." See de Gaulle 1954: 121.

(*caisse unique*) and to end the organizational fragmentation that had been characteristic of the French welfare state during the Third Republic.[16] In justifying this centralization of insurance, representatives of the government invoked the potential reduction in administrative costs and a better coordination among various providers of benefits and social services covering the various risks (Commission Délépine 1945–1946). The second change involved an increased role of labor representatives in the administration of social insurance (*conseils d'administration*). The draft bill proposed to give labor representatives a two-thirds majority in these institutions.

The debates of the extraparliamentary commission reveal that these proposals for institutional change were highly controversial. Although a significant consensus existed about the need to simplify the organizational framework of the French welfare state, the proposals to unify the administration of all social risks into one single institution were opposed by employers' delegates, some trade unionists, and the representatives of the voluntary institutions of social insurance, the *mutualités* (Commission Délépine 1945–1946). The spokesman of the Conseil National du Patronat Français denounced the "totalitarian character of the project, in total disagreement with the principles of freedom of association" (Barjot 1988: 19).[17] While the Confédération Générale du Travail supported the unification of social insurance, the second largest trade union federation, the Confédération Générale des Travailleurs Chrétiens favored a more decentralized system characterized by a "pluralism of social insurance funds" (Commission Délépine 1945–1946, Tessier 1946). Yet the opposition of these groups within the commission remained ineffective and led to only very small modifications of the draft bill. The only concession made by representatives of the Ministry of Labor concerned the separation of family policy from the unique fund and the creation of autonomous institutions administering these benefits (Barjot 1988: 21).

---

[16] According to the report of the Assemblée Consultative Provisoire, based on the law of 1930, one could find in France more than 1,000 institutions administering old-age benefits, including 911 *caisses de répartition*, 15 *unions régionales*, and 92 *caisses d'assurances-invalidite vieillesse*. One needs to add, of course, the institutions administering family benefits (*caisses de compensation d'allocation famililale*) and the multiple institutions of insurance against workplace accidents. Rapport sur le projet d'organisation de la Sécurite Sociale, Débats de l'assemblée consultative provisoire, no. 68, 31 July 1945, p. 1675.

[17] Déclaration du Conseil National du Patronat Français, annex to Rapport Mottin. See also Barjot 1988: 19.

In contrast to the cantankerous debates of the Délépine Commission, the draft bill encountered more enthusiastic support on the floor of the Consultative Provisory Assembly (Assemblée Consultative Provisoire). Here the debates were brief and trenchant so as to allow a vote before a new round of parliamentary elections. The favorable vote of the assembly allowed French reformers to accomplish a first legislative victory on the road to the universalization of insurance, a goal that had eluded policy makers in Germany. The most important changes to the policy status quo introduced by the *ordonnance* of 4 October 1945 were administrative in nature (*Journal Officiel* 1945: 6280–6288). By creating a national social security fund (*caisse nationale de sécurité sociale*), the law streamlined the administration of the subsystems of the French welfare state governing old-age, sickness, and accident insurance (*Journal Officiel* 1945, article 14). Simultaneously, this unification of social insurance attempted to equalize the level and provision of social policy benefits for all social risks among all social insurance funds. With regard to family benefits, the final version of the law accepted the policy recommendation of the Délépine Commission and allowed for the separate administration of this subsystem of the welfare state (*Journal Officiel* 1945, articles 19–23). Finally, the *ordonnance* increased the role and power of labor representatives and lowered the importance of employers in the administration of social insurance. The *ordonnance* assigned to labor representatives a two-thirds majority in the institutions administering social insurance and to employers the remaining one-third of the seats (*Journal Officiel* 1945, article 5).

For French policy reformers, the *ordonnance* of October 1945 established only the institutional and administrative infrastructure for more far-reaching policy transformations. The latter objective involved the extension of "the advantages of social insurance to independent workers ... who due to the uncertainties of the economic situation are incessantly threatened to lose their autonomy" (Assemblée Consultative, 1 August 1945).[18] In 1945 France, where economy was dominated by small production, the number of these "independents" – shopkeepers, artisans, wine growers and other agricultural smallholders – slightly exceeded the number of manufacturing employees. According to the estimates of the finance commission of the Chamber of Deputies, the extension of social insurance to independents potentially doubled the size of the risk pool. The number of persons immediately eligible for social policy benefits was estimated to increase from

---

[18] Intervention of Georges Buisson, rapporteur of the Labor Office (Comission de Travail).

1.7 million beneficiaries to a potential 3.5 million beneficiaries (Archives Nationales C15290, 25 April 1946).[19]

To carry out this second, more ambitious policy goal, the Ministry of Labor and Social Affairs developed a blueprint for a new social insurance bill and submitted it to the French legislature during the spring of the following year. The aim of this new legislation was the "generalization of social insurance" (Archives Nationales C15293).[20] The new draft bill contained a long and detailed list defining the conditions under which each new occupational group could become eligible for social policy benefits, as well as the minimum level of insurance contributions required from each occupation. These independents were included in social insurance on rather favorable terms: their insurance contributions were significantly lower than the contributions of salaried workers. The existing occupationally based institutions of social insurance developed by various professions (the *mutualités* that played such an important role in the provision of social insurance during the Third Republic) were assimilated within the *régime general* that had been established during the fall of the previous year (*Journal Officiel* 1946a).

Despite the change in the political composition of the French parliament and the gain in influence of the nonsocialist parties, the law encountered almost no political opposition from elected officials (Galant 1955: 80).[21] The entire political process became an exercise in political "credit-claiming" for the expansion of social policy benefits. As Viatte, the leading social policy expert of the Christian Democratic MRP and an opponent of the law characterized the parliamentary deliberations, "at the demand of President Auriol[22] who did not want one political party to attribute to itself the merit of having expanded old-age benefits, the law was voted without debate" (*Journal Officiel* 1946b: 3069). However, the lack of political consultation with the main economic associations representing trade unions, employers, and the newly enrolled "independents" proved to be a political

---

[19] Archives Nationale, Commission des finances, Ière Assemblée Constituante, 25 April 1946.

[20] See the following documents: Proposition de resolution tendant a inviter le gouvernement a soumettre a l'Assemblée Nationale Constituante un projet de loi étendant le benefice de la retraite des vieux aux artisans; Projet de loi portant la generalization de la Sécurité Sociale Archives Nationales C15293.

[21] At the time (2ème Assemblée Nationale Constituante), the Christian Democratic MRP had a legislative majority, of 163 deputies, as opposed to 150 communist and 128 socialist deputies (Galant 1955: 80).

[22] Reference to Vincent Auriol, the president of the 2ème Assemblée Nationale Constituante.

liability for the fate of the universalistic social policy. The initial objections of these groups to the design of the new institutions of social insurance could have been assuaged. During later episodes of social insurance reform, these groups succeeded in reversing some of the decisions taken by elected politicians in their effort to generalize social insurance.

French Employers and Universalistic Social Policies

The policy developments of the first years of the postwar period brought about a radical shift in the policy status quo. A social policy system characterized by decentralization and fragmentation into a large number of occupationally based institutions of social insurance was replaced by a compulsory and centralized social policy. This case of policy reform allows us to test the main propositions about the determinants of the preferences of employers toward different social policy arrangements in a situation in which firms remained confronted with a choice between a universalistic social policy, on the one hand, and either contributory insurance or occupationally based voluntary insurance, on the other hand. Do we see significant disagreement in the social policy preferences of employers and if so why? What are the major issues of disagreement and what variables help us explain the social policy preferences articulated by different associations of employers?

To test the propositions developed in Chapter 2, I have relied on three broad types of sources. The first is the archive of the Commission de Représentation Patronale (CRP), the peak association of the French business community. The CRP was founded in 1944 and was the forerunner of the Conseil National du Patronat Français (Commission de Représentation Patronale 1945–1946, Conseil National du Patronat Français 1946). To analyze the social policy demands of small firms (and to test the propositions about a difference between the social policy demands of large firms and small producers), I have relied on the archives of the social policy committee of the Chamber of Commerce of Paris and the Assembly of Presidents of French Chambers of Commerce (Assemblée des Présidents des Chambres de Commerce de France),[23] as well as on the statements of a host of other organizations representing the interests of small firms, such as the General

[23] Both of these sources can be found at the Archive of the Paris Chamber of Commerce. See Chamber de Commerce de Paris, III. 5. 70 (1) Organisation de la Sécurité Sociale; III. 5. 50 (13) and III 5. 50 (14) Assurance Vieillesse et Assurance Maladie des non-salariés.

Confederation of Small and Medium-Sized Enterprises, the Federation of French Retailers (Fédération des commerçants détaillants de France), or the General Confederation of French artisans (Confédération Générale de l'Artisanat Français). A third important source is the record of the policy deliberations of a commission appointed in the spring of 1947 to renegotiate the provisions of the law generalizing social insurance (Commission Surleau 1947).

The common theme expressed by nearly every single group representing employers is the strong defense of the status quo ante, the social policy regime of the Third Republic. Deploring the hasty and superficial manner with which policy makers approached the question of social insurance reform, employers hoped to reopen the policy debate on these issues and to delay the institutionalization of these policies.

Employers argued that the profound reorganization of social insurance was not a simple "technical issue, involving only changes in the ways social insurance contributions were collected, but a change with far-reaching financial, social, and political consequences" (Chambre de Commerce de Paris 1945). As the Paris Chamber of Commerce pointed out, "it would be a profound understatement to characterize the importance of social policy to employers as a question concerning the identity of the institution collecting the contributions for social insurance. On the contrary, the financial, social and political considerations prevail over the technical aspect of the problem" (Chambre de Commerce de Paris 1945: 2). These worrisome social and political considerations referred to the increased role of bureaucratic and labor representatives in the administration of social insurance (Chambre de Commerce de Paris 1946). This decline in the control of employers lowered both their collective ability to affect changes in the level of social insurance contributions and the ability of individual firms to tailor social policy benefits to their respective needs (Chambre de Commerce de Paris 1945). All employers concurred that the most problematic change brought about by the *ordonnance* of October 1945 was the increased presence of the state (*étatisation*) in the provision of social insurance (Chambre de Commerce de Paris 1945: 3). "Practically, the *ordonnance* has established an organization of the state, having all the inconveniences of an excessive bureaucracy: an impersonal administrative apparatus that excludes all differences and suppresses all efforts or initiatives to improve efficiency" (Chambre de Commerce de Paris 1946: 3).

With respect to "control," the distribution of responsibilities in the administration of social insurance among employers, unions, and the state, the most dramatic changes concerned the reorganization of accident insurance and, potentially, family benefits. In the case of accident insurance, the 1898 law represented the policy status quo. Given the noncompulsory nature of accident insurance, employers retained the freedom to insure their firm against potential liability in the case of workplace accidents with either private insurance companies or *syndicats de garantie*. In contrast to accident insurance, the provision of family benefits remained one of the few branches of social insurance that prior to 1945 was compulsory for all industries (Chambre de Commerce de Paris 1946: 7). Due to the fact that contributions to this subsystem of the welfare state were financed exclusively by employers, representatives of firms retained the ability to establish insurance contributions for firms in different regions (characterized by different levels of natality) and to determine yearly changes in the level of insurance contributions and benefits that could ensure the financial stability of this subsystem of the welfare state. What employers referred to as the "principle of unity of social insurance funds" (*le principe de l'unité de caisse*) threatened to unsettle this policy outcome. While accident insurance was merged with the other subsystems of the French welfare state (such as old-age and sickness insurance) into a unique institution, the *ordonnance* allowed for independent institutions of family benefits only for a temporary period. In contrast to the prewar policies, characterized by the exclusive control of employers in the administration of two branches of social insurance, labor representatives held now the majority in the administrative councils.

Employers raised strong objections against the loss in control brought about by the unification of all branches of social insurance. The chambers of commerce of Paris and Saint-Etienne denounced the "exclusion of business from the administration of family and accident insurance, two branches of social insurance financed primarily by employers" (Chambre de Commerce de Paris 1946, Chambre de Commerce et d'Industrie de Saint-Etienne 1945). The peak federation of French Industrialists and Retailers (Fédération des Industriels et des Commerçants Français) also expressed worries about the concentration of an immense sum of money (totaling about one-third of the budget of the French economy) into a unique fund "over which different political parties can exercise considerable control" (Fédération des Industriels et des Commerçants Français 1945: 2–3). The unification of social insurance was characterized by employers as an unjustified "trustification of the social," which was ironically attempted at a time when policy makers "declared war to the economic trusts" (Chambre de Commerce de Paris 1946: 3).

Employers rejected the argument of reformist policy makers that the administrative centralization of all branches of social insurance into a single insurance fund would bring about a reduction in the costs of administering social insurance. They argued that the creation of the new institutions of social insurance – as envisaged by the *ordonnance* of 1945 – could not be undertaken without a massive increase in costs and without further bureaucratic delays. "It is difficult to hope for an increase in the productivity on the part of a nonspecialized organization charged with administering three distinct and very different risks: a liability insurance, a social insurance, and family benefits" (Chambre de Commerce de Paris 1945: 3). An additional worry for employers was that the creation of a unique fund might lead policy makers to privilege some particular social policy expenditures (such as old-age expenditures). "If one centralizes in a unique insurance fund family benefits and the other social risks, one will see rapidly the old and sick dispute the benefits of the children" (Chambre de Commerce de Paris 1945: 3).

From the perspective of employers, the second problematic aspect of the social insurance reform was the unification of social insurance contributions. The unique contribution for all social benefits was set at 16 percent of the wage bill. Employers denounced this measure as "rigid, unjust, and irrational" (Chambre de Commerce de Paris 1945: 3). In the words of the Paris Chamber of Commerce, "at the moment a unique contribution is introduced, it has no longer a relationship to the risk that is being insured. Thus it is no longer possible to control the money that is being contributed. Today, employers are asked to pay 33 percent, tomorrow, they will be asked to pay 40 percent of the wage bill. One will no longer know how much each branch of social insurance costs, for example, how high old-age benefits of higher earning employees are as compared with the benefits of other groups" (Chambre de Commerce de Paris 1945: 3). Simultaneously, this unification of social insurance contributions had the function to redistribute some of the costs of social insurance between different industries that had previously paid differential contributions to accident or family insurance. This redistribution of the costs of social insurance among different industries (which remained one of the intentions of policy makers) opened up distributional conflict among employers. As one chamber of commerce pointed out, while this reform was expensive for all professions, it was particularly expensive for professions such as the food-processing and textile industries, whose contributions to family and accident insurance had been extremely limited. "The redistribution (*surcompensation*) across professions and regions realized by the unification of contributions to family . . . and accident insurance will be made in effect to the detriment of these industries" (Chambre de Commerce de Paris 1945: 3).

Rejecting both the administrative centralization of insurance and the unification of social insurance contributions, French employers recommended to maintain the separation of the various social risks. Due to the diversity in the causes and incidence of various risks, each risk required a different organizational solution (Chambre de Commerce de Paris 1945: 8). These proposals were made by representatives of large and small firms alike (Conseil National du Patronat Français 1946). The most detailed recommendations for the separation among the branches of social insurance were developed by the Social Policy Committee of the Paris Chamber of Commerce. In the case of sickness, old-age, and family benefits, this commission recommended the organization of social insurance on a "very limited scale" – either at the firm level (a solution recommended for large and "isolated" firms) or at the industry level (if an organization of employers existed that could take over the administration of these funds). If the second solution was adopted, the administration of these branches of social insurance was to be entrusted to committees grouping unions, employers, and representatives of the *mutualités* (Chambre de Commerce de Paris 1945: 9). With regard to accident insurance, these employers proposed a limited redistribution of risks at the industry level and rejected the solution of the unique insurance fund grouping "diverse industries for which the problem of workplace accidents requires different social insurance contributions to reflect the heterogeneity of risks" (Chambre de Commerce de Paris 1945: 9). The institutions governing accident insurance had to be administered by a council with a majority representation of employers, in addition to representatives of trade unions. In contrast to accident insurance, the organization of family benefits required a wide "territorial risk pool" and thus uniform insurance contributions across regions and occupations.

While the *ordonnance* of October 1945 programatically referred to the need to "generalize social insurance to all occupational categories," this radical measure was introduced only as a result of the social insurance law of May 1946. The universalization of social insurance doubled the size of the risk pool and made social insurance benefits available to a heterogeneous group of occupations and professions. First, this measure affected both small producers and employees in agriculture, a sector that in 1947 was employing over 36 percent of the French work force (Mitchell

1980: 163). It also included members of the "liberal professions," such as lawyers, doctors, or pharmacists. Next were the "artisans" – a nebulous category, including the self-employed and small shopowners but also high-skilled workers, employed in very small firms.[24] Due to the wide heterogeneity in the demographic and risk profiles of these groups, the attempt of policy makers to universalize social insurance by creating a unique occupational risk pool faced insurmountable technical and political difficulties.

What was the position of various producers toward this second aspect of reform, the generalization of social insurance? Which sectors opposed and which industries supported the creation of a system of social insurance that was compulsory and that mandated unique insurance contributions from all occupations? What variables influence the *sensitivity toward risk redistribution* (λ_R) of various firms?

Among French employers, the strongest opposition to the expansion of the risk pool was voiced by manufacturing firms. Old-age and sickness insurance had been compulsory for the manufacturing sector for almost two decades. Based on the provisions of the 1930 social insurance legislation, a worker became eligible for an old-age pension at age sixty-five after a long period of uninterrupted contributions of both the worker and the employer (Saly 1999: 209–243). From the perspective of these firms, the immediate extension of the right to social insurance to workers in other industries created an unjust advantage for these sectors, as the sum of their social insurance contributions (totaled over the employment history of a worker) were much lower. The provision for the generalization of social insurance introduced an unjust redistribution, which favored the newly included sectors over manufacturing employers. The strongest expression of this worry of employers can be found in a report of the employers in the metalworking and mining sectors (Union des Industries Métallurgiques et Minières), which denounced the expansion of social insurance coverage pool as a measure bringing about the "self-destruction of social security" (Reynaud 1975: 58, Guillemard 1986: 65). Representatives of the Conseil National du Patronat Français also regarded the "generalization of social

---

[24] On the difficulties in pinning down who actually belonged to the artisans and on the evolving legal and political clarification of this occupational category, see the study developed by the Paris Chamber of Commerce, Les differentes définitions légales de l'artisan, in Chambre de Commerce de Paris, III. 5. 50 (14). The widely accepted definition of the artisan was that the latter was "an autonomous worker who exercises a manual profession, sells the products of his labor and employs only a limited number of workers."

insurance" as the premature expansion of an unearned right and recommended the extension of social *assistance* benefits as a policy solution that was fiscally more prudent and distributionally less divisive (Commission Surleau 1945).

In contrast to large firms that opposed the generalization of social insurance, a host of professional associations representing the newly included industries welcomed the introduction of compulsory social insurance. Agricultural employers supported the extension of social insurance as an important provision that could stop the exodus from the countryside and that could create equal advantages among agriculture and industry (Ministère du Travail et de Sécurité Sociale 1946). Professional associations representing artisans expressed also the strong demands for social security of artisans, a "profession for which the appearance of stability dissimulates the true insecurity of professionals lacking the means of production" (Commission Surleau 1947).[25]

The support of compulsory insurance remained, however, the only issue on which artisans, agricultural employers, and other small producers agreed. The heterogeneity in the employment and demographic profiles of these industries opened up a distributional conflict over the magnitude of the gains and losses from the interoccupational risk redistribution that was envisaged by the proposal to equalize social insurance contributions. In the hierarchy of risk profiles of these industries, agriculture was clearly at the bottom. The exodus from the countryside of young workers had worsened considerably the demographic profile of this occupation (Commission Surleau 1947: 16 June). Thus, for many agricultural employers, a system of social insurance characterized by uniform insurance contributions was preferable to an occupationally based insurance. The situation was entirely different for industries with a younger employment structure and, thus, a better risk profile, which depicted themselves as potential subsidizers of agricultural employers. In a writing addressed to the Ministry of Labor, the Paris Chamber of Commerce issued the warning that "it is important to make sure that the agricultural professions that constitute more than a third of the active population do not fall at the charge of commerce and industry through the interplay of an unjust solidarity" (Chambre de Commerce de Paris 1945: 17). Voicing similar considerations, both the Confédération Générale des Petites et Moyennes Entreprises and the Assembly of the

---

[25] Statement of Hunault.

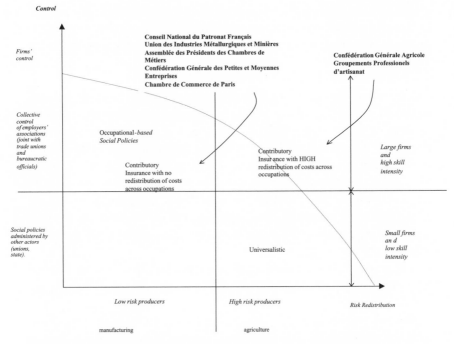

Figure 5.2 French employers and postwar social policy developments

Presidents of Professional Chambers (Assemblée des Présidents des Chambres de métiers) demanded the creation of distinct occupational risk pools (*caisses spéciales*) within social insurance (Ministère du Travail et de Sécurité Sociale 1946). Figure 5.2 locates the preferences of various employers' associations in the social policy space outlined in Chapter 2.

These statements articulated by different associations of employers allow us to test the propositions developed in Chapter 2 regarding the determinants of the social policy preferences of firms and the causes of intersectoral disagreement among employers over the introduction of a new social policy. As suggested in Chapter 2, a key expectation about the *sensitivity* of firms toward the control dimension of the social policy space (λ_C) was that λ_C should have positive sign for large firms, or firms employing high-skill workers, but that the sign of this sensitivity should be negative for small producers. As the preceding discussion indicates, this proposition is only partially confirmed. "Control" – the representation of employers in the administration of social insurance – remained a significant concern for *all* employers. Both the Confédération Nationale du Patronat Français, the peak federation representing large firms, and political associations representing small producers opposed the marginalization of employers from the administration of social insurance. Associations representing large and small firms alike demanded the creation of occupationally based risk pools within the universalist social policy introduced in May 1947. Why was control so important for small firms? To understand the importance of these issues for all French employers, it is important to situate the social insurance reforms within the broader political context of the period. A wave of other policy reforms introduced during the immediate postwar years – such as the introduction of *comités d'entreprise*, the nationalization of the key industrial sectors – increased the prospects of an impending "socialization of the means of production." These broader concerns about a possible marginalization of employers from the management of the postwar French economy explain the obstinate defense of the prewar status quo of social insurance institutions. In short, the fear of a social insurance system that was exclusively in the hands of trade unions explains why large and small firms alike favored social policies characterized by high levels of "control."

A second prediction of the theoretical model of business preferences is that we should encounter intersectoral conflict among employers over the degree of risk redistribution of different social policies. More specifically, the analysis has predicted that the *sensitivity for risk redistribution* (λ_R) should be positive for "high-risk" industries and negative for "low-risk" industries. As the analysis here has pointed out, questions about the reallocation of risks within social insurance have been extremely divisive for employers. Agricultural employers and representatives of the artisans – both industries characterized by an unfavorable demographic profile, due to exodus of younger workers to manufacturing jobs – supported the creation of compulsory insurance and the broadening of the risk pool. In contrast to these producers, associations representing large manufacturing employers (such as the Conseil National du Patronat Français or the Union des Industries Métallurgiques et Minières), characterized by a more favorable demographic profile, opposed the generalization of social insurance and policy decisions that introduced a high degree of interoccupational risk sharing. In short, the incidence of a risk remains a strong predictor of the position of different industries toward policy questions regarding the socialization of risks.

Employers' Influence and the Defeat of the Ordonnance

Both the *ordonnance* of October 1945 and the law generalizing social insurance had benefited from the strong intraparty consensus favoring social policy change that characterized the first years of the postwar period. This rare and unusual agreement created a safe political majority in support of the reorganization of social insurance, allowing elected politicians to ignore or dismiss the protests of various associations worried about the implications of reform. Both legal steps toward the universalization of social insurance had been taken without consultation or involvement of economic groups in the policy design of the new institutions of the French welfare state. But this political strategy based on the marginalization or dismissal of the worries of political groups that were opposed to the reform reached its limits after the enactment of the law generalizing social insurance. The cooperation of these various economic associations was necessary for the *implementation* and, thus, long-term success of this law. But this cooperation was not forthcoming.

As already established, independent producers were *not* opposed to the extension of social insurance and to the provision of benefits covering them during sickness or old age. What they opposed were the terms under which they became part of social insurance and, in particular, the dissolution of all occupationally based risk pools in the *régime general* instituted by the law generalizing social insurance. Their preferred outcome was an insurance solution that was universally available but which allowed each profession to administer its "risk pool" (Commission Surleau 1947).[26] In addition to political protest, the most important strategy available to these groups to express their opposition toward the dissolution of these occupational risk pools in the law generalizing social insurance was their refusal to enroll in the new insurance schemes and pay social insurance contributions. This strategy was highly effective. The universalization of social insurance had stretched the administrative capabilities of the French welfare state to its utmost. As Henri Galant's study of this political episode points out, "the great number and dispersion of artisans and independent workers, the evaluation of their revenues, and the determination of their contribution rate would have been difficult to solve even under more favorable circumstances" (Galant 1955: 108). In the spring of 1947, one prefect after another reported

---

[26] For a more detailed elaboration of this point, see the analysis of the demands of these professions expressed within the Surleau Commission and Galant 1955: 108.

to the General directorate of social security that the existing institutions of social insurance lacked the capacity to enforce the provisions of the law and collect social insurance contributions (Commission Surleau 1947: 4 June).[27] The government counted on the collection of 38 billion francs in social insurance contributions, out of which 28 billion francs were earmarked for the payment of old-age benefits to current retirees. In the spring of 1947, however, it realized that collecting these contributions and financing the much-awaited benefits was impossible. A statement of 19 June 1947 expressed this despair and resignation of officials in the ministry of social affairs with great clarity. "Due to the economic difficulties of the moment and due to an unfavorable psychological atmosphere created by various campaigns waged throughout the country, it has been impossible to collect contributions to social insurance. The application of the law of May 1946 needs to be in effect abandoned" (Barjot 1988: 87).[28]

Faced with the practical impossibility to *implement* the law generalizing social insurance, French policy makers reopened deliberations about social insurance reform. Charles Viatte, an influential member of the Commission of Labor and Social Affairs of the Chamber of Deputies, submitted a draft bill proposing the introduction of a wider number of occupational risk pools within the *régime general*. But the absence of societal support for the law generalizing social insurance prompted simultaneously a change in the method of political negotiation favored by French policy makers. To minimize the political opposition and the policy slippage at the implementation stage, it was important to involve societal associations in the broader process of policy deliberation and decision making. In the spring of 1947, the Ministry of Labor and Social Affairs appointed an extraparliamentary commission, the Commission Surleau, grouping representatives of all associations that shared an interest in the reform (Commission Surleau 1947). In addition to elected politicians, bureaucrats, and social reformers, this commission comprised delegates of trade unions (CFTC and agricultural employees, the Confédération Générale Agricole) and of all significant producer associations or economic associations of independents, including both representatives of large firms (Conseil National du Patronat Français) and small producers (Confédération Générale des Moyennes et Petites Enterprises), as well as agricultural producers (Confédération Générale Agricole)

---

[27] For an analysis of these "notes d'information" issued by the prefects, see Barjot 1988: 86–87.
[28] Archives de la Direction de la Sécurité Sociale, Cabinet du Directeur Général de la Sécurité Sociale, Note of 19 June 1947. Cf. Barjot 1988: 87.

and associations representing artisans and other independents (Groupe-ments Professionnels d'Artisans). The broad mandate of the commission was to study the policy preferences of various occupations and to forge a political compromise among these various groups. Thus, French employ-ers were involved in the process of policy deliberations only at this belated stage of the reform process, as part of the deliberations of the Surleau Commission.

The first issue investigated by this special commission was the extent to which representatives of different occupations supported the principle of compulsory insurance. De Lagarde, one of the delegates of the Conseil National du Patronat Français within this commission voiced the strong concern of his association about the financial costs of this rapid expansion of the risk pool (Commission Surleau 1947: 4 and 12 June). For large firms, the primary reason for their opposition to the generalization of social in-surance was their distrust of the ability of bureaucrats to collect insurance contributions from the newly enrolled professions (Commission Surleau 1947: 12 June).[29] The greater potential of independents to avoid the pay-ment of insurance contributions placed large firms at a comparative dis-advantage. As de Lagarde argued, "for the industrialists the collection of social insurance contributions will not pose any difficulties. On the contrary, the collection of contributions seems difficult to obtain from shopkeepers and the ideas of insurance and solidarity do not seem to facilitate things" (Commission Surleau 1947: 12 June).[30] A more prudent solution that was recommended by the Conseil National du Patronat Français was to make, at first, social *assistance* benefits available to those without support during old age and to delay the extension of insurance benefits until the financial stability of the insurance funds was assured (Commission Surleau 1947: 12 June).[31]

The objection of large firms to the principle of compulsory old-age in-surance found no support among the other members of the Surleau Com-mission. The agreement among representatives of all other professional associations to accept the introduction of compulsory contributory insur-ance was very advanced. The delegate of the professional associations of artisans, Hunault, signaled that these organizations supported the "prin-ciple of generalization of social insurance" (Commission Surleau 1947: 4

---

[29] Statement of De Lagarde, the representative of the CNPF.
[30] De Lagarde.
[31] De Lagarde.

June).[32] An even stronger support was expressed by the representatives of liberal professions, who endorsed a high redistribution of risks "among rich and poor funds" (Commission Surleau 1947).[33] Even representatives of the Confederation of Small and Medium-Sized Enterprises (Confédération Générale des Petites et Moyennes Entreprises) expressed a qualified support of the generalization of insurance benefits, provided the social charges required from small firms "were not excessive" (Commission Surleau 1947: 4 June).[34] Joining these voices, Pierre Laroque opposed the assistance solution that was proposed by employers and invoked the veto of the Ministry of Finance against any additional increase in social policy expenditures financed from the budget and not through social insurance contributions (Commission Surleau 1947: 12 June).[35] A subcommission, including only representatives of these professional associations and, surprisingly, no labor representative, was formed to discuss the technical details posed by the future organization of insurance.[36]

For this subcommission, the most controversial issue turned out to be the question of the future administration of social insurance. Two "extreme" solutions delimitated the range of available possibilities (Commission Surleau 1947: 12 July).[37] At one extreme was the unique insurance fund, as envisaged by the May 1946 legislation. This insurance fund covering the entire French population was to be financed by uniform insurance contributions paid by all occupations. The opposite possibility remained a decentralized solution, where each occupation would administer its own insurance, determining the contributions that were required to guarantee the financial equilibrium of this fund. This universe of available policy choices revealed strongly the trade-off between risk redistribution and control discussed in Chapter 2. As Pierre Laroque reminded the members of the subcommission, "the effect

---

[32] Hunault, the delegate of the professional associations of artisans.

[33] Hunault; Portes.

[34] Montaye.

[35] Laroque.

[36] The subcommission (which was ultimately responsible for drafting the occupationally based system of social insurance) had the following composition: one representative of the Conseil National du Patronat Français, two representatives of the Confédération Générale des Moyennes et Petites Entreprises (Montaye and Richard), one representative of agricultural employers (Confédération Générale de l'Agriculture) (Massot), four representatives of various organizations representing the artisans, two representatives of the liberal professions, and bureaucratic representatives from the social security institutions (their number varied based on meetings).

[37] Pierre Laroque.

of redistribution is to restrain the administrative autonomy and to attenu-
ate the financial responsibilities of the funds.... The redistribution among
insurance funds is incompatible with the principle of administrative
autonomy" (Commission Surleau 1947: 12 July).[38]

Consistent with the position advocating the introduction of assistance
benefits, large firms supported an outcome that involved no redistribution
of risks across occupations. As their representative pointed out, "there are no
other solutions but fiscal solidarity or the creation of autonomous regimes"
(Commission Surleau 1947: 12 July).[39] Risk redistribution had to be confined "to the no-man's land formed by a fraction of independent employees"
(Commission Surleau 1947: 12 July).[40] Elaborating on this rather opaque
policy recommendation, De Lagarde proposed that for independents in
dire need, social assistance benefits were necessary awaiting a gradual integration of these groups within social insurance (Commission Surleau 1947:
17 June).[41]

Representatives of agricultural employers, artisans, and the liberal professions continued to advocate the need for high interoccupational redistribution of risks. Voicing the interests of the liberal professions (totaling
about two hundred thousand members), Portes expressed the support for
"a system of compensation that will reestablish the equality between rich
and poor insurance funds" (Commission Surleau 1947: 4 and 12 June).[42]
Representatives of artisans also supported a unique insurance fund (*unifor-
mité de régime*), warning against the dangers posed by the fragmentation of
insurance into rich and poor funds (Commission Surleau 1947: 4 June).[43]
Agricultural employers demanded the creation of a financial arrangement
by which "the other insurance funds compensate annually the institutions
of social insurance in agriculture for the losses resulting from the exodus
of workers from the rural sector" (Commission Surleau 1947: 12 June).[44]

---

[38] Pierre Laroque.

[39] De Lagarde.

[40] De Lagarde.

[41] De Lagarde. In developing this policy recommendation, De Lagarde draws upon the example of Canada, which had introduced a special insurance fund covering the social policy
benefits of the independents (*les isolés*).

[42] Professor Portes.

[43] See, among others, the statement of Carrié, representing les Groupements Professionnels
d'Artisanat, 4 June 1947.

[44] Masot.

This privileged treatment of the social insurance institutions in agriculture was opposed, however, by Pierre Laroque, who pointed out that other professions, notably the artisanal profession, were also victims of "a similar exodus" (Commission Surleau 1947: 12 June).[45]

Associations representing small firms took an intermediary position between these two alternatives. For these professions, the ideal policy outcome was one that maintained the principle of compulsory insurance but which allowed different occupations or "professional families" to create and administer their own institutions of social insurance (Commission Surleau 1947: 12 June).[46] As the representatives of the Assembly of Presidents of Professional Chambers had argued in front of the Commission of Labor and Social Affairs of the French Chamber of Deputies, small producers "were partisans of the extension of social security but demand not to be deposessed from the administration of their insurance funds" (Archives Nationales C 15293).[47] Initially, Pierre Laroque and other bureaucratic reformers strongly opposed this solution, invoking the absence of foreign policy models that could serve as a blueprint for the creation of these funds. A compulsory system of old-age insurance organized on a professional basis was yet historically unknown and its introduction in France would constitute an audacious political experiment (Commission Surleau 1947).[48]

These proposals for the fragmentation of social insurance along professional lines, which were initially formulated by representatives of associations of small firms, became the focal point for a realignment of the other participants. In its initial formulation, this plan called for the creation of four different risk pools, grouping the liberal professions, agriculture, artisans, and retailers and the manufacturing sector (Commission Surleau 1947: 12 June). In the words of one of the advocates of this solution, the advantage of this "corporatization" of social insurance was that that it made the collection of insurance contributions easier, because these different professions "constitute closed sectors whose members are already compelled to pay professional contributions" (Commission Surleau 1947). Representatives of the Conseil National du Patronat Français overcame their initial opposition to the extension of social insurance to other occupational

---

[45] Laroque.

[46] Michel Gutel.

[47] Statement of Bellanger, vice-president of the Assemblée des Présidents des Chambres de Métiers en France, 25 April 1946.

[48] Pierre Laroque.

categories and pointed out that "the autonomy of the four insurance funds might overcome the resistance of the public to the institutions of social insurance" (Commission Surleau 1947: 17 June).[49] Agricultural employers, in turn, signaled their support for professional autonomy in the organization of social insurance, despite the fact that gain in "control" came at the cost of lower interoccupational redistribution of risks, which had been a policy priority for these occupations (Commission Surleau 1947: 17 June).[50]

The most significant drawback of this proposal was that it left out a large part of the population who could not be easily ascribed to these four professional categories. As a participant in these deliberations suggested with considerable concern, "it seems that in addition to these well-defined four sectors, a 'fifth sector' exists, whose essential characteristics are the *disorganization* and *isolation*" (Commission Surleau 1947: 17 June).[51] Among the occupations that could not be easily assigned to these four insurance funds were members of the Catholic clergy, artists, and the spouses of many of the newly enrolled independents. During the final stages of the deliberation, the question about the future position of these "unorganized" within a compulsory system of social insurance became the most divisive issue for the commission, giving rise to strong distributional conflict among the participants. The solution proposed by employers of large firms, to push these unorganized into the system of social assistance, was ultimately incompatible with the principle of generalized social insurance and rejected by many of the participants (Commission Surleau 1947: 25 June).[52] Representatives of the liberal professions volunteered to admit the "artists, writers, and clerical professions" into "their" insurance fund (Commission Surleau 1947: 25 June).[53] The solution was accepted, despite the drawback of "selecting" the low-risk, higher-earning occupations and leaving out the lower-earning, high-risk groups. Another possibility to "divide" and "redistribute" the disorganized among the four existing

[49] De Lagarde.

[50] Massot, 12 June 1947. It is significant to point out that, on this specific point, the representative of agricultural employers demanded both "control" (*autonomie de gestion*) *and* a subsidy on the part of the state or from the other insurance funds. This demand for both risk redistribution and control was opposed by Pierre Laroque, who reminded Massot that a "system of compensation" among the different occupations is incompatible with "autonomie de gestion."

[51] Lory.

[52] De Lagarde.

[53] Portes.

funds found no support, as each occupation jealously guarded the financial integrity of its fund (Commission Surleau 1947).[54]

The subcommission ultimately adopted a minimalist solution that proposed the creation of a "fifth insurance fund – the insurance fund of the unorganized (*caisse des inorganisées*), including all those who could not justify their enrollment in one of the other subsystems of social insurance" (Commission Surleau 1947: 17 June).[55] Despite practical worries that it might be very difficult to collect insurance contributions from these independents, the subcommission recommended the contributory method of financing, coupled with a subsidy from the government that could be phased out over time (Commission Surleau 1947). These recommendations of the subcommission were also adopted by the extended commission, despite the protest of labor representatives that joined the deliberations during their final stages.

The widely awaited recommendations of the Surleau Commission became public in the fall of 1947. The high legitimacy of the final report stemmed from the fact that they reflected the result of political bargains among the professional associations, expressing, as one of the participants noted, "the maximum that was compatible with the economic and psychological situation of the moment" (Galant 1955: 114, Assemblée des Presidents des Chambres de Métiers de France 1947). The government deferred to the decisions reached within the commission and adopted these recommendations in their entirety as part of a new draft bill for a new social insurance legislation (*Journal Officiel* 1947a: 2206–2208); so did the Commission of Labor and Social Affairs of the Chamber of Deputies (*Journal Officiel* 1947b: 2366–2368). Both chambers of the French parliament approved, with almost no public deliberations, the new draft bill, which became the building block of the French system of social insurance starting with January 1948 (*Journal Officiel* 1947c: 6663–6665).

During the first years of the postwar period, the process of social policy reform exhibited a back-and-forth movement between policy alternatives that differed dramatically in their policy design. In a first stage of reform, characterized by a strong autonomy of the French legislature from the demands of societal groups, policy makers enacted a law that radically departed from the policy status quo of the Third Republic. The *ordonnance* of October 1945 made social insurance benefits available to the entire

[54] Lory Report.
[55] See proposal of Marizis, 17 June 1947.

French population and promised to unify and centralize the administration of all institutions offering social policy benefits. This policy choice posed a severe threat to the existence of a broad variety of private-type institutions of social insurance that had characterized social policy provision during the Third Republic. French policy makers remained, however, unable to *implement* a policy change that marked such a radical departure from the prewar status quo. Faced with strong societal protest, opposition, and, most significantly, the refusal of many French independents to enroll in the new institutions of social insurance, policy makers were compelled to compromise on their original policy aspiration. In this second stage of reform, policy makers institutionalized a stronger policy consultation with a large number of groups representing the entire spectrum of interests in French society: retailers, small and large producers, artisans, and labor representatives. The final policy choice that resulted from the process of political negotiation among these actors recommended the extension of social insurance to a broad segment of the French population. With respect to the organization of social insurance, the final choice endorsed a decentralized policy outcome, in which different occupational groups were given broad prerogatives to administer their own institutions of social insurance.

The preexisting institutional fragmentation of the French welfare state was a critical variable affecting the social policy preferences of various groups. As discussed earlier, artisans, retailers, and small and large producers unanimously rejected the proposals of French policy makers to unify all institutions of social insurance and supported a policy outcome characterized by administrative decentralization among institutions of social insurance. The policy demands of these producer groups prevailed over alternative proposals of policy design advanced by important parts of the French trade union movement and reformist policy entrepreneurs. An important change to the policy status quo enacted during the first years of the postwar period expanded the "risk pool" of social insurance to include artisans, independents, and agricultural producers. As predicted by the model in Chapter 2, this policy change was supported by employers in high-risk occupations and opposed by low-risk producers.

Conclusion

This chapter has analyzed the reconstruction of the institutions of the French and German welfare state during the first years of the postwar period. In a first stage of reform, policy makers in both countries developed proposals that attempted to centralize and unify the administration of social insurance and to extend the provision of social policy benefits to the entire population. These reforms met, however, only with a modest degree of success. Political protest and opposition and the refusal of many independents to enroll in the new institutions of social insurance were factors that sharply curtailed the political ambition of these reforms. After the political disengagement of military authorities from the reform process, German policy makers abandoned the plans to replace the Bismarckian institutions of social insurance by an *Einheitsversicherung*. Reformers in France were more successful in broadening the scope of social insurance but abandoned plans to unify all preexisting occupationally based institutions of social insurance. The final policy outcome enacted in both countries was much closer to the prewar status quo than to the universalistic reforms enacted in Britain or Scandinavia.

The analysis of the political demands of employers confirms some of the theoretical propositions developed in Chapter 2. In both France and Germany, the most significant associations representing large manufacturing producers expressed a strong preference for either contributory insurance or for occupationally based institutions of social insurance and rejected the proposals of policy makers to centralize and unify the administration of social insurance. The incidence of a risk remained a strong predictor of the preferences of firms along the risk redistribution dimension of the social policy space. Employers in "low-risk" industries opposed an increase in the socialization of insurance, fearing the increase in costs that might result from an expansion of the risk pool. By contrast, high-risk producers supported either the progressive extension of social insurance or an increase in the financial subsidies to existing occupationally based social policies.

The correct specification of the policy preferences of various producers allows us to characterize the political dynamics that brought about the defeat of universalistic social policies. In Germany, the unattractiveness of the policy proposal of military authorities to the German labor movement contributed to the formation of a *strategic* alliance among German trade unions and large manufacturing producers in support of Bismarckian institutions of social insurance. In France, a political coalition among large and small producers supported a policy outcome characterized by a strong fragmentation of the institutions of social insurance. In the Surleau Commission, this coalition of French producers defeated the proposals calling for the administrative centralization of social insurance advanced by French trade unions. In both France and Germany, employers played a critical role in the reconstruction of the institutions of social insurance during the postwar period. Employers' involvement in the policy-making process at this critical juncture of political development shaped in important ways the postwar design of the German and French welfare state.

6

<hr>

Risk Redistribution in Mature Welfare States

THE POLITICS OF
EARLY RETIREMENT

Faced with the economic slowdown and the rise in the level of unemployment of recent decades, many European economies have favored a policy response that has encouraged the gradual withdrawal of elderly workers from the labor market (Clark and Anker 1990: 225: 257, Kohli et al. ed. 1991, Naschold and de Vroom 1994, Blondal and Pearson 1995). During the 1970s, elderly workers became the labor market group most vulnerable to the risk of unemployment and, during the 1980s, a rapidly growing new *clientèle* of the welfare state. Although the trend toward declining labor force participation rates at the end of the working life is more pronounced in continental European economies, it remains a pervasive phenomenon characteristic of all mature welfare states.

In many respects, early retirement policies are a hybrid policy outcome. They are situated at the interface of several subsystems of the welfare state (disability, old-age, and unemployment insurance) and of private, firm-level practices and public policies. A profound political uncertainty about the distribution of the costs of these policies has been central to political debates concerning the evolution of this policy. Two such distributional conflicts have shaped the development of early retirement. The first concerns the division of the costs of early retirement among the beneficiaries of these policies (firms and elderly workers) and the broader community of taxpayers to social insurance. The second conflict concerns the distribution of costs among the different subsystems of the welfare state. Are early retirees *unemployed* elderly workers or have they earned, by virtue of their participation in the efforts of postwar economic development, the right to an early *pension*? Should their benefits be financed by employers or by the public authorities? In an effort to characterize the development of these policies, several social policy scholars have used the metaphor of a welfare state in which various

213

risks are increasingly "blurred" (Gaullier 1992: 23–45, Guillemard 1993a: 266, Guillemard 1997: 15–30).

This chapter analyzes the development of early retirement policies in France and Germany during the 1970s and 1980s. These political episodes provide an ideal case allowing us to test the theoretical model of Chapter 2 in a policy context characterized by a very *high density* of existing policies and welfare state programs. As in previous chapters, I examine both the most significant factors shaping the preferences of employers toward these programs and the impact of preexisting policies and institutions on the cross-class alliances formed during the process of social policy reform.

From the Commission Laroque to the Eighth Plan: The Beginning of Early Retirement in France

During the early decades of the postwar period, the primary social policy objective of the French state toward elderly workers had been the effort to facilitate their employment and to increase their participation in the labor market (Guillemard 1986b, of Laroque 1985: 179–95, Garibal 1991). In 1960 French planning authorities appointed a commission, presided over by Pierre Laroque, one of the architects of the French system of social security, to study the economic and social problems of the third age (Haut Comité Consultatif de la Population et de la Famille 1962). The activities of the Laroque commission testify to the interventionist *élan* of the Gaullist state and represent an important attempt of the state to capture the political initiative on issues of old-age insurance (Guillemard 1986: 150–156). The Laroque report recommended "an increase in the number of active participants in the labor force as the only means to contain the increase in the charges of old-age insurance without raising contributions" (Haut Comité Consultatif de la Population et de la Famille 1962: 133). To achieve this objective, the commission proposed changes in policies regulating the employment and dismissal of elderly workers and changes in existing policies of vocational training and continuing education (Haut Comité Consultatif de la Population et de la Famille 1962: 138–149). For French planners, an increase in the participation of elderly workers in the labor market could serve a dual policy goal. On the one hand, this measure was an effort to address the problem of exclusion and marginalization of the elderly. On the other hand, this policy could improve the long-term financial soundness of the various subsystems of the French welfare state (Haut Comité Consultatif de la Population et de la Famille 1962: 116).

But these recommendations for an activist labor market policy toward elderly workers met with strong resistance from the social partners. During preliminary consultations, both unions and employers expressed skepticism and opposition to these proposals. From the perspective of trade unions, these policy guidelines were in direct contradiction to their demands for a shortening of the working life. The largest French trade union, the Confédération Générale du Travail (CGT), expressed the most vocal opposition to the recommendations of the Laroque commission, denouncing these measures, on repeated occasions, as "unacceptable" (Haut Comité Consultatif de la Population et de la Famille 1962: 125). The CGT openly supported the lowering of the retirement age, to reward a labor market group that had faced extremely harsh working conditions during the first decades of the postwar period (Haut Comité Consultatif de la Population et de la Famille 1962: 125). Other unions, such as the Confédération Générale du Travail "Force Ouvrière" (CGT – FO) and the Confédération Force Ouvrière (FO), remained more open to the introduction of a set of policies providing incentives for the lengthening of the working life, if these measures remained optional and if unions could exercise significant control during their introduction (Haut Comité Consultatif de la Population et de la Famille 1962: 126–130).

Employers expressed a profound reservation toward these policy initiatives as well. According to the Labor Market Committee of the Conseil National du Patronat Français (CNPF), it was impossible to establish a taxonomy of jobs in which elderly workers were preferable to younger employees: these were very particularistic decisions that had to remain within the discretionary realm of individual firms (Haut Comité Consultatif de la Population et de la Famille 1962: 123–125). Without a more expansionary macroeconomic policy regime, such policy measures that had as their goal the increase in the labor force participation rates of elderly employees could lead to "economic sclerosis" (Haut Comité Consultatif de la Population et de la Famille 1962: 125). From the perspective of employers, no policy remained the best policy: according to the CNPF under conditions of full employment an increase in the employment of elderly workers could occur "spontaneously"; in less auspicious times, the interference of the authorities in the employment decisions of firms was "unnecessary" and often "detrimental" (Haut Comité Consultatif de la Population et de la Famille 1962: 128–129).

Subsequent policy documents of the Commissariat Général du Plan reiterated the policy ambition of French planners to increase the participation in the labor market of elderly workers (Commissariat Général du Plan 1971, Commissariat Général du Plan 1980). In preparation for the Seventh Plan (1975–1980), the policy report of a new commission (Intergroupe Personnes Agées) suggested that the recommendations of the Laroque commission had retained their full validity, as the labor market situation of elderly workers had continued to deteriorate (Commissariat Général du Plan 1971: 65–87, Lombardot 1970: 87–92). French planners opposed both unions' demands for a lowering of the retirement age and the early retirement practices of firms (Commissariat Général du Plan 1971: 72, 8). Instead, they recommended an increase in the retirement age as the only solution that could guarantee a financial equilibrium of old-age insurance (Commissariat Général du Plan 1971: 77). To implement this policy goal, the commission proposed the introduction of a series of subsidies to firms hiring elderly employees and of measures improving the working conditions of elderly workers. From the perspective of French planners, a policy of sub-sidization of the *employment* of elderly workers was preferable to the subsi-dization of their unemployment (Commissariat Général du Plan 1971: 70).

The unexpected politicization of early retirement issues was the con-sequence of the strong political mobilization of French trade unions. This political offensive of French labor was initiated by the formulation of a joint platform of action between the Confédération Générale du Travail (CGT) and the Confédération Française Démocratique du Travail (CFDT) during the spring of 1971. The goal of the French unions was to refocus public opinion on the question of the intergenerational redistribution of the "fruits of three decades of economic growth" (*Journal Officiel* 1971: 1981).[1] In a number of political rallies conducted at the time, these unions demanded the lowering of the retirement age (to age sixty) and an "increase of the economic resources of the elderly"(Guillemard 1986: 254, *Le Syndicalisme* 10 February 1972).

In response to this strong political mobilization of unions, the French state introduced a number of policies that departed from recommendations that had been advocated by the Commissariat Général du Plan during the first two decades of the postwar period (*Journal Officiel* 1971: 1980–1997). A first policy, introduced at the end of 1971, increased pension replacement rates (Guillemard 1986b). A second measure (intended as a counterproposal

---

[1] According to unions' estimates, productivity had increased by 156% in the period 1949 to 1970 – a development that had not been counterbalanced by a commensurate increase in wages. See *Journal Officiel* 1971: 1981.

to the demands of the CGT and CFDT) increased the unemployment benefits of elderly workers in case of dismissals. This new policy instrument – called *garantie de ressources licenciement* – was first introduced as part of a corporatist agreement (*Accord Paritaire*) in March 1972 (Kerschen and Remniac 1981: 188–191, Kerschen 1983: 66, Latty 1973: 255). A subsequent policy – Law of July Fifth 1972 – established a framework enabling the negotiation of early retirement in all sectors (Gaullier and Gognalons-Nicolet 1983: 35–37). The costs of this measure, which guaranteed 70 percent of the previous wages of elderly workers, were financed by unemployment insurance. A third source of benefits for redundant elderly workers came from public subsidies to restructuring firms. These agreements were negotiated among individual firms in declining sectors and regions and a special bureaucratic agency – the Fonds National pour l'Emploi (FNE) (Lyon-Caen 1995: 160–170, Balmary 1969: 575–583, Husson 1994: 185–190). This policy instrument was less attractive to firms than the *garantie de ressources*, due to the higher costs incurred by firms (Kerschen and Remniac 1981: 195).

The introduction of early retirement policies in France was a response of policy makers to strong political pressures of the trade union movement. The *garantie de ressources licenciement* was a clear abdication from the policy goal of "insertion of elderly workers into the labor market" that had been advocated by various commissions of the plan. However, in attempting to steer a middle way between the Scylla of unions' demands and the Charybdis of employers' opposition to any form of state intervention over the employment practices of firms, the state initiated an ambivalent process of reform. The state did not lower the de facto retirement age, as trade unions demanded, nor did it unconditionally grant a green light to employers to dismiss elderly workers. Nonetheless, on a broad spectrum comprising all possible social policy solutions, the outcome was undoubtedly closer to employers' preferred policy than to the ideal point of trade unions. The generous levels of unemployment benefits provided by the *garantie de ressources licenciement* made firms' practices of labor shedding easier. And, although the state attempted to retain some control over the use of these policy instruments by firms, its monitoring capabilities were constrained by its limited participation in the financing of early retirement. The contribution of the state to the financing of early retirement declined from 12.7 percent of the costs of these policies in 1973 to 2.6 percent in 1978 (Guillemard 1991: 136). French early retirement policies shifted the costs of early retirement to unemployment insurance (for the financing of the *garantie de ressources*) and to the general budget (for the financing of early retirement policies negotiated by the Fonds National pour l'Emploi). While the financial equilibrium of old-age insurance appeared to be safeguarded, this stability was only illusory, because the exit of elderly from the labor market lowered the flow of insurance contributions to this subsystem of the French welfare state.

During the coming decade, French policy makers progressively extended the scope of these institutions of early retirement. The slowdown in economic growth and the overall deterioration of the economic conditions weakened both the determination of the state to implement a policy protecting the labor market situation of elderly workers and the ability of unions to defend the employment possibilities of labor market groups exposed to the risk of unemployment (Guillemard 1986b: chap. 6). Two policy changes testify to this underlying trend. The first was the extension of the *garantie de ressources*, through the introduction of an additional policy instrument covering the cases of "voluntary resignation" of elderly employees (the *garantie de ressources démission*) (Kerschen and Remniac 1981, Kerschen 1983: 63–74). The justification that prefaced this new agreement between the social partners suggested a subtle change of the political and economic motivations for early retirement policies. While the objective of the *garantie de ressources* had been to provide higher levels of unemployment benefits for elderly workers, the goal of the new accord was the "formation of new labor market positions" and "the creation of new jobs for younger workers" (Préambule de l'accord du 13 Juin 1977, quoted in Guillemard 1986b: 267, *Le Monde* 12 July 1977, *La Vie Française* 20 June 1977). This marked a clear subordination of the "social policy objectives" (income maintenance for the unemployed) to "labor market objectives." All French trade unions and even the CNPF welcomed the creation of this new social policy instrument, despite the fact that this expedient to fix the unemployment problems introduced a number of long-term liabilities for other subsystems of the French welfare state (*Le Figaro* 14 June 1977, *Les Échos* 13 June 1977)

During the same period, the second pathway of early retirement administered by the Fonds National pour l'Emploi underwent a significant change as well. Beginning with 1979, the state shifted the financing of these measures to unemployment insurance, a branch of the French welfare state, which is administered exclusively by the social partners. This change in financing of early retirement reflected a more profound disengagement of the state from its monitoring role over firms' employment policies and over potential discriminatory practices of employers with regard to elderly workers. By withdrawing public subsidies, the state abdicated control over the ways in which firms restructured their employment structure, opening a wider space for employers' discretionary practices. "Control" over the definition of the retirement age and over the broad terms of exit of elderly workers from the labor market shifted entirely to firms. This importance of this pathway into early retirement decreased significantly, due to higher attractiveness of the *garantie de ressources* to individual firms and early retirees. While in 1972, 38 percent of the early retirement cases were covered by the pathway administered by the Fonds National de l'Emploi, this number decreased to 8 percent in 1975 and to a mere 0.58 percent in 1981 (Commissariat Général du Plan 1991: appendix 6, table 1, Guillemard 1991: 138).

The early retirement policies developed in France during the 1970s were the result of a strategic compromise among unions, employers, and the state. Although the new policies were initiated in response to an offensive of trade unions for a right to a full pension at age sixty, the policies fell short of fulfilling unions' demands. In lieu of full pension rights, unions obtained higher unemployment benefits for workers in the age groups sixty to sixty-five. The state remained unable to implement its preferred social policy that increased the participation in the labor market of elderly workers. It consented to a "second-best" outcome, a policy that facilitated the exit of elderly workers from the labor market in the hope that this measure could increase the employment chances of younger workers. The state succeeded in reducing its financial obligations, by shifting the costs of this new policy to the subsystems of the French welfare state financed out of payroll taxes. The resulting policy outcome was, paradoxically, closest to the outcome that had been advocated by the peak association of French producers, the CNPF. This outcome increased the discretion of the firm and lowered the control over the initiation of early retirement held by labor market authorities.

What were the preferences of French employers toward early retirement? To what extent do the propositions developed in Chapter 2 explain the variation in the preferences of French firms? The following section analyzes these questions, by relying on a collection of studies conducted by French labor market authorities and several surveys among French employers.

The Preferences of French Employers

A first implication of the model of Chapter 2 suggests that early retirement should be very attractive for large firms as compared with small producers.

Initiating early retirement is costly for employers. It involves the creation of a compensation package that supplements the existing benefits that are financed by the public systems of social insurance. Other policy characteristics of various programs can further raise the costs of early retirement to firms. For example, the state can require employers to compensate various subsystems of the welfare state (such as old-age and sickness insurance) for the loss in revenues experienced as a result of early retirement. Alternatively, the state can raise the costs of early retirement for those firms that do not hire younger workers as substitutes for early retirees. Chapter 2 has suggested that large firms have a higher capability to finance this "private" aspect of early retirement, as compared with small producers.

A number of studies of the sectoral composition of early retirement have suggested that large firms were relying on the early retirement option more frequently than small producers. A survey conducted by French labor market authorities among 50,000 French employers found that 34 percent of firms employing over 500 workers had used the early retirement option (Dossiers statististiques du travail et d'emploi 1990: 132). Among firms employing less than 50 workers, the percentage was 13.9 percent, whereas for medium-sized enterprises (50–499 workers) the number was 17.05 percent (Dossiers statistiques du travail et d'emploi 1990: 132). A second study found a similar pattern, with 31.4 percent of firms with more than 500 employees using the early retirement option, as compared with 17 percent of firms employing less than 9 workers and 13.5 percent of firms with an overall work force between 10 and 49 workers (Gaullier 1993: 32). Similarly, a large-scale study of the policy intentions of French employers (administered in a sample of 1,002 firms) found a similar divergence among large and small producers (Guillemard 1994: 64). Asked whether firms "will consider early retirement in the case of an increase in the number of workers aged fifty or above," 38 percent of firms with more than 500 employees responded that the early retirement option was "possible." In contrast, only 18 percent of small firms (with a work force lower than 50 workers) considered the early retirement option as likely.

A second implication of the model developed in Chapter 2 is that large and small firms will prioritize different issues of policy design. Chapter 2 has hypothesized that "control" over the initiation of early retirement policies will be particularly important for large producers. In contrast, these considerations are unlikely to be significant for small firms. The model has hypothesized that small firms will express a stronger concern for the costs associated with the extension of early retirement benefits. Numerous policy statements formulated by the different associations of French producers (CNPF and CGPME) lend strong empirical support to this hypothesis. As early as 1964, during the deliberations of the Laroque commission, the central federation representing large manufacturing producers, CNPF, voiced its support of "individualized" early retirement policies administered by individual firms and opposed the "generalized" policy solutions that were favored by the French labor movement (Haut Comité Consultatif de la Population et de la Famille 1962: 123). In 1970 the Conseil National du Patronat Français published the first policy paper dedicated to the question of early retirement (Conseil National du Patronat Français 1971). In this document, large manufacturing producers strongly opposed unions' plans for a generalized lowering of the retirement age (Conseil National du Patronat Français 1971: 8–9). A statement of Yves Chôtard, the president of the CNPF, summarized the policy preferences of large firms: "The social strategy of the CNPF is founded on contractual policies [*politique contractuelle*] and social policies of the enterprise" (Conseil National du Patronat Français 1986). As Anne-Marie Guillemard characterized the policy preferences of the CNPF, "French employers strongly preferred a policy framework guaranteeing the possibility of *à la carte* retirement. Whereas the unions demanded a lowering of the retirement age across the board, arguing for the social entitlement to retirement and even its extension, employers preferred to see retirement as a component in their employment policy. They wanted to be able to get rid of older staff if compelled to do so by economic events, or if new quantitative or qualitative labor force needs were imposed by changes in, or the unavoidable reorganization of, production methods. Employers did not take the idea of a wide-ranging, definitive legal measure for bringing the retirement age down, as that would have affected the flexibility of the labor market; it would also have deprived them of a tool that provided conjunctural regulation over this market. They preferred to negotiate specific conditions in the framework of collective agreements" (Guillemard 2000: 186–187).

In contrast to large firms, small producers voiced a strong opposition to the policy status quo, which created a permissive environment for the early retirement practices of large firms. The general assembly of the association representing the interests of small and medium-sized enterprises denounced early retirement policies as "costly and contradictory" (Confédération Générale des Petites et Moyennes Entreprises 1984: 30). Small firms regarded early retirement policies as the source of an increase in their nonwage labor costs, especially in their contributions to unemployment insurance (Confédération Générale des Petites et Moyennes Entreprises 1980: 3). Small firms denounced early retirement as a "suicidal policy that has been pursued for a long time by successive governments, because it was a facile solution which appeared to impose no costs on anybody" (Confédération Générale des Petites et Moyennes Entreprises 1982).

A second hypothesis formulated in Chapter 2 has suggested that the skill composition of a firm will affect the cost-benefit calculations of employers toward different social policy arrangements and, thus, the social policy preferences of firms. In the case of early retirement policies, the impact of the skill composition of the work force on the social preferences of firms is ambiguous. On the one hand, one expects that early retirement will be an attractive policy instrument for firms employing a large number of unskilled or semiskilled workers. These policies create opportunities for firms to shed these workers with lower costs in terms of labor protest, union unrest (as compared with the dismissal option). However, firms might also use the early retirement option as an instrument for shedding highly skilled workers, due to the relatively higher costs of these workers. Thus, the prediction about the effect of skill on the policy preferences of firms is not as clear-cut as for other social policies.

Did French employers perceive elderly workers as a drag on the resources of firms or as a valuable resource, due to their higher levels of experience? The survey conducted by the French Ministry of Labor among 1,002 firms (discussed earlier) reveals that French producers had ambiguous and contradictory views about the contribution of elderly workers to the productivity of the firm (Ministère du Travail 1994: 66). Results showed that 64 percent of large firms[2] and 62 percent of small producers endorsed the statement that "an increase in the relative importance of elderly workers (> 50) will contribute to more experience for the firm"; and 45 percent of large firms and 42 percent of small producers shared the view that an increase in the number of elderly workers will lower the productivity of the firm. However, a number of additional responses to the same survey stand in partial conflict to these statements. Thus 76 percent of large producers (and 59 percent of small firms) considered that an increase in the percentage of elderly workers will contribute to a "weak acceptance of new technologies" and "a resistance to change"; and 72 percent of large firms and 56 percent of

---

[2] Large firms were defined as firms employing more than five hundred workers, small firms were defined as firms employing fewer than fifty workers.

small firms considered that an increase in the number of elderly workers will bring about an increase in the wage costs of the firm.

Available data on the skill composition of early retirees suggest that French firms used early retirement to shed both skilled and unskilled workers. A study of skill composition of the beneficiaries of the two early retirement policies – the *garantie de ressources démission* and the *garantie de ressources licenciement* – points to an almost even distribution of early retirement among high-skill and low-skill workers. Among blue-collar workers, 59 percent of early retirees were classified as "skilled blue-collar workers," whereas 31 percent were unskilled workers and 9 percent were manual laborers. The ratio was reversed for white collar workers: 59 percent of early retirees were "lower-level white-collar workers," whereas 41 percent were "middle- and top-level white-collar workers" (Bulletin de Liaison UNEDIC 1981: 21).

Finally, Chapter 2 has hypothesized that a third predictor of the social policy preferences of firms is incidence of a risk. For the policy context, the demographic composition of the work force of the firm (prior to early retirement) can be used as a measure of risk incidence. "High-risk producers" are those firms employing a higher percentage of elderly workers as part of their work force (as compared with the economy-wide average), whereas "low-risk producers" employ a lower number of elderly workers. We expect early retirement policies to be more attractive for high-risk producers.

A number of studies of the French demographic structure found that the two industries with the most aged work force were the chemical and the metalworking industry, respectively. Prior to the development of early retirement policies, the percentage of male workers aged forty-five and above as a total work force was 39 percent in the chemical industry and 36 percent in the metalworking industry, as compared with an average of 29.6 percent for the French economy as a whole (Gaullier and Goldberg 1993: 19, Volkoff 1989: 97–116). These two industries were using the early retirement option most extensively. A study of the sectoral distribution of early retirement conducted by the French Ministry of Labor in 1984 found that metalworking employers had made the highest use of the *garantie de ressources licenciement* (Marioni and Ricau 1984: 9). Of the workers in the metalworking industry who were eligible for the benefits of this policy, 69.1 percent had received this form of early retirement compensation (Marioni and Ricau 1984). Employers in the chemical industry also made extensive use of the early retirement option. In the chemical industry, the percentage of early retirees out of total workers eligible for early retirement

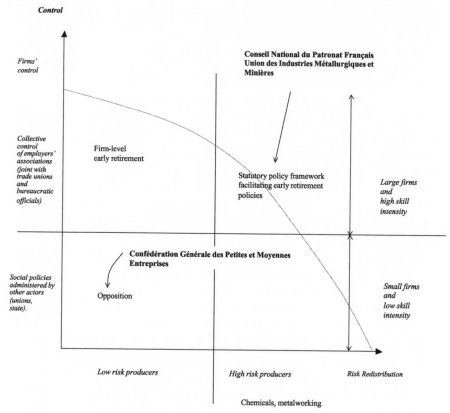

Figure 6.1 French employers and the development of early retirement policies

was 45.1 percent (as compared with an average of 23.1 percent for the French economy) (Marioni and Ricau 1984).

Figure 6.1 summarizes the preceding discussion. These findings support two out of the three hypotheses formulated in Chapter 2. The strongest predictors of the cleavages among French employers are size and risk incidence. Large firms with predominantly elderly workers benefited most from the introduction of early retirement policies. Among employers, the net losers from the process of early retirement were small firms and firms with a younger work force. Without using the early retirement option as extensively as large producers, these firms were adversely affected by the rise in employer contributions (that resulted from early retirement practices conducted by other employers). The association representing French small and medium-sized enterprises voiced the overall dissatisfaction of these producers with the externalization practices of large firms. "The expenditures of unemployment insurance which have increased from 30 billion to 90 billion francs . . . have resulted in part by the acceptance of expenditures that were outside the responsibility of this policy, such as the *garantie de ressources*. It is necessary to center unemployment insurance on its original principles. Unemployment insurance has to become an insurance system open only to the contributory and based on the redistribution of risks across industries [*solidarité interprofessionnelle*]. The specific redistributive issues posed by the existence of a structural unemployment have to be financed by the national community" (Confédération Générale des Petites et Moyennes Entreprises 1983: 39).

The Negotiation of Early Retirement Policies: The Ordonnance *of 26 March 1982*

The set of institutions created by French policy makers during the early 1970s encouraged the pervasive use of early retirement by firms. During this period, the labor force participation rates of elderly workers declined from 75.4 percent in 1970 to 64.6 percent in 1981 (OECD 1995). The introduction of the *garantie de ressources démission* and of the *garantie de ressources licenciement* had de facto established unemployment insurance as the subsystem of the welfare state financing the costs of early exit from the labor market. In contrast to Germany, where the risk of unemployment of elderly workers was distributed among several subsystems of the welfare state, in France this risk was shifted to the unemployment subsystem alone. At the beginning of the 1980s, social expenditures for the *garantie de ressources* constituted more than half of the total expenditures of unemployment insurance, leading to a severe deficit of unemployment insurance and to an increase in the level of payroll taxes (Commissariat Général du Plan 1991: annex 6, table 2, Amira and Roguet 1994).

This section analyzes the evolution of the institutions of early retirement during the early 1980s. During this period, labor force participation rates of elderly workers (aged fifty-five to sixty-five) continued to decline, from 64.6 percent in 1980 to 50.1 percent in 1985. What were the main political causes accounting for the persistence of early retirement? What were the most significant changes in the institutions and policies facilitating the early exit from the labor market? The study of this episode in the political history of the French welfare state will allow me to examine the mechanisms of employers' influence in a context characterized by a high

225

density of preexisting policies and programs. I seek to explore the reliance of French policy makers on public and private policies in an effort to forge a strategic alliance among French unions and employers around a policy outcome that was less costly to the French welfare state.

French planners continued to voice a strong opposition to the policy status quo that privileged early retirement. In preparation for the Eighth Plan (1981–1985), the Commissariat Général du Plan carried out a new study of the demographic and economic challenges facing the French system of social security (Commissariat Général du Plan 1980). The new report entitled *Aging Tomorrow* formulated a policy diagnosis that paralleled the conclusions expressed by the Laroque commission two decades earlier. According to French planners, the financial crisis of the system of social insurance was the consequence of highly unfavorable demographic developments, but demographics alone were not the entire story (Commissariat Général du Plan 1980: 96). These trends had been amplified by existing practices of unions and employers (carried out under the permissive eye of the state) and by existing policies that facilitated and encouraged the early exit from the labor market (Commissariat Général du Plan 1980: 64). The authors of the report regarded policies such as the *garantie de ressource* as a sign of "a collective resignation" and as a symptom of the inability of the French economy to find a solution to the problem of unemployment that either increased employment or distributed the incidence of this risk among different occupational and age groups (Commissariat Général du Plan 1980: 62). While "the economy succumbed to the temptation to use the retirement age to make unemployment more acceptable," the unintended effects of early retirement threatened the architecture of the entire system of social insurance (Commissariat Général du Plan 1980: 63).

In *Aging Tomorrow*, the community of French planners expressed a strong condemnation of the entire ensemble of policies and practices facilitating early retirement. In the words of the report, the introduction of the *garantie de ressources* contributed to a "blurring of risks" that was extremely problematic, as part of the risk of old age was now financed by unemployment insurance. The report recommended "to distinguish between retirement and unemployment" and reintroduce clearer separations between "boundaries" among the different risks in the welfare state (Commissariat Général du Plan 1980: chap. 3). To achieve this objective, the commission proposed to replace age by length of employment as a criterion for retirement (Commissariat Général du Plan 1980: 190–199). As in 1962 and 1971, however, the recommendations of the planning authorities remained, again, unrealized political goals. In contrast to these prior episodes, in 1981 the electoral calculations of the newly elected leftist government turned out to be the primary obstacle to the implementation of a social policy that attached greater considerations to the long-term financial stability of the French old-age insurance. Instead of tightening the eligibility criteria for an old-age pension, as the French planners demanded, the new government of Pierre Mauroy introduced a series of measures that increased the number of potential recipients of an old-age pension and that redistributed the costs of early retirement among the different branches of social insurance.

Immediately after their political victory, French Socialists announced their plans to lower the retirement age from sixty-five to sixty (*Le Monde* 27 June 1981, 13 August 1981). The measure was a fulfillment of an electoral promise of the Socialist Party (and presidential candidate François Mitterand) and a political response to a century-old desideratum of the trade union movement. In addition to these immediate electoral considerations, by lowering the retirement age French socialists hoped to eliminate the necessity of the *garantie de ressources*, to end the decentralized and chaotic "firm-level" early retirement regime, and to restore old-age insurance as the subsystem of the French welfare state regulating the exit from the labor market.

Negotiations between the minister of social solidarity, Nicole Questiaux, and the social partners began shortly after the electoral victory of the French left. However, these negotiations immediately stumbled on the question of the costs of this reform (*Le Monde* 13 August 1981, *Les Échos* 17 August 1981, *Le Matin* 29 September 1981). The lowering of the retirement age increased the number of beneficiaries of an old-age pension by 25 percent, raising significantly expenditures of the old-age insurance subsystem of the French welfare state. According to the calculations of the Ministry of Labor, this measure would contribute to a yearly increase in expenditures totaling 17.6 billion francs (*Le Monde* 6 June 1982, *Le Figaro* 26 March 1982, *Démocratie Moderne* 4 March 1982).[3] To finance these expenditures, French policy makers recommended an increase in old-age insurance contributions by 6 to 7 percent (*Le Monde* 6 June 1982).[4] To convince the social partners

---

[3] According to the Ministry of Social Affairs, these costs were distributed as follows: 11.6 billion francs for the *régime général* and 6.4 billion francs financed by the *régimes complémentaires* (*Le Monde* 6 February 1982).

[4] The same calculations estimated that the level of insurance contributions for the *régime général* would increase from 12.9% to 16.5%, and from 4.4% to 7% for the *régimes complémentaires* (*Le Monde* 6 February 1982).

227

to accept this increase in the level of payroll taxes, the socialist government pointed out that significant savings – estimated at about 15 billion francs – were also possible. These savings were based on the expectation that the lowering of the retirement age would make early retirement policies unnecessary. Given that early retirement policies (such as the *garantie de ressources licenciement*) were financed by unemployment insurance, the French social minister suggested to use some of the "savings" of the unemployment subsystem to subsidize the old-age insurance subsystem of the welfare state. In order to restore old-age insurance as subsystem of the French welfare state that regulated the early exit of elderly workers from the labor market, the minister of social affairs proposed a large transfer in expenditures from unemployment to pension insurance (*Le Monde* 26 March 1982).

Employers opposed these policy proposals as "improvised, costly, and difficult to implement" (*Le Monde* 13 March 1982, *La Croix* 26 March 1982, *Le Matin* 26 March 1982). Large manufacturing producers also disputed the estimations of the costs of a reduction of the retirement age that were presented by French policy makers. Based on the calculations of the Union des Industries Métallurgiques et Minières (UIMM), the real costs of the policy were much higher than the figures presented by the government, resulting in a 28 percent increase in the contributions to old-age insurance (UIMM 1981: 133).[5] Employers also rejected the proposals for a subsidization of old-age insurance by using funds from unemployment insurance. In light of the deficit of unemployment insurance, the suggestion that funds could be transferred to old-age insurance was deceptive. In the words of employers, it was an attempt to "cover a hole by another hole" (*Le Monde* 23 December 1983; cf. *L'Humanité* 23 December 1983). Refusing any additional increase in social insurance contributions, employers proposed the continuation of the existing regime of early retirement based on the *garantie de ressources* (UIMM 1981: 133, 1982: 133–134, *Le Monde* 23 December 1983). In contrast to a uniform retirement age, determined by administrative decree, this policy instrument that was more attuned to the swings of the business cycle gave firms a desirable and needed "flexibility" to adjust their work force during periods of economic

---

[5] According to the estimations of the UIMM employers, the increase in the number of recipients of an old age pension could lead to a 28% increase in the amount of pension insurance contributions. See, for example, Union des Industries Métallurgiques et Minières, *L'Année Métallurgique* (Paris) (1981): chap. 5.

downturns (Conseil National du Patronat Français 1981:3, Guillemard 1991: 148).

An additional possibility of cost-containment remained the lowering of pension benefits. But the recommendation of employers for a decrease of pension replacement rates from 70 to 60 percent triggered strong and vocal protest from trade unions and was quickly abandoned as a realistic policy goal during the negotiations between the state and the social partners (*Le Figaro* 26 March 1983, *Le Syndicalisme* 6 January 1983). Early retirement policies did actually guarantee a replacement rate of 70 percent. Thus, trade unions regarded a level of pension benefits that was lower than the *garantie de ressources* as a loss of a significant social gain and "as a social involution." If the socialist government wanted to go ahead with its plans for a lowering of the retirement age to sixty, it had to find a compromise solution that did not increase the social insurance contributions but that also did not lower the level of social policy benefits.

The institutional structure of the French pension system posed an additional obstacle to the negotiations of a policy compromise among employers, unions, and the state. The French old-age insurance is organized as a two-tiered system, consisting of a basic insurance, the *régime général*, administered by the state and a second tier of occupational pensions, *régimes de retraite complémentaires*, administered by the social partners (Lyon-Caen 1995: 159–170, Dupeyroux 1995, Reynaud 1994: 3–19). The actual pension is financed from these two different sources, with the basic pension of the *régime général* offering a replacement rate of 50 percent, supplemented by additional benefits (totaling around 20 percent of the average wage), financed by the *régimes complémentaires*. Given these two separate sources of funding of the old-age benefits, it was impossible for the state to *guarantee* a replacement rate of 70 percent, after the decrease in the retirement age. The state could persuade or pressure the social partners to "align" the pension benefits paid by the occupational pension funds to a new level, despite the contraction of the contributory base. Or, faced with the reluctance of both unions and employers to raise the level of contributions for occupational pensions, the state could agree to shoulder part of the financial burden by subsidizing the *régimes complémentaires* (Fournier and Questiaux 1989: 664–707).

The compromise solution achieved as the outcome of long negotiations between the social partners and the Ministry of Social Affairs accommodated the policy demands of both unions and employers (*Le Figaro* 28 January 1983, *Le Monde* 26 January 1983, 28 January 1983). To overcome employers' opposition to an increase in social costs and to counteract an increase of insurance contributions for the *régimes complémentaires*, the state agreed to subsidize the occupational pension funds. This generous aid from the state guaranteed at the same time a pension replacement rate of 70 percent that had been demanded by all trade unions. The state agreed to establish a "transitional fund," subsidizing the two major occupational pension funds (AGIRC and ARRCO) for a period of seven years, counteracting the financial disequilibria that resulted from the increase in the number of retirees. In exchange, those unions and employers who were involved in the administration of the second tier of the French pension system agreed to an increase in the level of pension benefits offered by the *régimes complémentaires*, guaranteeing a financially attractive pension to workers retiring at age sixty.

The result of these negotiations was publicly announced as a resounding success. Based on the *ordonnance* of 26 March 1982 (which was supplemented by an agreement among the state and the social partners covering the financial cross-subsidization outlined earlier), the retirement age was lowered to age sixty, without a corresponding loss in income for the retirees (*Journal Officiel* 1982, Mercereau 1982: 452–463, Durin 1982: 468–472, Bordeloup 1984: 656–662). The social policy benefits of elderly workers (more specifically workers in the age-group sixty to sixty-five) were no longer financed by unemployment insurance. Former recipients of the *garantie de resources* became now "retirees." However, unemployment insurance funds were now used to subsidize pension benefits paid by the *régimes complémentaires*. Because of this cross-subsidization, the risk of unemployment of elderly workers was not fully shifted to the pension system. French policy makers had to compromise on an important policy goal.

A few conclusions emerge from this narrative of the negotiations of the reduction in the retirement age. First, similar to earlier episodes in the political history of the French welfare state, representatives of the French state took active steps in forging a coalition among unions and employers. The cooperation of the social partners for the long-term success of the policy was of vital importance, because both unions and employers played a significant role in administering various subsystems of the French welfare state (such as unemployment insurance and the second tier of the pension system). To forge this *strategic alliance* among unions and employers, the French social minister offered important side payments to employers and unions. Among these side payments, the costliest measure for the state was the offer to subsidize the second-tier of the French pension system.

This offer attempted to prevent an explosion in the level of contributions (dreaded by employers) or a reduction in the level of benefits of the early retirees (opposed by trade unions).

The second conclusion of this analysis is that existing firm-level social policies constrained the set of policy choices that was open to reformers. A broader methodological implication is that the analysis of the pathways of business influence has to take into account both the influence exercised by employers as an interest group and the informal capacity of individual firms to change the policy status quo unilaterally through the creation of private social policies. Prior to 1982, the official retirement age was sixty-five, but only 40.6 percent of workers aged sixty to sixty-five were still working. Moreover, to the frustration of French labor market officials, the lowering of the retirement age failed to end firm-level early retirement practices. Because workers in the age-group sixty to sixty-five were now entitled to a pension, individual firms began to negotiate early retirement contracts with workers aged fifty-five to fifty-nine, who were now the eldest age-group within the enterprise. While the number of early retirement cases declined after 1982, they were not eliminated, as French labor market officials had hoped. In 1982, 399,356 French workers received the *garantie de ressources*; the number increased to 409,084 in 1983 and declined to 226,900 in 1987 (Guillemard 1990: 51).[6]

The Origin of Early Retirement Policies in Germany

In contrast to French planners, German policy makers attached a lower political priority to the development of a policy framework increasing the labor market participation of elderly workers (Schön and Rein 1994). To a large extent, this was the consequence of the policy success of German post-war pension reform, guaranteeing very high replacement rates for retirees (Hockerts 1980: 422).[7] The 1957 reform linked pension levels to the evolution of salaries, based on a complex indexation mechanism known as the "dynamic pension formula." Thus retirees became a group fully sharing

---

[6] The evolution of early retirement based on the *garantie de ressources* is as follows: 399,356 (1982); 434,084 (1983); 409,640 (1984); 350,382 (1985); 289,094 (1986); 226,900 (1987); 219,900 (1988).

[7] During the period between 1955 and 1960 the income of retirees rose faster than the income of any other socioeconomic group (Hockerts 1980: 422). During the period between 1955 and 1960, the income of blue-collar workers rose 47.4%, that of white-collar workers rose 48.7%, and the income of retirees rose 54.2%.

the benefits of postwar economic growth in Germany (Hockerts 1980, Nullmeier and Rüb 1993). Activist labor market policies targeted at elderly workers were never a high political priority in Germany, in part because the risk of poverty and social exclusion of the elderly was a much lower possibility.

German courts took the first steps toward the creation of early retirement policies. Faced with an increase in the number of unemployed elderly workers demanding pension benefits, the Federal Social Court modified the entitlement criteria for occupational disability pensions (*Erwerbsunfähigkeitsrenten*). In an influential case of 1969, the Federal Social Court faced the question whether a partially disabled person had the right to a pension if no part-time job was available (Bundessozialgericht 1970: 167–209).[8] The court ruled that an occupational disability pension could be granted to a partially disabled person unable to find a part-time job. According to the court, the real dilemma of this case was whether "the inability to find a part-time job was a risk that is to be covered by the pension or unemployment insurance" (Bundessozialgericht 1970: 176–177). In the justification prefacing the decision, the court expressed its belief that pension insurance (via the special occupational disability pensions) could, in fact, cover some of the risks associated with the worsening of labor market circumstances and that it could absorb some of the risk of unemployment (Bundessozialgericht 1970: 177).

The decision of the Federal Social Court, which involved a redefinition of the notion of "disability" as a legal category, had a number of far-reaching consequences for future labor market developments in Germany (cf. Stone 1984). The most immediate effect was an increase in the number of recipients of occupational disability pensions (Jacobs and Schmähl 1988: 196, *Handelsblatt* 13 July 1981, *Frankfurter Rundschau* 24 September 1981). The share of recipients of occupational disability pensions out of the total number of recipients of pensions increased from 33 percent in 1969 to 43 percent in 1979 (Jacobs, Kohli, and Rein 1991: 186). As a number of influential social insurance-experts noted, the court's ruling transformed the disability pension into a "disability *unemployment compensation*" (Jacobs and Schmähl 1988: 202). The second consequence for Germany's welfare state was the "blurring" of the boundary separating the pension, disability, and unemployment subsystems of the welfare state and the de facto shift

---

[8] Decision of 12 December 1969. See also the case of 10 December 1976 (Bundessozialgericht 1970).

of some of the risk of unemployment to other subsystems of the welfare state. Furthermore, the increase in the number of beneficiaries of pension benefits threatened to create a financial disequilibrium for the German old-age insurance, because this increase was not counteracted by an offsetting increase in the level of contributions to this subsystem of the German welfare state (Kaltenbach 1986, Müller 1981: 37–40).

The second policy facilitating the development of early retirement in Germany was a provision of the Employment Promotion Act (Arbeitsförderungsgesetz), a policy introduced by the SPD-CDU/CSU grand coalition government in 1969. Paragraph 128 of the Employment Promotion Act gave unemployed workers the right to a pension starting at age sixty, five years earlier than the official retirement age (Bundesanstalt für Arbeit 1985). At the time the policy was formulated, unemployment appeared as a problematic but short-lived interlude facing a full-employment economy. This shift of some of the risk of unemployment of elderly workers to the pension system appeared to German policy makers as an expedient and unproblematic solution. Moreover, this solution allowed elderly workers at the end of their career to avoid the stigma associated with unemployment.

The progressive worsening of the labor market circumstances increased the attractiveness of this policy instrument for both firms and employees and diminished the expectations of German policy makers about the short-term character of this policy. Using the legal provision of paragraph 128 of the Employment Promotion Act, large firms began to lay off workers aged fifty-nine and supplement their unemployment compensation for one year, until the former employee became eligible for early pension benefits at age sixty. The decade between 1970 and 1980 is characterized by a rapid expansion of firms' use of paragraph 128 of the Employment Promotion Act (Jacobs et al. 1991: 191, Nascold et al. 1994). The number of male workers receiving pensions at age sixty, after a short period of unemployment, increased from 3,880 in 1967 to 75,802 in 1984, a nineteen-fold increase (cf. Jacobs et al. 1991).

Firms' use of this social policy instrument mirrored largely the ups and down of the business cycles. Early retirement was both a cushion during economic downturns and a mechanism of stabilization of firms' demand for training (Jacobs and Schmähl 1988: 196–205). However, paragraph 128 of the Employment Promotion Act remained a social policy instrument used exclusively by large firms, which had the economic ressources to supplement the unemployment assistance for the elderly workers dismissed at age fifty-nine, by creating a financially attractive "private" social policy that induced elderly workers to retire early.

For almost a decade, early retirement remained confined to the realm of firm-level negotiations between management and works councils. At the beginning of the 1980s, political questions about the design of a national-level early retirement policy erupted on the center of the German political scene, driven by a political offensive for reduction in working time led by German trade unions. Faced with the deterioration of the employment performance of the German economy, trade unions demanded the introduction of a set of policies reducing working time and redistributing the available jobs to the growing numbers of unemployed. While the more radical metalworking union (IG Metall) favored a reduction of the working *week* (demanding a thirty-five-hour week with full compensation), more moderate unions proposed a reduction in working *life* as an appropriate distributional solution (Markovits 1986: 434–435, Swenson 1989: 222–223).[9] The latter "accommodationist" trade unions[10] comprised IG Chemie (the Chemical, Paper and Ceramic Workers' Union), IG Bau (the Construction Workers' Union), NGG (the Food-Processing Workers' Union), and GTB (the Textile Workers' Union). In opposition to IG Metall's demands for a thirty-five-hour week, these unions advocated early retirement as a solution compatible with the competitiveness constraints faced by German firms (Mayr and Jannsen 1984: 433).

The most elaborate plans for the implementation of early retirement were formulated by Günter Döding, the president of the Food-Processing Workers Union (Döding 1982, 1984a, 1984b, Bohner 1982). In contrast to prevailing firm-level early retirement solutions based on paragraph 128 of the Employment Promotion Act, the "Döding model" of early retirement proposed the negotiation of early retirement as part of general wage-bargaining agreements. These proposals recommended that elderly employees stop working at age sixty and receive a compensation package totaling 70 percent of their nominal wages. Unions recommended that the Federal Employment Office finance the compensation of elderly workers. Döding argued that the negotiation of early retirement at the level of the

---

[9] According to Swenson, "accommodationist unions led by the low-pay and organizationally weak Union of Food Processing Workers (Gewerkschaft Nahrung Genuss-Gaststätten) campaigned for state-subsidized early retirement. This approach represented no challenge to managerial prerogatives in production processes, unlike the seven-hour day, thirty-five-hour week favored by IG Metall" (Swenson 1989: 222).

[10] The term belongs to Andrei Markovits.

industry created advantages to all the actors: firms could be compensated for increases in the labor costs through collective wage restraint on the parts of unions, whereas unions could achieve their redistributive objective of work sharing, if the proper institutional guarantees that an unemployed person or a trainee would fill the vacancy resulting from early retirement were incorporated in the wage-bargaining agreement.

The recommendations of unions involved a double institutional change to the policy status quo, paragraph 128 of the Employment Promotion Act. On the one hand, these proposals were an effort to decrease the *control* enjoyed by individual firms over the timing and broad conditions of early retirement. By incorporating early retirement as part of industry-level agreements, these plans implied an increase in unions' control over the initiation of these policies. Second, unions' plans reopened the questions about the distribution of the costs of early retirement among unions, employers, and the different subsystems of the German welfare state. As such, these plans aroused understandable interest among policy makers of the Ministry for Social Affairs and the German business community.

The Preferences of German Employers

The previous discussion has characterized the policy context that has facilitated the emergence and rapid expansion of early retirement in Germany. German employers took strong advantage of the policy opportunities created by the Employment Promotion Act and of the loosening of the eligibility conditions for disability pensions. This section examines the factors affecting the policy preferences of German firms. Do we find disagreement among German employers about the usefulness of the early retirement option? What variables explain firms' use of this social policy instrument? To investigate these questions, I rely on two broad types of sources. Reports of German labor market authorities allow me to study the sectoral distribution of early retirement in Germany. To explore in greater depth the social policy preferences of German firms and their position toward policy proposals to shift to a corporatist negotiation of early retirement, I rely on a collection of documents found at the archive of the Central Confederation of German Employers (Bundesvereinigung der Deutschen Arbeitgeberverbände) and a series of publications of the Central Federation of German *Handwerk*.

Early retirement generates important, albeit intangible policy *benefits* to employers. These policies allow firms to circumvent existing employment protection regulations and shed elderly workers with no (or very low) opposition from trade unions. But early retirement involves also significant costs to the firm. To take advantage of the provisions of the Employment Protection Act and to make the early retirement option attractive to their employees, German firms had to supplement the unemployment benefits of elderly workers (for a period up to three years) (Schmähl and Gatter 1994). According to estimates of the German Ministry of Social Affairs, the costs of early retirement for a German firm totaled around 30,000 DM per employee (*Frankfurter Allgemeine* 5 January 1984). Due to these initial "setup" costs of early retirement policies, we expect large firms to take stronger advantage of the early retirement option as compared with small producers.

Large manufacturing producers exploited the opportunities for early retirement created by existing legislation. According to a study of the German Ministry of Social Affairs, every second large firm had used the early retirement option created by the Employment Promotion Act (*Süddeutsche Zeitung* 27 January 1984). Several other studies confirm the stronger incidence of early retirement among firms employing more than five hundred workers (Kühlewind 1986: 209–232, Hoffmann and Kühlewind 1984: 135–157). In describing the employment practices of large firms, Norbert Blüm, Germany's labor minister of the Christian Democratic government, characterized them as strategies of employers "to shift costs to unemployment and pension insurance" (Blüm 1995c: 12). In response to policy proposals to move to a sectoral negotiation of early retirement, the Central Confederation of German Employers (BDA) strongly defended the policy status quo, which was characterized by a high level of "flexibility" (*Der Arbeitgeber* 1984: 11, Bundesvereinigung der Deutschen Arbeitgeberverbände 1984a, 1984b). Given the very different labor market needs of enterprises within the same sector, the shift in the negotiation of early retirement to the level of the industry could result in immobilism and inflexibility and a significant rise in the social costs of firms (*Der Arbeitgeber* 1984: 12). Summarizing the policy position of large manufacturing producers, the BDA stated that "we cannot abandon the principle of absolute optionality [*Freiwilligkeit*] of employers" (*Der Arbeitgeber* 1984).

In contrast to large firms, the main association representing the interests of Germany's small and medium-sized enterprises strongly opposed all existing provisions facilitating early retirement. The Central Association of German *Handwerk* denounced on repeated occasions large firms' reliance on early retirement as a misuse of the generosity of the German social insurance system and demanded legislative action to end these practices

(Zentralverband des Deutschen Handwerks 1982a, 1983c, 1983d, 1983f). "We need to stop the trend toward early retirement," wrote the main publication of this association. Early retirement policies were characterized as a "dangerous boomerang" that led to an increase in the overall nonwage costs (Zentralverband des Deutschen Handwerks 1984a: 1). The Central Association of German *Handwerk* characterized early retirement as a policy that "posed a fundamental threat to the existence of the *Mittelstand*, by encouraging unemployment and by increasing the nonwage labor costs of all German firms" (Zentralverband des Deutschen Handwerks 1982a).

A study of the skill composition of the early retirement beneficiaries conducted by German labor market authorities found that 48.2 percent of early retirees were qualified skilled workers (*Facharbeiter*) and 24 percent unskilled workers (*nicht qualifiziert*) (Kühlewind 1986: 231). This distribution of early retirees seems to disconfirm the hypothesis of some welfare state scholars that German firms targeted this policy instrument exclusively to low-skill workers.

The third hypothesis formulated in Chapter 2 has suggested that the risk incidence of a firm is a predictor of the social policy preferences of the firms. The demographic composition of the work force can be used as a measure of the risk incidence of employers. High-risk industries have an elderly work force as compared with the economy-wide average, whereas low-risk industries have a younger work force. We expect firms with an elderly work force to rely on the early retirement option more extensively. A study of the demographic composition of the German work force found that in 1980, 8.7 percent of German employees were older than fifty-five (Schmähl and Gatter 1994: 448). Examining the variation of the age structure across German sectors, we find the highest percentage of elderly workers[11] in agriculture and forestry (27.7 percent). Among manufacturing industries, leather and textile (16.96 percent), chemical (11.58 percent), and basic metal (11.15 percent) industries have a more aged demographic structure than the economy-wide average (Kohli and Rein 1991: 80). The demographic composition of the work force explains only partially firms' use of the early retirement option. The only high-risk sector that made extensive use of the early retirement option comprised employers in the chemical industry. According to the estimations of German labor market authorities, the widest use of early retirement was in this sector (IAB 1986: 108). Other high-risk

---

[11] That is, workers aged over fifty-five.

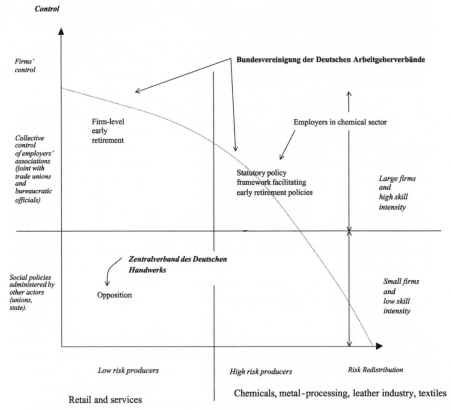

Figure 6.2 German employers and the development of early retirement policies

producers, such as those in agriculture or textiles, made only very low use of the early retirement option (IAB 1986).

Figure 6.2 summarizes the findings on business preferences. In the case of early retirement, the dominant sectoral conflict among German employers was the conflict among large and small firms. Large firms were the policy beneficiaries of a early retirement policies. Firms of the *Mittelstand* were losers of these policies. Unable to offer the same generous "private" compensation packages to induce elderly workers to stop working prior to the retirement age, they were, at the same time, disadvantaged by the rising pension and unemployment insurance contributions. The following section examines the political implications of this sectoral conflict among employers for the early retirement reforms introduced by the German government during the mid 1980s.

A Pyrrhic Victory of the State: The Negotiation of the Early Retirement Act (Vorruhestandsgesetz)

At the beginning of the 1980s, the question of early retirement moved to the center of policy debates in Germany. An important event that focused public deliberations on this issue was the publication of a report of Germany's Council of Economic Experts (Sozialbeirat) discussing the long-term trends facing Germany's old-age insurance (Sozialbeirat 1981, Borchert 1993). The report brought to public attention the precarious financial equilibrium of Germany's old-age insurance. Unfavorable demographic developments – such as increase in life-expectancy and a decrease in birthrates – had fundamentally altered the old-age dependency ratio of the German pension system.[12] The wide expansion of firm-level early retirement practices further accentuated the financial pressures faced by this subsystem of the German welfare state. The reduction of the number of persons contributing to pension insurance had not been counterbalanced by a corresponding reduction in the level of pension benefits, straining, thus, the financial resources of old-age insurance.

In response to this alarming report, German policy makers launched a political offensive to stop the financial hemorrhaging of the pension system. The first efforts toward policy change were initiated in 1982 by the coalition government led by the Social Democratic Party. A special commission, led by Labor Minister Ehrenberg, formulated a number of policy recommendations that borrowed heavily from the early retirement plans formulated by the Food-Processing Workers' Union (*Frankfurter Rundschau* 27 February 1982). The commission recommended to lower the social policy benefits of early retirees to 68 percent of their wages. It also suggested to increase the costs of early retirement to firms, by mandating firms' contributions for their early retirees to *both* unemployment and pension insurance (*Frankfurter Rundschau* 27 February 1982). The recommendations of the commission were at the basis of an early retirement legislation submitted by the Social Democratic government to the Bundestag in 1982 and to the Bundesrat in 1983.

These proposals met with strong opposition from employers. Large firms protested against the increase in their nonwage labor costs.[13] Furthermore, they opposed the proposal to negotiate early retirement as part

---

[12] This ratio was predicted to deteriorate to 3:2 in 2030 and to 1:1 in 2050 (Sozialbeirat 1981).

[13] In the case of a firm-level-negotiated early retirement (based on paragraph 128 of the Employment Promotion Act), a firm was not responsible for a continuing payment of

of wage-bargaining agreements, expressing a strong support for firm-based early retirement (Heck 1982, *Frankfurter Allgemeine* 6 January 1982). Small firms joined this protest against the Social Democratic proposals of reform. In a number of public statements, the Central Association of German *Handwerk* (ZDH) "warned" against the increase in nonwage labor costs that were an inevitable consequence of the proposals (Zentralverband des Deutschen Handwerks 1982a, 1982b). Furthermore, small firms feared that their policy demands would not carry much weight during industry-level wage bargaining and thus opposed the loss of the voluntary character (*Freiwilligkeit*) of early retirement.

Early retirement reform was one of the first political issues on the agenda of reform of the Christian Democratic coalition government. The policy proposals of the new government were remarkably similar to the proposals of its Social Democratic predecessor. The aim of these reforms was the effort to improve the financial equilibrium of the pension system, or, in the words of Labor Minister Norbert Blüm, to "defend the actuarial basis of the pension system threatened by so many alien claims." The goal of the state was to shift back to employers some of the costs "externalized by firms onto the welfare system," by mandating employers' contributions to *old-age insurance* for their early retirees. Simultaneously, early retirement reform was formulated as a political alternative to union proposals calling for a reduction in the working time.

To carry out these goals, Labor Minister Blüm submitted two early retirement bills to the Bundestag. The first law, the Law of the Adaptation of the Employment Promotion Act, mandated the obligation of employers to compensate the pension system for the loss in revenue associated with early retirement. The second law, the Early Retirement Act (*Vorruhestandsgesetz*), proposed to shift the negotiation of early retirement from the firm level to the industry level. An important fraction of the Christian Democratic coalition that represented the economic and policy interests of large firms (*Wirtschaftsflügel*) opposed both of these measures. Thus, to carry out his ambitious political project, Labor Minister Blüm had to enlist the political support of two important factions of the Christian Democratic coalition. These were the *Mittelstandsfraktion*, close to the interests of small firms and

contributions to pension and sickness insurance. In contrast, based on the Ehrenberg-Döding plan, the firm remained responsible for these costs. One of the goals of the plan was to counteract the decrease in the number of persons contributing to the different subsystems of the German welfare state.

the social committees (*Sozialausschüsse*), representing labor interests within the Christian Democratic Union (Winter 1989, 1990, Wood 1996).

The first element of the policy reform attempted to minimize the financial implications of early retirement for the German pension system. In a number of public statements attacking the labor-shedding practices of large firms, Labor Minister Blüm pointed out that every second large firm had made use of paragraph 128 of the Employment Promotion Act (*Süddeutsche Zeitung* 27 January 1984). "Although large firms collectively oppose the shortening of working life, they practice it individually, financed by the majority of taxpayers" (Blüm 1983a: 5). According to the estimates of the German Social Ministry, firm-level early retirement contributed to a yearly loss of 1.7 billion DM in unpaid pension insurance contributions (Blüm 1983b: 25–26, *Süddeutsche Zeitung* 12 January 1984). The crucial element of this political attack on the privileged practices of large firms was the "Law of the Adaptation of the Employment Promotion Act and of the Pension Insurance to the Introduction of Early Retirement Benefits" drafted by the Ministry of Labor and Social Affairs and approved by the cabinet in the fall of 1983 (Deutscher Bundestag 1983c). The law required employers who made use of the early retirement option (based on the existing provisions of the Employment Promotion Act) to pay contributions to pension insurance for their early retired workers for a period of three years *after* the termination of the employment relationship (Deutsches Institut für Wirtschaftsforschung 1984: 210–211). Under the provisions of the Employment Promotion Act, employers faced the obligation to repay to the Federal Employment Office (which administered unemployment insurance) the costs of unemployment compensation for one year. Under the proposed new law, large firms were responsible for *both* unemployment and pension contributions. This measure was estimated to raise the costs of early retirement to the firms from about 30,000 to 70,000 DM per employee (*Frankfurter Allgemeine* 21 December 1983, 5 January 1984).

In turning against large firms and against the economic wing (*Wirtschaftsflügel*) within the Christian-Democratic Coalition,[14] Norbert Blüm attempted to enlist the political support of the *Mittelstandsfraktion* in the Bundestag and of the economic associations of small firms, primarily that of the Central Association of German *Handwerk* (Zentralverband des

---

[14] On the opposition of employers of large firms, see, for example, the critique raised by employers of the chemical industry. See Informationsbrief Bundesarbeitgeberverband Chemie quoted in *Handelsblatt* 2 October 1984.

241

Deutschen Handwerks) (*Handelsblatt* 2 October 1984). This was a skillful political maneuver to exploit the strong policy disagreement among employers and to drive a wedge between the interests of large and small firms. On numerous occasions, *Mittelstand* firms had expressed their unambiguous hostility toward any forms of working time reduction (Zentralverband des Deutschen Handwerks 1982c: 649).[15] Small firms opposed both unions' demands for a thirty-five-hour working week and policy proposals considering the possibility of a shortening of working life (Zentralverband des Deutschen Handwerks 1983a: 290–291, 1983b: 407–408, 1983c: 416–420, 1983e: 735–739). According to small firms, any form of working-time reduction did not contribute to "the creation of new jobs but the destruction of existing ones" (Zentralverband des Deutschen Handwerks 1982a: 11). In attempting to win the political support of the skeptical representatives of the *Handwerk*, Labor Minister Blüm depicted the existing early retirement practices as "a conspiracy between management and works councils" and as "social policy with built-in privileges" that had been misused exclusively by large firms (*Volksblatt Berlin* 18 March 1984). As an important side payment to small firms, the Law of the Adaptation of the Employment Promotion Act excluded firms with less than sixty employees from the requirement to continue to pay insurance contributions to pension insurance in case of early retirement.

In their first public statement about the early retirement legislative initiative of the Christian Democratic coalition, representatives of the *Mittelstand* welcomed these policy changes. The Central Association of German *Handwerk* pointed out that by lowering the amount of "alien" claims on the pension system, the social insurance charges faced by employers could be de facto lowered (Zentralverband des Deutschen Handwerks 1983g: 760). Yet small firms opposed the proposal to shift the negotiation of early retirement to the industry level, arguing that this measure would inevitably contribute to an increase in the nonwage labor costs of firms. To prevent this increase in their nonwage labor costs, small firms demanded several compensation mechanisms. First, they called for a special provision, granting small firms the freedom to "opt out" of early retirement agreements that were negotiated at the industry level. As the Central Association of German *Handwerk* summarized this policy priority, "we demand the same optionality

---

[15] Source quotes a letter of the president of the Zentralverband des Deutschen Handwerks, Schnittler to Chancellor Helmut Kohl (Zentralverband des Deutschen Handwerks 1982c: 649).

[*Freiwilligkeit*] in the choice of early retirement both for employers and for employees" (Zentralverband des Deutschen Handwerks 1984b: 13). The second compensatory arrangement demanded by the *Mittelstandsfraktion* of the Christian Democratic coalition consisted of a combination of financial inducements and subsidies targeted exclusively at small firms (*Frankfurter Allgemeine* 13 December 1983). For example, *Mittelstandsfirms* demanded an increase in the subsidies paid by the Federal Employment Office to firms with less than sixty employees, if the firms hired new workers to replace early retirees. For firms employing fewer than ten workers, the *Mittelstandsfraktion* demanded a financial compensation for all costs associated with early retirement.

The second draft bill of the Early Retirement Act that resulted from negotiations in a cabinet meeting of December 1983 made concessions to some of the policy demands of small firms (*Frankfurter Allgemeine* 21 December 1983). Industry-level early retirement was not mandatory for firms with less than twenty employees. The requirement to compensate unemployment insurance for the loss in revenue associated with early retirement was also waived for small firms (*Süddeutsche Zeitung* 9 February 1984). Labor Minister Blüm used the opportunity created by the first deliberations of the Early Retirement Act on the floor of the Bundestag to praise the elements of the new law that were friendly to the interests of the *Mittelstand* (Deutscher Bundestag 1984a: 3425–3471). According to Blüm, what distinguished the policy proposal of the Christian Democratic Party from the competing policy proposal of the Social Democratic Party were special compensatory provisions for small firms (Deutscher Bundestag 1984a: 3454). The Christian Democrats, Blüm argued, were ready to "protect" small firms from an increase in the nonwage labor costs, by granting firms with less than twenty employees the freedom to opt out of industry-level early retirement agreements.

The Central Association of German *Handwerk* found these few concessions insufficient. Small firms continued the campaign of political opposition to the Early Retirement Act,[16] demanding the "strengthening of the *Mittelstandskomponente*." Some of the critical demands of the *Handwerk* were taken up during the policy deliberations of the Bundesrat (Zentralverband des Deutschen Handwerks 1984a: 2–13, 1984d: 107). The joint meeting of

---

[16] The Zentralverband des Deutschen Handwerks estimated that the Early Retirement Act could bring an increase in the nonwage labor costs of 18,000 to 27,000 DM per worker (Zentralveband des Deutschen Handwerks 1984b: 13).

the minister presidents of the *Länder* proposed two policy changes, which reflected the concerns and worries of small firms. The first change recommended the expansion of the optionality (*Freiwilligkeit*) or early retirement for a larger number of small firms (Zentralverband des Deutschen Handwerks 1984d: 107).[17] The second policy change recommended an additional increase in the financial compensation of those small firms that rehired a worker to fill the vacancy created as a result of early retirement (*Frankfurter Allgemeine* 1 February 1984). In addition, policy makers of the upper house demanded an increase in the amount of subsidies of the state to those small firms with a higher percentage of elderly workers (*Frankfurter Allgemeine* 4 February 1984). The political forces opposing the Early Retirement Act – consisting of an unusual coalition of interests of small firms and Social Democrats – achieved a resounding victory on the floor of the Bundesrat (Deutscher Bundesrat 1984: 1–18). In an effort to uphold the policy interests of small firms, Bayern abstained. This abstention brought about the defeat of the early retirement legislation on 6 February 1984.

This political setback in the Bundesrat increased the worries of Christian Democratic policy makers about a potential unraveling of this important policy initiative. After this defeat, important political figures of the conservative coalition called for the "mobilization and concentration of political forces" and demanded from the *Mittelstandsvereinigung* "a sacrifice to the *Zeitgeist*" (*Süddeutsche Zeitung* 9 February 1984). As a result of this rallying of political forces, the bargaining position of the association of small firms (*Mittelstandsvereinigung*) decreased after the defeat of the Early Retirement Act in the *Bundesrat* (*Süddeutsche Zeitung* 9 February 1984). These exhortations were effective: small firms moderated their policy demands. The Central Association of German *Handwerk* abandoned its demands for an increase in the subsidies paid by labor market authorities to small firms that made use of the early retirement option, a demand that was highly unpopular among CDU politicians (Zentralverband des Deutschen Handwerks 1984e: 171). By giving up these demands, the *Mittelstandsfraktion* concentrated their political efforts on formulation of protective mechanisms (*Härteklauseln*) for small firms with especially unfavorable age structure (Zentralverband des Deutschen Handwerks 1984e: 171, 1984f: 188–189). In a public hearing of the Committee for Social Affairs of the Bundestag, the Central Association of German *Handwerk* demanded

---

[17] More specifically, the proposal recommended to extend the optionality of the law to all firms employing less than sixty workers.

the right of employers to veto any early retirement proposals, if more than 5 percent of the work force within an enterprise were eligible for early retirement benefits. Christian Democratic policy makers accommodated this policy demand of small firms. A new draft bill approved by the cabinet after the political defeat in the Bundesrat approved an "exceptional clause" (*Ausnahmeregelung*) for small firms (*Volksblatt Berlin* 10 March 1984). This measure protected small firms with an unfavorable age structure from the adverse financial consequences of the Early Retirement Act (*Frankfurter Allgemeine* 28 November 1983).

After the defeat of the early retirement bill in the Bundesrat, the relationship between the labor minister and the *Mittelstandsfraktion* deteriorated sharply. Consequently, Labor Minister Blüm was forced to turn for political support to his own political base, the social committees (*Sozialausschüsse*). Social committees represented the interests of labor within the Christian Democratic coalition. Understanding their pivotal policy position after the political setback in the Bundesrat, social committees radicalized their policy demands (*Frankfurter Allgemeine* 28 November 1983). They demanded the lowering of the retirement age to fifty-eight in order to "increase the attractiveness of the early retirement option for employees" and "to enhance the employment effect of this labor market policy." This demand was in direct contradiction with the most significant policy objective of this political initiative, which was the effort to improve the long-term financial prospects of the pension system. However, social committees were granted this additional concession, because their support was critical for a political victory of the bill (*Frankfurter Allgemeine* 10 March 1984).

This intense effort of the labor minister to forge a political majority in support of the bill ultimately paid off. The Early Retirement Act was approved by the Bundestag on 29 March and by the Bundesrat on 4 April 1984 (Deutscher Bundestag 1984b: 4281–4307). Two important fractions of the Christian Democratic coalition, the *Mittelstandsfraktion* and the labor wing (*Sozialausschüsse*) supported the bill. The economic wing of the coalition (*Wirtschaftsflügel*) – representing the interests of large firms – joined the Social Democrats and the Greens, in opposing the bill. The numerous side payments and concessions obtained by small firms and the social committees in exchange for their support of the law diluted some of the desired fiscal implications of this legislation. The Early Retirement Act brought about two policy changes. The negotiation of early retirement was shifted to the industry level, as part of yearly wage bargaining agreements. Second, the bill increased the early retirement costs for employers and promised

245

to bring about a much-awaited improvement of the financial outlook of old-age insurance.

This highly contested political reform has important implications for our understanding of the politics of business influence. In this episode, German labor market authorities achieved a surprising political victory over the interests of large firms. What made this political victory possible was a carefully crafted political alliance among small firms and the labor wing of the Christian Democratic coalition. As a skillful political entrepreneur, Norbert Blüm used his agenda-setting power and significant inducements and side payments to these actors to forge this policy compromise. To sustain this strategic alliance, the German minister of social affairs was willing to deviate from a number of important policy objectives.

How consequential were these policy reforms? The early retirement act curtailed large firms' discretionary power over the introduction of these measures. As a result of this policy change, about 70 percent of the early retirement cases were negotiated as part of industry-level agreements (Schmähl and Gatter 1994: 441). Although the policy raised the costs of early retirement for firms, it did not stop the process of early withdrawal from the labor market. Labor force participation rates of male workers (aged fifty-five to sixty-five) continued to decline in Germany, from 60.9 percent in 1984 to 58.7 percent in 1988 (Mares 2001b: 299). As a result of the continuation of this externalization strategy of German firms, the level of contributions to old-age insurance did not decline. Employers' contributions to pension insurance experienced a slight overall increase from 9.25 percent of wages in 1982 to 9.6 percent in 1986 and 9.35 percent in 1988 (Bundesministerium für Arbeit und Sozialordnung 1998: table 7.7). Finally, early retirement policies failed to have a significant impact as a policy combating unemployment. The reemployment rates of firms who had made use of the early retirement option remained very small. Thus, the victory of the state against large firms was only a Pyrrhic victory. Due to the density of existing policies that facilitated early retirement, the efforts of the German state to close off the private early retirement option was largely unsuccessful.

Conclusion

This chapter has analyzed the role played by French and German employers in the development of early retirement policies. The analysis has revealed the existence of two distinct stages in the evolution of these policies. In a first stage, changes in the entitlement conditions for disability and unemployment insurance have opened up wide room for private early retirement practices of large firms. At this policy stage, individual firms were the primary driving force in the development of early retirement. The second stage of reform has been characterized by the concerted attempt of labor market authorities to regain control over the process of early retirement and to minimize the adverse financial implications of these policies for a variety of subsystems of the welfare state. While this offensive has led to the transformation of existing policies of early retirement, these measures were unsuccessful in reversing the trend toward early exit from the labor market.

The explanation for the development of early retirement policies presented in this chapter – stressing political bargaining among unions, employers, and representatives of labor market authorities – stands in contrast to the account of the welfare regime literature. Scholars such as Gøsta Esping-Andersen or Jan Kolberg have attributed the cross-national variation in the character of early retirement policies to the "hidden" institutional logic of different welfare regimes. For example, Esping-Andersen has suggested that "the Nordic cluster is characterized by low exit, the continental European welfare state by very high exit; the Anglo-Saxon world, except for Britain, by moderate exit" (Esping-Andersen 1990: 151, Esping-Andersen and Kolberg 1992a). These arguments postulating hidden institutional logics of welfare regimes as explanations of cross-national differences in early retirement policies are extremely problematic. First, these explanations are highly functionalistic, lacking coherent micrologics. Why do universalistic welfare regimes maximize total labor force participation rates, while conservative welfare regimes decrease participation in the labor market? Second, these explanations are static. They are unable to account for *change over time* in the character of early retirement policies. The preceding analysis has suggested that significant provisions of these policies have been repeatedly renegotiated. Finally, explanations stressing the determinant role of the welfare regime cannot account for differences in early retirement policies among countries belonging to the same "welfare regime," such as the difference among French and German institutions of early retirement.

This chapter complements the welfare-regime-based explanation in two important ways. In an effort to build in a micrologic to these analyses, I examine the policy preferences of different firms toward early retirement. The analysis reveals the existence of a strong, intersectoral conflict among employers over several dimensions of policy design. Large manufacturing

247

employers favored a policy outcome in which firms retained both a high discretion over the introduction of early retirement and the ability to externalize some of the costs of these policies to a number of subsystems of the welfare state. Because small firms lacked the resources to develop firm-level retirement policies, they did not benefit from the policy environment that made early retirement possible. In both France and Germany, small firms opposed the early retirement practices of large firms, which contributed to an increase in their social insurance contributions.

This specification of the policy preferences of employers allows us to characterize the coalitional dynamics of the stage of policy reform. An important policy objective of both German and French labor market authorities has been an effort to regain control over the process of early retirement. In both countries, labor market authorities have attempted to orchestrate cross-class alliances in support of a change to the policy status quo. The creation of these cross-class alliances was a costly process that involved significant side payments to various actors in exchange for their political support. The persistence of early retirement policies in France and Germany is a consequence of the willingness of French and German labor market authorities to incur these costs to *sustain* these cross-class alliances.

7

Conclusions

During the past four decades, research on the development of modern welfare states has been dominated by theories stressing the political centrality of class conflict. Marxist or neo-Marxist studies in the 1960s, power resource scholars in the 1970s, and more recent studies exploring the political determinants of various "welfare regimes" have characterized the political struggles over the enactment of a new social policy as a zero-sum conflict among labor-based political organizations and political associations representing the interests of capital (Stephens 1979, Esping-Andersen and Korpi 1985).

This literature has been premised on a set of assumptions that, at first, seem intuitively plausible. The first critical assumption made by these studies is that "the welfare state is a class issue. Logically and historically, its principal proponents and defenders are movements of the working class" (Shalev 1983: 319). Social policy compensates labor for its disadvantaged position in the labor market by reducing the income losses experienced by workers during employment-related risks. Using the terminology formulated by these studies, social policies "decommodify" workers: they weaken the dependence of workers on the labor market alone as a source of income (Esping-Andersen 1990: 20).

The second critical assumption underpinning this research is that employers have resisted the expansion of policies of social insurance and that they opposed the introduction of a new social policy. As Huber and Stephens argue, "business associations, like their political allies in the secular right, preferred as little legislation and as much flexibility in social and labor market policy as possible" (Huber and Stephens 2001: chap. 5). Most scholars justify the assumption of business opposition to social insurance by invoking both financial and labor market considerations of firms. Employers, these studies argue, oppose social policies because these are financed by payroll taxes and thus raise the nonwage labor costs of firms. Similarly, most studies assume that one of the goals of employers is to lower the bargaining power of workers. Consequently, firms will oppose policies that maintain income streams in the event of employment interruptions because these policies raise the reservation wages of their employees.

These two premises have been the foundation of a broad empirical literature examining cross-national variation in the character of social policy. Most scholars have explained cross-national differences in welfare state trajectories as the result of differences in the political mobilization of labor movements. Consider the often invoked comparison between Scandinavian social policy developments and policy developments in the United States. Even Theda Skocpol, a scholar who assigns an important role to differences in institutional arrangements, invokes the logic of class conflict to explain the different social policy outcomes. As Skocpol argues, "the political class struggle between workers and capital helps to explain why the United States has not developed a comprehensive welfare state along postwar Scandinavian lines" (Skocpol 1995: 18). Among the most significant empirical results generated by quantitative approaches to the study of the welfare state is that the two variables measuring labor strength – the degree of organizational centralization of the labor movement and the parliamentary strength of socialist parties – remain the strongest predictors of the size of the welfare state. Variables measuring labor strength are also strongly correlated with numerous indexes measuring more qualitative differences among welfare states, such as the level of "universalism" (absence of means testing in social policy) and the level of "decommodification" of social policy programs (measured as high income replacement rates, long benefit periods, and short waiting periods) (Esping-Andersen 1990: chap. 5).

This book has challenged the theoretical and empirical claims of these studies. An alternative model, developed in this book, suggests that capital and labor *can have common and converging preferences* over a broad range of questions of social policy design. Under some conditions, firms support the enactment of a new social policy, not out of altruism or generosity, but out of self-interest. A key theoretical objective has been to specify the conditions under which profit-maximizing firms, facing competition in domestic or international markets, support the enactment of a new social policy program, and to examine the type of social policies supported by different firms.

The starting point of the analysis has been the observation that policies of social insurance mitigate the reluctance of both firms and workers to invest resources in skill formation. For both firms and workers, decisions about investing in skills are fraught with uncertainty, because labor market contracts cannot specify in advance the obligations of each party during employment interruptions. During moments of employment loss – such as sickness, disability, or unemployment – workers who have invested in skills will face greater income losses than workers who have not made these investments. Hence, skilled workers will need some guarantees that their compensation during employment losses will be *proportional to their wages*. Social policies with earnings-related benefits that are either organized privately by individual firms or associations of employers or as contributory insurance policies provide these guarantees to workers. Thus, firms will either provide private-type social policies or support the introduction of compulsory social insurance programs to induce workers to make these investments in skills. In this alternative account of the origin of social insurance, institutions of social protection help employers overcome market failures in skill formation (cf. Estevez-Abe, Iversen, and Soskice 2001).

The institutional design of social policies matters to firms. The factors motivating employers to participate in the broad political negotiations leading to the introduction of a new social policy are not *only* defensive reasons, last-minute attempts to counteract the fiscal *largesse* of administrative officials and an increase in the bargaining power of workers. These considerations are important, but they do not capture the full range of motivations of employers. Firms have important concerns about the impact of social policies on their labor market practices – on their ability to recruit and retain skilled workers and to shed less productive workers quietly and without any confrontation with labor. Policy questions concerning the relationship between the level of social policy benefits and the wages of the workers, the length and duration of eligibility for policy benefits for different kinds of workers, and the restrictions on the kind of jobs that high-skill workers can accept during periods of employment interruption are very important to firms. The analysis of this book has developed (and tested) a range of predictions about the social policy preferences of employers and the details of policy design that are important to firms.

These concluding remarks summarize the two broad sets of findings of the book. The first results address questions about the social policy preferences of employers. What are the calculations made by firms during the enactment of a new social policy? What are the most important factors that predict differences in the social policy preferences of employers? The second set of findings concerns the type of cross-class alliances that form during the process of social policy reform. What sectors of the business community will participate in these cross-class alliances? What are the social policies supported by various cross-class alliances? The final section discusses the implication of the cross-class alliance perspective advanced in this book for understanding recent patterns of social policy change in advanced industrialized democracies.

Findings on Business Preferences

The model of business preferences for institutions of social insurance developed in this book has identified the questions of policy design that have a high salience for firms and the most significant policy trade-offs faced by employers during the process of social policy development. I have developed a number of propositions about the ideal social policy outcomes favored by different firms and about the most significant cleavages in the business community formed during the introduction of a new social policy.

The starting assumption of the model developed in Chapter 2 has been that existing social policies can be mapped in a two-dimensional social policy space. The axes of the social policy space represent the two issues that are distributionally most divisive during the introduction of a new social policy. The first set of questions concerns the scope of social policy. How broad should the level of social insurance coverage be? Should social policy be restricted to the participants of a single firm? Should social insurance be mandatory for the entire population of a country? What should be the relationship between the incidence of various risks and the level of social insurance contributions? The second divisive question of policy design concerns the distribution of responsibilities in the administration of social insurance among unions, employers, and state bureaucrats. What should be the role of the state and of private actors in the determination of insurance contributions and in the allocation of insurance benefits?

The empirical results confirm the main theoretical predictions of the model developed in Chapter 2. Figure 7.1 maps the major empirical findings of the book. The first result is that the peak associations dominated by large firms have supported either private-type or contributory insurance policies. These associations have favored these policies over alternative means-tested or universalistic social policies. This is a very robust empirical pattern that holds for all cases analyzed in the book. During the 1880s, the Central Federation of German Industrialists (Centralverband Deutscher

Findings on Business Preferences

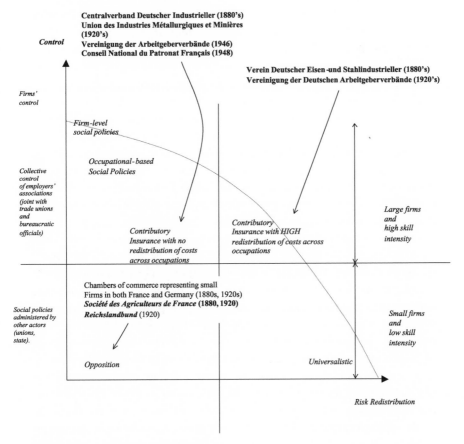

Figure 7.1 Possible strategic alliances

Industrieller) favored a "corporatist" organization of accident insurance administered by employers' associations and rejected proposals for an accident insurance policy financed and administered by the state (Centralverband Deutscher Industrieller 1884: 34). During the same period, large manufacturing employers in France (Comité des Forges, Comité Central des Houillères de France) also pursued a policy solution that guaranteed the autonomy of institutions of social insurance established by employers (Réforme Sociale 1894: 345). During the interwar period, the peak association representing large manufacturing employers in Germany (Vereinigung der Deutschen Arbeitgeberverbände) opposed the means-tested policy of unemployment assistance and demanded the introduction of a compulsory unemployment insurance that was administered by associations of labor

253

and capital. In France, the Union of Metallurgical and Mining Industries (Union des Industries Métallurgiques et Minières) also recommended to situate "the firm at the foundation of institutions of social insurance" (UIMM 1922). During the first years following World War II, the main associations representing manufacturing producers in both countries favored a return to contributory insurance policies. In Germany, the Federation of Employers' Associations (Vereinigung der Arbeitgeberverbände) defended the importance of parity representation of capital and labor in the administration of social insurance policies. French employers also opposed proposals of policy makers to exclude business from the administration of social insurance. Finally, as Chapter 6 has analyzed, private, firm-level social policies introduced by large manufacturing firms were at the basis of the development of early retirement policies in France and Germany.

A second empirical result is that firms with a more skilled work force have favored private-type or contributory insurance policies. The important policy considerations for employers that rely on a skilled work force are considerations about the *relative* levels of policy benefits of high-skill and low-skill workers. These firms do not attempt to lower the reservation wage of all workers (as previous studies have assumed). On the contrary, they favor social policies that raise the relative reservation wage of high-skill workers. A statement of the Federation of German Employers' Associations (Vereinigung der Deutschen Arbeitgeberverbände) in support of a contributory insurance policy with earnings-related benefits illustrates this linkage between social policies and the skill needs of these firms. As these employers argued, "The condition of unemployment leads to changes in the profession of the unemployed, which is an extremely unfavorable situation for employers who can hold on to their skilled workers only with great difficulty. These hardships will become extremely severe during those years when the problem of skill formation of workers will become extremely severe.... Purely insurance based considerations call for the importance of the gradation of the insurance benefits on the level of wages and the introduction of a *Lohnklassensystem*" – that is, a policy of unemployment insurance with earnings-related benefits (Vereinigung der Deutschen Arbeitgeberverbände 1925). Similarly, during the postwar period, associations of employers in mining and railways defended the existing institutions of social insurance administered by the federations of employers in these industries. As these employers argued, social policies with earnings-related benefits played an important role in recruiting new generations of workers to these professions (Wirtschaftsvereinigung Bergbau 1956).

The third empirical finding of the book is that associations representing small firms have opposed private-type or contributory insurance policies. As Henri Hatzfeld has characterized the policy among large firms and small producers, while large firms have been the motor behind the expansion of social policies, small firms acted as a brake on social policy development (Hatzfeld 1971). For these firms, concerns about costs of these programs have outweighed the potential institutional advantages provided by social policies. The opposition of associations representing small firms to various legislative proposals that recommended the introduction of compulsory insurance emerges as a *leitmotif* across the cases investigated in this book. During the 1880s, both German and French producers raised vocal concerns about the "incalculable and highly dangerous consequences of social insurance" (Francke 1881). During the interwar period, various associations representing small firms greeted legislative proposals for compulsory unemployment insurance (Germany) and compulsory social insurance (France) with opposition and hostility (Chapter 4). As discussed in Chapter 6, small firms in both France and Germany have opposed the development of early retirement policies during recent years.

As Figure 7.1 illustrates, the relative incidence of a risk affecting the firm's work force is an important factor affecting the location of the preferences of employers along the risk redistribution dimension of the social policy space. Recall that the relative incidence of a risk is computed as the difference between the economy-wide average of the risk and the risk facing the firm. Employers in high-risk industries have favored highly redistributive social insurance policies. For these firms, private forms of insurance were often too costly, because sharing "good" and "bad" risks was rarely possible in these narrow risk pools. In contrast, employers in low-risk industries have favored private or occupationally based social policies or contributory insurance policies in which the social insurance contributions are determined based on actuarial considerations alone. These employers have feared that social insurance policies that redistributed risks across occupations would turn them into subsidizers of high-risk industries.

In the case of accident insurance reform, iron and steel producers and employers in mining – representing industries facing a high incidence of workplace accidents – have pushed for the introduction of compulsory social insurance. These policies had the immediate advantage of sharing risks across all industries and, thus, lowering their social insurance charges. In both France and Germany, these producers supported policy proposals for compulsory insurance and demanded the extension of the law to all occupations. In contrast, employers in industries facing a low incidence of workplace accidents – such as textiles – denounced compulsory insurance policies as a conspiracy of high-risk producers (see Verein Süddeutscher Baumwollindustrieller in Tennstedt and Winter 1993). Similarly, agricultural employers (Société des Agriculteurs de France) also opposed the intention of lawmakers to enlist agricultural producers as part of social insurance, denouncing this measure as a policy that brought no immediate advantage but which created only "unbearable" financial burdens.

The incidence of the risk of unemployment predicts some of the variation in the preferences of employers toward different policies of unemployment compensation. In both France and Germany, the volatility of employment was highest in manufacturing industries dependent on export markets, such as metal-processing and metalworking industries. In contrast, agriculture was facing a low incidence of unemployment.[1] In Germany, high-risk producers favored the introduction of a compulsory unemployment insurance. These employers supported "the expansion of the scope of social insurance legislation" and "the inclusion of good risks [günstige Risiken] as part of unemployment insurance – in other words, the inclusion of occupations in which the risk of unemployment is lower" (Vereinigung der Deutschen Arbeitgeberverbände 1923: 35). They opposed policy proposals for the fragmentation of unemployment insurance along occupational lines and the creation of "occupational risk pools" (Gefahrenklassen) within unemployment insurance (Vereinigung der Deutschen Arbeitgeberverbände 1923). These employers argued that it was impossible for industries facing high and recurrent levels of unemployment to pay higher unemployment insurance contributions, because "the financial existence of these firms is endangered, both as a result of an uncertainty in their labor relations and as a result of an uncertainty in demand" (Vereinigung der Deutschen Arbeitgeberverbände 1920). In contrast to these producers, employers in industries facing a low incidence of unemployment opposed highly redistributive social policies. In Germany, the peak associations representing agricultural producers opposed the proposals of lawmakers to extend the provisions of unemployment insurance law to agriculture and argued that "the labor market

[1] In Germany, average unemployment rates in agriculture were 10.7% in metalworking as compared to 0.3% in agriculture (see Chapter 4).

contract of agricultural employees is the best insurance against the risk of unemployment" (Führer 1990: 324). The two main associations grouping French agricultural producers, the Society of French Farmers (Société des Agriculteurs de France) and the National Confederation of Agricultural Associations (Confédération Nationale des Associations Agricoles) strongly opposed the intention of lawmakers to extend social insurance to agriculture and favored a policy outcome that relied on voluntary institutions of private insurance, such as mutual aid societies (sociétés de secours mutuels) and agricultural mutual insurance companies (mutuelles agricoles) (Augé-Laribé 1950).

Until World War II, manufacturing sectors pushed for the expansion of social insurance, while agriculture resisted policy initiatives recommending compulsory social policies. The assessment by these sectors of the optimal degree of risk redistribution changed during the postwar period. The factor accounting for the change in the relative location of the ideal point of these sectors along the risk redistribution dimension of the social policy space is the worsening of the demographic profile of agriculture. According to calculations of social policy experts of the period, agriculture was characterized by a much higher old-age dependency ratio than industry (Schieckel 1947). During the first postwar years, agricultural producers in both France and Germany demanded the expansion of social insurance to the countryside. French agricultural producers supported the extension of social insurance, arguing that this policy change could stop the exodus from the countryside to the city and create equal advantages for agriculture and industry (Commission Surleau 1946). German agricultural producers also favored the expansion of social insurance to the countryside, arguing that the "load of old-age insurance is particularly burdensome in agriculture" (Die zwei Seiten der bäuerlichen Altersversicherung n.d.).

Finally, the relative incidence of a risk is one of the variables that predict the use of the early retirement option by German and French employers. Employers in industries characterized by a very unfavorable age structure – such as the chemical sector in both France and Germany and the metalworking sector in France – made extensive use of the early retirement option. These policies created a window of opportunity for these firms that allowed them to circumvent the rigid dismissal laws of both countries and shed elderly workers at a relatively low cost. Employers in industries with a more favorable demographic burden made less extensive use of these policies.

257

The research on the role played by employers in the development of institutions of social insurance is only in its beginning and additional studies need to test the robustness of the findings of this book in other political contexts. The theoretical propositions advanced in this book are confirmed by a number of studies on the determinants of business preferences for social insurance institutions. The studies of "welfare capitalism" – or enterprise-based provision of social protection – in countries such as the United States, the United Kingdom, or Japan suggest that these firm-level institutions of social protection were established primarily by large manufacturing employers in an effort to cement the attachment of their high-skill workers to the firm and to reduce interfirm mobility of workers. The most significant factors that contributed to the establishment of these private social policies was the attempt of employers to structure the career incentives of their skilled workers and to lengthen the tenure of employees within the firm. Social policy benefits were thus contingent on a continuous presence of workers within the firm (Dore 1973, Hannah 1986, A. Gordon 1990, C. Gordon 1994, Jacoby 1997). As Swenson characterizes the mix of motives of employers in establishing these institutions, "in pursuit of their strategy to mollify workers and attach them physically and emotionally to their companies, many employers sought to elevate themselves above other firms in the labor market by providing paternalistic extras like housing, recreational, educational and cultural services. . . . Less overbearingly paternalist were vacation time, profit sharing payments and insurance benefits for retirement, illness, disability and unemployment. These "welfare capitalists" often introduced more professional management practices to replace the mean and capricious authoritarianism of foremen. Often they endeavored to "regularize" employment. Things like careful production and inventory planning to cope with seasonal and cyclical variation in demand increased workers' annual earnings beyond prevailing standards" (Swenson 2002: 83). Firm size and skill intensity of the work force remain important predictors of the development of private-type institutions of social protection (Hacker 2000: 138, Hannah 1986: 18).

Existing comparative studies also provide preliminary support for the importance of risk incidence in predicting whether the firm will support or oppose socialized insurance. Employers in occupations characterized by a high risk-incidence have supported the introduction of policies socializing risks, whereas employers in low-risk industries have favored social policies involving lower levels of redistribution of costs across occupations. In the United Kingdom and United States, employers in industries prone to a high incidence of workplace accidents have supported the introduction of compulsory social insurance, whereas low-risk producers opposed it (Hay 1977: 435–455, Ritter 1986: 171–172, Asher 1969: 447–455, Castronovici 1980: 268–269). Peter Swenson's analysis of the development of unemployment insurance policies in the United States also reveals that "seasonal and otherwise unstable industries like rubber, clothing, construction, mining, and textiles, favored cross-subsidization," hence the introduction of a redistributive policy of unemployment insurance (Swenson 2002: 393). As Swenson argues, in Ohio representatives of the rubber industry "which suffered heavy cyclical and seasonal unemployment pleaded for national legislation with pooling" (Swenson 2002: 393). "In Rhode Island, employers from the ailing textile industry and its important jewelry industry, whose output fluctuated seasonally, successfully joined forces with labor in sharp conflict with other employers on this issue. State-level, cross-class alliance politics also affected outcomes in Utah, where steel, oil, retail merchandising and auto dealers clashed with mining and seasonal industries like construction favoring the more liberal pooling system" (Swenson 2002: 395). Thus, the findings of this book concerning the determinants of business interests toward different social policies "travel" across different political contexts.

Findings on Cross-Class Alliances

Employers voiced these policy demands during various stages of the policy process preceding the enactment of a new social policy. We find employers' representatives at every step of the policy-making process: in various commissions appointed by the labor market authorities, in front of parliamentary and bureaucratic commissions, in secret meetings with pivotal policy makers (such as Bismarck), and, sometimes, pleading their case directly on the floor of the lower or upper chambers of parliament. Employers were not "agenda setters." They were not responsible for introducing a social policy proposal on the broad agenda of reform (the one exception is the case of disability insurance reform in Germany in the 1880s). The impetus for reforms came from bureaucratic or elected politicians or, in some cases, from the courts. But employers' representatives were involved in the broad political negotiations of social insurance legislation and influenced the minute details of policy design of the legislation that was, ultimately, adopted. We cannot explain the policy outcome that was ultimately adopted without specifying the policy preferences of employers.

The empirical chapters of the book have identified systematic differences in the composition of political coalitions that have supported various social policies. This study has generated four general findings that can be further tested in different political contexts. First, in all cases analyzed in the book, the social insurance bill that was introduced enjoyed the political support of *some* sectors of the business community. The cases span nearly a century of social policy development and include the most critical subsystems of the welfare state – old-age, unemployment, and disability insurance. I control for a broad range of institutional and political variables, such as strength of labor movement, political composition of government, and variety in the number of policy veto players (associated with a variation in the level of policy disagreement among the upper and lower chambers of parliament). The empirical evidence disconfirming the proposition that the welfare state has been enacted against the opposition of employers is simply overwhelming.

The second result on the dynamics of political coalitions is that most social policy outcomes were supported by broad *cross-class alliances* that comprised both trade unions and representatives of the business community. (The only exceptions are the cases analyzing the introduction of disability insurance cases, when labor representatives did not formally participate in the policy deliberations.) Neither representatives of capital nor trade unions were able to secure their preferred policy choice (or, using the concepts of Chapter 2, the ideal combination of "risk redistribution" and "control"). During the process of bargaining, both employers and unions were forced to retreat from their policy goals and accept a compromise on several questions of policy design. Thus, we can characterize these cross-class alliances as "strategic alliances."

A third important finding of the book is that preexisting private and public social policies influence the policy strategies adopted by labor and business associations during the process of bargaining. As historical-institutionalist scholars have observed, preexisting policies exercise important feedback effects, precluding political coalitions around particular outcomes and, at the same time, facilitating cross-class alliances in support of other policies (Pierson 1996). To illustrate the impact of policy legacies, consider the example of policy reforms during the first years of the postwar period in Germany. Given the unfavorable old-age dependency ratio of the German *Handwerk*, small firms were potential winners under a universalistic social policy. Many policy experts hoped that a cross-class alliance among small firms and labor around a universalistic policy would be feasible. These policy experts underestimated, however, the impact of policies introduced during the period of National Socialism. Preexisting policy legacies precluded this cross-class alliance around a universalistic social policy. As analyzed in Chapter 5, the Nazi regime had introduced a social policy that allowed *Handwerk* firms to choose between private insurance and social insurance of the white-collar employees (*Angestelltenversicherung*). This policy was highly advantageous to the *Handwerk*: very generous social policy benefits available at a low cost in terms of insurance contributions. Therefore, representatives of the *Handwerk* favored the policy status quo over the introduction of a universalistic social policy. *Handwerk*'s opposition to a change in status quo was an important factor that contributed to the defeat of the policy proposals for the introduction of a universalistic social policy in postwar Germany.

A final empirical finding of the book is that the political composition of cross-class alliances explains differences in social policy outcomes. We can identify two broad cases. A cross-class alliance comprising large manufacturing producers and the most important sectors of the labor movement will support the introduction of a contributory compulsory social insurance. Conversely, if the decisive cross-class alliance comprises labor and small firms, the resulting policy outcome will be a social policy characterized by incomplete coverage and institutional fragmentation.

To illustrate these differences, we can refer back to two of the cases discussed in the book. During the Weimar period, a cross-class alliance comprising large manufacturing employers and the socialist trade union movement supported the introduction of contributory unemployment insurance. In the period following World War I, the German trade union movement realized that preexisting union-based institutions of social support in case of unemployment were too fragile to cope with the high and persistent levels of unemployment. Consequently, the Federation of German Trade Unions demanded the introduction of a compulsory unemployment insurance and abandoned its earlier plans that called for the introduction of a Ghent system. Beginning in 1920, the main federation representing large manufacturing employers also supported a contributory unemployment insurance, as part of an effort to lower the income losses experienced by high-skill workers during periods of unemployment. To consolidate this initially fragile cross-class alliance, policy makers of the Imperial Employment Office formulated proposals that increased the role and responsibilities of associations representing employers and unions in the administration of unemployment insurance. These features of policy design that introduced parity administration of unemployment insurance thus anchored this cross-class alliance within the institutional design of the German welfare state.

This proposition is confirmed by studies examining social policy development in other political contexts. In Belgium, the policy of contributory unemployment insurance introduced in 1944 was supported by a cross-class alliance comprising the socialist trade unions and the main association representing large manufacturing producers, the Central Industrial Committee (Vanthemsche 1990: 369). As Vanthemsche argues, employers "argued for a bipartite management of the new public institution, with representatives of both employers' organizations and trade unions jointly running the system" (Vanthemsche 1990: 369). The Socialist Trade Union Federation, "attracted by the technocratic element of a simple, rationalized state apparatus," also supported the replacement of the preexisting Ghent policy with contributory unemployment insurance (Vanthemsche 1990: 370). Peter Swenson's research on social policy developments in postwar Sweden indicates that the key policies of social insurance were supported by a broad cross-class alliance between the Swedish Labor Confederation (LO) and the peak association of Swedish producers (SAF). The policies that were supported by this broad, cross-class alliance ultimately prevailed over alternative proposals supported by important members of the Swedish Social Democratic Party as well as by the Swedish Conservatives. Large manufacturing producers supported the introduction of statutory health and pension policies and of solidaristic wage practices – characterized by a high level of interoccupational wage leveling – in an effort to preempt inter-firm competition for scarce labor on the basis of private provision of social policy benefits. As Swenson argues, employers supported the major policies of the Swedish welfare state "not out of resignation, but out of self-interest. In Sweden, the historical facts suggest that the enduring political success of the Social Democratic labor movement and the durability of its famous social and labor market policy reforms would not have been possible had they been imposed against the interests of capital" (Swenson 2002: 493).

A second important finding of the analysis is that cross-class alliances that include small producers alongside labor representatives lead to social policies characterized by incomplete coverage, loopholes, and wide occupational fragmentation. Consider the introduction of a Ghent system of unemployment insurance in France in 1905. The analysis of the archival records of the deliberations of the Conseil du Travail in 1903 has allowed me to establish that this policy outcome was supported by a cross-class alliance of small firms and trade unions. The Ghent solution was appealing to French producers because it was a voluntary outcome that involved no extension of the administrative role of the state and thus no increase in the level of social charges (Fagnot 1905: 123). To limit a potential increase in the strength of trade unions – resulting from the subsidization of union unemployment funds – French employers demanded and obtained the subsidization of *all* associations offering benefits in case of unemployment (Fagnot 1905: 131). The list of associations eligible for subsidies from the state was extended to include philanthropic organizations, the *mutualités* and unemployment funds organized by a local chamber of commerce. The main institutional characteristics of this policy outcome were a wide institutional fragmentation and a very limited coverage.

Policy developments in postwar Japan provide another example where a political coalition comprising small firms and labor was successful in imposing its desired social policy against the interests of large manufacturing producers (Estevez-Abe 1999). As Estevez-Abe argues, large manufacturing producers supported the introduction of a compulsory family policy, in an effort to "alleviate the burden of family expenses on the middle-aged cohort of workers" (Estevez-Abe 1999: 350) and as a policy instrument that could correct some of the problems associated with the seniority-wage system, which imposed constraints on the ability of large firms to reward younger workers. In contrast, employees and employers in small firms, independents, and farmers opposed the policy proposals advocated by large firms, disliking the potential increase in the tax burden associated with the introduction of this policy (Estevez-Abe 1999). Instead, these actors favored the introduction of a family policy characterized by tax incentives, hence, an outcome characterized by selectivity and not by a socialization of costs. This coalition prevailed in the policy-making process and the legislation introduced by Japan in the 1970s reflected the preferences of employers and workers of Japan's small enterprises. Thus, the variation in the political composition of cross-class alliances explains not only cross-national variation across social policies but also variation in the institutional characteristics of social policies within the same country.

Concluding Remarks

I began this book by noting a striking bifurcation in the scope of social policy reforms experienced by advanced industrialized democracies during the past two decades. The magnitude of welfare state retrenchment has been much greater in countries characterized by meager and market-conforming institutions of social protection. In contrast, countries with generous welfare states have experienced lower levels of policy cutbacks. The degree of hostility or support shown by employers toward these reforms has varied dramatically across countries. In liberal market economies, such as the United Kingdom, employers have waged a radical assault against existing social insurance and labor market institutions. As Wood has shown, "in liberal market economies, employers' preference is to weaken organized labor as much as possible. Where firms do not rely upon production strategies that render organized labor a virtue – in collective bargaining or managing process innovation, for example – they see strong trade unions and strong employment protection as fetters on their ability to compete on the basis of lowering production costs" (Wood 2001: 250). In contrast, German employers have approached "the issue of bargaining decentralization very gingerly" and have resisted radical proposals calling for radical labor market deregulation (Thelen 2001: 85, Thelen and Kume 1999). On numerous occasions, employers in "coordinated market economies" have defended a variety of non-market-based institutions protecting labor (Manow 2000: 161, Thelen 2000: 138–172, Wood 2001: 247–274).

The analysis developed in this book provides the tools that allow us to understand the conditions under which some sectors of the business community will join cross-class alliances in support of existing policies of social insurance. Social policies allow employers and employees to solve commitment problems associated with decisions over investments in skills. For a particular firm, the "institutional benefits" provided by social policies increase if the share of its work force that has firm- or industry-specific skills increases. The number of firms that will support institutions of social insurance will be higher in those economies in which the percentage of workers who have made investments in skills is larger. In these economies, a positive feedback loop exists between the welfare state and the level of skills in the economy. While the welfare state makes possible investment in training, an increase in the number of workers with high levels of skills needed by firms contributes to greater support for the welfare state among employers. Thus, we expect that in economies characterized by high levels of investment in training and skill formation, welfare states will be less vulnerable to attacks from employers.

Second, the analysis of the book provides insights about the type of social policy programs that will be more vulnerable to attacks from employers. Both the theoretical and empirical analyses have shown that for large manufacturing firms that have made significant investments in the training of

264

workers, the social policies that are most beneficial are those that maintain income streams that are proportional to the wages of workers. These are the policies that "protect" the investment in skills. Universal programs, in which benefits are flat rate, and means-tested social policies, awarded on the basis of need, do not provide the same guarantees to these firms that their investment in the skills of their workers will be protected. We have seen that during formative periods in the development of institutions of social insurance, large manufacturing producers have favored contributory social insurance and private-type social policies over universalistic social policies. We expect that these firms will *prioritize* contributory insurance policies over means-tested programs during current periods of fiscal strain and retrenchment.

For more than four decades, scholars of the welfare state have attributed the genesis and development of institutions that protect citizens against the most significant employment-based risks to the triumph of labor-based organizations over a community of employers forced into retreat. These theories suggest that during the current period of welfare state austerity, labor-based organizations remain the only defense against political and economic forces pushing for welfare state retrenchment. The analysis of this book generates different implications about the preferences of actors and lines of political conflict that are likely to emerge during future social insurance reforms. Future battles over the shape and design of institutions of social protection will not be the outcome of a struggle between labor and capital. Rather, reforms will result from a process of piecemeal negotiations among cross-class alliances comprising different sectors of unions and employers. In many economies with well-developed systems of social protection, support for the welfare state is much broader, reaching deep in the business community. The finding of this book that business is not irrevocably opposed to the development of institutions of social insurance brings, I submit, good news for many welfare states.

References

Abel, Wilhelm. 1959. *Soziale Sicherheit in den Grenzbereichen des selbständigen Mittelstandes.* Stuttgart: Kohlhammer.

Abelshauser, Werner. 1996. Erhard oder Bismarck? Die Richtungsentscheidung der deutschen Sozialpolitik am Beispiel der Reform der Sozialversicherung in den fünfziger Jahren. *Geschichte und Gesellschaft,* 22, 350–375.

Abraham, David. 1981. *The Collapse of the Weimar Republic.* Princeton: Princeton University Press.

Abramowski, Günter, ed. 1988. *Die Kabinette Marx III und IV.* Boppard am Rhein: Boldt.

Ahrend, Peter. 1996. Pension Financial Security in Germany. In Bodie Zvi, Olivia Mitchell, and John Turner, eds., *Securing Employer-Based Pensions: An International Perspective.* Philadelphia: University of Pennsylvania Press, 73–113.

Alber, Jens. 1981. Government Responses to the Challenge of Unemployment: The Development of Unemployment Insurance in Western Europe. In Peter Flora and Arnold Heidenheimer, eds., *The Development of Welfare States in Europe and America.* New Brunswick: Transactions Books, 151–186.

1982. *Vom Armenhaus zum Wohlfahrtsstaat.* Frankfurt: Campus.

Aldrich, R. 1987. Late-Comer or Early Starter? New Views on French Economic History. *Journal of European Economic History,* 16, 1, 89–101.

Allgemeiner Deutscher Gewerkschaftsbund, ed. 1896. *Protokoll der Verhandlungen des 2. Kongresses der Gewerkschaften Deutschlands.* Berlin: ADGB.

1902a. *Correspondenzblatt der Generalkommission der Gerwerkschaften Deutschlands,* 12, 308.

1902b. *Protokoll der Verhandlungen des 4. Kongresses der Gewerkschaften Deutschlands.*

1903. Die deutschen Krankenkassen und die Krankenkassenversicherungsnovelle. *Correspondenzblatt der Generalkomission der Gewerkschaften Deutschlands,* 13, 12, 177–180.

1918. Leitsätze für eine Arbeitslosenversicherung. *Correspondenzblatt der Generalkommission der Gerwerkschaften Deutschlands,* 28, 1, 6.

References

1920a. Zur Frage der künftigen Form unserer Arbeitslosenversicherung. *Korrespondenzblatt des Allgemeinen Deutschen Gewerkschaftsbundes*, 30, 12–13, 159–161.

1920b. Ein Gesetzentwurf über Arbeitslosenversicherung. *Correspondenzblatt des Allgemeinen Deutschen Gewerkschaftsbundes*, 30, 20, 251.

1921. Zur Arbeitslosenversicherung. *Korrespondenzblatt des Allgemeinen Deutschen Gewerkschaftsbundes*, 31, 53, 745–747.

1922a. Zum Entwurf einer Arbeitslosenversicherung. *Korrespondenzblatt des Allgemeinen Deutschen Gewerkschaftsbundes*, 32, 35, 504.

1922b. Zum Entwurf einer Arbeitslosenversicherung II. *Correspondenzblatt der Generalkomission der Gewerkschaften Deutschlands*, 32, 36, 521.

1924. Die preussische Gefahrengemeinschaft für die Erwerbslosenfürsorge. *Die Gewerkschaftszeitung*, 34, 37, 342–343.

1926. *Protokolle der Verhandlungen der 13. Kongresses der Gewerkschaften Deutschlands*. Berlin: 1926.

Ambler, John S. 1988. Ideas, Interests and the French Welfare State. In J. S. Ambler, ed., *The French Welfare State: Surviving Social and Ideological Change*. New York: New York University Press, 1–31.

Ed. 1991. *The French Welfare State: Surviving Social and Ideological Change*. New York: New York University Press.

Amira, Selma, and Brigitte Roguet. 1994. Le coût des politiques publiques actives et passives en faveur des travailleurs vieillissants. In Ministère du Travail, ed., *Emploi et Vieillissement*. Paris: La Documentation Française.

Anderson, Karen. 2001. The Politics of Retrenchment in a Social Democratic Welfare State: Reform of Swedish Pensions and Unemployment Insurance. *Comparative Political Studies*, 34, 9, 1063–1091.

Arbeitsgemeinschaft der bayerischen Industrie- und Handelskammern. 1947. Rundschrift an dem Bayerischen Landtag und an die Bayerische Staatsregierung und den Herrn Ministerpräsidenten Dr. Erhard, 10.1.1947, Bundesarchiv Koblenz, Z1/941/177–179.

Arbeitsgemeinschaft der bayerischen Industrie- und Handelskammern, Bayerischer Handwerkskammertag und Arbeitsgemeinschaft der Arbeitgeberverbände Bayerns. 1947. Stellungnahme zu den Reformplänen für die deutsche Sozialversicherung, Rheinisch-Westfälisches Archiv, Köln, Archiv der Industrie- und Handelskammer Wuppertal, RWWA 22 800/00.

Archives Nationales. C15290. Commission des Finances. 25 April, 28 August.

Archives Nationales. C15293. Commission du Travail, Première Assemblée Constituante.

Archives Nationales. F7 13594. Revendications syndicales sur le chômage.

Arnold, R. Douglas. 1990. *The Logic of Congressional Action*. New Haven: Yale University Press.

Asher, Robert. 1969. Business and Workers' Welfare in the Progressive Era: Workmen's Compensation Reform in Massachusetts, 1880–1911. *Business History Review*, 447–455.

Ashford, Douglas E. 1982. *Policy and Politics in France: Living with Uncertainty*. Philadelphia: Temple University Press.

1986. *The Emergence of the Welfare States*. Oxford: Basil Blackwell.

References

1988. Advantages of Complexity: Social Insurance in France. In J. Ambler, ed., *The French Welfare State: Surviving Social and Ideological Change.* New York: New York University Press, 32–57.

Assemblée Consultative. 1945. Débats de l'Assemblée Consultative, Archives Nationales, C 15293.

Assemblée des Présidents des Chambres de Commerce en France. 1927. *Compte-Rendu in extenso de la Séance tenu à Paris le 15 mars 1927 sous la présidence de M. Kempf.* Paris: Librairies Imprimeries Réunies, Archives de la Chambre de Commerce de Paris, IX.

Assemblée des Presidents des Chambres de Métiers de France. 1947. Rapport sur les travaux de la Commission Surleau. Centre d'Archives Contemporaines, SS 07921, 760228, box 45, Ministère du Travail et de Sécurité Sociale.

Association Catholique. 1899. Congrès International des Accidents du Travail. *L'Association Catholique,* 27, 6, 735–739.

Augé-Laribé, Michel. 1950. *La politique agricole de la France de 1880 à 1940.* Paris: Presses Universitaires de France.

Baccaro, Lucio. 1984. The Organizational Consequences of Democracy: Labor Unions and Economic Reforms in Contemporary Italy. Ph.D. dissertation, Sloan School of Management, MIT.

Bäcker, Gerhard. 1984. Bewältigung der Beschäftigungskrise auf Kosten der Frauen? *Die Mitbestimmung,* 1, 29–31.

Bäcker, Gerhard, and Gerhard Naegele. 1984. Ältere Arbeitnehmer zwischen Erwerbstätigkeit und Ruhestand. *Die Mitbestimmung,* 6, 245–247.

Baldwin, Peter. 1990. *The Politics of Social Solidarity: Class Bases of the European Welfare State, 1875–1975.* Cambridge: Cambridge University Press.

Balmary, D. 1969. Le fonds national pour l'emploi. *Droit social,* 12, 575–583.

Barenberg, Mark. 1993. The Political Economy of the Wagner Act: Power, Symbol, and Workplace Cooperation. *Harvard Law Review,* 106, 1381–1496.

Barjot, Alain, ed. 1988. *La sécurité sociale: Son histoire à travers les textes.* Paris: Association pour l'étude de la Sécurité Sociale.

Barr, Nicholas. 1993. *The Economics of the Welfare State.* Stanford: Stanford University Press.

Barthélémy, Jacques. 1986. Contributions patronales aux régimes de retraite et de prévoyance et cotisations de sécurité sociale. *Droit Social,* 4, 332–335.

Bartholomai, Reinhart. 1977. Der Volksversicherungsplan der SPD. In Reinhard Barholomai, ed., *Sozialpolitik nach 1945: Geschichte und Analysen.* Bonn: Verlag Neue Gesellschaft, 161–172.

Bavarez, Nicolas. 1991. Chômage des années 1930, chômage des années 1980. *Le Mouvement Social,* 154, 103–130.

Bec, Colette. 1994. *Assistance et République: La recherche d'un nouveau contrat social sous la IIIe République.* Paris: Editions de l'Atelier.

Bellom, Maurice. 1894. La question des accidents du travail. État actuel devant le parlement français. *Revue Politique et Parlementaire,* July, 65–78.

1899. La loi sur les accidents du travail et les difficultés présentes. *Revue Politique et Parlementaire,* July, 59–91.

Benöhr, H. 1981. Soziale Frage, Sozialversicherung und Sozialdemokratische Reichstagsfraktion. *Zeitschrift der Savigny-Stiftung für Rechtsgeschichte. Germanistische Abteilung*, 98, 95–156.

Berenz, Claus, Gabriele Borck, and Michael Worzalla. 1991. Verfassungsrechtliche Grenzen überschritten. *Der Arbeitgeber*, 43, 10, 381–382.

Berger, Suzanne. 1977. D'une boutique à l'autre: Changes in the Organization of the Traditional Middle Classes from the Fourth to Fifth Republics. *Comparative Politics*, 10, 1, 121–136.

    1980. Reflections on Industrial Society: The Survival of the Traditional Sectors in France and Italy. In Suzanne Berger and Michael Piore, eds., *Dualism and Discontinuity in Industrial Societies*. Cambridge: Cambridge University Press.

    1981a. Lame Ducks and National Champions. In Stanley Hoffmann and William G. Andrews, eds., *The Fifth Republic at Twenty*. Brockport, N.Y.: SUNY Press, 292–310.

    1985. The Socialists and the Patronat: The Dilemmas of Coexistence in a Mixed Economy. In H. Machin and Vincent Wright, eds., *Economic Policy and Policy-Making under the Mitterand Presidency, 1981–1984*. New York: St. Martin's Press, 225–244.

    Ed. 1981b. *Organizing Interests in Western Europe*. Cambridge: Cambridge University Press.

Berger, Suzanne, and Michael Piore. 1980. *Dualism and Discontinuity in Industrial Societies*. Cambridge: Cambridge University Press.

Berichte zur Zonenkonferenz. 1946. Berichte zur Zonenkonferenz am 21–23. 8. 1946. Archive of the Friedrich Ebert Foundation, Bonn.

Bernard, André. 1926. *Observations sur le projet de loi sur les assurances sociales*. Archives de la Chambre de Commerce de Paris, III. 5. 50 (10).

Béraud, Jean-Marc. 1992. La mise à la retraite: Un droit qui se cherche. *Droit Social*, 9–10, 812–817.

Bieber, Hans-Joachim. 1981. *Gewekschaften in Krieg und Revolution. Arbeiterbewegung, Industrie, Staat und Militär in Deutschland 1914–1920*. Hamburg: Christians.

Biernacki, Richard. 1995. *The Fabrication of Labor: Germany and Britain, 1640–1914*. Berkeley: University of California Press.

Bivière, Louis. 1912. Les subventions municipales aux caisses de chômage. *La Réforme Sociale*, 344–379.

Block, Fred. 1977. The Ruling Class Does Not Rule: Notes on the Marxist Theory of the State. *Socialist Revolution*, 33, 1, 6–27.

Blondal, Sveinbjorn, and Mark Pearson. 1995. Unemployment and Other Non-Employment Benefits. *Oxford Review of Economic Policy*, 11, 1, 136–152.

Blüm, Norbert. 1983a. Flexible Altersgrenzen: Weiter senken. *Bundesarbeitsblatt*, 1, 25–26.

    1983b. Sozialpolitik: Wende ohne Ende. *Bundesarbeitsblatt*, 2, 5–9.

    1993. Mißbrauchbekämpfung: Sozialstaatliche Pflicht. *Bundesarbeitsblatt*, 11, 16–17.

    1995a. Fünf gute Botschaften. *Bundesarbeitsblatt*, 3, 5–12.

References

1995b. Vor einer grundlegenden Reform, *Bundesarbeitsblatt*, 2, 15–19.

1995c. Konkurrenzfähig bleiben. *Bundesarbeitsblatt*, 9, 12.

Bogs, Walter. 1955. *Grundfragen des Rechts der Sozialen Sicherheit und seiner Reform*. Berlin: Duncker & Humblot.

Böhm, Gustav. 1924. Bedeutet die Ersetzung der Erwerbslosenfürsorge durch die Arbeitslosenversicherung eine Mehrbelastung der Wirtschaft? *Reichsarbeitsblatt*, 24, 8 November, 591–593.

Bohner, E., C. Müller. 1982. Aktive Beschätigungspolitik – aber wie? *Die Mitbestimmung*, 10, 354–355.

Boira, François. 1939. *Accidents du travail et responsabilité du droit commun*. Paris: Librairie generale de droit et de jurisprudence.

Boissard, A. 1900. La loi du 9 avril 1898. Quelques résultats des six premiers mois d'application. *Revue d'économie politique*, 14, 265–295.

Bollache, Pierre. 1967. *Les responsabilités de l'entreprise en matière d'accidents du travail*. Paris: Sirey.

Bonoli, Giuliano. 2000. *The Politics of Pension Reform: Institutions and Policy Change in Western Europe*. Cambridge: Cambridge University Press.

Borchert, Jürgen. 1993. *Renten vor dem Absturz. Ist der Sozialstaat am Ende?* Frankfurt: Fischer.

Bordeloup, Jean. 1984. Les rayons et les ombres de la politique sociale actuelle menée en direction des personnes âgées. *Droit Social*, 11, 656–662.

1992. La réforme des régimes de retraîte: Une ardente obligation. *Droit Social*, 4, 399–404.

Born, Karl Erich. 1957. *Staat und Sozialpolitik seit Bismarck's Sturz. Ein Beitrag zur Geschichte der Innenpolitischen Entwicklung des deutschen Reiches 1890–1914*. Wiesbaden.

Boyer, Robert. 1990. *The Regulation School: A Critical Introduction*. New York: Columbia University Press.

1991. Le particularisme de années trente à la lumière de recherches récentes. *Le Mouvement Social*, 154, 3–40.

1994. Wage Reforms Imposed by the State: Some Paradoxes of French Incomes Policy. In Ronald Dore, ed., *The Return to Incomes Policy*. New York: St. Martin's Press, 47–70.

Brandt, T. 1919. Bericht über die sozialpolitische Gesetzgebung in der Zeit von April bis Oktober 1919 erstattet in der außerordentlichen Mitgliederversammlung der Vereinigung der Deutschen Arbeitgeberverbände am 22. Oktober 1919. In Vereinigung der Deutschen Arbeitgeberverbände, ed., *Berichte der Vereinigung der Deutschen Arbeitgeberverbände*. Berlin: VDA.

Braun, Rudolf, et al., eds. 1973. *Gesellschaft in der industriellen Revolution*. Cologne: Kiepenheuer & Witsch.

Breger, Monika. 1982. *Die Haltung der Industriellen Unternehmer zur staatlichen Sozialpolitik in den Jahren 1878–1891*. Frankfurt: Haag & Herchen.

1994. Der Anteil der Deutschen Großindustriellen and der Konzeptualisierung der Bismarckschen Sozialgesetzgebung. In Lothar Machtan, ed., *Bismarcks Sozialstaat:Beiträge zur Geschichte der Sozialpolitik und zur sozialpolitischen Geschichtsschreibung*. Campus: Frankfurt, 25–60.

271

Brentano, Lujo. 1877a. *Das Arbeitsverhältnis gemäß dem heutigen Recht*. Leipzig: Duncker & Humblot.

1877b. Die Arbeiterversicherung gemäß der heutigen Wirtschaftsordnung. In Lujo Brentano, ed., *Handbuch der politischen Ökonomie*. Leipzig: Duncker & Humblot.

Broecker, Bruno. 1926. Arbeitsbeschaffung und Erwerbslosenunterstützung. *Die Arbeit*, 3, 8, 477–483.

1927a. Das Gesetz über Arbeitsvermittlung und Arbeitslosenversicherung. *Die Arbeit*, 4, 8, 571–574.

1927b. Forderungen an die Arbeitslosenversicherung, *Die Arbeit*, 4, 5, 313–321.

Büchtemann, Christoph F., and Helmut Neumann, eds. 1990. *Mehr Arbeit durch weniger Recht? Chancen und Risiken der Arbeitsmarktflexibilisierung*. Berlin: Sigma.

Bueck, Henry Axel. 1901. *Der Centralverband Deutscher Industrieller 1876–1905*. Berlin: Druck Deutscher Verlag.

Bulletin de Liaison UNEDIC. 1981. Garantie de ressources et emplois salariés du secteur privé. *Bulletin de Liaison UNEDIC*, December, 83, 21.

Bundesanstalt für Arbeit. 1985. *Arbeitsförderungsgesetz mit angrenzenden Gesetzen, Verordnungen und BA-Regelungen*, Nuremberg: Bundesanstalt für Arbeit.

Bundesarbeitsblatt. 1984a. Ältere Arbeitnehmer: Viele Vorurteile. *Bundesarbeitsblatt*, 3, 8–10.

Bundesarbeitsblatt. 1984b. Alterssicherung: Empfehlungen der Kommission. *Bundesarbeitsblatt*, 2, 5–24.

Bundesarchiv Koblenz. Z40 Zentralamt für Arbeit in der britischen Zone.

Bundesministerium für Arbeit und Sozialordnung, ed. 1998. *Statistisches Taschenbuch*. Bonn: BMAS.

Bundessozialgericht, ed. 1970. *Entscheidungen des Bundessozialgerichtes*. Vol. 30. Cologne: Carl Heymans.

Bundesvereinigung der Deutschen Arbeitgeberverbände. 1984a. Rentenzugang und Frühinvalidität, Anlage zum Rundschreiben VI/7 vom 16.1. 1984, box IV-1-4-1. Archiv der Bundesvereinigung der Deutschen Arbeitgeberverbände, Cologne.

1984b. Niederschrift über die Sitzung des Ausschusses Soziale Sicherung am 30. Januar 1984 in Köln, box IV-1-4-1. Archiv der Bundesvereinigung der Deutschen Arbeitgeberverbände, Cologne.

Bunel, Jean, and Jean Saglio. 1979. *L'action patronale. Du CNPF au petit patron*. Paris: Presses Universitaires de France.

1980. La redéfinition de la politique sociale du patronat français. *Droit Social*, 12, 489–498.

Carlton, Dennis, and Jeffrey Perloff. 1992. *Modern Industrial Organization*. New York: Harper Collins.

Castleiner, Erwin. 1984. Vorsorge für den Vorruhestand – der Lebensabend muß gesichert sein. *Die Mitbestimmung*, 6, 238–240.

Castles, Francis. 1982. "The Impact of Parties on Public Expenditures." In Francis Castles, ed., *The Impact of Parties: Politics and Policies in Democratic Capitalist States*. Beverly Hills: Sage, 21–96.

References

Castronovici, Joseph. 1980. Prelude to Welfare Capitalism: The Role of Business in the Enactment of Workmen's Compensation Legislation in Illinois, 1905–1912. In Frank Breul and Steven Diner, eds., *Compassion and Responsibility: Readings in the History of Social Welfare Policy in the United States*. Chicago: University of Chicago Press.

Caurier, G. 1909. *La législation sur les accidents du travail*. Paris: Rousseau.

Cazajeux, J. 1895. La loi sur les accidents du travail et le socialisme d'Etat devant le Sénat. *La Réforme Sociale*, 5, 971–974.

CDU. 1947. Richtlinien von dem für die Sozialversicherung bestellten Ausschuses der Zonenparteileitung in einer Sitzung am 13. September 1947 in Köln. Archive of the Friedrich Ebert Foundation, Auerbach Papers, box 208, Bonn.

Centralverband Deutscher Industrieller. 1881. Beschlüsse der Ausschuss-Sitzung der Centralverbandes vom 30. Januar 1881. In Centralverband Deutscher Industrieller, *Verhandlungen, Mitteilungen und Berichte des Centralverbandes Deutscher Industrieller*. Berlin: CDI.

1882. *Verhandlungen, Mitteilungen und Berichte des Centralverbandes Deutscher Industrieller*. Berlin: CDI.

1883. *Verhandlungen, Mitteilungen und Berichte des Centralverbandes Deutscher Industrieller*. Berlin: CDI.

1884. *Verhandlungen, Mitteilungen und Berichte des Centralverbandes Deutscher Industrieller*. Berlin: CDI.

Chadelat, Jean-François. 1994. Le fonds de solidarité viellesse. *Droit Social*, 727–733.

Chambre de Commerce d'Abbeville. 1898a. *Les accidents du travail, rapport présenté à la Chambre de commerce de 'arrondissement d'Abbeville, sur la loi votée par la Chambre et le Sénat et promulguée le 29 mars 1898*. Abbeville: C. Paillart.

1898b. *Les Accidents du travail. Rapport présenté à la chambre de commerce d'Abbeville par M. Paillart*. Archives de la Chambre de Commerce de Paris.

Chambre de Commerce d' Auxerre. 1889. *Rapport sur le projet de loi concernant les accidents dont les ouvriers sont victimes présenté dans la séance du 4 avril 1889*.

Chambre de Commerce de Beauvais et de l'Oise. 1895. *Projet de loi concernant la responsabilité des accidents du travail et l'organisation de l'assurance obligatoire. Rapport de M. Noël et délibération de la Chambre de Commerce (9 novembre 1895)*. Beauvais: Schmutz.

Chambre de Commerce de Belfort. 1925. *Rapport sur le Regime des Assurances Sociales en preparation devant le Sénat*. Archives de la Chambre de Commerce de Paris, III. 5. 50 (9).

Chambre de Commerce de Chalon-sur-Saone, Autun et Louhan. 1884. *Responsabilité des patrons en matiére d'accidents*. Chalon-sur-Saone.

Chambre de Commerce de Nevers. 1893. *Assurances contre les accidents du travail*. Nevers: Vallière.

1895. *Séance du 25 octobre 1895. Assurances contre les accidents du travail*. Rapport de M. Cladière. Nevers: Vallière.

Chambre de Commerce de Paris. 1880–1890. *Les Accidents du Travail*. Archives de la Chambre de Commerce de Paris, III. 5. 60 (1).

1883a. *Responsabilité des patrons en cas d'accidents*. 2 March. Archives de la Chambre de Commerce de Paris, III. 5. 60 (1).

1883b. *Responsabilité des patrons en matière d'accidents.* 18 April. Archives de la Chambre de Commerce de Paris, III. 5. 60 (1).

1894. *Projet de loi adopté par la Chambre des Députés et soumis actuellement au Sénat concernant le responsabilités des accidents dont les ouvriers sont victimes dans leur travail et l'organisation de l'assurance obligatoire. Rapport présenté au nom de la Commission nr. 3 par M. Fumouze.* 6 June. Archives de la Chambre de Commerce de Paris, III. 5. 60 (1).

1896. *De la responsabilité des accidents dont les ouvriers sont victimes dans leur travail. Rapport adopté par la chambre du commerce de Paris dans sa séance du 17 juin 1896.* Archives de la Chambre de Commerce de Paris, III. 5. 60 (1).

1897. *Examen du projet de loi adopté par la Chambre des Députés concernant la résponsabilité des accidents dont les ouvriers sont victimes dans leur travail. Rapport présenté au nom de la Commission No. 3 par M. A. Fumouze et converti en délibération par la Chambre du Comerce de Paris dans sa séance du 22 décembre 1897.* Archives de la Chambre de Commerce de Paris, III. 5. 60 (1).

1926. *Les Assurances Sociales. Rapport Présenté au nom de la Commission de Législation, Questions financiers et fiscales par M. Jules Loebnitz.* Archives de la Chambre de Commerce of Paris, III. 5. 50. (10).

1945. *Un projet d'unification et d'étatisation des institutions de Sécurité Sociale.* Archives de la Chambre de Commerce de Paris, III. 5. 70 (1).

1946. *L'organisation de la Sécurité Sociale. Rapport présenté au nom de la Commission du Travail et des Questions Sociales par M. André Brossard, Paris.* Archives de la Chambre de Commerce de Paris, III. 5. 70 (1).

Chambre de Commerce de Rennes. 1922. *Vouex emis par le groupement économique régionale de Rennes sur le projet de loi Daniel Vincent relatif aux assurances socials.* 13 January. Archives de la Chambre de Commerce de Paris, III 5. 50 (9).

Chambre de Commerce de Troyes. 1921. *Les assurances sociales. Rapport par M. Alfred Ploye et délibération. Séance du 4 octobre 1921.* Archives de la Chambre de Commerce de Paris, III. 5. 50 (9).

Chambre de Commerce du Havre. 1922. *Rapport de la Chambre de Commerce du Havre.* 10 January 1922. In Archives de la Chambre de Commerce de Paris, III. 5. 50 (9).

Chambre de Commerce et d'Industrie de Saint-Etienne. 1945. *Projet d'unification des institutions de Sécurité Sociale, (Séance du 28. 06. 1945).* Archives de la Chambre de Commerce de Paris, III. 5. 70 (1).

Chambre Syndicale de Marseille. 1897. *Séance de la Chambre Syndicale de Marseille du 17 novembre 1897. Loi des accidents du travail, rapport présenté au nom de la commission spéciale.* Archives de la Chambre de Commerce de Paris, III. 5.60 (1).

1921. *Séance de la Chambre syndicale de Marseille sur le projet de loi sur les assurances sociales.* Archives de la Chambre de Commerce de Paris, III. 5. 50 (10).

Charpentier, François. 1990. *Retraites et fonds de pension: L'état de la question en France et a l'étranger.* Paris: Economica.

References

Chevalier, François. 1998. *Le sénateur français 1875–1995. Essai sur le recrutement et la représentativité des membres de la seconde chamber.* Paris: Librairie Générale de Droit et de Jurisprudence.

Cheysson, E. 1892a. Les Assurances Ouvrières. *La Réforme Sociale,* 3, 797–817.

1892b. L'évolution du patronage. *La Réforme Sociale,* 3, 170–189.

1895a. Les assurances ouvrières. *La Réforme Sociale,* 5, 513–525.

1895b. Le congrès international des accidents à Milan et la garantie obligatoire de l'indemnité. *Revue Politique et Parlamentaire,* March, 415–432.

Clark, Robert, and P. Anker. 1990. Labor Force Participation Rates of Older Persons: An International Comparison. *International Labor Review,* 129, 2, 227–255.

Clement, Joseph. 1870. L'accident Professionnel. *Journal des économistes,* 17, January, 91–97.

Cohen, Elie. 1988. Formation, modéles d'action et performance de l'élite industrielle. *Sociologie du travail,* 4, 587–614.

1988. Patrons, entrepreneurs et dirigeants: Avant-Propos. *Sociologie du travail,* 4, 509–514.

Comité des Forges. 1891. Réunion mensuelle du groupe de Paris. Séance du 28 Décembre 1891. *La Réforme Sociale,* III, 14, 218–233.

Commissariat Général du Plan, ed. 1971. *Rapport de l'intergroupe "Problèmes relatifs aux personnes agées."* Paris: La Documentation Française.

1980. *Vieillir demain. Preparation du huitième plan 1981–1985.* Paris: La Documentation Française.

1991. *Livre blanc sur les retraites.* Paris: La Documentation Française.

Commission de Représentation Patronale. 1945–1946. Archives d'histoire Contemporaine, Fondation Nationale de Science Politique, Paris.

Commission Délépine. 1945–1946. *Commission chargée d'éxaminer les dispositions d'un projet relatif à l'organisation de la Sécurité Sociale.* Centre des Archives Contemporaines, Archives de la direction de la Sécurité Sociale.

Commision Surleau. 1946. *Note résumant les entretiens avec les différentes organizations des travailleurs independents au sujet de la modification de la loi du 28 mai 1946.* Centre d'Archives Contemporaines, SS07921 760228, box 45, Ministère du Travail et de Sécurité Sociale.

1947. *Rapport sur les travaux de la Commission d'Etudes nommée par la commission chargée d'étudier les modifications a apporter à la loi du 22 mai 1946 portant generalization de la Sécurité Sociale.* Centre d'Archives Contemporaines, SS 07921, 760228, box 45, Ministère du Travail et de Sécurité Sociale.

Confédération Générale des Petites et Moyennes Entreprises. 1982. *Assemblée Générale de la CGPME. Un contre-sens socio-économique.* Paris: CGPME.

1984. Assemblée Générale de la CGPME du 19 novembre 1984, allocation de M. Jean Brunet, vice président. Paris: CGPME.

Ed. 1980. *Observations de la CGPME sur l'abaissement de l'age de la retraite.* Paris: Flash PME.

1983. *Assemblée Générale de la CGPME du 15 novembre 1983.* Paris: CGPME.

Confédération Générale du Travail. 1902. *Compte-rendu officiel des travaux du Congrès.*

1904. *Compte-rendu des travaux du Congrès.* Paris.

1921. *Compte-rendu officiel des travaux du Congrès.* Lille, 25–30 July.

Ed. 1923 Rapport de la Commission Administrative de la Confédération Générale du Travail sur les Assurances Sociales. In *Compte-Rendu Officiel des travaux du Congrès.* Paris.

Conseil National du Patronat Français. 1946. Note résumant les entretiens avec les différentes organizations des travailleurs independents au sujet de la modification de la loi du 28 mai 1946. Centre d'Archives Contemporaines, SS 07921, 760228, box 45, Ministère du Travail et de Sécurité Sociale.

1971. *L'abaissement de l'âge de la retraite.* Paris: CNPF.

1981. Préretraite volontaire: Ou en est-on? *CNPF: La Revue des Entreprises,* 3.

1986. Minutes of the General Assembly of the CNPF, January. In *Revue de l'entreprise,* no. 475, January.

Conseil Supérieur du Travail. 1892. Rapport du Conseil Supérieur du Travail. In *Bulletin de l'office du travail.* Paris: Office du Travail.

Crouch, Colin, and Wolfgang Streeck, eds. 1997. *Political Economy of Contemporary Capitalism: Mapping Convergence and Diversity.* London: Sage.

Culpepper, Pepper. 1998. Rethinking Reform: The Politics of Decentralized Co-operation in France and Germany. Ph.D. dissertation, Harvard University.

Dansette, Jean-Lambert. 2000. *Histoire de l'entreprise et des chefs de l'entreprise en France.* Paris: Harmattan.

Darcy, H. 1896. *La question des accidents du travail devant le Sénat.* Paris: Chaix.

1898. *La loi des accidents du travail devant le Sénat en 1898.* Paris: Comité Central des Houillières de France.

deBoyer Montegut, Robert. 1912. Les bureaux de placement municipaux et les bourses du travail. *La Réforme Sociale,* 529–543.

de Gaulle, Charles. 1954. *Mémoires de Guerre. Le salut 1944–1946.* Paris: Plon.

Dejace, Charles. 1889. *La responsabilité des accidents du travail et le risque professionnel.* Paris: Baudry.

Der Arbeitgeber. 1910a. Das Problem der Arbeitslosenversicherung. 1 January.

1910b. Zur Arbeitslosenfürsorge. 1 August.

1911. Der Deutsche Städtetag und die Arbeitslosenversicherung. 1 October.

1912. Erfahrungen aus der kommunalen Arbeitslosenversicherung. 1 August.

1913a. Von der Arbeitslosenversicherung. 1 November.

1913b. Die Stellung der Arbeitgeber zur Arbeitslosenversicherung. 15 November.

1913c. Von der Arbeitslosenversicherung II. 1 December.

1914. Zur Frage der Arbeitslosigkeit. 15 January.

1920. Zur Frage der Reichsarbeitslosenversicherung. 15 March.

1921a. Der Referentenentwurf des Gesetzes über ein vorläufige Arbeitslosenversicherung. 15 October.

1921b. Zum Referentenentwurf des Gesetzes über eine vorläufige Arbeitslosenversicherung. 1 November.

References

1927. Das Gesetz über Arbeitsvermittlung und Arbeitslosenversicherung. 1 August.

1949a. Einheitsversicherung widerlegt. *Der Arbeitgeber*, 1, 2, 17–19.

1949b. Warum keine Einheitsverischerung? *Der Arbeitgeber*, 1, 3, 6–7.

1949c. Selbstverwaltung in der Sozialversicherung. *Der Arbeitgeber*, 1, 1, 5.

1949d. Soziale Selbstverwaltung als Gemeinschaftsaufgabe. *Der Arbeitgeber*, 1, 1, 9–12.

1949e. Umstrittene Selbstverwaltung in der Sozialversicherung. *Der Arbeitgeber*, 1, 6, 14–15.

1984. Probleme eines vorgezogenen Ruhestandes. *Der Arbeitgeber*, 36, 1, 11.

Deutsche Arbeitgeberzeitung. 1920. Zur Frage der Erwerbslosenfürsorge. 11 January.

Deutsche Eisenbahnhauptverwaltung. 1947a. 12. Vollsitzung des Hauptbetriebsrates bei der Hauptverwaltung der Eisenbahnen, 8 March 1947. Archive of the Friedrich Ebert Foundation, Auerbach Papers, box 208, Bonn.

1947b. Schrift der Eisenbahnhauptverwaltung an das Zentralamt für Arbeit, 1 April 1947. Archive of the Friedrich Ebert Foundation, Auerbach Papers, box 208, Bonn.

Deutscher Bundestag. 1984a. *Stenographische Berichte des deutschen Bundestages*. 10. Wahlperiode, 48. Sitzung, 20 January, 3425–3471.

1984b. *Stenographische Berichte Deutscher Bundestag*. 10. Wahlperiode, 61. Sitzung, 29 March, 4281–4307.

1983c. Gesetz zur Anpassung des Rechts der Arbeitsförderung und der gesetzlichen Rentenversicherung an die Einführung von Vorruhestandsleistungen. *Drucksachen des Bundestages*, 10/893.

Deutscher Bundesrat. 1984. *Stenographische Berichte des Bundesrates*, 531. Sitzung, 3 February, 1–18.

Deutscher Gewerkschaftsbund. N.d. Dringende Forderungen zur Sozialversicherung. Archive of the Friedrich Ebert Foundation, 5/55, Bonn.

N.d. 1. Tagung der arbeitsrechtlichen und sozialpolitischen Arbeitgemeinschaft in Lehenstedt. Archive of the Friedrich Ebert Foundation, 118/3, Bonn.

Ed. 1982. Gewerkschafliche Forderungen zur Arbeitszeitpolitik im Überblick. *Die Mitbestimmung*, 4–5, 163–165.

1984a. Arbeitszeitflexibilisierung – die große Alternative? *Die Mitbestimmung*, 1, 26–28.

1984b. Argumente gegen eine Verkürzung der Arbeitszeit. *Die Mitbestimmung*, 1, 24–25.

1984c. Die Arbeit auf alle verteilen. *Die Mitbestimmung*, 1, 3.

1985. Flexibilisierung order Arbeitszeitverkürzung für alle?, *Die Mitbestimmung*, 6, 216–218.

Deutscher Gewerkschaftsbund Bundeskongreß, ed. 1982a. An die Spitze der Bewegung stellen. *Die Mitbestimmung*, 7, 227–228.

1982b. Beschlüsse des 12. ordentlichen DGB-Bundeskongresses. *Die Mitbestimmung*, 7, 229–235.

Deutscher Gewerkschaftsbund der britischen Besatzungszone, ed. 1947. Gründungskongress des Deutschen Gewerkschaftsbundes, 22–25 April 1947. Archive of the Friedrich Ebert Foundation, Bonn.

Deutscher Industrie- und Handelstag. 1920a. *Entwurf eines Gesetzes uber die Arbeitslosenversicherung.* Zentrales Staatsarchiv Potsdam, Reichswirtschaftsministerium 2078.

1920b. Entwurf eines Gesetzes über die Arbeitslosenverischerung, Zentrales Staatsarchiv Potsdam, Reichsarbeitsministerium 2073.

Ed. 1920c. Bericht der Sitzung des Deutschen Industrie und Handelstages vom 28.–29. Oktober 1920. Zentrales Staatsarchiv Potsdam: RWM 2078.

1920d. Erklärung des Deutschen Industrie- und Handelstages an das Reichsarbeitsministerium am 25. November 1920. Zentrales Staatsarchiv Potsdam: RAM 4311/197–198.

1922. *Verhandlungen des Deutschen Industrie und Handelstages. Sitzung des Sozialpolitischen Ausschusses am 15. September 1922.* Berlin: Liebheit & Thießen.

1924. *Verhandlungen des Deutschen Industrie und Handelstages. Sitzung des Sozialpolitischen Ausschusses am 22. Oktober 1924.* Berlin: Liebheit & Thießen.

1926a. Rundschreiben an das Reichsarbeitsministerium. Zentrales Staatsarchiv Potsdam: RAM 1137.

1926b. *Verhandlungen des Deutschen Industrie und Handelstages. Sitzung des Hauptausschusses, Leipzig, 18. Juni 1926.* Berlin: Liebheit & Thießen.

1926c. *Verhandlungen des Deutschen Industrie und Handelstages. Sitzung des Sozialpolitischen Ausschusses.* Berlin: Liebheit & Thießen.

1926d. *Verhandlungen des Deutschen Industrie und Handelstages. Sitzung des Sozialpolitischen Ausschusses am 11. November 1926.* Berlin: Liebheit & Thießen.

1926e. *Verhandlungen des Deutschen Industrie und Handelstages. Sitzung des Sozialpolitischen Ausschusses am 16. Februar 1926.* Berlin: Liebheit & Thießen.

1927a. *Verhandlungen des Deutschen Industrie und Handelstages. 47. Vollversammlung des Deutschen Industrie- und Handelstages.* Berlin: Liebheit & Thießen.

1927b. *Verhandlungen des Deutschen Industrie und Handelstages. Sitzung des Sozialpolitischen Ausschusses am 23. Februar 1927.* Berlin: Liebheit & Thießen.

Deutscher Reichstag. 1881a. *Drucksachen des Reichstages Nr. 159.* 4. Legislaturperiode, 4. Session, 846.

1881b. Bericht der 13. Kommission des Reichstages über den Gesetzentwurf betreffend die Unfallversicherung der Arbeiter. *Drucksachen des Reichstages Nr. 41,* 4. Legislaturperiode, 4. Session, 1–66.

1881c. Stenographische Berichte des Reichstages, 1 April.

1882. Entwurf eines Gesetzes betreffend die Unfallversicherung der Arbeiter. *Drucksachen des Reichstages,* 5. Legislaturperiode, 2. Session, 1–86.

1884a. Stenographische Berichte des Reichstages, 14 March.

1884b. Entwurf eines Gesetzes betreffend die Unfallversicherung. *Drucksachen des Reichstages,* Nr. 4, 1–86.

1926. *Drucksachen des Reichstages,* Nr. 3622.

1927. *Drucksachen des Reichstages,* Nr. 2885. (Entwurf eines Gesetzes über die Arbeitslosenversicherung.)

Deutsches Institut für Wirtschaftsforschung. 1984. Mögliche Beschäftigungseffekte der Vorruhestandsregelung. *Wochenberichte des Deutschen Instituts für Wirtschaftsforschung,* 51, 18, 210–211.

References

Die Wirtschaft und die deutsche Sozialversicherung. N.d. Archive of the Friedrich Ebert Foundation, Auerbach Papers, box 207, 11/1, Bonn.

Die zwei Seiten der bäuerlichen Altersversicherung. N.d. Archive of the Friedrich Ebert Foundation, Auerbach Papers, box 240, Bonn.

Difourq, Nicolas. 1994. Sécurité Sociale: Le mythe de l'assurance. *Droit Social*, 3, 291–297.

Dobbernack, Wilhelm. 1947. Betrachtungen über die Neuordnung der deutschen Sozialversicherung und ihre Problematik. *Arbeitsblatt für die britische Zone*, 1, 58–63.

1949. Die Bedeutung des Sozialversicherungs-Anpassungsgesetzes für die Krankenversicherung. *Die Ortskrankenkasse*, 31, 1, 66–68.

Döding, Günter. 1982. Überzeugendes Handeln ist gefragt. *Die Mitbestimmung*, 4–5, 157–158.

1984a. Das gewerkschafliche Ziel verkürzter Lebensarbeitszeit. *Die Mitbestimmung*, 6, 232–233.

1984b. Mit 58 – Ja bitte! *Die Mitbestimmung*, 9, 380–382.

Dore, Ronald, 1973. *British Factory – Japanese Factory: The Origins of National Diversity in Industrial Relations*. Berkeley: University of California Press.

Dossiers statistiques du travail et d'emploi. 1990. Les preretraités en 1989. *Dossiers statistiques du travail et d'emploi*, nos. 63–64.

Dötsch, Werner. 1985. Reformdruck in der Krankenversicherung. *Der Arbeitgeber*, 37, 23, 936.

Ducourtieux, P. 1898. *Cinquième Congrés des maîtres imprimeurs de France. La nouvelle loi relative aux accidents dont les ouvriers sont victimes dans leur travail*. Limoges: Charles Lavauzelle.

Dumons, Bruno, and Gilles Pollet. 1991. La naissance d'une Politique Sociale: Les Retraites en France 1900–1914. *Revue Française de Science Politique*, 41, 4, 627–648.

1993. Politiques de la vielleisse et rationalisation dans l'entreprise: La gestion des vieux travailleurs en France au début du siècle. *Sociologie du travail*, 3, 241–255.

1994. *L'État et les retraites: Genèse d'une politique*. Paris: Bellin.

Dupeyroux, Jean-Jacques. 1995. *Droit de la Securité Sociale*. Paris: Dalloz.

Durin, François. 1982. L'abaisement de l'âge de la retraite: Aspects sociaux et financiers. *Droit Social*, 6, 468–472.

Ebert, Reinhard. 1988. Die Politik bleibt weiterhin gefordert. *Der Arbeitgeber*, 12, 40, 462.

Ehrmann, Henry. 1957. *Organized Business in France*. Princeton: Princeton University Press.

Einaudi, Mario, and François Goguel, eds. 1952. *Christian Democracy in Italy and France*. Notre Dame, Ind.: University of Notre Dame Press.

Erdmann, Karl-Dietrich, and Martin Vogt, eds. 1978. *Die Kabinette Stresemann I und II*. Boppard am Rhein: Boldt.

Erdmann, Lothar. 1925. Zu den Richtlinien für eine künftige Wirksamkeit der Gewerkschaften. *Die Arbeit*, 2, 390–392.

279

Erkelenz, Anton. 1927. Fehler des Arbeitslosenversicherungsgesetzes. *Die Arbeits-losenversicherung und Erwerbslosenfürsorge*, 4, 1, 1–5.

Esping-Andersen, Gøsta. 1985. *Politics against Markets: The Social Democratic Road to Power*. Princeton: Princeton University Press.

Esping-Andersen, Gøsta. 1990. *Three Worlds of Welfare Capitalism*. Princeton: Princeton University Press.

1994. The Eclipse of the Social Democratic Class Struggle? European Class Structures at Fin de Siècle. Paper presented to the Study Group on Citizenship and Social Policy, Center for European Studies, Harvard University.

1996a. Welfare States without Work: The Impasse of Labor-Shedding and Famil-ialism in Continental European Social Policy. In Gøsta Esping-Andersen, ed., *Welfare States in Transition: National Adaptations in Global Economies*. London: Sage, 66–87.

Ed. 1996b. *Welfare States in Transition: National Adaptations in Global Economies*. London: Sage.

Esping-Andersen, Gøsta, and Jan Eivind Kolberg, eds. 1992. Welfare States and Employment Regimes. In Gøsta Esping-Andersen and Jan Eivind Kolberg, eds., *Between Work and Social Citizenship*. London: Sharpe, 3–35.

Esping-Andersen, Gøsta, and Walter Korpi. 1984. Social Policy as Class Politics in Post-War Capitalism. In John Goldthorpe, ed., *Order and Conflict in Contem-porary Capitalism*. Oxford: Oxford University Press, 179–208.

1985. From Poor Relief towards Institutional Welfare States: The Development of Scandinavian Social Policy. In E. Eriksson, ed., *The Scandinavian Model: Welfare States and Welfare Research*. New York: M. E. Sharpe, 39–74.

Esping-Andersen, Gøsta, Martin Rein, and Lee Rainwater, eds. 1987. *Stagnation and Renewal in Social Policy: The Rise and Fall of Policy Regimes*. Armonk, N.Y.: M. E. Sharpe.

Estevez-Abe, Margarita. 1998. Changes to the Japanese Model of Welfare: Becom-ing More Like the US? Paper presented at the annual meeting of the American Political Science Association, Boston, 3–6 September.

1999. Welfare and Capitalism in Contemporary Japan. Ph.D. dissertation, De-partment of Government, Harvard University.

2001. The Forgotten Link: the Financial Regulation of Pension Funds. In Philip Manow and Bernhard Ebbinghaus, *The Varieties of Welfare Capitalism: Social Policy and Political Economy in Europe, Japan and the USA*. London: Routledge, 190–216.

Estevez-Abe, Margarita, Torben Iversen, and David Soskice. 2001. Social Protection and the Formation of Skills: A Reinterpretation of the Welfare State. In Peter Hall and David Soskice, eds., *Varieties of Capitalism: The Institutional Foundations of Comparative Advantage*. Oxford: Oxford University Press, 145–183.

Esser, Josef. 1941. *Grundlagen und Entwicklung der Gefährdungshaftung*. Munich: Beck.

Ewald, François. 1981. Formation de la notion d'accident du travail. *Sociologie du travail*, 23, 1, 3–13.

1983. Old Age as Risk. In Anne-Marie Guillemard, ed., *Old Age and the Welfare State*. London: Sage, 115–127.

References

1985. Le droit du travail: Une légalité sans droit? *Droit Social*, 11, 723–728.

1986. *L'État providence*. Paris: Grasset.

1991. Insurance and Risk. In G. Burchell, ed., *The Foucault Effect: Studies in Governmentality*. London: Harvester, 197–211.

1996. *Histoire de l'État providence. Les origines de la solidarité*. Paris: Grasset.

Eycken, P. 1900. *Du fondement de la responsabilité patronale en matière d'accidents de travail*. Lille: A. Masson.

Fagnot, François. 1905. *Le Chômage*. Paris: Société nouvelle de librairie et d'édition.

Faupel, Georg. 1985. Rentenversicherung nahe am Abgrund. *Die Mitbestimmung*, 8, 348–349.

Faust, Anselm. 1981. Funktion und Soziale Bedeutung des Gewerkschaftlichen Unterstützungswesens. Die Arbeitslosenunterstützung der Freien Gewerkschaften im Deutschen Kaiserreich. In Hans Mommsen and W. Schulze, eds., *Vom Elend der Handarbeit: Probleme historischer Unterschichtenforschung*. Stuttgart: Klett-Cotta, 395–417.

1986. *Arbeitsmarktpolitik im deutschen Kaiserreich: Arbeitsvermittlung, Arbeitsbeschaffung und Arbeitslosenunterstützung 1890–1918*. Stuttgart: Franz Steiner.

1987. Von der Fürsorge zur Arbeitsmarktpolitik: Die Errichtung der Arbeitslosenversicherung. In Werner Abelshauser, ed., *Die Weimarer Republik als Wohlfahrtsstaat*. Stuttgart: Steiner, 260–279.

Fédération des Industriels et des Commerçants Français. 1945. Réunion du 16 mai 1945 sur la réforme des institutions sociales. Archives de la Chambre de Commerce de Paris, III. 5 (70). 1.

Fédération du Livre. 1895. *Histoire d'une Caisse de Chômage*. Paris: Fédération du Livre.

Feldman, Gerald. 1977. *Iron and Steel in the German Inflation*. Princeton: Princeton University Press.

Feldman, Gerald, and Ulrich Nocken. 1975. Trade Associations and Economic Power: Interest Group Development in the German Iron and Steel and Machine Building Industries, 1900–1933. *Business History Review*, 49, 4, 413–445.

Feldman, Gerald, and Irmgard Steinisch. 1973. The Origin of the Stinnes-Legien Agreement: A Documentation. *Internationale Wissenschaftliche Korrespondenz zur Geschichte der deutschen Arbeiterbewegung*, 20, 45–103.

Fère, Isabelle. 1996. *Strategies de l'entreprise*. Mémoire DEA, Université Paris II, Paris.

Ferlemann, Erwin. 1985. Arbeitszeitverkürzung statt Arbeitszeitflexibilisierung. *Die Mitbestimmung*, 6, 211–212.

Fiedler, Martin. 1996. Betriebliche Sozialpolitik in der Zwischenkriegszeit. Wege der Interpretation und Probleme der Forschung im Deutsch-Französischen Vergleich. *Geschichte und Gessellschaft*, 22, 350–376.

Fischer, Wolfram. 1972. *Wirtschaft und Gesellschaft im Zeitalter der Industrialisierung*. Göttingen: Vandenhoeck & Ruprecht.

1978. Die Pionierrolle der betrieblichen Sozialpolitik im 19. und im beginnenden 20. Jahrhundert. In Wilhelm Treue and Hans Pohl, eds., *Betriebliche Sozialpolitik Deutscher Unternehmen seit dem 19. Jahrhundert*. Wiesbaden: Franz Steiner.

Flora, Peter, and Arnold Heidenheimer, eds. 1981. *The Development of the Welfare State in Europe and America*. New Brunswick, N.J.: Transaction Books.

Flora, Peter, and Jens Alber. 1983. *State, Economy and Society in Western Europe*, Frankfurt: Campus.

Fournier, Jacques, and Nicole Questiaux. 1989. *Traité du social. Situations, luttes, politiques, institutions*. Paris: Dalloz.

Francke, L. 1881. Die Stimmen der deutschen Handels- und Gewerbekammern über das Haftpflichtgesetz vom 7. Juni 1871 und den Reichs-Unfallsversicherungs-Gesetzentwurf vom 8. 03. 1881. *Zeitschrift des Königlich-Preussischen Statistischen Büros*, 21, 397–416.

Frank, Daniel, Raymond Hara, Gérard Magnier, and Olivier Villey. 1982. Entreprises et contrats de solidarité de préretraite-démission. *Travail et emploi*, 13, 75–89.

Frankfurter Allgemeine. 6 January 1982. Das Rentenalter soll herabgesetzt werden. Parteien diskutieren Verkürzung in Lebensarbeitszeit.

28 November 1983. Sozialausschüsse für Vorruhestandsrente.

13 December 1983. Mittelstand der Union lehnt Blüm's Entwurf ab.

21 December 1983. Blüm: Angebot an Staat, Arbeitnehmer und Arbeitgeber.

5 January 1984. Es wird teurer Arbeitnehmer mit 59 Jahren zu entlassen.

1 February 1984. Änderungsvorschläge zum Vorruhestandsgeld.

4 February 1984. Der Vorruhestand soll attraktiver gemacht werden: Vorschläge des Bundesrates.

10 March 1984. Der Vorruhestand soll mit 58 Jahren beginnen.

Frankfurter Rundschau. 24 September 1981. Berufunfähige drücken auf die Rentenkassen.

27 February 1982. Bonner Pläne zur Umverteilung der Arbeit – mit 58 Jahren aufs Altenteil.

Fridenson, Patrick, and Straus André. 1987. *Le capitalisme français XIX–XX siècle*. Paris: Fayard.

Führer, Carl Christian. 1990. *Arbeitslosigkeit und die Enstehung der Arbeitslosenversicherung in Deutschland 1902–1927*. Berlin: Colloqium.

Galant, Henri. 1955. *Histoire politique de la Sécurité Sociale française*. Paris: Armand Colin.

Galland, Olivier, Jocelyne Gaudin, and Philippe Vrain. 1984. Contrats de solidarité de préretraite et stratégies d'entreprises. *Travail et emploi*, 22, 7–20.

Garibal, Michel. 1991. *La France malade du vieillissement*. Paris: Economica.

Gaßmann, Peter. 1984. Rationalisierung in der Metallwirtschaft: Eine Bestandsaufnahme. *Die Mitbestimmung*, 17–9.

Gaullier, Xavier. 1992. Le risque vieillesse, impossible paradigme. *Sociétés Contemporaines*, 10, 23–45.

1993. *Âge et Emploi. De la discrimination à la gestion des âges*. Paris: Iresco.

Gaullier, Xavier, and Maryvonne Gognalons-Nicolet. 1983. Crise économique et mutations sociales: Les cessations anticipées d'activité. *Travail et Emploi*, 15, 1, 33–45.

References

Gaullier, Xavier, and Arlette Goldberg. 1993. *Salariés âgés: Conditions de travail et transition vers la retraite. Rapport sur la France pour le Bureau International du Travail.* Paris: Iresco.

Gewerkschaftsbewegung der britischen Besatzungszone. 1949. *Geschäftsbericht des Deutschen Gewerkschaftsbundes (britische Besatzungszone).* Cologne: Bund-Verlag.

Gewerkschaftsrat der vereinten Zonen. 1948. Grundsätze für die Wiederherstellung der Selbstverwaltung in der Sozialversicherung, Materialsammlung Adolf Ludwig zur Sozialpolitik und zum Arbeitsrecht 13/76. Archive of the Friedrich Ebert Foundation, Bonn.

Geyer, Martin. 1987. *Die Reichsknappschaft. Versicherungsreformen und Sozialpolitik im Bergbau 1900–1945.* Munich: Beck.

Giaimo, Susan, and Philip Manow. 1999. Welfare State Adaptation or Erosion? The Case of Health Care Reform in Britain, Germany and the United States. *Comparative Political Studies*, 32, 8, 933–967.

Gibon, A. 1895. *Les retraites organisées par les companies houillères au profit des ouvriers mineurs.* Paris: Guillaumin.

Gierke, Otto von. 1888. *Die Soziale Aufgabe des Privatrechtes.* Berlin. Springer.

Gigot, Albert. 1895. Les assurances ouvrières et le socialisme d'état. *La Réforme Sociale*, 5, 829–846.

Gitter, Wolfgang. 1969. *Die Soziale Unfallversicherung als Teil des Allgemeinen Rechts.* Tübingen: Mohr.

Goguel, François. 1946. *La Politique des Partis sous la IIIème République*, Paris: Seuil.
    1952. *Histoire des institutions politiques de la France de 1870 à 1940.* Paris: Les Cours du Droit.
    1958. *La politique des partis sous la IIIe République.* Paris: Editions du Seuil.

Goldthorpe, John H., ed. 1984. *Order and Conflict in Contemporary Capitalism.* Oxford: Oxford University Press.

Gordon, Andrew. 1990. *Labor and Imperial Democracy in Japan.* Berkeley: University of California.

Gordon, Colin. 1994. *New Deals: Business, Labor and Politics in America, 1920–1935.* Cambridge: Cambridge University Press.

Gorges, Karl-Heinz. 1989. Der Christlich Geführte Industriebetrieb und das Modell Villeroy und Boch. In H. Pohl and W. Treue, eds., *Zeitschrift für Unternehmensgeschichte*. Wiesbaden: Franz Steiner.

Gottschalk, Marie. 2000. *The Shadow Welfare State: Labor, Business and the Politics of Health Care in the United States.* Ithaca: Cornell University Press.

Gresle, François. 1985. Le Patronat: Analyses et réflexions sur la literature récente. *Revue Française de Sociologie*, 26, 661–694.

Guillemard, Anne-Marie. 1983. La dynamique sociale des cessations anticipées d'activité. *Travail et emploi*, 15, 15–31.
    1984. Jalons pour une sociologie des politiques sociales: Le cas de la politique française de la vielleise. *Sociologie et sociétés*, 16, 2, 119–128.
    1986a. Formation et crise d'une politique sociale: Le case de la politique de la viellesse. *Sociologie du travail*, 2, 156–172.

1986b. *Le déclin du social.* Paris: Presses Universitaires de France.

1989. Les transformations de la sortie définitive d'activité au niveau international: Vers un réexamen du role de la retraite? *Droit Social,* 12, 851–860.

1990. Les nouvelles frontières entre travail et retraite en France. Bilan et perspectives des cessations anticipées d'activité. *Revue de l'IRES,* 2, 41–98.

1991. France: Massive Exit through Unemployment Compensation. In M. Kohli, ed., *Time for Retirement: Comparative Studies of Early Exit from the Labor Market.* Cambridge: Cambridge University Press, 127–180.

1993a. Emploi, protection sociale et cycle de vie: Résultats d'une comparaison internationale des dispositifs de sortie anticipée d'activité. *Sociologie du travail,* 3, 257–284.

1993b. Travailleurs viellissants et marché du travail en Europe. *Travail et emploi,* 57, 60–79.

1994. Attitudes et opinions des entreprises à l'égard des salariés agés et du vieillissement de la main-d'oeuvre. In Ministére du Travail, ed., *Emploi et vieillissement.* Paris: La Documentation Française, 143–149.

1997. Sorties précoces d'activité. *Projet,* 249, 15–30.

2000. *Aging and the Welfare State Crisis.* Newark: University of Delaware Press, 186–187.

Guyot, Yves. 1894. Le congrès international des accidents à Milan et la garantie obligatoire à l'indemnitè. *Revue Politique et Parlamentaire,* November, 281–302.

Hacker, Jacob. 2000. Boundary Wars: The Political Struggle over Public and Private Social Policy Benefits in the United States. Ph.D. dissertation, Department of Political Science, Yale University.

Hacker, Jacob, and Paul Pierson. 2000. Business Power and Social Policy: Employers and the formation of the American Welfare State. Paper presented at the annual meeting of the American Political Science Association.

Hall, Peter A., ed. 1989. *The Political Power of Economic Ideas: Keynesianism across Nations.* Princeton: Princeton University Press.

Hall, Peter A., and David Soskice. 2001a. An Introduction to Varieties of Capitalism. In Peter A. Hall and David Soskice, eds., *Varieties of Capitalism: The Institutional Foundations of Comparative Advantage.* Oxford: Oxford University Press, 1–68.

2001b. *Varieties of Capitalism: The Institutional Foundations of Comparative Advantage.* Oxford: Oxford University Press.

Handel und Gewerbe. 1888. Mangel des Unfallversicherungsgesetzes. *Handel und Gewerbe,* 32, 373–374.

1920. Arbeitslosenversicherung. *Handel und Gewerbe,* 28, 6, 56–57.

Handelsblatt. 13 July 1981. Mehr Frührentner.

2 October 1984. Herbe Kritik am sozialpolitischen Verschiebebahnhof.

Handelskammer zu Altona. 1922. Entwurf eines Gesetzes über eine vorläufige Arbeitslosenversicherung, 25 October 1922. Zentrales Staatsarchiv Potsdam, Reichswirtschaftsrat 664.

Handelskammer zu Hannover. 1922. Entschliessung zum Referentenentwurf über eine vorläufige Arbeitslosenversicherung, 11 April 1922. Zentrales Staatsarchiv Potsdam, Reichswirtschaftsrat 664.

References

Handwerkskammer von Oberbayern. 1920. Einschreiben betreffend der Arbeitslosenversicherung, 9 April. Zentrales Staatsarchiv Potsdam, Reichsarbeitsamt 4310.

Haneberg, Eva. 1993. Lebensarbeitszeit: Größere Flexibilität. *Bundesarbeitsblatt*, 7–8, 9–12.

Hanley, D., ed. 1994. *Christian Democracy in Europe: A Comparative Perspective*. London: Pinter.

Hannah, Leslie. 1986. *Inventing Retirement: The Development of Occupational Pensions in Britain*. Cambridge: Cambridge University Press.

Harris, J. 1972. *Unemployment and Politics*. Oxford: Clarendon Press.

Hatzfeld, Henri. 1971. *Du paupérisme à la sécurité sociale*. Paris: Armand Colin.

Hauck, Karl, and Werner Niemeyer. 1983. Haushaltbegleitgesetz 1983: Rentenpolitische Bilanz. *Bundesarbeitsblatt*, 3, 11–16.

Hauck, Karl, and Klaus Schenke. 1985. Rentenstrukturereform: Voraussetzungen geschaffen. *Bundesarbeitsblatt*, 12, 5–9.

Haupt, Heinz-Gerhard. 1996. Bemerkungen zum Vergleich staatlicher Sozialpolitik in Deutschland und Frankreich 1880–1920. *Geschichte und Gesellschaft*, 22, 299–310.

Haut Comité Consultatif de la Population et de la Famille, ed. 1962. *Politique de la vieillesse. Rapport de la commission d'étude des problèmes de la vieillesse*. Paris: La Documentation Française.

Hay, Roy. 1977. Employers and Social Policy in Britain: The Evolution of Welfare Legislation, 1905–1914. *Social History*, 4, 435–455.

Heck, Heinz. 1982. Mit 58 Jahren in die Rente? *Die Welt*, 5 March.

Heclo, Hugh. 1974. *Modern Social Politics in Britain and Sweden: From Relief to Income Maintenance*. New Haven: Yale University Press.

Heinz, Hans-Michael. 1973. *Entsprechungen und Abwandlungen des privaten Unfall und Haftversicherungsrechtes in der gesetzlichen Unfallversicherung nach der Reichsversicherungsordnung*. Berlin: Duncker & Humblot.

Hempel, Frank. 1984. 59-er Regelung geändert. *Bundesarbeitsblatt*, 7–8, 8–11.

Henning, Hans-Joachim. 1974. Arbeitslosenversicherung vor 1914: Das Genter System und seine Übernahme in Deutschland. In H. Kellenbenz, ed., *Wirtschaftspolitik und Arbeitsmarkt*. Munich: Oldenberg, 271–287.

Hentschel, Volker. 1978. *Wirtschaft und Wirtschaftspolitik im wilhelminischen Deutschland. Organisieter Kapitalismus und Interventionsstaat?* Stuttgart: Klett-Cotta.

Herder-Dorneich, Philipp. 1985. Die Kostenexplosion wäre nicht aufzuhalten. *Der Arbeitgeber*, 37, 5, 148–149.

Héreil, Georges. 1932. *Le chômage en France, étude de legislation sociale*. Paris: Librairie du Recueil Sirey.

Herrigel, Gary. 1995. *Industrial Constructions: The Sources of German Industrial Power*. Cambridge: Cambridge University Press.

Herrmann, Erich. 1985. Von der Humanisierung zur Beschäftigungspolitik: Arbeitszeitverkürzung und Arbeitszeitflexibilisierung in der Nahrungs- und Genußmittelindustrie. *Die Mitbestimmung*, 6, 247–248.

Hesse, Philippe-Jean, and Yvon Le Gall. 1999. L'assurance-accident du travail. In Michel Laroque, ed., *Contribution à l'histoire financière de la Sécurité Sociale*. Paris: La Documentation Française.

Hicks, Alexander. 1999. *Social Democracy and Welfare Capitalism: A Century of Income Security Politics*. Ithaca: Cornell University Press.

Hilbert, Ernst. 1947. Was erwarten die Arbeitgeber von der Neuordnung der deutschen Sozialversicherung. *Arbeitsblatt für die britische Zone*, 285–287.

Hitze, Franz. 1880. *Kapital und Arbeit und die Reorganisation der Gesellschaft*. Paderborn: Verl. der Bonifacius-Dr.

Hockerts, Hans Günter. 1980. *Sozialpolitische Entscheidungen im Nachkriegsdeutschland. Allierte und Deutsche Sozialversicherungspolitik*. Stuttgart: Klett-Cotta.

Höfler, Ludwig. 1984. Vorruhestand: Spielraum erweitern. *Bundesarbeitsblatt*, 7–8, 5–7.

Hofman, Claus F. 1992. Sozialpolitik im gesamtwirtschaftlichen Kontext. *Bundesarbeitsblatt*, 7–8, 5–7.

———. 1984. Gut im Rennen, *Bundesarbeitsblatt*, 7–8, 12–16.

———. 1993. Witschaftsstandort Deutschland: Mehr als nur eine Kostenfrage. *Bundesarbeitsblatt*, 11, 10–13.

Hoffmann, Edeltraud, and Gerhard Kühlewind. 1984. Arbeitsmarkt und Kostenaspekte zur Vorruhestandsregelung. Datenmaterial und Modellrechnungen. *Mitteilungen aus der Arbeitsmarkt- und Berufsforschung*, 2, 135–157.

Hoffmann, Walther. 1965. *Das Wachstum der deutschen Wirtschaft seit der Mitte des 19. Jahrhunderts*. Berlin: Springer.

Höffner, Josef. 1959. *Die Handwerkerversorgung im Hinblick auf die berufsständische Eigenart des Handwerks*. Stuttgart: Kohlhammer.

Hofmann, G. 1982. Die Deutsche Sozialdemokratie und die Sozialreformen von 1889. *Zeitschrift für Geschichtswissenschaft*, 30, 511–523.

Hollingsworth, J., and Robert Boyer, eds. 1997. *Contemporary Capitalism: The Embeddedness of Institutions*. Cambridge: Cambridge University Press.

Huber, Evelyne, and John Stephens. 2001. *Development and Crisis of the Welfare State: Parties and Policies in Global Markets*. Chicago: University of Chicago Press.

Hubert, René, and René Leproust. 1929. *Les assurances sociales*. Paris: Dalloz.

Hubert-Valleroux, P. 1883. De la responsabilité des patrons en matière d'accidents arrivés à leurs ouvriers. *Journal des économistes*, 22, April, 18–34.

———. 1896. Les accidents du travail et l'assurance obligatoire. *Le Correspondant*, 182, 25 March, 1152–1164.

Huet, Maryse. 1994. Les attitudes des entreprises via-à-vis des travailleurs vieillissants. In Ministère du Travail, ed., *Emploi et Vieillissement*. Paris: La Documentation Française.

Husmann, Jürgen. 1991. Pflegeabsicherung: Aus Strukturfehlern lernen. *Der Arbeitgeber*, 43, 10, 376.

Husmann, Jürgen. 1992. Koalition im Argumentationskrampf. *Der Arbeitgeber*, 44, 15–16, 524.

Husson, Raymond. 1994. Les préretraites du Fonds National de l'Emploi. *Revue Pratique du Droit Social*, 590, 185–190.

References

Hutton, Patrick H., eds. 1986. *Historical Dictionary of the French Third Republic.* Westport, Conn.: Greenwood Press.

IAB. 1986. Aktualisierte Befunde zur Vorruhestandsregelung: Globale und wirtschaftszweigspezifische Ergebnisse. IAB Kurzbericht. Nuremberg.

IG Metall, ed. 1980. *Fünfundsiebzig Jahre Industriegewerkschaft 1891 bis 1966: Vom Deutschen Metallarbeiterverband zur Industriegewerkschaft Metall – Ein Bericht in Wort und Bild.* Cologne: Bund.

Immergut, Ellen. 1992. *Health Politics: Interests and Institutions in Western Europe.* Cambridge: Cambridge University Press.

Industrie und Handelskammer Bochum. 1881. Bochumer Gesetzentwurf zur Errichtung einer Anrebeiterunfallversicherungskasse. In *Bericht der Industrie- und Handelskammer zu Bochum.* Bochum, 15–22.

Industrie- und Handelskammer München. 1947. Schreiben der Industrie- und Handelskammer München an den Länderrat der amerikanischen Beseatzungszone, 1. 10. 1947. Bundesarchiv Koblenz, Länderrat der Amerikanischen Besatzungszone, Z1/952/9–11.

Industrieverband Bau, Steine und Erde. 1947. Resolution der Delegierten des Industrieverbandes Bau, Steine und Erde. Bundesarchiv Koblenz, Z1/952/219–220.

International Labor Organization. 1927. Employers' Organizations in France. *International Labor Review,* 16, 1, 50–77.

Jacobs, Klaus, Martin Kohli, and Martin Rein. 1991. Germany: The Diversity of Pathways. In Martin Kohli, Martin Rein, Anne-Marie Guillemand, and Herman van Gunstern, eds., *Time for Retirement: Comparative Studies of Early Exit from the Labor Force.* Cambridge: Cambridge University Press, 181–221.

Jacobs, Klaus, and Winfried Schmähl. 1988. Der Übergang in den Ruhestand: Entwicklung, öfftentliche Diskussion und Möglichkeiten seiner Umgestaltung. *Mitteilungen aus dem Arbeitsmarkt und Berufsforschung,* 2, 196–205.

Jacoby, Sanford. 1997. *Modern Manors: Welfare Capitalism since the New Deal.* Princeton: Princeton University Press.

Jacquey, J. 1897. A propos de la loi sur les accidents du travail. *Revue Politique et Parlamentaire,* November, 533–542.

Jaillet, Renée. 1980. *La faute inexcusable en matière d'accident du travail et de maladie professionnelle.* Paris: Pichon and Durand-Auzias.

Jallade, Jean-Pierre, ed. 1988. *The Crisis of Distribution in European Welfare States.* Stoke-on-Trent: Trentham Books.

Janoski, T. 1990. *The Political Economy of Unemployment.* Berkeley: University of California Press.

Jay, Raoul. 1895. Un projet d'assurance contre le chômage dans le canton de Bale-Ville. *Revue d'Économie Politique,* 9, 368–386.

Jellinek, Georg. 1919. *System der Öffentlichen Subjektiven Rechte.* Tübingen: Mohr.

Jentsch, Peter. 1992. Koalition auf dem Weg zum Konsens. *Das Parlament,* 24 January.

Johr, Walter Adolf. 1933. *Die öffentlich-rechtlichen Formen der Arbeitslosenfürsorge auf Grund der Gesetzgebungen Deutschlands, der Schweiz und Frankreichs.* Aarau: H. R. Sauerlander.

Join-Lambert, Marie Thérèse, Anne Bolot-Gittler, Christine Daniel, Daniel Lenoir, and Dominique Méda, eds. 1997. *Politiques sociales.* Paris: Presses de Sciences Po.

Jourdain, René. 1899. *De l'intervention des tribunaux pour la fixation des indemnités en cas d'accidents du travail bénéficiaires de l'indemnité suivant l'état civil des victimes.* Evreux: C. Hérissey.

Journal Officiel. 1879. Secours aux ouvriers sans travail de Flers, de Condé-sur-Noireau et de leur rayon. Texte de la proposition de Mn. Delafosse et de Mackau, tendant a ouvrir a cet effet un credit extraordinaire de 200 000 F. Chambre des Députés, no. 1323.

—— 1880. Proposition de loi sur les responsabilités des accidents dont les ouvriers sont victimes dans l'exercice de leur travail. Chambre des Députés, Nr. 2660.

—— 1882a. Proposition de loi sur la responsabilité des accidents dont les ouvriers sont victimes dans l'exercise de leur travail, présentée par M. Léon Peulevey. Chambre des Députés, no. 283.

—— 1882b. Rapport fait au nom de la commission sur quatre propositions précédentes. Chambre des Députés, no. 694.

—— 1882c. Propositions de loi … présentées par M. Felix Faure. Chambre des Députés, no. 399.

—— 1884. Exposé des motifs et texte de la proposition de loi, presentée par M. Laroche-Joubert, ayant pour objet d'atténuer le chômage qui subsissent les travailleurs Français. no. 2815.

—— 1888a. Première Délibération du texte du projet de loi relatif a la responsabilité des accidents dont les ouvriers sont victimes dans leur travail, 15–29 mai.

—— 1888b. Deuxième délibération du texte du projet de loi relatif à la responsabilité des accidents dont les ouvriers sont victimes dans leur travail, 21–30 juin, 2–10 juillet.

—— 1889. 1ère Déliberation sur le projet de loi relatif aux accidents dont les ouvrières sont victimes dans leur travail, Sénat, 8–12 mars.

—— 1890a. Exposé des motifs et texte du projet de loi, modifié par le Sénat, concernant la responsabilité des accidents dont les ouvriers sont victimes dans leur travail. Chambre des Députés, no. 745.

—— 1890b. Projet de loi relatif au droit a indemnité des ouvriers victmies d'un accident dans leur travail, présenté au nom de M. Carnot, Président de la République Française, par M. Jules Roche, ministre du commerce, de l'industries et des colonies. Chambre des Députés, no. 746.

—— 1890c. 1ère déliberation sur le projet de loi relatif aux accidents dont les ouvrières sont victimes dans leur travail, Sénat, 8 mars.

—— 1893. 2ème déliberation sur le projet de loi relatif aux accidents dont les ouvrières sont victimes dans leur travail Chambre des Députés, 3 juin.

—— 1895. Déliberation sur le projet de loi relatif aux accidents dont les ouvrières sont victimes dans leur travail, Sénat, 10 juin, 582.

—— 1904a. Exposé des motifs et texte de la proposition de loi, présentée par MM. F. Dubief et Millerand, tendant à allouer des subventions aux Caisses de secours contre le chômage involontaire. Chambre des Députés, no. 1698.

References

1904b. Discussion de l'interpellation de M. Vaillant sur la nécéssité d'une enquête parlementaire et de mesures immédiates relatives au chômage. Chambre des Députés, 30 novembre.

1905a. Loi portant fixation du budget des dépenses et des recettes de l'exercise 1905, 23 avril.

1905b. Ministère du commerce, de l'industrie, des postes et des télégraphes. Rapport au Président de la République Française, 13 septembre.

1907. Ministère du travail et de la prévoyance sociale. Rapport au Président de la République Française, 1 janvier.

1913. Ministère du Travail et de la Prévoyance sociale. Rapport sur les subventions aux caisses de chômage pour l'année 1912, 28 août.

1921. Projet de loi sur les assurances sociales, par M. Daniel-Vincent. Chambre des Députés, no. 2369.

1922. Rapport de la Commission Permanente de l'Office du Travail, 16 novembre.

1923a. Ministère du Travail. Rapport sur les subventions aux caisses de chômage pour l'année 1922, présenté au Président de la République par le Ministre de Travail, 5 octobre.

1923b. Rapport fait au nom de la Commission d'assurance et de prévoyance sociale chargée d'éxaminer le projet de loi sur les assurances sociales par M. Edouard Grinda. Chambre des Députés, no. 5505.

1926. Rapport Supplémentaire fait au nom de la Commission de l'hygiène, de l'asistance, de l'assurance et de prévoyance sociale chargée d'examiner le projet de loi sur les assurances sociales adopté par la Chambre de Députées par M. Chaveau, Sénateur. Sénat, no. 628.

1928. Loi sur les assurances sociales, 12 avril.

1930. Rapport Antonelli-Grinda. no. 3187.

1945. Ordonnance no. 45–2250 du 4 octobre 1945 portant organization de la Sécurité Sociale.

1946a. Loi no. 46–1146 du 22 mai 1946 portant la generalization de la Sécurité Sociale.

1946b. Débats de l'Assemblée Nationale Constituante, 8–9 août.

1947a. Document no. 2805, 9 décembre.

1947b. Document no. 2948, 19 décembre.

1947c. Débats, Assemblée Nationale, 31 décembre.

1971. Abaisement de l'âge de la retraite. Questions orales avec débats, Assemblée Nationale, 19 mai, 1980–1997.

1982. Ordonnance no. 82–270 du 26 mars 1982 relative à l'abaissement de l'âge de la retraite des assurés du régime général et du régime des assurances sociales agricoles.

Kaelble, Hartmut. 1967. *Industrielle Interessenpolitik in der Wilhelminischen Gesellschaft: Der Centralverband Deutscher Industrieller 1895–1914.* Berlin: De Gruyter.

Kalle, Fritz, and Ludwig-Wolf Zilmer, eds. 1874. *Über Alters-und Invalidenkassen für Arbeiter. Gutachten auf Veranlassung des Vereins für Sozialpolitik.* Leipzig: Duncker & Humblot.

Kaltenbach, Helmut. 1986. Probleme der Rentenversicherung bei den BU/EU Renten, einschließlich die Zukunftsperspektiven. *Die Angestelltenversicherung,* 33, 10, 357–361.

Kammertöns, Johannes. 1952. *Die knappschaftliche Rentenversicherung.* Cologne: Bund.

Katzenstein, Peter. 1984. *Coporatism and Change.* Ithaca: Cornell University Press.

1985. *Small States in World Markets.* Ithaca: Cornell University Press.

1987. *Policy and Politics in West Germany: The Growth of a Semi-Sovereign State.* Philadelphia: Temple University Press.

Ed. 1978. *Between Power and Plenty.* Madison: University of Wisconsin Press.

Keller, Berthold. 1984. Beschäftigungswirksame Arbeitszeitverkürzung duch Vorruhestands- Tarifverträge. *Die Mitbestimmung,* 9, 386–388.

Kerschen, Nicole. 1983. Cessation anticipée d'activité et droit social. *Travail et Emploi,* 15, 63–74.

1994. Politique de l'emploi et droit: La préretraite comme statut et comme instrument. *Revue Française des Affaires Sociales,* 48, 1, 45–49.

Kerschen, Nicole, and Anne-Valérie Nenot. 1993. La fin des pré-retraites ou l'éternel recommencement? *Droit Social,* 5, 470–479.

Kerschen, Nicole, and Huguette Reminiac. 1981. Les systèmes de "pré-retraite": Classification juridique et pratique. *Droit Social,* 2, 175–201.

Killat, Arthur. N.d. *Zur Reform der Sozialversicherung.* DGB Archive of the Friedrich Ebert Foundation, 13/118, Bonn.

King, Desmond. 1995. *Actively Seeking Work? The Politics of Unemployment and Welfare Policy in the United States and Britain.* Chicago: University of Chicago Press.

King, Desmond, and Bo Rothstein. 1993. Institutional Choices and Labour Market Policy: A British-Swedish Comparison. *Comparative Political Studies,* 26, 147–177.

King, Desmond, and Stewart Wood. 1999. Neo-Liberalism and the Conservative Offensive: Britain and the United States in the 1980s. In Herbert Kitschelt, Peter Lange, Gary Marks, and John D. Stephens, eds., *Change and Continuity in Contemporary Capitalism.* Cambridge: Cambridge University Press, 371–397.

King, Gary, Robert Keohane, and Sidney Verba. 1994. *Designing Social Inquiry: Scientific Inference in Qualitative Research.* Princeton: Princeton University Press.

Kitschelt, Herbert, Peter Lange, Gary Marks, and John D. Stephens, eds. 1999. *Continuity and Change in Contemporary Capitalism.* Cambridge: Cambridge University Press.

Kleeis, Friedrich. 1911. *Die Sozialpolitik der Sozialdemokratie.* Halle: Hallesche Genossenschaftsbuchdruckerei.

Kocka, Jürgen. 1967. *Unternehmensverwaltung und Angestelltenschaft am Beispiel Siemens 1847–1914.* Stuttgart: Ernst Klett.

1980. The Rise of the Modern Industrial Enterprise in Germany. In Alfred Chandler and H. Daems, eds., *Managerial Hierarchies: Comparative Perspectives on the Rise of the Modern Industrial Enterprise.* Cambridge, Mass.: Harvard University Press, 77–116.

References

Kocka, Jürgen, and Siegrist Hannes. 1979. Die hundert deutschen Großunternehmen im späten 19. und frühen 20. Jahrhundert: Expansion, Diversifikation und Integration im internationalen Vergleich. In N. Horn and J. Kocka, eds., *Recht und Entwicklung der Großunternehmen 1860–1920*. Göttingen: Vandenhock & Ruprecht, 55–122.

Kocka, Jürgen, and Michael Prinz. 1983. Vom neuen Mittelstand zum angestellten Arbeitnehmer: Kontinuität und Wandel der deutschen Angestellten seit der Weimarer Republik. In Werner Conze, and M. Rainer Lepsius, eds., *Sozialgeschichte der Bundesrepublik Deutschland*. Stuttgart: Klett-Cotta, 239–247.

Köhler, Peter. 1979. Entstehung von Sozialversicherung: Ein Zwischenbericht. In Hans Zacher, ed., *Bedingungen für die Entstehung und Entwicklung von Sozialversicherung*. Berlin: Duncker & Humblot.

Köhler, Peter, and Hans Zacher, eds. 1982. *The Evolution of Social Insurance*. New York: St. Martin's Press.

Kohli, Martin, and Martin Rein. 1991. The Changing Balance of Work and Retirement. In Martin Kohli, Martin Rein, Anne-Marie Guillemand, and Herman van Gunstern, eds., *Time for Retirement: Comparative Studies of the Early Exit from the Labor Force*. Cambridge: Cambridge University Press, 1–35.

Kohli, Martin, Martin Rein, Anne-Marie Guillemand, and Herman van Gunstern, eds. 1991. *Time for Retirement: Comparative Studies of the Early Exit from the Labor Force*. Cambridge: Cambridge University Press.

Kolberg, Jan Eivind, ed. 1992. *Between Work and Social Citizenship*. London: Sharpe.

1992. *The Study of Welfare State Regimes*. London: Sharpe.

Kolboom, Ingo. 1983. *Frankreichs Unternehmer in der Periode der Volksfront*. Rheinfelden: Schauble.

Korpi, Walter. 1978. *The Working Class in Welfare Capitalism: Work, Unions and Politics in Sweden*. London: Routledge and Kegan Paul.

1983. *The Democratic Class Struggle*. London: Routledge and Kegan Paul.

1995. Un État Providence contesté et fragmenté. Le développement de la citoyenneté sociale en France. *Revue Française de Science Politique*, 45, 4, 17–35.

Kott, Sandrine. 1996. Gemeinschaft oder Solidarität? Unterschiedliche Modelle der französischen und deutschen Sozialpolitik am Ende des 19. Jahrhunderts. *Geschichte und Gesellschaft*, 22, 311–330.

Krieger, Wolfgang. 1980. Das Gewerkschaftliche Unterstützungswesen in Grossbritanien in den zwanziger Jahren. *Archiv für Sozialgeschichte*, 20, 119–146.

Kühlewind, Gerhard. 1986. Beschäftigung und Ausgliederung älterer Arbeitnehmer. Empirische Befunde zu Erwerbsbeteiligung, Rentenübergang, Vorruhestandsregelung und Arbeitslosigkeit. *Mitteilungen aus der Arbeitsmarkt- und Berufsforschung*, 2, 209–232.

Kuisel, R. 1981. *Capitalism and the State in Modern France*. Cambridge: Cambridge University Press.

Labi, Maurice. 1964. *La grande division des travailleurs*. Paris: Les Editions Ouvrières.

La Croix. 26 March 1982. Le droit à la retraite a 60 ans ouvre une controverse.

Lalou, Henri. 1955. *Traité pratique de la responsabilité civile*. Paris: Dalloz.

291

Landesrat der amerikanischen Besatzungszone. N.d. Bundesarchiv Koblenz, Z1/939.

1946a. *Vorschlag für eine Neuauffassung des Gesetzes über die pflichtmäßige Sozialversicherung der Arbeiter und Angestellten in Deutschland.* Bundesarchiv Koblenz, Landesarchiv der amerikanischen Besatzungszone, Z1/ 939, 39–67.

1946b. *Gesetz über die pflichtmässige Sozialversicherung der Arbeiter und Angestellten in Deutschland.* Fassung vom 14. 12. 1946. Bundesarchiv Koblenz, Landesrat der amerikanischen Besatzungszone, Z 1/961/71–89.

Landesverband Südwestdeutschland der gewerblichen Berufsgenossenschaften. 1946. 18 April. Bundesarchiv Koblenz, Z1/939.

Lang, Klaus. 1985. Neue Wochenarbeitszeit in der Metallindustrie ab 1. April 1985, *Die Mitbestimmung*, 6, 219–221.

Laroque, Marie-France. 1985. La protection sociale des personnes âgées. *Revue Française des Affaires Sociales*, 39, 3, 179–195.

Laroque, Michel, ed. 1999. *Contribution à l'histoire financière de la Sécurité Sociale.* Paris: La documentation Française.

Laroque, Pierre. 1946. Le plan français de Sécurité Sociale. *Revue Française du Travail*, 1, 1, 16.

Ed. 1983. *The Social Institutions of France.* New York: Gordon and Breach.

Lasseron, Paul. 1928. *L'assurance contre le chômage.* Bordeaux: L'imprimerie de l'Université.

Latty, Philippe. 1973. Les systèmes de pré-retraite en France. *Droit Social*, 4, 255–268.

La Vie Française. 20 June 1977. La Préretraite à 60 ans: Du provisoire qui peut durer.

Lee, W. R., ed. 1991. *German Industry and German Industrialization: Essays in Economic and Business History in the Nineteenth and Twentieth Century.* London: Routledge.

Le Figaro. 14 June 1977. Préretraite: Accord signé par tous les syndicats.

26 March 1982. Déception générale. Le CNPF: Une mesure improvisée coûteuse et difficilement applicable.

28 January 1983. Retraites: Les Régimes Complémentaires Préservés.

Lefranc, Georges. 1963. *Le mouvement socialiste sous la Troisième République.* Paris: Payot.

1976. *Les organisations patronales en France.* Paris: Payot.

Leibfried, Stefan, and Florian Tennstedt, eds. 1985. *Politik der Armut und die Spaltung des Sozialstaates.* Frankfurt: Suhrkamp.

Leibfried, Stephan. 1977. Die Institutionalisierung der Arbeitslosenversicherung in Deutschland. *Kritische Justiz*, 10, 2, 189–201.

Leienbach, Volker. 1984. Experimente wären gefährlich, *Der Arbeitgeber*, 36, 18, 689–690.

Le Matin. 29 September 1981. Retraite: La Carrière comptera plus que l'âge.

26 March 1982. Retraite à 60 ans: Critiques tous azimuts. Patrons commes syndicalistes jugent l'ordonnance insuffisante ou trop onereuse.

Le Monde. 12 July 1977. Comment les salariés de soixante à soixante-cinq ans peuvent toucher la préretraite.

27 June 1981. La retraite à 60 ans: Projet de loi a l'automne.

References

13 August 1981. Retraite à 60 ans: Les difficultés du dossier.

13 March 1982. Le patronat et le pouvoir.

26 March 1982. Sept ordonnances et quatre projets sur la retraite.

6 June 1982. Ordonnances risquent d'alourdir gravement le déficit des régimes sociaux.

23 December 1983. L'ouverture des négotiations entre patronat et syndicats. Qui paiera la retraite à soixante ans?

26 January 1983. La négotiation sur la retraite a soixante ans. D'importants progrès ont été réalisés sur le dossier du financement.

28 January 1983. La retraite a soixante ans: Les derniers obstacles semblent levés.

Le Nouveau Journal. 18 May 1977. La retraite à soixante ans?

Le Pluart, Alain. 1992. Gestion de main d'œuvre et departs en preretraite dans les grands etabilissements en 1987–1988 et 1989. *Dossiers statistiques du travail et de l'emploi,* 84, 101–107.

Les Échos. 13 June 1977. Une nouvelle étape pour la politique contractuelle.

17 August 1981. L'abaissement de l'âge de la retraite aura de répercussions couteuses sur les régimes complémentaires.

Le Syndicalisme. 10 February 1972. Retraites: Pour le developpement et la permanence de l'action.

6 January 1983. Retraite à 60 ans: La bataille des complémentaires.

Lévy-Leboyer, Maurice. 1980. The Large Corporation in Modern France. In Alfred Chandler and H. Daems, eds., *Managerial Hierarchies: Comparative Perspectives on the Rise of the Modern Enterprise.* Cambridge: Harvard University Press, 117–160.

Lévy-Leboyer, Maurice, and Jean-Claude Casanova, eds. 1991. *Entre l'état et le marché.* Paris: Gallimard.

Lewek, Peter. 1992. *Arbeitslosigkeit und Arbeitslosenversicherung in der Weimarer Republik 1918–1927.* Stuttgart: Franz Steiner.

L'Humanité. 23 December 1983. Premier tour de table pour la retraite à 60 ans.

Lidtke, Vernon. 1966. *The Outlawed Party: Social Democracy in Germany, 1878–1890.* Princeton: Princeton University Press.

Lincoln, Andrew. 1981. Le syndicalisme patronal à Paris de 1815 à 1848: Une étape de la formation d'une classe patronale. *Le Mouvement Social,* 114, 11–34.

Lombardot, Michel. 1970. Les problèmes sociaux des personnes âgées. *Revue Française des Affaires Sociales,* 24, 2, 87–92.

Lowi, Theodore. 1964. American Business, Public Policy, Case Studies and Political Theory. *World Politics,* 16, 677–715.

Lüttich, A. 1924. Befreiung von den Beiträgen zur Erwerbslosenfürsorge. *Die Arbeit,* 1, 4, 213–217.

Lyon-Caen, Gérard. 1995. *Droit Social.* Paris: Librairie Générale du Droit et Jurisprudence.

Machtan, Lothar. 1985. Risikoversicherung statt Gesundheitsschutz für Arbeiter: Zur Entstehung der Unfallversicherungsgesetzgebung im Bismarck-Reich. *Leviathan,* 13, 3, 420–441.

Mackie, Thomas, and Richard Rose. 1974. *The International Almanac of Electoral History.* New York: Facts on File.

Malivoire de Camas, Jacques. 1933. *La France et le chômage. Étude de législation (moyens mis en œuvre par l'État et les collectivités pour venir en aide aux chômeurs involontaires par manque de travail)*. Paris: Librairie du Recueil Sirey.

Manes, Alfred. 1905. *Die Arbeiterversicherung*. Leipzig: Duncker & Humblot.

Manow, Philip. 1997. Social Insurance and the German Political Economy. Paper presented at the Seminar on State and Capitalism since 1800, Center for European Studies, Harvard University, 16 April.

——— 1998. Individuelle Zeit, institutionelle Zeit, Soziale Zeit. Das Vertrauen in die Sicherheit der Rente und die Debatte um die Kapitaldeckung und Umlage in Deutschland. *Zeitschrift für Soziologie*, 27, 3, 193–211.

——— 2000a. Capitalist Production, Social Protection. Max Planck Institute, Cologne. Unpublished manuscript.

——— 2000b. Comparative Institutional Advantage of Welfare State Regimes and New Coalitions in Welfare State Reform. In Paul Pierson, *The New Politics of the Welfare State*. Oxford: Oxford University Press, 146–164.

Mansfield, M., R. Salais, and N. Whileside, eds. 1994. *Aux sources du chômage 1880–1914*. Paris: Belin.

Mares, Isabela. 1997. Is Unemployment Insurable? Employers and the Institutionalization of the Risk of Unemployment. *Journal of Public Policy*, 17, 3, 299–327.

——— 1999. Negotiated Risks: Employers' Role in Social Policy Development. Ph.D. dissertation, Department of Government, Harvard University.

——— 2000. Strategic Alliances and Social Policy Reform: Unemployment Insurance in Comparative Perspective. *Politics and Society*, 26, 2, 223–244.

——— 2001a. Strategic Bargaining and Social Policy Development: Unemployment insurance in France and Germany. In Bernhard Ebbinghaus and Philip Manow, eds., *Comparing Welfare Capitalism: Social Policy and Political Economy in Europe, Japan and the USA*. London: Routledge, 52–74.

——— 2001b. Enterprise reorganization and social insurance reform: the development of early retirement in France and Germany. *Governance*, 14, 3, 295–318.

Mariaux Franz. 1981. Gedenkwort zum hunderjährigen Bestehen der Industrie- und Handelskammer zu Bochum. *Mitteilungen. Industrie- und Handelskammer zu Bochum*, 37, 10, 537–544.

Marichy, Jean-Pierre. 1969. *La deuxième chambre dans la vie politique française depuis 1875*. Paris: Librairie Générale de droit et de jurisprudence.

Marin, Bernd. 1988. Qu'est-ce que le patronat? Enjeux théoriques et résultats empiriques. *Sociologie du travail*, 4, 515–544.

Marioni, Pierre, and Marc Ricau. 1984. Préretraites et politiques de gestion du personnel: Approche sectorielle. *Dossiers statistiques du travail et de l'emploi*, 7, 7–23.

Markovits, Andrei. 1986. *The Politics of the West German Trade Unions*. Cambridge: Cambridge University Press.

Martin, Cathie Jo. 1995a. Nature or Nurture? Sources of Firm Preferences for National Health Reform. *American Political Science Review*, 89, 4, 898–913.

——— 1995b. Stuck in Neutral: Big Business and the Politics of National Health Reform, *Journal of Health Politics, Policy and Law*, 20, 2, 431–436.

——— 2000. *Stuck in Neutral*. Princeton: Princeton University Press.

References

Massé, Jacqueline, and T. Marie-Marthe. 1984. Sociétés et viellissement. *Sociologie et Sociétés*, 16, 2, entire issue.

Mataja, Victor. 1888. *Das Recht des Schadensersatzes vom Standpunkt der Nationalökonomie*. Leipzig: Duncker & Humblot.

Matzner, Egon, and Wolfgang Streeck, eds. 1991. *Beyond Keynesianism*. London: Edward Elgar.

Mayr, Hans, and Hans Jannsen, eds. 1984. *Perspektiven der Arbeitszeitverkürzung: Wissenschaftler und Geastarbeiter zur 35-Stunden Woche*. Cologne: Bund.

Melchior, Eric. 1993. *Le PS, du projet au pouvoir. L'impossible concordance*. Paris: Editions de l'Atelier.

Mercereau, François. 1982. La retraite à 60 ans. *Droit Social*, 6, 452–463.

Michel, H., and B. Mirkine-Guetzevich. 1954. *Les idées politiques et sociales de la Résistance*. Paris: PUF.

Michel, Jules. 1892. A propos de la question des accidents du travail. *Réforme Sociale*, 3, 397–408.

Ministère du Commerce. 1903. *Conseil Supérieur du Travail. Commission Permanente. Extraits des Procès-Verbaux*. Paris: Imprimerie Nationale.

Ministère du Travail. 1922. *Rapport présenté au nom de la minorité de la commission permanente par M. Pralon*. 15 novembre 1922. Archive of the Chambre de Commerce de Paris, III. 5. 50 (9).

——— Ed. 1994. *Emploi et vieillissement*. Paris: La Documentation Française.

Ministère du Travail et de Sécurité Sociale. 1946. Note résumant les entretiens avec les différentes organizations des travailleurs independents au sujet de la modification de la loi du 28 mai 1946. Centre d'Archives Contemporaines, SS 07921, 760228, box 45.

Mistral, Jacques. 1995. Politique Sociale: Un cas de schizophrénie patronale?, *Droit Social*, 1, 3–8.

Mitchell, B. 1980. *European Historical Statistics*. London: Butler & Tann.

Mittelrheinischer Fabrikantenverein. 1920. Erklärung betreffend des Gesetzentwurfes der Arbeitslosenversicherung. Zentrales Staatsarchiv Potsdam, Reichsarbeitsamt 4311/87–88.

Molitor, Bruno. 1980. Ein trojanisches Pferd. Argumente gegen die im Arbeitsministerium favorisierte Umstellung der Arbeitgeberbeiträge. *Deutsches Handwerksblatt*, 5, 179–181.

Mommsen, Hans, Dietmar Petzina, and Bernd Weisbrod, eds. 1974. *Industrielles System und Politische Entwicklung in der Weimarer Republik*. Düsseldorf: Droste.

Mommsen, Wolfgang, ed. 1981. *The Emergence of the Welfare State in Britain and Germany*. London: Croom Helm.

Monchois, Xavier, and Didier Gélot. 1994. Les bénéficiaires de la politique de l'emploi de 50 ans et plus. In Ministere du Travail, ed., *Emploi et Vieillissement*. Paris: La Documentation Française.

Monse, Stefan. 1993. Große Herausforderungen. *Bundesarbeitsblatt*, 11, 14–15.

Moss, Bernard. 1976. *The Origins of the French Labor Movement, 1830–1914: The Socialism of Skilled Workers*. Berkeley: University of California Press.

Mossé, Robert. 1929. *L'assurance obligatoire contre le chômage au point de vue social. Étude de législation comparée et d'économie sociale*. Paris: Thèse Droit.

Müller, Eugen. 1981. Frühinvalidität: Zwischen Behauptungen und Fakte. *Der Arbeitgeber*, 33, 1, 37–40.

Müller, Hermann. 1878. *Die Organisation der Lithographen, Steindruckero und verwandten Berufe*, Berlin: Dietz.

Muth, Wolfgang. 1985. *Berufsausbildung in der Weimarer Republik*. Stuttgart: Franz Steiner.

Myles, John, and Jill Quadagno, eds. 1991. *States, Labor Markets and the Future of Old-Age Policy*. Philadelphia: Temple University Press.

Nachtigal, Gert. 1987. Langfristiges Konzept gesucht. *Der Arbeitgeber*, 39, 8, 317.

Nagel, Paul. 1920. Reichsarbeitslosenversicherung. *Deutsche Arbeitgeberzeitung*, 8 August.

———. 1921. Das Genter System. *Deutsche Arbeitgeberzeitung*, 20 November.

Namgalies, Brigitte. 1981. *Das französische Arbeitsunfallsrecht. Eine Darstellung mit rechtsvergleichenden Hinweisen zum deutschen Arbeitsunfallsrecht*. Berlin: Duncker & Humblot.

Naschold, Frieder, and Bert de Vroom, eds. 1994. *Regulating Employment and Welfare: Company and National Policies of Labor Force Participation Rates at the End of Worklife in Industrial Countries*. Berlin: Walter de Gruyter.

Naschold, Frieder, Maria, Oppen, Holger Peinemann, and Joachim Rosenow, 1994. Germany: The Concerted Transition from Work to Welfare. In Frieder Naschold and Bert de Vroom, eds., *Regulating Employment and Welfare: Company and National Policies of Labor Force Participation at the End of Worklife in Industrial Countries*. Berlin: Walter de Gruyter, 117–182.

Nerb, Gernot. 1986. Arbeitslosigkeit in Europa. Überwindung durch Flexibilisierung? *Bundesarbeitsblatt*, 6, 5–10.

Neuloh, Otto. 1957. *Hundert Jahre Staatliche Sozialpolitik 1839–1939*. Stuttgart: Kohlhammer.

Niemeyer, Werner. 1989. Kernstück Rentenversicherung, *Bundesarbeitsblatt*, 6, 5–9.

Noiriel, Gérard. 1988. Du "patronage" au "paternalisme": La restructuration des formes de domination de la main-d'oeuvre ouvrière dans l'industrie métallurgique française. *Le Mouvement Social*, 144, 17–35.

———. 1990. *Workers in French Society in the 19th and 20th Century*. New York: Berg.

Nolan, Many. 1986. Economic Crisis, State Policy and Working Class Formation in Germany, 1870–1900. In Ira Katznelson and Aristide Zolberg, eds., *Working-Class Formation: Nineteenth Century Patterns in Western Europe and the United States*. Princeton: Princeton University Press, 352–396.

Nord, Philip. 1981. Le mouvement des petits commerçants et la politique en France de 1888 à 1914. *Le Mouvement Social*, 33–55.

———. 1994. The Welfare State in France, 1870–1914. *French Historical Studies*, 18, 3, 821–838.

Nullmeier, Frank, and Friedebert Rüb. 1993. *Die Transformation der Sozialpolitik: Vom Sozialstaat zum Sicherungsstaat*. Frankfurt: Campus.

OECD. 1995. *The Labor Market and Older Workers*. Paris: OECD.

———. 1999. *Taxing Wages: Taxes on Wages and Salaries, Social Security Contributions for Employees and Their Employers*. Paris: OECD.

References

Office du Travail, ed. 1896. *Documents sur la question du chômage*. Paris: Imprimerie Nationale.

1898. *Les caisses patronales de retraites des établissements industriels*. Paris: Imprimerie Nationale.

Ortlepp, Hanns-Peter. 1987. Arbeitgeber zur Strukturreform. *Der Arbeitgeber*, 20, 748–750.

Pactet, Pierre. 1995. *Institutions Politiques. Droit Constitutionnel*. Paris: Armand Collin.

Pascaud, H. 1885. Recours de l'ouvrier contre le patron en cas d'accident. *Journal des économistes*, 31, September, 365–371.

Pavard, Francis. 1980. A propos du minimum vieillesse. *Droit Social*, 3, 225–232.

Pedersen, Susan. 1993. *Family, Dependence and the Origin of the Welfare State: Britain and France, 1914–1945*. Cambridge: Cambridge University Press.

Peiter, Henry. 1976. Institutions and Attitudes: The Consolidation of the Business Community in Bourgeois France. *Journal of Social History*, 9, 4, 510–525.

Piachaud, David. 1986. Disability, Retirement and Unemployment of Older Men. *Journal of Social Policy*, 15, 2, 145–162.

Pic, Paul. 1895. La question des accidents du travail devant le Parlement Français. *Revue Politique et Parlementaire*, June 502–517.

1898. Étude critique de la loi du 9 avril 1898. *Revue d'Économie Politique*, 12, 513–537.

Picard, Roger. 1924. Le marché du travail, le syndicalisme et la législation sociale. *Revue d'Économie Politique*, 38, 382–392.

1925. Le mouvement ouvrier. *Revue d'Économie Politique*, 675–697.

Picot, Georges. 1892. La solution française de la question sociale. *La Réforme Sociale*, 2, 40–48.

Pierson, Paul. 1993. When Effect Becomes Cause: Policy Feedback and Political Change. *World Politics*, 45, 3, 595–628.

1994. *Dismantling the Welfare State? Reagan, Thatcher and the Politics of Retrenchment*. Cambridge: Cambridge University Press.

1995a. Fragmented Welfare States: Federal Institutions and the Development of Social Policy. *Governance*, 8, 4, 447–478.

1995b. The Scope and Nature of Business Power: Employers and the American Welfare State, 1900–1935. Paper presented at the annual conference of the American Political Science Association, Chicago.

1996. The New Politics of the Welfare State. *World Politics*, 48, 2, 143–179.

2000a. Three Worlds of Welfare State Research. *Comparative Political Studies*, 33, 6–7, 791–821.

Ed. 2000b. *The New Politics of the Welfare State*. Oxford: Oxford University Press.

Pierson, Paul, and Jacob Hacker. 2000. Business Power and Social Policy: Employers and the Formation of the American Welfare State. Paper presented at the annual meeting of the American Political Science Association, Washington, D.C.

Piloty, Robert. 1890. *Das Reichs-Unfallversicherungsrecht, dessen Entstehungsgeschichte und System*. Würzburg: Stürtz.

Pinon, H. 1898. La responsabilité des accidents du travail. *Revue d'Économie Politique*, 12, 827–856.

Pinot, Robert. 1924. *Les œuvres sociales des industries métallurgiques*. Paris: Colin.

Piore, Michael. 1987. Historical Perspectives and the Interpretation of Unemployment. *Journal of Economic Literature*, 25, 4, 1934–1950.

Pohl, Hans, and Treue Wilhelm. 1970. *Betriebliche Sozialpolitik Deutscher Unternehmen seit dem 19. Jahrhundert*. Wiesbaden: Franz Steiner.

Polanyi, Karl. 1944. *The Great Transformation: The Political and Economic Origins of Our Time*. Boston: Beacon Hill.

Pollet, Gilles, and Renard Didier. 1995. Genèses et usages de l'idée paritaire dans le système de protection sociale français. *Revue Française de Science Politique*, 45, 4, 545–569.

    1996. Entstehung und Umsetzung des paritätischen Gedankens im System der sozialen Sicherung Frankreichs. *Geschichte und Gesellschaft*, 22, 331–349.

Pontusson, Jonas. 1992. *The Limits of Social Democracy: Investment Politics in Sweden*. Ithaca: Cornell University Press.

Pontusson, Jonas, and Peter Swenson. 1996. Labor Markets, Production Strategies and Wage Bargaining Institutions: The Swedish Employer Offensive in Comparative Perspective. *Comparative Political Studies*, 29, 4, 223–250.

Porte, Marcel. 1927. Les assurances sociales devant le Sénat. *Revue d' Économie Politique*, 41, 1054–1087.

Post, Alfred. 1956. *Handwerkerversorgung, Soziale Rentenversicherung und Rentenreform*. Hamburg: Paulsen und Lannsen.

Potthoff, Heinrich. 1979. *Gewerkschaften und Politik zwischen Revolution und Inflation*. Düsseldorf: Droste.

Poulantzas, Nicos. 1973. *Political Power and Social Classes*. London: Verso.

Pridham, Geoffrey. 1977. *Christian Democracy in Western Germany: The CDU/CSU in Government and Opposition*. London: Croom Helm.

Priouret, Roger. 1963. *Origines du patronat français*. Paris: Bernard Grasset.

Puppke, Ludwig. 1966. *Soziale Anschauungen frühindustrieller Unternehmen*. Cologne: Rheinisch- Westfälisches Wirtschaftsarchiv.

Purwien, Peter. 1984. Defizite des Vorruhestandsgesetzes und Mindestanforderungen für dessen tarifvertragliche Ausgestaltung. *Die Mitbestimmung*, 6, 234–237.

Quandt, Otto. 1938. *Die Anfänge der Bismarckschen Sozialgesetzgebung und die Haltung der Parteien: das Unfallversicherungsgesetz, 1881–1884*. Vaduz: Kraus.

Rabinbach, Anson. 1996. Social Knowledge, Social Risk and the Politics of Industrial Accidents in Germany and France. In Dietrich Rueschemeyer and Theda Skocpol, eds., *States, Social Knowledge and the Origin of Modern Social Policies*. Princeton: Princeton University Press, 48–89.

Rappe, Hermann. 1984. Tarifpolitik zwischen Geld und Zeit. *Die Mitbestimmung*, 9, 369–371.

Recker, Marie. 1985. *Nationalsozialistische Sozialpolitik im zweiten Weltkrieg*. Munich: Oldenbourg.

References

Réforme Sociale. 1892a. Réunion mensuelle du groupe de Paris. Séance du 28 décembre 1891. *La Réforme Sociale*, 3, 14, 218–233.

1892b. Les caisses syndicales d'assurance mutuelle contre les incendies. *La Réforme Sociale*, 2, 218–233.

1892c. Chronique du mouvement social. *La Réforme Sociale*, 3, 458–460.

1892d. La compagnie de gaz de Paris et son personnel. *Réforme Sociale*, 3, 720–721.

1893. L'assurance libre contre les accidents du travail. *La Réforme Sociale*, 3, 960–963.

1921. Un projet grandiose d'assurances sociales. *La Réforme Sociale*, 81, 342–344.

Ed. 1894. L'assurance obligatoire allemande et l'assurance libre. *La Réforme Sociale*, 4, 341–353.

Reichsarbeitsblatt. 1920. Entwurf zum Gesetz der Arbeitslosenversicherung. *Reichsarbeitsblatt*, 18, 391–410.

1921. Referentenentwurf des Gesetzes über eine vorläufige Arbeitslosenversicherung. *Reichsarbeitsblatt*, 839–845.

1922. Entwurf eines Gesetzes über eine vorläufige Arbeitslosenversicherung nebst allgemeiner Begründung. *Reichsarbeitsblatt*, 329–346.

1923. Entwurf eines Gesetzes über eine vorläufige Arbeitslosenversicherung. *Reichsarbeitsblatt*, 187–194.

1924. Die Soziale Belastung der Deutschen Wirtschaft. *Reichsarbeitsblatt*, 135–140.

1925. Entwurf des Gesetzes zur Arbeitslosenversicherung. *Reichsarbeitsblatt*, Sonderheft 34.

Reichsgesetzblatt. 1871. Reichshafspflichtgesetz, *Reichsgesetzblatt*, 7 June, 207–209.

1918. Verordnung über Erwerbslosenfürsorge. *Reichsgesetzblatt*, Nr. 6530, 1305–1308.

1938. Gesetz über die Altersversorgung für das deutsche Handwerk. *Reichsgesetzblatt*, 21 December 1900.

Reichsverband des Deutschen Handwerks. 1923. *Beiträge zu den Mitteln der Erwerbslosenfürsorge.* Zentrales Staatsarchiv Potsdam, Reichsarbeitsministerium 1017.

1925. Zum Entwurf eines Gesetzes über die Arbeitslosenversicherung. *Das Deutsche Handwerksblatt*, 19, 1, 12–14.

1926a. Entwurf eines Gesetzes über die Arbeitslosenversicherung. *Das Deutsche Handwerksblatt*, 21, 2, 17–20.

1926b. *Tätigkeitsbericht des Reichsverbands des Deutschen Handwerks 1926.* Zentrales Staatsarchiv Potsdam, Reichswirtschaftsministerium 2073.

1926c. Handwerk und Arbeitslosenversicherung. *Das deutsche Handwerksblatt*, 20, 21, 322.

1927. Entwurf eines Gesetzes über Arbeitslosenversicherung. *Das deutsche Handwerksblatt*, 21, 2, 17–20.

Reichsverband der Deutschen Industrie. 1920. *Zur Frage der Arbeitslosenversicherung.* Zentrales Staatsarchiv Potsdam, Reichsarbeitsministerium 4311.

Remmers, Werner. 1983. Subsidiarität: Mit der Zukunft rechnen. *Bundesarbeitsblatt*, 3, 5–10.

Renard, Didier. 1995. Assistance et assurance dans la constitution du système de protection sociale française. *Genèses*, 18, 30–46.

Reynaud, Emmanuel. 1993. Le chômage de longue durée; la théorie et l'action. *Revue Française de Sociologie*, 34, 271–291.

1994. Les grandes tendances de la retraite complémentaire en France. *Revue Française des Affaires Sociales*, 48, 3, 3–19.

Reynaud, Jean Daniel. 1975. *Les syndicats en France*. Paris: Seuil.

Rhein- Kress, Gaby. 1993. Coping with Economic Crisis: Labour Supply as a Policy Instrument. In Francis Castles, ed., *Families of Nations*. Aldershot: Dartmouth Publishing.

Rhodes, Martin. 2000. The Political Economy of Social Pacts: Competitive Corporatism and European Welfare Reform. In Paul Pierson, ed., *The New Politics of the Welfare State*. Oxford: Oxford University Press, 165–196.

Ridley, F. 1970. *Revolutionary Syndicalism in France: The Direct Action of Its Time*. Cambridge: Cambridge University Press.

Rimlinger, Gaston. 1973. Sozialpolitik und wirtschaftliche Entwicklung: Ein historischer Vergleich. In Rudolf Braun, ed., *Gesellschaft in der Industriellen Revolution*. Cologne: Kiepenheuer & Witsch, 113–126.

Ritter, Erich. 1933. *Die Stellungnahme der Gewerkschaften zu den Problemen der Sozialversicherung in Deutschland*. Frankfurt: Wertheim.

Ritter, Gerhard. 1980. *Wahlgeschichtliches Arbeitsbuch. Materialen zur Statistik des Deutschen Kaiserreichs*. Munich: Beck.

1986. *Social Welfare in Germany and Britain: Origins and Development*. New York: Berg.

1996. Probleme und Tendenzen des Sozialstaates in den neunziger Jahren. *Geschichte und Gesellschaft*, 22, 393–408.

Rist, Charles. 1900. Sur la responsabilité des accidents dont les ouvriers sont les victimes dans leur travail. *Revue d' Économie Politique*, 14, 91–95.

Rivaud-Danset Dorothée, and Robert Salais. 1992. Les conventions de financement des entreprises. Premières approches théoriques et empiriques. *Revue française d'économie*, 7, 4, 81–120.

Robak, Brigitte, and Michael Schlecht. 1982. Arbeitszeitverkürzung: Formen und Auswirkungen. *Die Mitbestimmung*, 7, 241–243.

Robinson, M. 1913. *The Spirit of Association*. London: Murray.

Romano, Joseph. 1995. *La modernisation des PME: L'expert, le patron et le politique*. Paris: PUF.

Rosanvallon, Pierre. 1990. *L'état en France de 1789 à nos jours*. Paris: PUF.

Rosin, Heinrich. 1893. *Das Recht der Arbeiterversicherung*. Berlin.

Rothfels, Hans. 1938. Bismarck's Social Policy and the Problem of State Socialism in Germany. *Sociological Review*, 30, 81–94, 288–302.

Rothstein, Bo. 1985. The Success of Swedish Labor Market Policy: The Organizational Connection to Politics. *European Journal of Political Research*, 13, 153–165.

1992. Labor Market Institutions and Working Class Strength. In Sven Steinmo Kathleen Thelen, and Franh Longstreth, eds., *Structuring Politics: Historical*

References

Institutionalism in Comparative Analysis. Cambridge: Cambridge University Press, 33–56.

Rougé, Charles. 1912. *Les syndicats professionnels et l'assurance contre le chômage*. Paris: M. Rivière.

Rueschemeyer, Dietrich, and Theda Skocpol, eds. 1996. *States, Social Knowledge and the Origins of Modern Social Policies*. Princeton: Princeton University Press.

Rust, Michael. 1973. Business and Politics in the Third Republic: The Comité des Forges and the French Steel Industry. Ph.D. dissertation, Department of History, Princeton University.

Saint-Jours, Yves. 1982. France. In Peter Köhler and Hans Zacher, eds., *The Evolution of Social Insurance*. New York: Saint Martin's Press.

1994. La sécurité sociale et la prévention des risques sociaux. *Droit Social*, 6, 594–599.

Salais, Robert. 1988a. Les stratégies de moderninsation des entreprises de 1983 à 1986. *Économie et Statistique*, 213, 51–74.

1988b. Why Was Unemployment So Low in France during the 1930s? In Barry Eichengreen and T. Hatton, eds., *Interwar Unemployment in International Perspective*. Dordrecht: Kluwer, 247–288.

1992. Modernisation des entreprises et Fonds National de l'Emploi. Une analyse en terme de mondes de production. *Travail et emploi*, 51, 49–69.

Salais, Robert, Nicholas Bavarez, and Bénédicle Reynaud. 1986. *L'invention du chômage*. Paris: PUF.

Saly, Pierre. 1999. Les retraites ouvrières et paysannes (loi de 1910) et les retraites dans le cadre des assurances socials (loi de 1928–1930). In Michel Laroque, ed., *Contribution à l'histoire financière de la Sécurité Sociale*. Paris: La documentation française, 209–243.

Salzberg, Liliane. 1992. Le dispositif sur l'indemnisation du chômage et des preretraites en France. *Dossiers statistiques du travail et de l'emploi*, 84, 5–31.

Sauzet, Marc. 1883. De la responsabilité des patrons vis-à-vis des ouvriers dans les accidents industriels. *Revue critique de législation et de jurisprudence*, 32, 12, 596–640.

Savatier, Jean. 1987a. Les clauses conventionelles sur l'âge de la retraite. *Droit Social*, 1, 7–10.

1987b. Les dispositions de la loi du 30 juillet 1987 sur la rupture du contrat de travail à l'âge de la retraite. *Droit Social*, 11, 723–730.

Schalla, Karl-Heinz. 1985. Gleitender Ruhestand. *Bundesarbeitsblatt*, 5, 14–16.

Scharrer, Manfred. 1976. *Arbeiterbewegung im Obrigkeitsstaat: SPD und Gewerkschaften nach dem Sozialistengesetz*. Berlin: Rotbuch.

Schatz, H. 1947. Die Bedeutung der Innungskrankenkassen für das Handwerk aus ihrer geschichtlichen Entwicklung. Archive of the Friedrich Ebert Foundation, Bonn.

Schellhaaß, Horst. 1984. Unternehmerische Reaktionsmuster auf das Tarifrentengesetz. *Die Mitbestimmung*, 6, 241–243.

Schenke, Klaus, and Josef van Almsick. 1981. Alterssicherung: Systemwechsel nicht nötig. *Bundesarbeitsblatt*, 10, 5–10.

Schieckel, Horst, ed. 1947. *Gegenwartsprobleme der Sozialversicherung*. Munich: Richard Pflaum.

Schmähl, Winfried, and Jutta Gatter. 1994. Options for Extending the Working Period and Flexibilising the Transition to Retirement in the German Insurance Industry – the Current Situation and Assessment for the Future. *Geneva Papers on Risk and Insurance*, 19, 73, 433–474.

Schmid, J. 1990. *Die CDU. Organisationsstrukturen, Politiken und Funktionsweise der Partei im Föderalismus*. Opladen: Leske & Budrich.

Schmoller, Gustav. 1874. *Die Natur des Arbeitsvertrages und der Kontraktbruch*. Leipzig: Duncker & Humblot.

1881. *Jahrbuch für Gesetzgebung, Verwaltung und Volkswirtschaft im Deutschen Reich*. Leipzig: Duncker & Humblot.

1904. *Grundriss der Allgemeinen Volkswirtschaftslehre*. Leipzig. Duncker & Humblot.

1899. *Vier Briefe über Bismarcks Sozialpolitische Bedeutung*. Leipzig: Duncker & Humblot.

Schön, Donald, and Martin Rein, eds. 1994. *Frame Reflection: Toward the Resolution of Intractable Policy Controversies*. New York: Basic Books.

Schönhoven, Klaus. 1980. Selbsthilfe als Form der Solidarität. Das gewerkschaftliche Unterstützungswesen im Deutschen Kaiserreich bis 1914. *Archiv für Sozialgeschichte*, 20, 147–193.

Schöttler, Peter. 1985. *Naissances des bourses du travail*. Paris: Presses Universitaires de France.

Seffen, Achim. 1991. Die beste Lösung des Problems ist noch nicht gefunden. *Der Arbeitgeber*, 43, 3, 94–96.

Shalev, Michael. 1983. The Social Democratic Model and Beyond: Two Generations of Comparative Research on the Welfare State. *Comparative Social Research* 6, 315–351.

Simon, Dominique. 1986. Le patronat face aux assurances sociales 1920–1930. *Le Mouvement Social*, 137.

Simons, Gerda. 1919. *Die Erwerbslosenfürsorge während des Krieges*. Berlin.

Skocpol, Theda. 1985. Bringing the State Back In: Strategies of Analysis in Current Research. In Peter Evans, Dietrich Rueschemeyer, and Theda Skocpol, eds., *Bringing the State Back In*. Cambridge: Cambridge University Press.

1992. *Protecting Soldiers and Mothers: The Political Origns of Social Policy in the United States*. Cambridge: Cambridge University Press.

1995. *Social Policy in the United States: Future Possibilities in Historical Perspective*. Princeton: Princeton University Press.

Ed. 1984. *Vision and Method in Historical Sociology*. Cambridge: Cambridge University Press.

Skocpol, Theda, and Edwin Amenta. 1986. States and Social Policies. *Annual Review of Sociology*, 12, 131–157.

Skocpol, Theda, and John Ikenberry. 1983. The Political Formation of the American Welfare State in Historical and Comparative Perspective. *Comparative Social Research*, 6, 87–147.

References

Société industrielle du Nord de la France. 1887. *Communication sur les accidents industriels*. Lille: Daniel.

1888. *Rapport sur la nouvelle loi des accidents*. Lille: Daniel.

Sorge, Arnd, and Wolfgang Streeck. 1988. Industrial Relations and Technological Change. In Richard Hyman and Wolfgang Streeck, eds., *New Technology and Industrial Relations*. Oxford: Blackwell, 19–47.

Soskice, David. 1990a. Reinterpreting Corporatism and Explaining Unemployment: Coordinated and Non-Coordinated Market Economies. In R. Brunetta and C. Dell'Ariga, eds., *Labour Relations and Economic Performance*. London: Macmillian, 170–214.

1990b. Wage Determination: The Changing Role of Institutions in Advanced Industrialized Countries. *Oxford Review of Economic Policy*, 6, 4, 36–61.

1991. The Institutional Infrastructure for Industrial Competitiveness: A Comparative Analysis of the UK and Germany. In A. Atkinson and R. Brunetta, eds., *Labour Relations and Economic Performance*. London: Macmillan, 45–66.

1994. Reconciling Markets and Institutions: The German Apprenticeship System. In Lisa Lynch, ed., *Training and the Private Sector: International Comparisons*. Chicago: Chicago University Press, 25–60.

1997. German Technology Policy, Innovation and National Institutional Frameworks. *Industry and Innovation*, 4, 1, 75–96.

1998. Divergent Production Regimes: Coordinated and Uncoordinated Market Economies in the 1980s and 1990s. In Herbert Kitschelt, Peter Lange, Gary Marks, and John D. Stephens, eds., *Continuity and Change in Contemporary Capitalism*. New York: Cambridge University Press, 101–134.

Sozialaussschuss der Hauptpersonalvertretung bei der Reichsbahngeneraldirektion [britische Zone]. 1946. Stellungnahme zur Schaffung einheitlicher Sozialversicherungsanstalten. 3 April. Archive of the Friedrich Ebert Foundation, Auerbach Papers, box 208, Bonn.

Sozialbeirat. 1981. Gutachten des Sozialbeirates über langfristige Probleme der Alterssicherung in der Bundesrepublik Deutschland: Bundestags-Drucksachen 9/632, Bonn.

Spliedt, Franz. 1924. Einheitliche Gefahrengemeinschaft in der Arbeitslosenfürsorge. *Die Arbeit*, 1, 5, 257–266.

1925. Die Soziale Belastung der deutschen Wirtschaft. *Die Arbeit*, 2, 3, 143–152.

Standing, Guy. 1986. La flexibilité du travial et la marginalisation des travailleurs âgés. Pour une nouvelle stratégie. *Revue Internationale du Travail*, 125, 3, 363–387.

Stegman, Dirk, and Bernd-Jürgen Wendt. 1978. *Industrielle Gesellschaft und politisches System*. Bonn: Neue Gesellschaft.

Steinmetz, George. 1991. Workers and the Welfare State in Germany. *International Labor and Working-Class History*, 40, 1, 18–46.

1993. *Regulating the Social: The Welfare State and Local Politics in Imperial Germany*. Princeton: Princeton University Press.

Stellungnahme der Landwirtschaft zur Socialversicherung. N.d. Archive of the Friedrich Ebert Foundation, Auerbach Papers, box 206, Bonn.

Stephens, John. 1979. *The Transition from Capitalism to Socialism*. London: Macmillan.

Stone, Deborah. 1984. *The Disabled State*. Philadelphia: Temple University Press.

Storch, Anton. 1947. Was erwarten die Arbeitnehmer von der Neuordnung der deutschen Sozialversicherung. *Arbeitsblatt für die britische Zone*, 1, 1, 140.

Stürmer, Michael. 1967. *Koalition und Opposition in der Weimarer Republik*. Düsseldorf: Droste.

Süddeutsche Zeitung. 27 January 1984. Heftige Kontroverse um 59-er Regelung.

12 January 1984. Bonn will Sozialversicherung entlasten.

9 February 1984. Regierung halt an Vorruhestandsgesetz fest.

Sueur, Jean-Pierre. 1985. *Changer la retraite: Rapport au premier ministre*. Paris: La Documentation Française.

Supiot, Alain. 1989. Déréglementation des relations de travail et autoréglementation de l'entreprise. *Droit Social*, 3, 195–205.

1994. *Critique du droit du travail*. Paris: PUF.

Swenson, Peter. 1989. *Fair Shares: Unions, Pay and Politics in Sweden and West Germany*. Ithaca: Cornell University Press.

1991. Bringing Capital Back In, or Social Democracy Reconsidered: Employer Power, Cross-Class Alliances and Centralization of Industrial Relations in Denmark and Sweden. *World Politics*, 43, 4, 513–544.

1997. Arranged Alliance: Business Interests in the New Deal. *Politics and Society*, 25, March, 66–116.

2002. *Capitalists against Markets*. Oxford: Oxford University Press.

Syrup, Friedrich, and Otto Neuloh. 1957. *Hundert Jahre Staatliche Sozialpolitik*. Stuttgart: Kohlhammer.

Tänzler, Fritz. 1928. Die Soziale Belastung der Deutschen Wirtschaft. *Reichsarbeitsblatt*, 28, 608–612.

Tennstedt, Florian. 1977. *Soziale Selbstverwaltung: Geschichte der Selbstverwaltung in der Sozialversicherung*. Bonn: Verlag der Ortskrankenkassen.

Tennstedt, Florian, and Heidi Winter, eds. 1993. *Quellensammlung zur Geschichte der deutschen Sozialpolitik 1867 bis 1914. Von der Haftpflichtgesetzgebung zur ersten Unfallversicherungsvorlage*. Stuttgart: Fischer.

1995. *Quellensammlung zur Geschichte der deutschen Sozialpolitik 1867 bis 1914. Von der zweiten Unfallversicherungsvorlage bis zum Unfallversicherungsgesetz vom 6. Juli 1884*. Stuttgart: Fischer.

Tessier, Gaston. 1946. Contre la caisse unique. In Fondation Nationale des Sciences Politiques, Dossiers de Presse, 420/1.

Thelen, Kathleen. 1991. *Union of Parts*. Ithaca: Cornell University Press.

1993. West European Labor in Transition. *World Politics*, 46, 23–49.

1994. Beyond Corporatism: Towards a New Framework for the Study of Labor in Advanced Capitalism. *Comparative Politics*, 27, 3, 107–124.

2000. Why German Employers Cannot Bring Themselves to Dismantle the German Model. In Torben Iversen et al., eds., *Unions, Employers and Central Banks: Macroeconomic Coordination and Institutional Change in Social Market Economies*. Cambridge: Cambridge University Press, 138–169.

References

2001. Varieties of Labor Politics in the Developed Democracies. In Peter Hall and David Soskice, eds., *Varieties of Capitalism: The Institutional Foundations of Comparative Advantage*. Oxford: Oxford University Press, 75–103.

Thelen, Kathleen, and Ikuo Kume. 1999. The Rise of Non-Market Training Regimes: Germany and Japan Compared. *Journal of Japanese Studies*, 25, Winter, 33–64.

Thelen, Kathleen, and Sven Steinmo. 1992. Historical Institutionalism in Comparative Politics. In Sven Steinmo, Kathleen Thelen, and Frank Longstreth, eds., *Structuring Politics: Historical Institutionalism in Comparative Perspective*. Cambridge: Cambridge University Press, 1–33.

Thelen, Kathleen and Christa van Wijnbergen. 2000. The Paradox of Globalization: Turning the Tables on Labor and Capital in German Industrial Relations. Northwestern University. Unpublished manuscript.

Thierry, Dominique. 1996. *L'entreprise face à la question de l'emploi*. Paris: Harmattan.

Tollard, E. 1911. *Des actions du droit commun sous le régime de la loi du 9 avril 1898*. Paris: Rousseau.

Topalov, Christian. 1985. *Aux origines de l'assurance chômage. L'état et les secours de chômage syndicaux en France, Grande-Bretagne et Etats-Unis*. Paris: Centre de Sociologie Urbaine.

1994a. Inventing the Language of Unemployment: Britain, France and the United States. Paper presented at the Seminar on State and Capitalism since 1800, Center for European Studies, Harvard University, December.

1994b. *Naissance du chômeur*. Paris: Albin Michel.

1996. Langage de la réforme et déni du politique: Le débat entre assistance publique et bienfaissance privée 1889–1903. *Genèses*, 23, 30–52.

Tschirbs, Rudolf. 1982. Das Ruhrgebiet zwischen Privilegierung und Staatsverlust: Lohnpolitik von der Inflation bis zur Rationalisierung 1919–1927. In G. Feldman et al., eds., *Die deusche Inflation: Eine Zwischenbilanz*.

Ullmann, Hans Peter. 1979a. *Der Bund der Industriellen: Organisation, Einfluss und Politik klein- und mittelbetrieblicher Industrieller im Deutschen Kaiserreich 1895–1914*. Göttingen: Vandenhoeck & Ruprecht.

1979b. Industrielle Interessen und die Entstehung der deutschen Sozialversicherung 1880–1889. *Historische Zeitschrift*, 229, 3, 574–610.

1981. German Industry and Bismarck's Social Security System. In Wolfgang Mommsen, ed., *The Emergence of the Welfare State in Britain and Germany*. London: Croom Helm.

1983. *Interessenverbände in Deutschland*. Frankfurt: Suhrkamp.

Union des Chambres Syndicales Lyonnaises. 1921. Rapport sur le projet de loi sur les assurances socials. 16 June. Archives de la Chambre de Commerce de Paris III. 5. 50 (10).

Union des Corporations Françaises. 1926. Le Projet de Loi des Assurances Sociales devant le Sénat. Archives de la Chambre de Commerce de Paris, III. 5. 50 (10).

Union des Intérêts Economiques and Confédération des Groupes Commerciaux. 1926. Ordre du jour 21 decembre. *Revue Politique et Parlementaire*, 33, 1, 156.

Union des Industries Métallurgiques et Minières [UIMM]. N.d. Bibliothèque Nationale, Paris.

1922. *Déposition devant la Commission des Assurances et de Prévoyance Sociale de la Chambre des Députés (23 décembre 1921) et le Conseil Supérieur du Travail (9 janvier 1922)*. Document no. 1273.

1981. *L'année métallurgique*. Paris: UIMM.

Uusitallo, Hannu. 1984. Comparative Research on the Determinants of the Welfare State: The State of the Art. *European Journal of Political Research*, 12, 4, 403–422.

Van Kersbergen, Kees. 1995. *Social Capitalism: A Study of Christian Democracy and the Welfare State*. London: Routledge University Press.

Vanthemsche, Guy. 1990. Unemployment Insurance in Interwar Belgium. *International Review of Social History*, 35, 3, 349–376.

Varlez, Louis. 1903. *Les formes nouvelles de l'assurance contre le chômage*. Paris: M. Rivière.

Verein Deutscher Eisen- und Stahlindustrieller. 1884a. Vorstandssitzung des Vereins Deutscher Eisen- und Stahlindustrieller, Berlin. 10 February. *Stahl und Eisen*, 11, 1884, 177–179.

1884b. Die Grundzüge für den Entwurf eines Gesetzes über die Unfallversicherung der Arbeiter. *Stahl und Eisen*, 11, 1884, 190–192.

Vereinigung der Arbeitgeberverbände. 1949a. Stellungnahme zu dem Entwurf eines Gesetzes zur Wiederherstellung der Selbstverwaltung in der Sozialversicherung. 18 May. BDA Archiv, Cologne.

1949b. Selbstverwaltung in der Sozialversicherung. 19 December. BDA Archive, Cologne.

1949c. Wiederherstellung der Selbstverwaltung in der Sozialversicherung. BDA Archive, Cologne.

1949d. Rundschreiben an den Bundesarbeitsminister Storch betreffend der Wiederherstellung der Selbstverwaltung in der Sozialversicherung. 29 November. BDA Archive, Cologne.

Vereinigung der Deutschen Arbeitgebervberbände. 1919. *Bericht über die sozialpolitische Gesetzgebung*. Berlin: VDA.

1920. *Denkschrift der Vereinigung der Deutschen Arbeitgeberverbände an das Reichsarbeitsministerium*. 24 April. Zentrales Staatsarchiv Potsdam: Reichsarbeitsamt 4310.

1927. *Geschäftsbericht der Vereinigung der Deutschen Arbeitgeberverbände 1925–1926*. Berlin: VDA.

Ed. 1921. *Geschäftsbericht der Vereinigung der Deutschen Arbeitgeberverbände 1920*. Berlin: VDA.

1923. *Geschäftsbericht über das Jahr 1922*. Berlin: VDA.

1924. *Geschäftbericht der Vereinigung der Deutschen Arbeitgeberverbände 1923*. Berlin: VDA.

1925. *Stellungnahme zu den Grundfragen der Arbeitslosenversicherung*. Zentrales Staatsarchiv Potsdam, DAF 2575/36–43.

Vereinigung der Handwerkskammern in der britischen Zone. N.d. *Vereinigung der Handwerkskammern in der britischen Zone zu der SPD*. Archive of the Friedrich Ebert Foundation, Kurt Schumacher Papers, J74, Bonn.

References

Vereinigung der Industrie- und Handelskammern in der britischen Besatzungszone. 1948. Rundschreiben an das Hauptamt der Arbeitsverwaltung für die britische Zone. 9 December. Rheinisch-Westfälisches Wirtschaftsarchiv, Cologne, Archive of Chamber of Commerce Wuppertal, RWWA 22 800/00.

Verkindt, Pierre-Yves. 1993. Le travailleur viellissant. *Droit Social*, 12, 932–941.

Vermont, H. 1922. La loi d'assurances sociales. *La Réforme Sociale*, 82, 10–38.

Vertreter der Gewerkschaften im Länderrat. 1947. Neuaufbau der Sozialversicherung, 5. 10. 1947. Archive of the Friedrich Ebert Foundation, Bonn.

Villey, Edmond. 1923a. Réflexions sur le projet de loi relatif aux assurances sociales. *Revue d'Economie Politique*, 37, 373–383.

1923b. *L'organisation professionnelle des employeurs dans l'industrie française*. Paris: Alcan.

1924. Chronique législative. *Revue d'Économie Politique*, 38, 558.

Vincens, Jean. 1993. Réflexions sur le chômage de longue durée. *Revue Française de Sociologie*, 34, 327–344.

Vinen, Richard. 1991. *The Politics of French Business*. Cambridge: Cambridge University Press.

Vogel, Walter. 1951. *Bismarck's Arbeiterversicherung: Ihre Entstehung im Kräftespiel der Zeit*. Berlin.

Volkoff, S. 1989. Le travail après 50 ans: Quelques chiffres et plusieurs inquiétudes. *Travail Humain*, 52, 2, 97–116.

Volksblatt Berlin. 10 March 1984. Ausnahmeregel für kleine Betriebe.

18 March 1984. Beim Vorruhestand ist der finanzielle Abstieg eingeplant.

von Strandmann, Hartmut Pogge. 1978. Widersprüche im Modernisierungsprozess Deutschlands: Der Kampf der verarbeitenden Industrie gegen die Schwerindustrie. In D. Stegman and B. Wendt, eds., *Industrielle Gesellschaft und Politsches System*. Bonn: Neue Gesellschaft.

Wagner, Adolph. 1910. *Die Strömungen in der Sozialpolitik und der Katheder- und Staatssozialismus*. Berlin.

Wagner, M. 1920. Die Träger der Reichsarbeitslosenversicherung. *Deutsche Arbeitgeberzeitung*, Nr. 35, 29 August.

Walker, Alan, et al., eds. 1993. *Older People in Europe: Social and Economic Policies: The 1993 Report of the European Observatory*. Brussels: Commission of the European Communities.

Warnken, Jürgen. 1993. Alterstätigkeit: Bislang unausgeschöpfte Potentiale. *Bundesarbeitsblatt*, 4, 5–10.

Weber, Eugen. 1976. *Peasants into Frenchmen: The Modernization of Rural France 1870–1914*. Stanford: Stanford University Press.

Weber, Henri. 1986. *Le parti des patrons: Le CNPF 1946–1986*. Paris: Seuil.

Weir, Margaret. 1992. *Politics and Jobs*. Princeton: Princeton University Press.

Ed. 1988. *The Politics of Social Policy in the United States*. Princeton: Princeton University Press.

Weir, Margaret, Ann Shola Orloff, and Theda Skocpol. 1988. Introduction: Understanding American Social Politics. In Margaret Weir et al., eds., *The Politics of Social Policy in the United States*. Princeton: Princeton University Press, 1–37.

Weir, Margaret, and Theda Skocpol. 1985. State Structures and the Possibilities for "Keynesian" Responses to the Great Depression in Sweden, Britain and the United States. In Peter Evans et al., eds., *Bringing the State Back In*. New York: Cambridge University Press, 107–163.

Weisbrod, Bernd. 1974. *Schwerindustrie in der Weimarer Republik: Interessenpolitik zwischen Stabilisierung und Krieg*. Wuppertal: Hammer.

Weisz, Christoph, and Hans Woller, eds. 1977. *Wörtliche Berichte und Drucksachen der Wirtschaftsrates des Vereinigten Wirtschaftsgebietes*. Munich: Oldenburg.

Wermel, Michael, and Roswitha Urban. 1949. Arbeitslosenfürsorge und Arbeitslosenversicherung. *Neue Soziale Praxis*, 6, 1–3.

Winter, Thomas von. 1989. Die CDU im Interessenkonflikteine Fallstudie zur Parteiinternen Auseinandersetzung über den Paragraph 116 AFG. *Leviathan*, 17, 46–84.

1990. Die Sozialausschüsse der CDU. Sammelbecken für christlich-demokratische Arbeitnehmerinteressen oder linker Flügel der Partei? *Leviathan*, 18, 322–345.

Wirtschaftsvereinigung Bergbau. 1956. Die Sozialreform aus der Sicht des Bergbaus, Bad Godesberg, 14. 08. 1956. Archive of the Friedrich Ebert Foundation, Auerbach Papers, box 215, Bonn.

1956. Die Sozialreform aus der Sicht des Bergbaus. Archive of the Friedrich Ebert Foundation, Auerbach Papers, box 215, Bonn.

Witt, Peter-Christian. 1983. Das Verhältnis von Regierung, Bürokratie und Parlament in Deutschland. In Gerhard Ritter, ed., *Bürokratie und Parlament in Deutschland nach 1948 bis zur Gegenwart*. Düsseldorf: Droste, 117–149.

Wood, Stewart. 1996. Labour Power and Employers' Preferences: The Ambiguous Reform of the West German Strike Payments Law. Paper presented at the Conference of Europeanists, Chicago.

2001. Business, Government and Patterns of Labor Market Policy in Britain and the Federal Republic of Germany. In Peter Hall and David Soskice, eds., *Varieties of Capitalism*. Oxford: Oxford University Press, 247–274.

Woronoff, Denis. 1998. *Histoire de l'industrie en France: Du XVIème siècle à nos jours*. Paris: Editions du Seuil.

Wulf, Peter. 1972. *Das Kabinett Fehrenbach*. Boppard am Rhein: Boldt.

Württembergischer Gewerkschaftsbund. 1947. Entschliessung zur Sozialversicherung. Bundesarchiv Koblenz, Z1/952/134–135.

Zacher, Hans, ed. 1979. *Bedingungen für die Entstehung und Entwicklung der Sozialversicherung*. Berlin: Duncker & Humblot.

Zahnbrecher, Franz. 1914. *Arbeitslosenversicherung und Arbeitgeber*. Nurenberg Schrag.

Zentralamt für Arbeit. N.d. Memorandum zur Begründung von Änderungen der geltenden Regelung zur Handwerkerversicherung. Archive of the Friedrich Ebert Foundation, box 240, Bonn.

Zentralamt für Arbeit in der britischen Zone. 1947. Denkschrift an die Social Branch Manpower Division Headquarters. 14 March. Archive of the Friedrich Ebert Foundation, Auerbach Papers, box 208, Bonn.

References

Zentralanstalt für Arbeit Lemgo. N.d. Finanzielle und organisatorische Schwierigkeiten bei der Sozialversicherung der Reichsbahn. Archive of the Friedrich Ebert Foundation, Auerbach Papers, box 208/1, Bonn.

1947a. Organisation der kanppschaftlichen Versicherung bis 1933. Archive of the Friedrich Ebert Foundation, Auerbach Papers, box 215, Bonn.

1947b. Niederschrift für die Sitzung der Vorbereitenden Konferenz für Knappschaftsfragen am 29. November 1947 in Düsseldorf. Archive of the Friedrich Ebert Foundation, Auerbach Papers, box 215, Bonn.

1948. Stellungnahme zur Begründung von Änderungen der geltenden Regelung der Handwerkerversicherung. Archive of the Friedrich Ebert Foundation, Auerbach Papers, box 240, Bonn.

Zentralverband des Deutschen Handwerks. 1949. Forderungen zur Altersversorgung des Handwerks, Beratungen des Sozialversicherungsausschusses der Zentralarbeitsgemeinschaft des Handwerks vom März. 1949. Archive of the Friedrich Ebert Foundation, Walter Auerbach Papers, box 240, Bonn.

1982a. Verkürzung der Lebensarbeitszeit – kein Beitrag zur Bekämpfung der Arbeitslosigkeit. In *Argumente zur Handwerkspolitik*. Bonn: Bundesvereinigung der Fachverbände des Deutschen Handwerks.

1982b. Schmittker lehnt Verkürzung erneut ab. *Deutsches Handwerksblatt*, 18, 590.

1982c. Den Neubeginn wagen. Ein Brief vom *Handwerk* an Bundeskanzler Kohl. *Deutsches Handwerksblatt*, 19, 649.

1983a. Arbeitzeitverkürzung löst keine Arbeitsmarktprobleme. *Deutsches Handwerksblatt*, 18.

1983b. Klare Absage an Arbeitszeitverkürzung. *Deutsches Handwerksblatt*, 12, 407–408.

1983c. Kürzere Arbeitszeit: Alle Gründe und Überlegungen sprechen dagegen. *Deutsches Handwerksblatt*, 1983, 12, 416–420.

1983d. Das ZDH nimmt zu den Beschäftigungspolitischen Leitlinien und anderen Anträgen Stellung. *Deutsches Handwerksblatt*, 18, 591–593.

1983e. *Handwerk*: 35-Stunden Woche vernichtet Arbeitsplätze. *Deutsches Handwerksblatt*, 1983, 22, 735–739.

1983f. Handwerk bekräftigt sein Nein zu Arbeitszeitverkürzungen. *Deutsches Handwerksblatt*, 23–24, 754.

1983g. Arbeitszeitverkürzung: Kostenwirksame Vorruhestandsregelung vorgesehen. *Deutsches Handwerksblatt*, 1983, 23–24, 760.

1984a. Politik der Vernunft – Chance für das Handwerk! *Deutsches Handwerksblatt*, 1, 11.

1984b. *Handwerk*: Bedenken nicht ausgeräumt. *Deutsches Handwerksblatt*, 1, 13.

1984c. Vorruhestandsgesetz: Arbeitsplatz und Existenzgefährdend. *Deutsches Handwerksblatt*, 1, 13.

1984d. Bundesrat greift Vorschläge des *Handwerk*s auf. *Deutsches Handwerksblatt*, 4, 107.

1984e. Härteregelung dringend erforderlich. *Deutsches Handwerksblatt*, 5, 171.

1984f. Ablehnung der 35-Stunden Woche und Vorbehalte gegen Vorruhestandsregelung bekräftigt. *Deutsches Handwerksblatt*, 6, 188–189.

1984g. *Handwerk* über Verabschiedung enttäuscht. *Deutsches Handwerksblatt*, 8, 270.

Ziegler, Nicholas. 2000. Corporate Governance and the Politics of Property Rights in Germany. *Politics and Society*, 28, 2, 195–222.

Zimmermann, Lothar. 1985. Solidarisierung- das Gebot der Stunde. *Die Mitbestimmung*, 6, 209–210.

Zöllner, Detlev. 1982. Germany. In Peter Köhler et al., eds., *The Evolution of Social Insurance*. New York: St. Martin's Press, 1–92.

Zumpe, Lotte. 1961. Zur Geschichte der Unfallverhältnisse in der deutschen Industrie. Wirtschaftswissenschafliche Fakultät, Humboldt Universität, Berlin.

Zysman, John. 1977. *Political Strategies for Industrial Order*. Berkeley: University of California Press.

1983. *Governments, Markets and Growth*. Ithaca: Cornell University Press.

Index

Abraham, David, 151
accident insurance: development of, 64–5;
France's post-WWII social policy reform
and, 191, 195, 197; overview, 64–5,
255–6; private social policies and, 57;
statistics on (early 1900s), 15–16
accident insurance (France/19th century):
agricultural workers and, 94, 97, 100–1,
103; business preferences of, 89–96;
business preferences summary, 95f;
chambers of commerce preferences, 91,
93; Chamber vs. Senate and, 96–104;
control and, 92–3; financing of, 96, 98,
102–3; legal reforms and, 86–9; overview,
104–5; policy-making process in, 96–104;
private preexisting institutions and, 92–3,
95, 96, 99–100, 101–2; risk incidence and,
93–5; risk pools of, 96, 103, 104; risk
redistribution and, 93–5, 101–2; scope of,
98–9, 100–1; size of firms and, 92–3,
94–5, 97, 98, 99–100; small-business
preferences and, 97, 104, 105; state's role
in, 99, 100, 103; théorie du risque
professionnel, 97–8, 100–1, 103
accident insurance (Germany/19th century):
agricultural sector and, 73, 74–5, 79, 80,
85; business influence on, 78–85; business
preferences of, 71–6, 77f; chambers of
commerce preferences, 71, 76; control of,
79, 80, 81–5; financing of, 79, 80, 83–4,
85; labor preferences of, 104;
policy-making process of, 76–85;
politicization of, 65–71; risk "classes of
danger," 83, 84; risk incidence and, 72–3,
74; risk pool, 79–80, 84–5; risk
redistribution and, 72, 72–3, 74; size of
firm and, 71, 75–6, 105; strategic alliances
and, 85

Accident Insurance Fund (France), 99, 100
accidents (France/19th century): burden of
proof in, 86–7, 88; "categories of danger"
with, 89; contractual responsibility and,
86–7; reversal of burden of proof, 87;
théorie du risque professionnel, 87–9,
89–90, 91–2, 94, 95; unknown causes of,
87, 97–8
accidents (Germany/19th century): burden
of proof in, 66–8; employer obligations
and, 67; reversal of burden of proof, 67–8;
statistics on fatalities, 72; supervising
personnel and, 66–7; unknown causes of,
66
agricultural sector: accident insurance
(France), 94, 97, 100–1, 103; accident
insurance (Germany), 73, 74–5, 79, 80,
85; compulsory social insurance (France),
126–7, 128, 134, 257; demographic
structure (Germany), 174–5; post-WWII
social policy (France), 197–8, 199, 201,
204, 206–7, 208; post-WWII social policy
(Germany), 174–5; price controls (U.S.),
53; unemployment insurance (Germany),
150–1, 158, 256–7
alliances: cross-national variation in, 1–2;
overview, 41–2, 50–62; politicians and,
42n14; preexisting policies and, 42n14,
50, 52–62. See also cross-class alliances;
prestrategic alliances; strategic alliances
American Federation of Labor (AFL), 47
Association of Employers' Organizations in
Agriculture and Forestry (Germany), 150,
151
Association of French Industry, 89
Association of German Industry, 144
Association of German Iron and Steel
Industrialists, 70

311

Index

Baare, Louis, 57, 69, 70–1, 76, 83
Baldwin, Peter, 5–8, 12, 14, 15, 18, 49–50, 52, 183, 186–7, 187–8
Baron, Julius, 68
Bauer, Gustav, 158
Belgian Christian Democratic union federation, 45
Belgium: development of unemployment insurance, 262; Ghent system, 115; trade union benefits, 44
Beutner, Georg, 76–7
Beveridge reforms (Britain), 15, 166, 167, 188
Bismarck, Chancellor: accident liability, 57, 70–1, 73; compulsory accident insurance, 77, 78, 79, 82–3, 85; coverage of agriculture, 74; old-age insurance, 58; paternalism, 79
Bloc des Gauches, 117
Blohm, Rudolf, 159
Blüm, Norbert, 236, 240, 241–2, 243, 245, 246
Brauns, Heinrich, 155, 165
business: assumption of opposition to social insurance, 2–3, 5, 22–3, 41, 62, 249–50; business-centered research, 8–9, 12–13, 41; social policy preferences overview, 2–3, 9, 21–5, 250–1, 260
business social policy preferences: for accident insurance (France), 89–96; for accident insurance (Germany), 71–6, 77f; analyses of, 32–3, 34f, 35f, 36–7; business preference for compulsory social insurance (France), 121–8, 129f, 135; change in, 37–9, 40f; of early retirement policies (France), 215, 216, 217, 219–25, 224f, 228, 229–30; of early retirement policies (Germany) and, 235–8; in liberal market economies, 264; location in the social policy space, 32–40; overview, 21–39, 40f, 252–9; of post-WWII social policy (France), 193–201; of post-WWII social policy (Germany), 171–9, 212; summary of, 38f, 62; for unemployment insurance (France), 113, 114, 116, 263; for unemployment insurance (Germany), 140, 142–3, 144–53

Caisse des Forges, 19
cartels, 22
Central Committee of Coal-Mining Producers (France), 93–4
Central Federation of German Industrialists, 26–7, 58, 70, 72, 75, 78, 80, 153, 252–3

Central Industrial Committee (Belgium), 262
Chaveau Report (France), 120, 121–2, 124, 135–7
Chôtard, Yves, 221
Christian-Democratic MRP (France), 188–9, 192
Christian Democratic Party (Germany): early retirement policy and, 240–1, 241–2, 243, 244, 245, 246; universalistic social policy and, 185, 186
Christian Democratic political parties, 52
Christian Social Union (Germany), 185
Civil Code (France) and accidents, 86, 98
Civil Code (Germany) and accidents, 65–8
coalitions. *See* alliances
Commission of Assistance and Social Insurance (France), 133
Commission of Social Insurance (France), 117
Committee of Producers in Coal Mining (France), 90–1
compulsory social insurance (France): agricultural sector and, 126–7, 128, 134; chambers of commerce preferences, 124–5; control issues and, 122–4, 125, 129f, 131, 132–3, 135, 137; disability and, 130–1; employer preferences in, 121–8, 135; employer preference summary in, 129f; family benefits and, 123, 130, 136; hostility toward, 128–9; labor preferences in, 132; negotiations/legislation on, 128–38; old-age benefits and, 120–1, 122, 123, 124, 130, 131–2, 136; preexisting private policies and, 122–3, 131, 132–3, 134; risk determination and, 135–6; risk pool of, 131; risk redistribution and, 125–8, 129f, 130, 133–4, 137–8; sickness benefits and, 120–1, 122, 123, 130–1, 136; size of firms and, 122, 124–5, 126, 127–8, 138; tax evasion from, 127–8; unemployment insurance and, 120–1, 125, 126, 136–7
Confédération Générale du Travail, 112, 130, 132, 190, 215, 216
Confederation of Commercial Groups, 135
Congress of German Industry and Commerce, 146
Conseil National du Patronat Français (CNPF): early retirement policies and, 215, 219, 221; universalization of policies and, 190, 198–9, 201, 204, 207
Conservative political bloc (Germany), 78, 80, 82

Index

construction industry, 72, 92
contributory policies: effect on employers, 26; financing of, 26; social policy preferences of firms, 36–7, 252, 254, 265; social policy space and, 18, 19; unemployment insurance and, 108; unemployment insurance (France) and, 109, 111–12, 113, 114–15; unemployment insurance (Germany) and, 143–4, 145, 153, 154, 165
control: accident insurance (France) and, 92–3; accident insurance (Germany) and, 79, 80, 81–5; business cost-benefits of, 25–8; compulsory social insurance (France) and, 122–4, 125, 129f, 131, 132–3, 135, 137; description of, 17, 25; early retirement policies (France) and, 218–19, 220; in Ghent unemployment policies, 107; labor and, 45, 48–9, 54; post-WWII social policy (France) and, 188, 191, 194–6, 200–1, 205–6; post-WWII social policy (Germany) and, 170, 172–3, 178, 181; social policy space and, 15f, 16–20, 25–8; unemployment insurance and, 17n1, 28, 107–8; unemployment insurance (France) and, 109, 112–13, 115; unemployment insurance (Germany) and, 146–7, 148–9, 154, 156, 159, 161–2, 163. *See also* sensitivity to control (of a firm)
Council of Economic Experts (Germany), 239
cross-class alliances: in different political contexts, 259; early retirement policies (France), 248; early retirement policies (Germany), 248; failure of, 58; general findings of, 260–3; overview, 2, 3, 5, 8, 50–9, 259–63; political composition of, 261–2; preexisting social policies and, 42n14, 50, 52–62, 260–1; unemployment insurance (Germany), 155–8; universalistic policies and, 49–50, 58–9. *See also* strategic cross-class alliances

Dalle, Victor, 111
decommodification, 5, 249, 250
Délépine Commission, 190, 191
Democratic Party (Germany), 185
Denmark: social policy developments, 49–50; wage-bargaining institutions, 8
Döding, Günter, 234
Dore, Ronald, 54

Duisburg, Carl, 151–2

Early Retirement Act (Germany): negotiations of, 239–46; policy changes of, 245–6; significance of, 246
early retirement policies: as hybrid policies, 213; positioning in social policy space, 15f, 19–20
early retirement policies (France): contributions of elderly workers and, 222–3; cost issues and, 220, 221–2; cross-class alliances and, 248; economy and, 215, 218, 228–9; employer social policy preferences of, 215, 216, 217, 219–25, 228, 229–30; financing of, 217–19, 226, 227–8; firm size and, 220; *garantie de ressources*, 217, 218, 223, 225, 226, 227, 230, 231; labor market authorities and, 248; labor preferences of, 215, 216–17, 218, 229–30; Laroque commission/report, 214–15, 216; negotiation of, 225–31; old-age insurance and, 228, 229; old-age pension rates and, 216, 229, 230; *ordonnance* of March 1982, 230; overview, 246–8; preexisting policies and, 225–6, 231, 254; risk redistribution and, 223–5, 257; size of firms and, 220–2, 224–5; skill composition of work force and, 222, 223; strategic alliances and, 219, 230; subsidies and, 216, 218–19, 229–31; unemployment insurance and, 216–17, 226, 228, 230; voluntary resignation and, 218
early retirement policies (Germany): "blurring of risks" in, 232–3; cross-class alliances and, 248; disability benefits and, 232–3; Early Retirement Act negotiations, 239–46; economy and, 233; employer preferences of, 235–8; Employment Promotion Act and, 233–4, 241; German courts and, 232–3; industry risk profiles, 237; labor market authorities and, 248; labor preferences for, 234–5; large- vs. small-firm conflict, 241–6; Law of the Adaptation of the Employment Promotion Act, 242; old-age insurance and, 239; overview, 246–8; preexisting policies and, 242, 246, 254; priority of, 231–2; retirement age and, 233; risk redistribution and, 237–8, 257; size of firm and, 233–4, 236–7, 238, 239–40, 241–6; skill composition of work force and, 237; unemployment benefits and, 232–3; working time reduction and, 234, 242

Index

Index

railway industry (France): labor and, 54; private policies and, 23

railway industry (Germany), 54, 67–8, 174, 175–6

Reichslandbund, 150

reservation wage, 27; gradation of reservation wage and investment in skills, 24, 28

Richter, Willi, 167

risk incidence: definition, 30; impact on social policy preferences of firms, 31–2, 33–7; risk of old-age, 31; risk of unemployment, 31; risk of workplace accidents, 31; sources of variation in, 31

risk redistribution: accident insurance (France) and, 93–5, 101–2; accident insurance (Germany) and, 72–3, 74; compulsory social insurance (France) and, 125–8, 129f, 130, 133–4, 137–8; in different political contexts, 259; early retirement policies (France) and, 223–5, 257; early retirement policies (Germany) and, 237–8, 257; in Ghent unemployment policies, 107–8; labor preferences in, 45–6, 47n16, 48, 49; post-WWII social policy (France) and, 197–200, 201, 202, 203, 204–9, 210, 211; post-WWII social policy (Germany) and, 170, 173, 174–8, 180, 211; social policy space and, 10, 15f, 16, 30–40; unemployment insurance (Germany) and, 147, 150–2, 162–3; unemployment insurance and, 31, 46, 107. *See also* sensitivity to risk redistribution

Robertson, General, 184

Roche, Jules, 102

Ruhr industrial region, 69

Salais, Robert, 106, 126

Say, Léon, 88

Schmoller, Gustav, 57

Schönhoven, Klaus, 43–4

Schumpeter, Joseph, 12

"second-best" outcome. *See* strategic alliances

sensitivity to control (of a firm): factors affecting, 28–30, 30–2; social policy space, 32–40; unemployment insurance and, 146, 147. *See also* control

sensitivity to risk redistribution (of a firm): factors affecting, 30–2; firm sector and, 126; low/high-risk business and, 37, 39; social policy space, 15f, 16, 30–2, 32–40; unemployment insurance and, 147. *See also* risk incidence; risk redistribution

Shalev, Michael, 4, 5, 249

sickness benefits/insurance: after World War II, 16; compulsory social insurance (France), 120–1, 122, 123, 130–1, 136; post-WWII social policy (France), 189–90, 191, 198; post-WWII social policy (Germany), 181, 183; unemployment insurance (Germany), 158, 159, 160

size of firms: accident insurance (France), 92–3, 94–5, 97, 98, 99–100; accident insurance (Germany), 71, 75–6, 105; compulsory social insurance (France), 122, 124–5, 126, 127–8, 138; control and, 29–30, 32; early retirement policies (France), 220–2, 224–5; early retirement policies (Germany), 233–4, 236–7, 238, 239–40, 241–6; Ghent system and, 117–18; large/small cleavage, 39, 255; market power and, 29; policy preferences and, 10, 211, 252–4; post-WWII social policy (France), 197–8, 199, 200–1, 203–4, 205, 206, 207; post-WWII social policy (Germany), 170–1, 172–3; small-firm cost concerns, 29–30, 220, 221–5, 255; unemployment insurance (France), 117–18; unemployment insurance (Germany), 145–9, 152–3

skill formation: social policies and, 9–10, 24–5, 27–8, 32, 250–1, 264–5; social protection and, 258; unemployment insurance (Germany) and, 145–6, 147–8

skill profile of business: control and, 28–30, 32; early retirement policies (France), 222, 223; early retirement policies (Germany), 237

skill shortages, 24–5

Skocpol, Theda, 4, 23, 51, 52, 53, 250

social committees (Germany), 240–1, 245

Social Democratic Party (Germany): administration centralization and, 180; Early Retirement Act and, 239–40, 243, 245; proposals for higher social policy benefits, 185; unemployment insurance and, 140, 141, 163, 164, 180

Social Democratic political parties: Scandinavia social policy and, 6; social policy preferences, 51–2, 53

Social Insurance Code (Germany), 176

Socialist Party (France), 188–9

Socialist Trade Union Federation (Belgium), 262

social policy: major types of, 19; variation in the level of coverage, 15–16

social policy retrenchment, 1, 263–4